PCCN EXAM PREP:

Disclosure: This publication, including all text, graphics, and information contained herein, is provided for educational purposes only and is not intended as a substitute for professional medical advice, diagnosis, or treatment. The authors, editors, and publishers of this book have made extensive efforts to ensure the accuracy and completeness of the information provided, but make no warranties, expressed or implied, regarding the performance or use of the information herein and shall not be liable for any direct, indirect, incidental, or consequential damages, or any damages whatsoever arising from or in connection with the use of this publication.

The practices, procedures, and protocols described in this book may not reflect the most current clinical or legal standards and are subject to change. Healthcare professionals are encouraged to consult a wide range of sources and adhere to the guidelines and standards set forth by their professional governing bodies, institutions, and applicable health authorities.

This book does not endorse any specific tests, physicians, products, procedures, opinions, or other information that may be mentioned. Reliance on any information provided by this book is solely at your own risk. The content is provided on an "as is" basis and the reader assumes full responsibility for the use of the information.

The views expressed in this publication are those of the authors and do not necessarily reflect the views of the publisher. The mention of specific companies, organizations, or authorities in this book does not imply endorsement by the publisher, nor does the exclusion of others imply disapproval.

Any trademarks, service marks, product names, or named features are assumed to be the property of their respective owners and are used only for reference. There is no implied endorsement if one of these terms is used.

Readers are advised to keep in mind that laws, regulations, and medical practices for pharmaceuticals and medical devices vary from country to country. As such, they are advised to consult the current literature and product information in their country of practice.

Table of Contents

INTRO..PAGE 3
Cardiovascular..PAGE 5
Pulmonary..PAGE 32
Renal/Gastrointestinal..PAGE 56
Musculoskeletal/Multisystem/Psychosocial..PAGE 63
Professional Aspects of Critical Care Nursing....................................PAGE 80
Practice Questions..PAGE 89

INTRO:

This isn't just another textbook. It's your roadmap for passing the PCCN exam and becoming the critical care nurse you've always envisioned.

Think back to why you chose this path – the adrenaline rush when things get intense, the knowledge that you're making a difference in those life-and-death moments. Maybe you saw how skilled critical care nurses helped a loved one, and now it's your turn to step up.

Whatever brought you here, it wasn't just for a good paycheck. You crave that deep understanding that makes even the toughest cases a bit less overwhelming. Sometimes, though, it's tough to know where to even start. Textbooks are a jumble of information, and who has the time to sort through it all?

That's where this guide comes in. We've broken down the PCCN exam, topic by topic. You'll find clear explanations, not fluffy theory. We're talking real-world scenarios, what the examiners are looking for, and insider tips on how to prioritize those overwhelming patient needs.

The PCCN isn't easy, and critical care nursing is even tougher. But you're determined, and you're not alone. Consider this guide your study partner, your mentor whispering in your ear as you face down even the scariest cases. Your goals are within reach – let's get to work.

Picture this: a patient's status suddenly spirals, every alarm is clamoring, and the whole team looks to you. With your PCCN certification, you're the one with the in-depth knowledge to make split-second decisions and the proven expertise to lead. Let's break down why this certification matters, and how to make sure you're eligible to take the test.

Why Become a PCCN-Certified Nurse?
- **Career Advancement:** PCCN certification is your ticket to specialized units and leadership roles. It demonstrates your commitment to excellence and opens doors.
- **Respect and Recognition:** Colleagues and patients alike trust your advanced skills. It's validation of your dedication to providing the best possible care.
- **Potential for Higher Pay:** Many organizations recognize PCCN certification with competitive salaries and bonuses.
- **Personal Growth:** Preparing for the exam deepens your critical care knowledge, transforming you into a more confident and decisive clinician.

Am I Eligible? The Two Pathways:

The AACN offers two ways to prove you're ready to sit for the PCCN exam:
- **Direct Care Pathway:**
    - You need an active, unrestricted RN license in the U.S. or its territories.
    - Your job involves handing on care of critically ill adults.
    - Here's the key: you must have clocked enough hours in direct care. The AACN website breaks this down (see the PCCN handbook for detailed requirements).
- **Knowledge Professional Pathway:**
    - This is for nurses who influence patient outcomes but don't primarily provide direct care – think educators, managers, or researchers in the critical care field.
    - You need the same active RN license, along with a whole different set of hour requirements focused on your expertise.

The PCCN exam isn't just about knowing your stuff, it's about understanding how to apply your knowledge under pressure. Knowing the format of the test will give you an edge, letting you focus on the critical thinking, not the clock.

Here's the Breakdown:
- **Computer-Based Exam:** You'll take the exam at a designated testing center, not pen and paper style. Get familiar with the computer interface beforehand to avoid any surprises that day.
- **Multiple-Choice Mayhem:** The entire PCCN exam is multiple-choice. But don't be fooled, these aren't simple recall questions. Expect to analyze patient scenarios and choose the most appropriate interventions.
- **Questions Galore:** Get ready for 125 questions. But here's the twist: only 100 of them actually count towards your score. The extra 25 are the AACN trying out new questions for future tests.
- **Timed Battle:** You have three hours to tackle all 125 questions. That averages to about 1.5 minutes per question. Practice tests are crucial to developing your pacing strategy.
- **Content Breakdown:** The PCCN exam focuses on these key areas of critical care nursing – we'll tackle each in the guide individually:
    - Cardiovascular
    - Pulmonary
    - Endocrine/Hematology
    - Neurology
    - Renal/Gastrointestinal
    - Musculoskeletal/Multisystem/Psychosocial
    - Behavioral / Crisis Intervention
    - Advocacy, Caring Practices, Response to Diversity, Facilitation of Learning
    - Collaboration, Systems Thinking, and Clinical Inquiry.

Key Takeaways:
- **Scenario-Based is King:** This isn't about memorizing facts. It's about applying knowledge to real-world situations.
- **Time is Your Enemy:** Practice managing your time effectively so you don't run out of steam on the last section.

The PCCN exam is a marathon, not a sprint. Having a solid study plan and knowing which resources to tap into can make all the difference – let's get strategic!

Developing Your Personalized Study Plan
- **Honesty is the Best Policy:** Be brutally honest about your strengths and weaknesses. Do you rock at cardiac but struggle with neurology? Your plan needs to reflect that.
- **Time is of the Essence:** How many weeks or months do you have until your exam date? This determines the intensity and how much content you can realistically cover each day.
- **Your Learning Style:** Are you a visual learner? Note-taker? Practice-question junkie? Tailor your study methods to what works best for you.
- **Practice, Practice, Practice:** The more practice quesions you try the odds of scoring higher are increased.

Beyond the Books: Real-world Prep
- **Shadow a PCCN Nurse:** If possible, spend a shift with an experienced PCCN nurse to see the knowledge in action.
- **Study Groups:** Find motivated peers and hold each other accountable. Talking through concepts out loud can be incredibly helpful.

- **Self-Care Isn't Optional:** Sleep deprivation and burnout make the PCCN even harder. Schedule breaks, healthy meals, and even short moments of mindfulness into your study plan.

Remember: There's no one-size-fits-all recipe for PCCN success. But with dedication, strategic planning, and the right resources, you can walk into that testing center with confidence.

Cardiovascular:

Think of the cardiovascular system as your body's superhighway, with the heart as its tireless engine. Understanding how this system functions - and malfunctions - is critical when patients' lives hang in the balance. Let's get ready to dive into the nitty-gritty of cardiac care.

Why the Cardiovascular System Matters in Critical Care

Whether it's a heart attack, life-threatening bleeding, or severe infection, the cardiovascular system is almost always impacted in critically ill patients. Our ability to quickly assess, interpret data, and intervene makes a profound difference in patient outcomes.

What We'll Cover in this Section

- **The Building Blocks:** We'll start with cardiac output, preload, afterload, and the other factors that determine how well the heart moves blood. Think of these as the individual settings on your car's engine.
- **Rhythms Gone Wild:** Arrhythmias can range from minor annoyances to life-threatening chaos. You'll learn to recognize them on an EKG, understand the risks, and know the treatments.
- **Plumbing Problems:** Heart failure, heart attacks, shock states... we'll break down these diagnoses, how to spot them, and interventions that range from medications to advanced devices.
- **Beyond the Heart:** We'll look at the plumbing too – how to assess fluid status, use blood vessel tone to our advantage, and the role of blood itself (think electrolytes!).

This section isn't about memorizing isolated facts. You'll learn to connect dots – a low heart rate with changes in blood pressure, telltale lab results, and a patient's clinical picture. This integrated thinking is what makes excellent critical care nurses.

Picture your heart as a powerful, adaptable muscle—not just a simple pump. The Frank-Starling Law is the key to understanding how your heart adjusts its force of contraction based on how full it is. Here's the breakdown:

The Basic Idea: The more a muscle fiber is stretched (like a rubber band), the stronger it will contract. Your heart applies the same principle.

The Heart's Version: Increased blood return to the heart means that the heart's muscle fibers (especially in the ventricles) are stretched more before they contract. This stretch translates to a stronger squeeze (or increased stroke volume). Think of it as the heart giving an extra "oomph" to send more blood out into the body.

stronger squeeze ↑ stroke volume

Why This Matters in Critical Care: Picture a patient in shock – low blood pressure means organs and tissues aren't getting enough blood. The Frank-Starling mechanism is one way the heart tries to compensate. By pumping more forcefully with each beat, it aims to improve circulation even when there's less blood volume overall.

But There's a Limit: Like any muscle, your heart can be overstretched. Too much blood volume for too long weakens the contractions over time. This is where medications or support devices come into play in critical care.

Frank-Starling Law = Stretch = Stronger Contraction

It's a compensatory mechanism, helping the heart adjust to changing blood volume.

Critical care patients often have drastic fluid shifts, which makes the Frank-Starling Law extremely relevant.

Cardiac output (CO) is the lifeblood of critical care – literally! Here's the breakdown:

- **What It Is:** Cardiac output is the amount of blood your heart pumps out each minute. Think of it as the volume of blood your heart is shipping through the body to deliver oxygen and nutrients.
- **Why It Matters:** A patient's cardiac output is a major indicator of how well their organs and tissues are getting what they need. Too low? It's a red flag that the body might be heading into shock. Too high? It might be overworking the heart.
- **Simple Math, Big Impact:** We calculate cardiac output with a straightforward formula:

$CO = HR \times SV$

- HR = Heart Rate (beats per minute)
- SV = Stroke Volume (the amount of blood ejected with each beat)

Let's Use an Example:

Say a patient has a heart rate of 80 beats per minute. Each beat pushes out around 70 mL of blood (a typical stroke volume). Their cardiac output would be:

80 beats/minute x 70 mL/beat = 5,600 mL/minute (or about 5.6 liters pumped per minute!)

Critical Care Caveat: We can measure cardiac output directly in critical care with special devices, but this simple calculation gives us a quick ballpark idea of the patient's cardiovascular status. It's a starting point that we then pair with other assessments to get the full picture.

Cardiac output (CO) serves as a fundamental indicator of cardiovascular function, offering a comprehensive snapshot of the heart's efficiency in circulating blood throughout the body. This parameter is pivotal for assessing the hemodynamic status of patients, especially in critical care settings where cardiovascular stability often hangs in the balance.

Role of Cardiac Output in Cardiovascular Assessment

Indicator of Circulatory Health: CO quantifies the heart's ability to meet the body's metabolic demands. A normal cardiac output ensures adequate delivery of oxygen and nutrients to tissues, which is crucial for maintaining cellular function and organ health.

Diagnostic Tool: Variations in CO can signal underlying cardiac issues. For instance, a reduced CO might indicate heart failure, cardiogenic shock, or other conditions impairing the heart's pumping capability. Conversely, an elevated CO could be seen in scenarios like sepsis or hyperthyroidism, where peripheral vasodilation or increased metabolic demands elevate the heart's workload.

Guiding Interventions: In critical care, interventions often aim to optimize CO to ensure vital organ perfusion. Decisions regarding fluid management, inotropic support, and vasopressor use are frequently based on CO measurements, alongside other hemodynamic parameters.

Implications for Critical Care Interventions

Fluid Management: Careful administration of fluids in critical care aims to optimize preload (end-diastolic volume), enhancing CO based on the Frank-Starling law. However, it's a delicate balance; excessive fluid can lead to volume overload, reducing CO and exacerbating heart failure symptoms.

Inotropic Support: Medications that increase myocardial contractility (inotropes) can be employed to boost CO in patients with heart failure or cardiogenic shock. These interventions directly enhance stroke volume, thereby increasing CO.

Vasopressor and Vasodilator Therapy: Vasopressors can be used to increase systemic vascular resistance (SVR), aiding in the elevation of blood pressure in hypotensive states. Vasodilators, conversely, can reduce SVR and afterload, potentially increasing CO in conditions like acute heart failure, provided that preload is adequately managed.

Mechanical Assistance: In severe cases, mechanical circulatory support devices (like intra-aortic balloon pumps or ventricular assist devices) can be used to temporarily support or augment cardiac output, ensuring organ perfusion in critically ill patients.

Understanding and managing CO is fundamental in critical care, where interventions often hinge on the dynamic interplay between volume status, myocardial contractility, and vascular tone. Mastery of these concepts allows healthcare professionals to tailor their approach to each patient's unique physiology, optimizing outcomes in complex clinical scenarios.

Think of preload as the "filling pressure" of the heart before it squeezes. It's the amount of blood the heart has available to pump out with each beat. Understanding preload is essential in critical care, as it impacts how much blood the heart can send to the rest of the body.
Here's a breakdown:
What is Preload?
- It's the stretch placed on the heart's muscle fibers (especially the ventricles) right before contraction. Remember, the Frank-Starling Law tells us that a greater stretch usually translates to a stronger contraction.
- Imagine a water balloon: the more water you fill it with (volume), the more stretched and tense it becomes. Your heart operates similarly.

What Determines Preload?
1. Blood Volume: More circulating blood = more blood returning to the heart = higher preload. This is why we carefully monitor fluid balance in critical care – it directly impacts preload.
2. Venous Return: This is the blood flowing back to the heart through the veins. Think of veins as the highways carrying blood towards the heart. Factors that increase venous return (like giving fluids) will also increase preload. Conversely, factors that decrease venous return (like bleeding) will decrease preload.

Critical Care Connection:
- Dehydration leads to low preload: The patient doesn't have enough circulating volume to fill the heart adequately.
- Heart failure can lead to high preload: Blood backs up into the veins and over-stretches the heart muscle over time.

- Assessing preload: While we can't directly measure a number, we use clues like central venous pressure (CVP) along with the patient's clinical presentation to gauge if preload is low, normal, or high.

Key Takeaway: Preload is a dynamic factor, constantly changing based on a patient's condition. Managing preload is a balancing act – too low or too high can negatively impact cardiac output.

Central Venous Pressure (CVP) monitoring is a widely used clinical tool to assess preload, providing insights into the right atrial pressure and, by extension, the volume status and venous return to the heart. It serves as an indirect marker of the heart's filling pressure, offering valuable information for guiding fluid management and optimizing cardiac function, particularly in critically ill patients.

CVP as an Indicator of Preload
CVP reflects the pressure in the thoracic vena cava near the right atrium, offering an approximation of right ventricular end-diastolic pressure, which correlates with preload under certain conditions. By monitoring CVP, clinicians can infer whether the preload is potentially high or low, aiding in decisions regarding fluid administration or removal. For instance, a low CVP might suggest that a patient could benefit from fluid resuscitation, while a high CVP might indicate fluid overload or right ventricular dysfunction.

Limitations of CVP Monitoring
Despite its utility, CVP monitoring comes with several limitations that can affect its accuracy and reliability in assessing preload:

Intrathoracic Pressure Changes: Conditions that alter intrathoracic pressure, such as mechanical ventilation or tension pneumothorax, can influence CVP readings, making them less reflective of true preload.

Right Heart Function: CVP is more directly related to right ventricular function and may not accurately reflect left ventricular preload, especially in the presence of left-sided heart dysfunction or valvular abnormalities.

Venous Tone: Changes in venous tone due to medications or autonomic nervous system activity can alter CVP without reflecting changes in blood volume.

Individual Variability: There is considerable individual variability in the relationship between CVP and preload, making it difficult to define absolute CVP values that apply universally to all patients.

Alternative Preload Assessment Methods
Given the limitations of CVP monitoring, several alternative methods are utilized to assess preload and guide fluid management:

Echocardiography: This non-invasive technique provides real-time images of the heart, allowing direct assessment of ventricular volumes, wall motion, and filling patterns. It can more accurately estimate preload and cardiac function, guiding fluid and inotropic therapy.

Pulmonary Artery Catheterization: The use of a pulmonary artery catheter can measure pulmonary artery occlusion pressure (PAOP), which more closely approximates left ventricular preload than CVP. However, this invasive method is reserved for specific clinical scenarios due to its associated risks.

Passive Leg Raise (PLR) Test: The PLR test is a dynamic bedside maneuver that transiently increases venous return, simulating a fluid bolus. Observing the hemodynamic response to PLR can help predict fluid responsiveness in patients, particularly when combined with echocardiography or continuous cardiac output monitoring.

Volume Responsiveness Indices: Advanced hemodynamic monitoring technologies offer dynamic indices like stroke volume variation (SVV) and pulse pressure variation (PPV), which can predict volume responsiveness more accurately than static pressures in selected patients, particularly those under mechanical ventilation.

Incorporating a multimodal approach to assess preload, considering both the limitations of CVP and the utility of alternative methods, allows for more nuanced and effective management of fluid therapy in critically ill patients, ultimately improving outcomes by tailoring interventions to individual patient needs.

Afterload refers to the load against which the heart must contract to eject blood during systole. In simpler terms, it's the resistance the left ventricle must overcome to circulate blood throughout the body. Afterload is a critical determinant of cardiac function and is closely intertwined with the concept of systemic vascular resistance (SVR), which plays a significant role in influencing afterload.

Understanding Afterload

Afterload is not just a single value or pressure but a dynamic factor that reflects the complexities of arterial blood flow, vessel elasticity, and the overall vascular tone of the systemic circulation. It's pivotal in the context of cardiac health and disease management, as excessive afterload can lead to ventricular hypertrophy and exacerbate conditions like hypertension and heart failure.

The Role of Systemic Vascular Resistance (SVR) in Afterload

SVR is the resistance offered by the systemic circulatory system (excluding the pulmonary circulation) to the ejection of blood by the left ventricle. It is influenced by various factors, including the diameter and elasticity of blood vessels, blood viscosity, and the overall length of the vascular system. Mathematically, SVR can be calculated using the formula:

$$SVR = \frac{(MeanArterialPressure - CentralVenousPressure)}{CardiacOutput} \times 80$$

This equation highlights how SVR is directly proportional to the mean arterial pressure (minus central venous pressure) and inversely proportional to cardiac output. The constant factor (80) is used to convert the units to dynes·sec·cm^{-5}, a conventional unit for measuring resistance.

Implications of SVR on Afterload

1. **Increased SVR**: Conditions that elevate SVR, such as hypertension, vasoconstriction, or atherosclerosis, increase afterload. This requires the left ventricle to exert more force to eject blood, which can lead to myocardial strain and, over time, ventricular hypertrophy.
2. **Decreased SVR**: Conversely, a decrease in SVR, which might occur due to vasodilation from medications or septic shock, reduces afterload. While initially this may seem beneficial, excessively low afterload due to diminished SVR can lead to inadequate perfusion pressures and organ underperfusion.

Understanding and managing afterload and SVR is crucial in treating various cardiovascular disorders. Therapeutic interventions often aim to modulate SVR to optimize afterload, thereby improving cardiac efficiency and patient outcomes. For instance, antihypertensive medications that induce vasodilation can effectively reduce SVR and, consequently, the afterload, easing the burden on the heart.

Systemic Vascular Resistance (SVR) is a critical parameter in understanding the hemodynamic state and cardiac function, representing the resistance offered by the systemic circulation against the blood ejected from the left ventricle. Calculating SVR not only provides insights into afterload but also helps in diagnosing, monitoring, and managing various cardiovascular conditions.

Calculation of SVR
SVR is calculated using the following formula:

$$SVR = \frac{(MAP - CVP)}{CO} \times 80$$

Where:

- SVR = Systemic Vascular Resistance (usually expressed in dynes·sec·cm^{-5})
- MAP = Mean Arterial Pressure (in mmHg)
- CVP = Central Venous Pressure (in mmHg), often considered to be negligible or zero in clinical settings where it's not measured
- CO = Cardiac Output (in L/min)
- The constant 80 is a conversion factor used to convert the units from mmHg·min/L to dynes·sec·cm^{-5}.

Mean Arterial Pressure (MAP) can be calculated from systolic and diastolic blood pressure (SBP and DBP) using the formula:

$$MAP \approx DBP + \tfrac{1}{3}(SBP - DBP)$$

Impact on Cardiac Function
SVR directly influences cardiac function by affecting the afterload, which is the resistance the heart must overcome to eject blood. A high SVR increases afterload, making it more challenging for the heart to pump blood, potentially leading to left ventricular hypertrophy and exacerbating conditions like heart failure. Conversely, a low SVR decreases afterload, which can ease the work of the heart but might also lead to inadequate perfusion pressure if too low.

Impact on Blood Pressure
SVR is intricately linked to blood pressure regulation. An increase in SVR, assuming constant cardiac output, typically leads to an increase in blood pressure. This is often seen in conditions like hypertension, where vasoconstriction or arterial stiffness increases resistance. On the other hand, a decrease in SVR, which can occur with vasodilation from certain medications or in septic shock, can lead to a drop in blood pressure.

Understanding and monitoring SVR is crucial in the clinical setting, especially in critical care, where precise hemodynamic management can significantly affect patient outcomes. Interventions may include fluid management, vasopressors, or vasodilators, tailored to optimize SVR, thereby improving cardiac function and stabilizing blood pressure according to the individual patient's needs.

Contractility refers to the intrinsic ability of cardiac muscle fibers to contract, independent of changes in muscle length or preload. It is a crucial determinant of the heart's pumping efficiency, reflecting the strength of myocardial contraction. This property is influenced by the intracellular calcium availability and the sensitivity of the contractile apparatus to calcium, which are modulated by various neurohormonal factors, including sympathetic stimulation and certain medications.

Impact on Stroke Volume
Stroke volume, the amount of blood ejected by the left ventricle with each heartbeat, is influenced by three primary factors: preload, afterload, and contractility. Of these, contractility plays a pivotal role in determining the heart's capacity to eject blood effectively:

Enhanced Contractility: An increase in contractility leads to a more forceful ventricular contraction, resulting in a greater volume of blood being ejected with each beat, thereby increasing stroke volume. This can be observed during sympathetic stimulation, where catecholamines such as adrenaline enhance myocardial contractility, or with the administration of positive inotropic agents like digoxin.

Diminished Contractility: Conversely, a decrease in contractility, as seen in myocardial ischemia or heart failure, can lead to a reduced stroke volume. In these conditions, the impaired contractile function of the heart muscle compromises its ability to pump blood efficiently, necessitating medical intervention to support cardiac output.

Clinical Relevance
The clinical assessment of contractility is often indirect, inferred from measures such as ejection fraction, ventricular pressure-volume relationships, or the response to inotropic agents. Enhancing contractility is a common therapeutic goal in heart failure management, aiming to improve stroke volume and overall cardiac output. However, it's crucial to balance the benefits of increased contractility with potential risks, such as heightened myocardial oxygen demand or arrhythmias.

Contractility is a fundamental aspect of cardiac function, directly impacting stroke volume and, by extension, cardiac output. Its modulation, whether through physiological mechanisms or pharmacological interventions, is central to managing various cardiovascular conditions, underscoring the importance of understanding this dynamic component of cardiac performance. In the critical care setting, manipulating contractility is often necessary to manage acute heart failure, cardiogenic shock, and other conditions where the heart's pumping efficiency is compromised. This is where inotropic drugs play a pivotal role.
Inotropic Drugs and Their Mechanisms
Inotropic drugs affect contractility by altering the intracellular calcium concentration, which is the key regulator of cardiac muscle contraction. These agents can be classified into two main types based on their effect on contractility:
1. **Positive Inotropes**: These drugs increase myocardial contractility, thereby enhancing stroke volume and cardiac output. They work through various mechanisms, including:

- Increasing intracellular calcium availability, as seen with digoxin, which inhibits the Na^+/K^+-ATPase pump, indirectly increasing calcium influx.
- Stimulating adrenergic receptors ($β_1$-adrenergic agonists like dobutamine), leading to increased cyclic AMP and calcium levels within cardiac cells.
- Phosphodiesterase inhibitors (such as milrinone) prevent the breakdown of cyclic AMP, prolonging its positive inotropic effect.

2. **Negative Inotropes**: These agents decrease myocardial contractility and are used less frequently in critical care. They may be employed in specific scenarios, such as hypertrophic cardiomyopathy, to reduce the force of cardiac contractions and alleviate obstructive symptoms. Examples include beta-blockers and non-dihydropyridine calcium channel blockers.

Clinical Application in Critical Care

The judicious use of positive inotropic drugs is critical in managing patients with acute heart failure or shock states where enhanced cardiac output is necessary to maintain tissue perfusion. For example:

- **Dobutamine**: Often the first choice in cases of acute heart failure with reduced ejection fraction, dobutamine improves contractility without significantly increasing heart rate or oxygen demand.
- **Milrinone**: Used in patients with heart failure who are also experiencing significant afterload, as it provides both inotropic and vasodilatory effects, improving contractility and reducing ventricular filling pressures.

Considerations and Monitoring

While inotropic drugs can be lifesaving, their use requires careful consideration of the patient's overall hemodynamic status and monitoring for potential side effects, such as arrhythmias, increased myocardial oxygen consumption, and hypotension. The choice of inotropic support is tailored to the individual patient's clinical scenario, underlying pathophysiology, and response to initial treatments.

Inotropic drugs are powerful tools in critical care for modulating heart contractility, enhancing cardiac output, and improving perfusion. Their use, guided by a thorough understanding of their mechanisms and vigilant monitoring, can significantly impact patient outcomes in the acute care setting.

Pulsus paradoxus is like a detective story inside your patient's chest. It's a subtle sign with big implications! Let's break it down:

What is Pulsus Paradoxus?

The Drop: Pulsus paradoxus is an exaggerated decrease in blood pressure (more than 10 mmHg) during inspiration (when someone breathes in).

Feel the Difference: You would notice this as a weaker pulse when the patient takes a deep breath. If you're measuring blood pressure, the reading would drop significantly during inspiration.

Mechanism of Pulsus Paradoxus

The mechanism underlying pulsus paradoxus involves complex interactions between intrathoracic pressure changes, ventricular interdependence, and alterations in cardiac filling:

Inspiratory Intrathoracic Pressure Decrease: During inspiration, the intrathoracic pressure decreases, leading to increased venous return to the right side of the heart. However, the negative pressure also expands the lung tissue, increasing pulmonary vascular capacitance and thus, sequestering more blood in the pulmonary circulation.

Ventricular Interdependence: The increased right ventricular filling during inspiration, combined with a fixed total cardiac volume due to the pericardial constraint, shifts the interventricular septum towards the left ventricle, reducing its filling capacity (preload).

Decreased Left Ventricular Output: The reduced left ventricular filling during inspiration leads to a significant drop in stroke volume and, consequently, systolic blood pressure, manifesting as pulsus paradoxus.

Assessment Techniques
Pulsus paradoxus is traditionally assessed using a sphygmomanometer and stethoscope:

Blood Pressure Measurement: Inflate the blood pressure cuff to a point above the systolic pressure, then slowly deflate it.

Identification of Korotkoff Sounds: Note the pressure at which Korotkoff sounds are first heard only during expiration (this is the higher systolic pressure). Continue to slowly deflate the cuff until the Korotkoff sounds are heard throughout the respiratory cycle (this is the lower systolic pressure).

Calculation: The difference between the higher systolic pressure (heard only during expiration) and the lower systolic pressure (heard throughout the respiratory cycle) is the magnitude of pulsus paradoxus.

Modern methods can involve more sophisticated hemodynamic monitoring equipment, providing continuous measurements that can detect subtler variations in intrathoracic pressure and cardiac output.

Clinical Significance in Cardiac Tamponade and Severe Asthma
Pulsus paradoxus is a hallmark sign in conditions like cardiac tamponade and severe asthma, where intrathoracic pressures and cardiac filling are significantly affected:

Cardiac Tamponade: The accumulation of fluid in the pericardial space restricts cardiac filling, amplifying the effects of intrathoracic pressure changes on ventricular filling and leading to marked pulsus paradoxus. In this context, pulsus paradoxus is a critical diagnostic clue and an indicator of the severity of tamponade physiology.

Severe Asthma: The increased negative intrathoracic pressure due to forceful inspiratory efforts, combined with air trapping and hyperinflation, exacerbates the venous return and ventricular interdependence dynamics, leading to pulsus paradoxus. Its presence in asthma can indicate a severe airway obstruction and impending respiratory failure.

Recognizing pulsus paradoxus and understanding its underlying mechanisms are essential in diagnosing and managing conditions with altered cardiac filling and intrathoracic pressures, guiding timely and appropriate interventions to mitigate the hemodynamic consequences.

Stroke Volume Variations (SVV) are fluctuations in the stroke volume (the amount of blood ejected by the left ventricle of the heart during a single contraction) that occur during the respiratory cycle. In mechanically ventilated patients, these variations can be particularly pronounced and have been recognized as valuable indicators in assessing fluid responsiveness, an essential aspect of dynamic fluid management in critical care settings.

Understanding Stroke Volume Variations

SVV is influenced by the interplay between intrathoracic pressure changes during mechanical ventilation and the preload condition of the heart. During positive pressure ventilation, the increase in intrathoracic pressure during inspiration reduces venous return to the heart, leading to a decrease in left ventricular preload and, consequently, a reduced stroke volume. Conversely, during expiration, the decrease in intrathoracic pressure facilitates venous return, increasing preload and stroke volume. This cyclical change constitutes stroke volume variation.

Interpretation of SVV

The magnitude of SVV is directly related to the patient's fluid status and ventricular function. A high SVV (typically >12-15%) often indicates that the patient is in a fluid-responsive state, meaning that their stroke volume—and thus cardiac output—would likely increase with fluid administration. Conversely, a low SVV suggests that the patient is less likely to benefit from additional fluid loading, as they may be on the flat portion of the Frank-Starling curve where further increases in preload do not significantly enhance stroke volume.

SVV in Dynamic Fluid Assessment

Dynamic fluid assessment using SVV offers several advantages over traditional static measures of preload, such as Central Venous Pressure (CVP) or Pulmonary Artery Occlusion Pressure (PAOP), which have not consistently correlated well with fluid responsiveness. SVV provides a real-time, beat-to-beat analysis of how intrathoracic pressure changes affect cardiac filling and output, making it a more sensitive and specific indicator for guiding fluid therapy in critically ill patients, especially those who are mechanically ventilated.

Clinical Implications

1. **Cardiac Tamponade**: In conditions like cardiac tamponade, where external compression on the heart restricts ventricular filling, SVV may be elevated due to the heart's impaired response to changes in preload. Recognizing elevated SVV can be a diagnostic clue, prompting further investigation for tamponade physiology.
2. **Severe Asthma**: Similarly, in severe asthma or conditions associated with high intrathoracic pressures, the impact on venous return can exaggerate SVV. This highlights the need for cautious fluid management, guided by dynamic indices like SVV, to avoid fluid overload while managing the underlying respiratory condition.

Assessment Techniques

SVV is typically measured using advanced hemodynamic monitoring systems that can derive stroke volume from arterial waveform analysis. These systems calculate SVV by analyzing the variations in pulse pressure or stroke volume over a defined number of respiratory cycles, providing a quantitative measure of SVV. Stroke volume variations offer a dynamic and insightful approach to assessing fluid responsiveness in critically ill patients. By integrating SVV into the broader clinical context, healthcare providers can make more informed decisions about fluid management, optimizing cardiac output and tissue perfusion while minimizing the risks associated with inappropriate fluid administration.

Systematic EKG (electrocardiogram) analysis is an essential skill in diagnosing and managing a wide array of cardiovascular conditions. A meticulous, step-by-step approach ensures no vital information is overlooked. Here's a structured method to interpret an EKG:

1. Rate Determination

Start by calculating the heart rate, which can be done by counting the number of QRS complexes in a 6-second strip and multiplying by 10 for the beats per minute (bpm). Alternatively, for regular rhythms, measure the distance between R waves in small squares, and divide this into 1500 for the rate in bpm.

2. Rhythm Analysis

Assess the rhythm's regularity by measuring the interval between successive R waves. Check if this interval remains constant across the EKG. Identify the rhythm's origin by observing P wave presence and morphology - regular P waves before each QRS complex suggest sinus origin.

3. Axis Evaluation

The heart's electrical axis gives insight into the overall direction of electrical activity. It's determined by analyzing the QRS complex in leads I and aVF:

- Normal axis: Positive QRS in both leads I and aVF.
- Left axis deviation: Positive QRS in lead I, negative in aVF.
- Right axis deviation: Negative QRS in lead I, positive in aVF.
- Extreme axis deviation: Negative QRS in both leads I and aVF.

4. P Wave Assessment

P waves represent atrial depolarization. Evaluate for:

- Presence: Absent P waves may indicate atrial fibrillation.
- Morphology: Abnormal shapes can suggest atrial enlargement.
- Relationship to QRS: A P wave preceding each QRS complex indicates normal atrioventricular conduction.

5. QRS Complex Analysis

The QRS complex reflects ventricular depolarization. Examine for:

- Duration: A QRS duration > 0.12 seconds suggests bundle branch block.
- Morphology: Abnormal QRS shapes can indicate conduction delays, ventricular hypertrophy, or previous myocardial infarctions.

6. ST-T Segment and T Wave Evaluation

The ST segment and T wave indicate ventricular repolarization. Look for:

- ST elevation or depression: These can be signs of myocardial infarction or ischemia.
- T wave inversion: This may suggest ischemia, especially if localized in specific leads corresponding to certain heart regions.

7. Identification of Hypertrophy and Infarction

- Left Ventricular Hypertrophy (LVH): Look for increased voltage in the QRS complexes, particularly in the left-sided leads (V5, V6, aVL, and I).
- Right Ventricular Hyparthy (RVH): May show a dominant R wave in lead V1.
- Infarction: ST elevation, Q waves, and T wave inversion in contiguous leads can indicate a myocardial infarction's location and age.

By systematically following these steps, you can perform a comprehensive analysis of an EKG, allowing for accurate diagnosis and appropriate management of various cardiac conditions. Remember, practice and familiarity with a wide range of EKG patterns are key to mastering EKG interpretation.

Arrhythmias, or irregular heart rhythms, can range from benign to life-threatening. Understanding their EKG features, clinical presentations, and treatment principles is crucial for effective management. Here's an overview of common arrhythmias:

Atrial Fibrillation (AFib)

EKG Features: Irregularly irregular rhythm, absent P waves, replaced by fibrillatory waves. **Clinical Manifestations**: Palpitations, fatigue, dyspnea, or may be asymptomatic. **Treatment Principles**: Rate control (beta-blockers, calcium channel blockers), rhythm control (antiarrhythmic drugs, electrical cardioversion), anticoagulation to prevent thromboembolic events, and potentially ablation therapy.

Atrial Flutter

EKG Features: Sawtooth-like flutter waves, particularly in leads II, III, and aVF, with a regular or variable ventricular response. **Clinical Manifestations**: Similar to AFib, including palpitations and shortness of breath. **Treatment Principles**: Rate control, rhythm control (often through catheter ablation), and anticoagulation based on risk factors for stroke.

Supraventricular Tachycardias (SVTs)
EKG Features: Narrow QRS complexes with a rapid rate (>150 bpm), P waves may be buried within the QRS or appear after the QRS. **Clinical Manifestations**: Rapid palpitations, dizziness, chest discomfort. **Treatment Principles**: Vagal maneuvers, adenosine (to help diagnose and potentially treat), beta-blockers, or calcium channel blockers for rate control, and possible electrophysiology study with ablation.

Ventricular Tachycardia (VTach)
EKG Features: Wide QRS complexes (>0.12 sec) with a fast rate (>100 bpm), often regular rhythm. **Clinical Manifestations**: May be stable with palpitations or unstable with severe hypotension, syncope, or cardiac arrest. **Treatment Principles**: Immediate synchronized cardioversion if unstable, antiarrhythmic drugs (like amiodarone), and ICD (Implantable Cardioverter Defibrillator) evaluation for secondary prevention.

Ventricular Fibrillation (VFib)
EKG Features: Chaotic rhythm with no discernible P waves, QRS complexes, or T waves. **Clinical Manifestations**: Sudden collapse, loss of consciousness, no pulse. **Treatment Principles**: Immediate CPR and defibrillation, followed by ACLS protocols including epinephrine and potential antiarrhythmic drugs.

Heart Blocks
- **First-Degree**: Prolonged PR interval (>0.20 sec) consistently across all beats.
- **Second-Degree Type 1 (Wenckebach)**: Progressive lengthening of the PR interval until a beat is dropped.
- **Second-Degree Type 2**: Sudden dropped beats without change in PR interval.
- **Third-Degree (Complete Heart Block)**: Complete disassociation between P waves and QRS complexes. **Clinical Manifestations**: Can be asymptomatic or present with fatigue, dizziness, or syncope. **Treatment Principles**: Observation for first-degree and some type 2, pacemaker for symptomatic type 2 and third-degree blocks.

Life-Threatening Arrhythmias Requiring ACLS Interventions
For arrhythmias like VTach, VFib, and unstable SVTs, Advanced Cardiac Life Support (ACLS) protocols provide a structured approach, including drug therapy, electrical cardioversion/defibrillation, and other advanced interventions tailored to the arrhythmia's type and the patient's stability.

Understanding the nuances of these arrhythmias enables healthcare providers to initiate timely and appropriate interventions, optimizing patient outcomes in both acute and chronic care settings. Arrhythmias, or abnormal heart rhythms, arise from disruptions in the heart's electrical conduction system, which can lead to irregular heartbeats. These disruptions can result from various electrophysiological mechanisms, including altered automaticity, triggered activity, and re-entry.

Altered Automaticity
Automaticity refers to the heart cells' inherent ability to generate electrical impulses spontaneously. In a healthy heart, this property is primarily confined to pacemaker cells in the sinoatrial (SA) node. However, under certain pathological conditions, other cardiac tissues can exhibit enhanced automaticity, leading to arrhythmias.

Enhanced Automaticity: This occurs when cells outside the SA node start firing impulses more rapidly than normal, potentially due to ischemia, electrolyte imbalances, or pharmacological agents. This can lead to ectopic beats or tachycardia originating from atrial or ventricular tissues.

Depressed Automaticity: Reduced automaticity in the SA node can lead to bradycardia, where the heart rate slows down, potentially causing inadequate blood circulation.

Triggered Activity
Triggered activities arise from afterdepolarizations, which are abnormal depolarizations following a regular action potential. These are classified into:

Early Afterdepolarizations (EADs): Occur during the repolarization phase, often under conditions of prolonged action potentials, as seen with electrolyte imbalances or certain medications. EADs can lead to torsades de pointes, a type of polymorphic ventricular tachycardia.

Delayed Afterdepolarizations (DADs): Occur after the cell has repolarized, typically due to intracellular calcium overload, which can be seen in digitalis toxicity or catecholaminergic states. DADs can trigger atrial or ventricular tachycardias.

Re-entry
Re-entry is the most common mechanism underlying arrhythmias and occurs when an electrical impulse continues to circulate within a circuitous pathway in the heart tissue, repeatedly activating the same areas. This can happen due to:

Anatomic Re-entry: Involves a fixed anatomical pathway with unidirectional block and slow conduction, allowing the tail of the impulse to re-activate tissue that has recovered from refractoriness. Common examples include atrial flutter and AV nodal re-entrant tachycardia (AVNRT).

Functional Re-entry: Does not rely on a fixed anatomical pathway but rather on functional differences in refractory periods and conduction velocity within cardiac tissue, often seen in atrial fibrillation and ventricular fibrillation.

Clinical Implications
Understanding these electrophysiological mechanisms is crucial for diagnosing and managing arrhythmias effectively. Treatments may involve medications to stabilize the heart's electrical activity, interventions to correct electrolyte imbalances, or procedures like catheter ablation to disrupt re-entrant circuits or pacemaker/defibrillator implantation to manage bradyarrhythmias or prevent sudden cardiac death.

Pharmacological treatment of arrhythmias involves a range of antiarrhythmic drugs, each classified based on its primary mechanism of action. Understanding these drug classes, their mechanisms, indications, side effects, and necessary monitoring parameters is crucial for effective and safe management of arrhythmias.

Class I: Sodium Channel Blockers
- **Mechanism**: Inhibit fast sodium channels, slowing phase 0 depolarization and conduction velocity.
- **Indications**: Atrial and ventricular arrhythmias.
- **Side Effects**: Proarrhythmia, dizziness, blurred vision, and worsening of heart failure.
- **Monitoring**: ECG for QRS duration, signs of toxicity, liver function tests.
    - **Subclasses**:
        - IA (e.g., Quinidine, Procainamide) - Prolongs repolarization.
        - IB (e.g., Lidocaine, Mexiletine) - Shortens repolarization, used more for ventricular arrhythmias.

- IC (e.g., Flecainide, Propafenone) - Minimal effect on repolarization but significant slowing of conduction, used in atrial fibrillation/flutter.

Class II: Beta-Blockers
- **Mechanism**: Block beta-adrenergic receptors, reducing sympathetic influence on the heart, decreasing heart rate and contractility.
- **Indications**: Atrial fibrillation, atrial flutter, ventricular rate control, prevention of recurrent MI and sudden cardiac death.
- **Side Effects**: Bradycardia, hypotension, fatigue, bronchospasm in asthmatics.
- **Monitoring**: Heart rate, blood pressure, respiratory status.

Class III: Potassium Channel Blockers
- **Mechanism**: Inhibit potassium channels, prolonging repolarization and refractory period.
- **Indications**: Atrial fibrillation, ventricular tachycardia.
- **Side Effects**: Torsades de pointes, QT prolongation, liver and lung toxicity (amiodarone).
- **Monitoring**: ECG for QT interval, liver and thyroid function tests (for Amiodarone), pulmonary function tests.

Class IV: Calcium Channel Blockers
- **Mechanism**: Inhibit L-type calcium channels, reducing calcium influx during phase 2 of the action potential, slowing heart rate and conduction through the AV node.
- **Indications**: Atrial fibrillation/flutter for ventricular rate control, supraventricular tachycardia.
- **Side Effects**: Hypotension, constipation (Verapamil), peripheral edema, bradycardia.
- **Monitoring**: Blood pressure, heart rate, signs of heart failure.

Other Antiarrhythmics
- **Digoxin**: Increases vagal tone, slowing AV conduction. Used in atrial fibrillation for rate control.
- **Adenosine**: Temporarily blocks AV node conduction. Used in acute termination of supraventricular tachycardia (SVT).
- **Side Effects**: Nausea, vomiting, bradycardia, AV block.
- **Monitoring**: ECG monitoring during administration, especially for adenosine due to its short half-life.

Monitoring and Considerations
- **Electrolytes**: Imbalances in potassium and magnesium can affect drug efficacy and risk of toxicity; regular monitoring is essential.
- **Renal and Liver Function**: Many antiarrhythmics are metabolized in the liver or excreted by the kidneys; impaired function can increase toxicity risk.
- **Drug Interactions**: Antiarrhythmics can interact with numerous other medications, affecting their metabolism and increasing the risk of adverse effects.
- **Patient-Specific Factors**: Age, comorbidities, and the presence of structural heart disease significantly influence drug choice and dosing.

The selection and management of antiarrhythmic drugs require a thorough understanding of their pharmacological properties, patient-specific factors, and potential interactions. Regular monitoring and adjustment based on clinical response and side effect profile are crucial for optimizing treatment outcomes.

Electrical therapies are pivotal interventions in the management of various arrhythmias and cardiac conditions. They include cardioversion, defibrillation, and cardiac pacing, each serving distinct purposes and utilized under different clinical scenarios.

Cardioversion

Cardioversion is a procedure used to restore a normal heart rhythm in patients with certain types of arrhythmic disorders, particularly atrial fibrillation or atrial flutter. It can be performed using either synchronized electrical shocks or pharmacological agents.

- **Electrical Cardioversion**: Involves delivering a synchronized electrical shock to the heart, timed with the R wave on the ECG to avoid the vulnerable period of repolarization, which could precipitate ventricular fibrillation. This shock depolarizes a large portion of the heart muscle simultaneously, allowing the sinoatrial node to resume its role as the primary pacemaker.
- **Indications**: Symptomatic atrial fibrillation or flutter, supraventricular tachycardias not responsive to medical therapy.
- **Preparation and Monitoring**: Anticoagulation therapy is often required before and after the procedure to reduce the risk of thromboembolic events. Continuous ECG monitoring is essential during the procedure.

Defibrillation

Defibrillation is an emergency procedure used in life-threatening situations such as ventricular fibrillation (VF) or pulseless ventricular tachycardia (VT). Unlike cardioversion, the electrical shock is delivered immediately, without synchronization to the ECG, with the goal of depolarizing the entire myocardium to halt the arrhythmia and allow the sinoatrial node to re-establish a normal rhythm.

- **Indications**: Ventricular fibrillation, pulseless ventricular tachycardia.
- **Procedure**: High-energy shocks are delivered through paddles or adhesive pads placed on the chest. The energy levels and number of shocks are determined based on protocols and the patient's response.

Cardiac Pacing

Cardiac pacing involves the use of a pacemaker to regulate the heart's electrical activity and maintain an adequate heart rate. Pacemakers can be temporary or permanent, depending on the patient's condition.

- **Temporary Pacing**: Used in acute settings where bradycardia or heart block is reversible or awaiting permanent pacemaker implantation. Can be transcutaneous (external pacing pads) or transvenous (leads inserted into a central vein and positioned in the right heart chambers).
- **Permanent Pacing**: Involves implanting a pacemaker device under the skin, with leads placed in direct contact with the heart tissue. Used for chronic conditions such as symptomatic bradycardia, heart blocks, and certain heart failure cases.

Pacing Modes:

- **Single Chamber Pacing**: Stimulates either the right atrium or ventricle.
- **Dual Chamber Pacing**: Simultaneously stimulates the right atrium and ventricle, maintaining physiological coordination between atrial and ventricular contractions.
- **Rate-Responsive Pacing**: Adjusts pacing rate based on the patient's activity level or physiological needs.

Monitoring and Considerations

- **Electrolytes and Medication**: Ensure optimal electrolyte balance and review medications that might affect the procedure's efficacy or the patient's arrhythmia.
- **Device Checks**: Regular monitoring and programming of pacemakers are essential to ensure appropriate function and to adjust settings as the patient's condition changes.
- **Post-Procedure Care**: For invasive procedures, monitoring for complications such as infection, bleeding, or lead displacement is crucial.

Electrical therapies are integral components of arrhythmia management and cardiac care, requiring careful patient selection, preparation, and post-procedure monitoring to maximize efficacy and safety.

Acute Coronary Syndromes (ACS) encompass a spectrum of conditions associated with sudden, reduced blood flow to the heart, including ST-Elevation Myocardial Infarction (STEMI), Non-ST-Elevation Myocardial Infarction (NSTEMI), and Unstable Angina (UA). Understanding the pathophysiology, diagnostic workup, and management priorities of these conditions is crucial for effective treatment and improving patient outcomes.

Pathophysiology
1. **STEMI**: Characterized by full-thickness myocardial damage due to complete occlusion of a coronary artery. The hallmark is ST-segment elevation on an ECG, indicating transmural ischemia. The loss of blood flow leads to necrosis of the myocardial tissue in the affected area.
2. **NSTEMI**: Results from partial occlusion of a coronary artery or complete occlusion of a smaller artery, leading to partial-thickness myocardial damage. The ECG may show ST-segment depression, T-wave inversion, or no changes, but cardiac biomarkers (e.g., troponins) are elevated, indicating myocardial injury.
3. **Unstable Angina**: Similar to NSTEMI in that the coronary artery is partially occluded, but without the biochemical markers of myocardial injury. Patients present with chest pain, typically at rest or with minimal exertion, indicating worsening coronary ischemia.

Immediate Diagnostic Workup
The initial assessment includes a thorough history and physical examination, ECG, and cardiac biomarkers:
1. **ECG**: Performed immediately to identify ST-segment elevation in STEMI or other changes suggestive of NSTEMI or unstable angina.
2. **Cardiac Biomarkers**: Troponins are the most sensitive and specific markers for myocardial injury, rising within hours of symptom onset and remaining elevated for days.
3. **Risk Stratification**: Tools like the GRACE and TIMI scores can help assess the risk of adverse cardiac events, guiding management decisions.

Management Priorities
Reperfusion Strategies
- **STEMI**: Prompt reperfusion is critical. Primary percutaneous coronary intervention (PCI) is the preferred method if it can be performed within 90-120 minutes of first medical contact. If PCI is not available, fibrinolytic therapy should be considered within 12 hours from symptom onset, provided there are no contraindications.
- **NSTEMI/Unstable Angina**: Early invasive strategy (angiography with possible PCI) is recommended for high-risk patients, typically within 24-48 hours. Conservative management may be considered for low-risk patients.

Guideline-Directed Medical Therapies
- **Antiplatelets**: Aspirin is administered to all ACS patients unless contraindicated, with dual antiplatelet therapy (DAPT) initiated in patients undergoing PCI.
- **Anticoagulants**: Unfractionated heparin, low molecular weight heparin, or bivalirudin are used to prevent further thrombosis.
- **Beta-Blockers**: Reduce myocardial oxygen demand and are indicated unless contraindicated (e.g., severe heart failure, bradycardia).
- **ACE Inhibitors/ARBs**: Recommended within the first 24 hours for patients with STEMI, particularly those with left ventricular systolic dysfunction, heart failure, or hypertension.
- **Statins**: High-intensity statin therapy is initiated as soon as possible to stabilize atherosclerotic plaques and reduce cholesterol levels.

The management of ACS requires a rapid and coordinated approach to restore coronary blood flow and minimize myocardial damage. Early diagnosis, risk stratification, and prompt implementation of reperfusion strategies and guideline-directed medical therapies are key to improving outcomes for patients with ACS.

Imagine your heart as a tireless pump, but sometimes it gets worn out. That's the essence of heart failure (HF). Let's break down how it happens and the different ways we categorize it.
Heart failure (HF) is a complex clinical syndrome resulting from any structural or functional impairment of ventricular filling or the ejection of blood. The pathophysiology of heart failure involves a combination of hemodynamic abnormalities, neurohormonal activation, and cellular changes, leading to the heart's inability to pump sufficient blood to meet the body's needs.

Pathophysiology
1. **Hemodynamic Changes**: Initially, heart failure may stem from conditions that overwork the heart, such as hypertension, valve diseases, or myocardial infarction. These conditions increase the heart's workload, leading to hypertrophy and remodeling, which can eventually impair the heart's pumping ability.
2. **Neurohormonal Activation**: In response to reduced cardiac output, the body activates several neurohormonal systems, including the renin-angiotensin-aldosterone system (RAAS) and the sympathetic nervous system. While initially compensatory, chronic activation of these systems leads to vasoconstriction, fluid retention, and further cardiac remodeling, worsening heart failure.
3. **Cellular and Molecular Changes**: Heart failure is associated with alterations at the cellular level, including changes in calcium handling, energy metabolism, and myocyte contractility, contributing to the progressive nature of the disease.

Classifications of Heart Failure
Heart failure is classified based on the left ventricle's ejection fraction (EF), which is the percentage of blood the left ventricle pumps out with each contraction.
1. **Heart Failure with Reduced Ejection Fraction (HFrEF)**: Also known as systolic heart failure, HFrEF is characterized by a weakened heart muscle that cannot contract effectively, leading to an EF of 40% or less. The reduced contractility results in inadequate blood being pumped out to the body.
2. **Heart Failure with Preserved Ejection Fraction (HFpEF)**: Also known as diastolic heart failure, HFpEF occurs when the heart muscle is stiff and cannot relax normally, leading to impaired filling of the ventricles. Despite this, the EF may be normal or near normal (greater than 50%), as the heart can still contract well, but the amount of blood pumped is less due to poor filling.
3. **Heart Failure with Mid-Range Ejection Fraction (HFmrEF)**: This category includes patients with an EF that falls between HFrEF and HFpEF, specifically an EF between 41% and 49%. These patients share characteristics with both HFrEF and HFpEF.

New York Heart Association (NYHA) Functional Classification
The NYHA classification system is used to describe the severity of symptoms in patients with heart failure and how those symptoms affect daily activities:
- **Class I**: No limitation of physical activity. Ordinary physical activity does not cause undue fatigue, palpitation, or dyspnea (shortness of breath).
- **Class II**: Slight limitation of physical activity. Comfortable at rest, but ordinary physical activity results in fatigue, palpitation, or dyspnea.
- **Class III**: Marked limitation of physical activity. Comfortable at rest, but less than ordinary activity causes fatigue, palpitation, or dyspnea.
- **Class IV**: Unable to carry on any physical activity without discomfort. Symptoms of heart failure are present even at rest, with increased discomfort with any physical activity.

Understanding the pathophysiology and classifications of heart failure is crucial for diagnosing, managing, and treating this condition. Management strategies vary depending on the type of heart failure, its severity, and the underlying cause, aiming to improve symptoms, enhance quality of life, and extend survival.

The treatment of heart failure is multifaceted, aiming to alleviate symptoms, improve quality of life, and reduce mortality. A comprehensive approach involves a combination of lifestyle modifications, pharmacologic therapy, device therapy, and in some cases, surgical interventions. Here's an overview of the primary therapeutic strategies:

Diuretics
- **Purpose**: Diuretics are used to reduce fluid overload, a common symptom in heart failure, thereby alleviating congestion, edema, and dyspnea.
- **Types**: Loop diuretics (e.g., Furosemide) are most commonly used due to their efficacy in reducing volume. Thiazide diuretics may be used in some patients, while Aldosterone antagonists (e.g., Spironolactone, Eplerenone) offer both diuretic and neurohormonal blocking benefits.
- **Monitoring**: Electrolyte levels, renal function, and fluid status need to be closely monitored to avoid dehydration, electrolyte imbalances, and worsening renal function.

Inotropes
- **Purpose**: Inotropes, such as Dobutamine and Milrinone, enhance the contractility of the heart muscle, improving cardiac output and organ perfusion.
- **Use**: Primarily used in acute decompensated heart failure or chronic heart failure patients with refractory symptoms.
- **Considerations**: Long-term use is limited due to risks of arrhythmias and increased mortality; thus, they are often reserved for palliative care or as a bridge to more definitive therapy like heart transplantation.

Vasodilators
- **Purpose**: Vasodilators reduce systemic vascular resistance (afterload) and venous tone (preload), decreasing the work the heart must do to pump blood.
- **Agents**: ACE inhibitors (e.g., Enalapril) or ARBs (e.g., Losartan) are first-line therapies for HFrEF. Nitrates and Hydralazine can be added, especially in patients who cannot tolerate ACE inhibitors or ARBs.
- **Benefits**: Besides afterload reduction, these agents have been shown to improve survival and reduce hospitalizations in heart failure patients.

Beta-Blockers
- **Purpose**: Beta-blockers (e.g., Carvedilol, Metoprolol succinate, Bisoprolol) reduce the harmful effects of excessive sympathetic stimulation, a hallmark of chronic heart failure.
- **Impact**: They have been shown to improve survival, reduce hospitalizations, and ameliorate symptoms in patients with HFrEF.
- **Titration**: Initiated at low doses and gradually titrated up to target doses as tolerated, to avoid initial worsening of symptoms.

Aldosterone Antagonists
- **Purpose**: Aldosterone antagonists offer diuretic effects and counteract the adverse effects of aldosterone on the heart, including fibrosis and electrolyte imbalances.
- **Indications**: Recommended in patients with HFrEF, especially after an acute MI, to reduce mortality and hospitalization.

Angiotensin Receptor-Neprilysin Inhibitors (ARNIs)

- **Example**: Sacubitril/Valsartan is a newer class of medication that combines neprilysin inhibition with angiotensin receptor blockade.
- **Benefits**: ARNIs have been shown to be superior to ACE inhibitors in reducing cardiovascular death and hospitalizations for heart failure in patients with HFrEF.

Device Therapy
- **Implantable Cardioverter-Defibrillators (ICDs)**: For patients at high risk of sudden cardiac death due to ventricular arrhythmias.
- **Cardiac Resynchronization Therapy (CRT)**: For patients with HFrEF and evidence of ventricular dyssynchrony (e.g., wide QRS complex), CRT can improve symptoms and survival by optimizing the timing of ventricular contractions.

Advanced Therapies

For patients with refractory heart failure not amenable to conventional therapies, advanced options like heart transplantation or mechanical circulatory support devices (e.g., left ventricular assist devices) may be considered.

Lifestyle and Supportive Measures
- **Lifestyle Modifications**: Dietary sodium restriction, fluid intake management, regular physical activity tailored to the patient's tolerance, and smoking cessation are crucial.
- **Management of Comorbidities**: Optimal control of hypertension, diabetes, and ischemic heart disease is vital in managing heart failure.

Heart failure management requires a personalized approach, taking into account the type of heart failure, symptom severity, comorbidities, and patient-specific factors. Regular follow-up and adjustments to the treatment regimen are essential to ensure optimal patient outcomes.

Valvular heart diseases (VHD) involve abnormalities in one or more of the heart valves, leading to disrupted blood flow patterns within the heart. Among these, aortic stenosis and aortic regurgitation are two prevalent conditions, each with distinct pathophysiology, hemodynamic consequences, clinical presentations, and management strategies. This overview will also touch upon other significant valvular diseases for a comprehensive understanding.

Aortic Stenosis (AS)
- **Pathophysiology**: AS is characterized by the narrowing of the aortic valve orifice, usually due to calcific degeneration or congenital abnormalities, leading to obstruction of blood flow from the left ventricle to the aorta.
- **Hemodynamics**: The obstruction increases the pressure gradient across the aortic valve, leading to left ventricular hypertrophy as a compensatory mechanism to maintain cardiac output.
- **Clinical Presentations**: Patients may present with the classic triad of exertional dyspnea, angina, and syncope. Symptoms typically manifest when the stenosis is severe.
- **Management**: Symptomatic severe AS warrants aortic valve replacement, which can be surgical (SAVR) or transcatheter (TAVR). Asymptomatic patients with severe AS require careful monitoring for the development of symptoms, significant LV dysfunction, or other indications for intervention.

Aortic Regurgitation (AR)
- **Pathophysiology**: AR involves the backflow of blood from the aorta into the left ventricle during diastole, due to aortic valve leaflet malcoaptation. Causes include aortic root dilation, bicuspid aortic valve, rheumatic heart disease, and infective endocarditis.
- **Hemodynamics**: Chronic volume overload in the left ventricle leads to dilatation and eccentric hypertrophy, initially maintaining cardiac output through Frank-Starling mechanisms.

- **Clinical Presentations**: Patients may be asymptomatic for years before developing symptoms like exertional dyspnea and fatigue. Acute AR presents more dramatically with pulmonary edema and hypotension.
- **Management**: Chronic severe AR with symptoms or LV dysfunction typically requires aortic valve replacement. Acute AR necessitates emergency management, potentially including urgent valve surgery.

Mitral Stenosis (MS)
- **Pathophysiology**: Most commonly caused by rheumatic heart disease, MS is characterized by narrowing of the mitral valve orifice.
- **Clinical Presentations**: Dyspnea, orthopnea, and paroxysmal nocturnal dyspnea are common. Patients may also present with symptoms of right heart failure and systemic embolization.
- **Management**: Interventional procedures like percutaneous mitral balloon valvotomy may be indicated in symptomatic patients with favorable valve anatomy. Surgical repair or replacement is considered for others.

Mitral Regurgitation (MR)
- **Pathophysiology**: MR is the backflow of blood from the left ventricle to the left atrium during systole, caused by mitral valve leaflet prolapse, rheumatic heart disease, or myocardial infarction leading to papillary muscle dysfunction.
- **Clinical Presentations**: Fatigue and exertional dyspnea are typical. Severe MR can lead to pulmonary hypertension and right heart failure.
- **Management**: Management includes vasodilators for symptomatic relief and surgical repair or replacement for severe symptomatic MR or asymptomatic patients with signs of LV dysfunction.

Tricuspid Regurgitation (TR)
- **Pathophysiology**: Often secondary to right ventricular dilation, TR entails the backflow of blood into the right atrium during systole.
- **Clinical Presentations**: Symptoms include fatigue, peripheral edema, and ascites.
- **Management**: Primary management focuses on treating the underlying cause. Diuretics can help manage volume overload. Surgical intervention is reserved for severe cases, often during surgery for left-sided valve diseases.

Management Considerations

Management of valvular heart diseases is highly individualized, considering the severity of valve dysfunction, symptomatology, and the presence of comorbid conditions. Interventional strategies range from medical therapy for symptom management to percutaneous interventions and surgical valve repair or replacement, guided by a multidisciplinary heart team approach. Advances in diagnostic imaging, minimally invasive techniques, and valve repair technologies continue to evolve, offering improved outcomes for patients with VHD.

The management of arrhythmias often involves the use of antiarrhythmic medications, which are categorized into classes based on their primary mechanism of action. Here's a chart summarizing the main classes, their mechanisms, indications, common side effects, and essential monitoring parameters:

Class	Mechanism of Action	Indications	Common Side Effects	Monitoring
I: Sodium Channel Blockers	Block fast Na^+ channels, slowing conduction	Ventricular arrhythmias, some supraventricular arrhythmias	Dizziness, blurred vision, arrhythmias, nausea	ECG (QRS duration), liver function tests

Class	Mechanism of Action	Indications	Common Side Effects	Monitoring
IA (e.g., Quinidine, Procainamide, Disopyramide)	Moderate Na⁺ channel blockade; delay repolarization	Atrial fibrillation, flutter; ventricular arrhythmias	Tinnitus, headache, thrombocytopenia (Quinidine), lupus-like syndrome (Procainamide)	Blood counts, antinuclear antibody (ANA) for Procainamide
IB (e.g., Lidocaine, Mexiletine)	Mild Na⁺ channel blockade; shorten repolarization	Ventricular arrhythmias, especially post-MI	CNS effects, seizures (Lidocaine), GI disturbances	Serum levels (especially for Lidocaine)
IC (e.g., Flecainide, Propafenone)	Strong Na⁺ channel blockade; minimal effect on repolarization	Supraventricular arrhythmias, atrial fibrillation	Visual disturbances, dizziness, worsening heart failure	ECG, symptoms of heart failure
II: Beta-Blockers (e.g., Propranolol, Metoprolol)	Block β-adrenergic receptors, reducing sympathetic effects on the heart	Supraventricular arrhythmias, ventricular rate control in AF, prevention of SCD	Fatigue, bradycardia, hypotension, bronchospasm	Heart rate, blood pressure, respiratory status
III: Potassium Channel Blockers (e.g., Amiodarone, Sotalol)	Block K⁺ channels, prolonging repolarization	Atrial fibrillation, ventricular arrhythmias	Thyroid dysfunction, pulmonary toxicity (Amiodarone), torsades de pointes, bradycardia	ECG (QT interval), thyroid and liver function tests (especially for Amiodarone), pulmonary function
IV: Calcium Channel Blockers (e.g., Verapamil, Diltiazem)	Block L-type Ca²⁺ channels, slowing AV node conduction	Supraventricular tachycardia, rate control in AF	Constipation (Verapamil), edema, hypotension, bradycardia	Blood pressure, heart rate, signs of heart failure
Others: Digoxin	Increases vagal tone, reducing AV nodal conduction; positive inotropic effect	Atrial fibrillation (rate control), heart failure	Nausea, visual disturbances, arrhythmias, confusion	Serum digoxin level, electrolytes (K⁺, Mg²⁺), renal function

When prescribing antiarrhythmic medications, it's crucial to consider the patient's overall clinical picture, including underlying cardiac conditions, comorbidities, and potential drug interactions. Regular monitoring, both clinical and through laboratory tests, is essential to optimize therapy, minimize side effects, and ensure patient safety.

Inotropes and vasopressors are critical components of managing acute cardiovascular conditions, especially in critical care settings. Their use requires a thorough understanding of their mechanisms, indications, contraindications, and essential nursing considerations.

Inotropes

Dobutamine

- **Mechanism**: Dobutamine is a synthetic catecholamine that primarily stimulates $β_1$-adrenergic receptors, leading to increased myocardial contractility and stroke volume without significantly increasing heart rate.

- **Indications**: Used in cases of acute heart failure, cardiogenic shock, and inotropic support during cardiac stress testing.
- **Contraindications**: Hypertrophic obstructive cardiomyopathy, idiopathic subaortic stenosis, and caution in arrhythmias.
- **Nursing Considerations**: Monitor blood pressure, heart rate, and signs of ischemia. Titrate based on clinical response and hemodynamic parameters. Continuous cardiac monitoring is essential.

Milrinone
- **Mechanism**: Milrinone is a phosphodiesterase-3 inhibitor, increasing intracellular cAMP and calcium, leading to improved myocardial contractility and vasodilation.
- **Indications**: Acute decompensated heart failure, especially in patients with beta-blocker therapy, as it does not rely on adrenergic receptor stimulation.
- **Contraindications**: Severe obstructive aortic or pulmonic valvular disease.
- **Nursing Considerations**: Monitor for hypotension and arrhythmias. Renal function should be monitored, as milrinone is renally excreted. Use cautiously in patients with renal impairment.

Vasopressors

Norepinephrine
- **Mechanism**: Norepinephrine acts primarily on α_1-adrenergic receptors, causing potent vasoconstriction, and to a lesser extent on β_1-adrenergic receptors, increasing cardiac output.
- **Indications**: First-line agent for septic shock and other forms of shock where vasodilation is a primary problem.
- **Contraindications**: Hypotensive patients with hypovolemia not corrected by fluid resuscitation.
- **Nursing Considerations**: Monitor for peripheral ischemia, and ensure adequate fluid resuscitation before initiation. Continuous blood pressure and cardiac monitoring are necessary.

Dopamine
- **Mechanism**: Dopamine's effects are dose-dependent: low doses primarily stimulate dopaminergic receptors, medium doses stimulate β_1-adrenergic receptors, increasing contractility and heart rate, and high doses stimulate α_1-adrenergic receptors, causing vasoconstriction.
- **Indications**: Used in shock and acute heart failure, especially when increased renal perfusion is desired.
- **Contraindications**: Tachyarrhythmias, pheochromocytoma.
- **Nursing Considerations**: Monitor for tachyarrhythmias and extravasation, which can cause necrosis. Titrate based on response and monitor renal function.

Phenylephrine
- **Mechanism**: Phenylephrine is a pure α_1-adrenergic agonist, causing vasoconstriction and increasing systemic vascular resistance and arterial blood pressure.
- **Indications**: Used for vascular support in shock, particularly when tachyarrhythmias are a concern with other agents.
- **Contraindications**: Severe hypertension, bradycardia, narrow-angle glaucoma.
- **Nursing Considerations**: Closely monitor blood pressure and signs of decreased organ perfusion. Phenylephrine may increase afterload significantly, potentially worsening heart failure.

General Nursing Considerations
- **Titration**: Inotropes and vasopressors should be titrated to the lowest effective dose to achieve the desired hemodynamic effect while minimizing side effects.
- **Central Venous Access**: Preferably administer through a central line to reduce the risk of extravasation and tissue necrosis.

- **Multimodal Monitoring**: Continuous monitoring of vital signs, cardiac rhythm, urine output, and laboratory markers (lactate, base deficit) to assess the response to therapy and organ perfusion.
- **Patient Safety**: Ensure rapid recognition and management of adverse effects, including arrhythmias, ischemia, and extravasation.

The use of inotropes and vasopressors requires a delicate balance between improving hemodynamics and minimizing potential adverse effects. Careful patient selection, dosing, and vigilant monitoring are key to optimizing patient outcomes.

Anticoagulants and thrombolytics are pivotal in managing various cardiovascular conditions, particularly those involving thromboembolic events. Understanding their indications, mechanisms, administration routes, contraindications, and monitoring requirements is crucial for safe and effective patient care.

Anticoagulants

Anticoagulants prevent the formation of new clots and the growth of existing clots, playing a crucial role in conditions like atrial fibrillation, deep vein thrombosis (DVT), pulmonary embolism (PE), and in the prevention of stroke.

Mechanisms and Types

1. **Vitamin K Antagonists (e.g., Warfarin)**: Inhibit the synthesis of vitamin K-dependent clotting factors.
2. **Direct Oral Anticoagulants (DOACs) (e.g., Apixaban, Rivaroxaban)**: Inhibit specific clotting factors (Factor Xa or Thrombin) directly.
3. **Heparins (Unfractionated Heparin, Low Molecular Weight Heparin [LMWH])**: Enhance the activity of antithrombin, leading to the inactivation of thrombin and Factor Xa.

Administration
- Warfarin is administered orally, while heparins can be given intravenously (unfractionated) or subcutaneously (LMWH). DOACs are also taken orally.

Contraindications
- Active bleeding, recent surgery, severe thrombocytopenia, and specific patient populations (e.g., pregnancy for warfarin) are common contraindications.

Monitoring
- Warfarin requires regular INR monitoring to ensure therapeutic anticoagulation levels. Unfractionated heparin often necessitates aPTT monitoring, whereas LMWH and DOACs require less frequent laboratory monitoring but may need renal function assessment.

Thrombolytics

Thrombolytics, or "clot busters," are used in acute settings to dissolve significant thromboembolic occlusions, such as in acute myocardial infarction (AMI), acute ischemic stroke, and massive PE.

Mechanism
- Thrombolytics, including alteplase, reteplase, and tenecteplase, catalyze the conversion of plasminogen to plasmin, which then degrades fibrin clots.

Administration
- These agents are typically administered intravenously in acute care settings, often within specific time windows from symptom onset to maximize efficacy and reduce the risk of complications.

Contraindications
- Contraindications include recent surgery, active internal bleeding, history of hemorrhagic stroke, severe uncontrolled hypertension, and known bleeding disorders.

Monitoring

- Monitoring involves careful observation for signs of bleeding, hemodynamic stability, and neurological status, depending on the thrombolytic's indication. Serial imaging studies might be required for ischemic stroke patients to assess for hemorrhagic transformation.

Nursing Considerations
1. **Assessment**: Thorough patient history to identify contraindications to therapy.
2. **Bleeding Precautions**: Implement measures to minimize the risk of bleeding, including careful monitoring of access sites, minimizing invasive procedures, and regular inspection of potential bleeding sites.
3. **Education**: Patient and family education on the signs of bleeding, the importance of adherence to follow-up appointments, and dietary considerations, especially with warfarin therapy.

Anticoagulants and thrombolytics are cornerstone therapies in cardiovascular care, necessitating judicious use and vigilant monitoring to optimize outcomes and minimize risks.

Pacemakers are electronic devices that stimulate the heart to maintain or restore a normal rhythm. They are vital in managing various cardiac arrhythmias and conduction disorders. Understanding the indications, differences between temporary and permanent pacemakers, potential complications, and essential nursing care is crucial for effective patient management.

Indications
Pacemakers are indicated in several conditions where the heart's natural pacemaking and conduction system is compromised, including:

Bradycardia: Persistent slow heart rates leading to symptoms like fatigue, dizziness, or syncope.
Heart Blocks: Delays or blocks in the heart's electrical conduction pathways, particularly higher-degree blocks (second-degree type II, third-degree).
Sick Sinus Syndrome: Dysfunction of the sinoatrial node resulting in alternating bradycardia and tachycardia.
Atrial Fibrillation with Slow Ventricular Response: Particularly after medication management to control ventricular rate.

Temporary vs. Permanent Pacemakers
Temporary Pacemakers: Used in acute settings for transient bradycardia or blocks, such as after a myocardial infarction or during surgery. They can be external, transvenous, or epicardial (post-cardiac surgery) and are intended for short-term use until the underlying condition resolves or a permanent pacemaker is implanted.

Permanent Pacemakers: Implanted subcutaneously, usually in the pectoral region, with leads threaded through the venous system into the heart. They are used for chronic conduction system diseases, providing long-term pacing support.

Modes of Pacemakers
Pacemakers can operate in various modes, tailored to the patient's needs, including:

Single Chamber: Pacing either the atrium or ventricle.
Dual Chamber: Pacing both the atrium and ventricle, allowing for more physiological heart rhythm coordination.
Rate-Responsive: Adjusting pacing rate based on the patient's physical activity or physiological needs.
Complications

Potential complications from pacemaker implantation include:

Infection: At the device site or along the lead pathway.
Lead Displacement: Leads may move from their original position, affecting the device's efficacy.
Pneumothorax: Particularly with transvenous lead insertion.
Device Malfunction: Including battery depletion or electronic failure.
Nursing Care
Effective nursing care for patients with pacemakers involves:

Monitoring: Regular checks for device function, heart rhythm, and signs of complications, especially after initial implantation.
Wound Care: Managing the surgical site to prevent infection.
Education: Instructing the patient on activity restrictions, wound care, recognizing signs of infection or device malfunction, and the importance of regular follow-up appointments for device checks.
Psychosocial Support: Assisting patients in adjusting to living with a pacemaker, addressing concerns about device visibility, sensations of pacing, and lifestyle modifications.
Pacemakers significantly improve quality of life for patients with arrhythmias or conduction disorders. Careful monitoring, patient education, and timely management of complications are key to ensuring optimal outcomes with pacemaker therapy.

The Intra-aortic Balloon Pump (IABP) is a mechanical circulatory support device used to augment cardiac output and myocardial oxygen supply in patients with severe cardiac conditions. Understanding its mechanism, indications, timing and waveform analysis, and nursing care priorities is essential for effective patient management.

IABP Mechanism
The IABP consists of a balloon catheter inserted into the thoracic aorta. Its operation is synchronized with the cardiac cycle:

Diastole: The balloon inflates immediately after the closure of the aortic valve, increasing diastolic pressure, which enhances coronary artery perfusion and myocardial oxygen supply.
Systole: Just before ventricular ejection, the balloon deflates, creating a vacuum effect that reduces afterload and augments forward blood flow, thereby decreasing myocardial oxygen demand.
Indications
IABP therapy is indicated for various acute cardiac conditions, including:

Acute Myocardial Infarction (AMI): Especially with cardiogenic shock.
Cardiogenic Shock: Not responsive to medical therapy.
Complications of AMI: Such as acute mitral regurgitation or ventricular septal defect.
Support During High-Risk Percutaneous Coronary Interventions (PCI).
Bridge to Further Therapy: Such as cardiac surgery or transplantation in patients with refractory heart failure.
Timing and Waveform Analysis
Proper timing of IABP inflation and deflation is critical for its effectiveness:

Inflation: Should occur just after the dicrotic notch on the arterial waveform, indicating the closure of the aortic valve and the onset of diastole.

Deflation: Should be timed just before the onset of systole, ideally at the end of the T-wave on the ECG, to ensure reduced afterload during ventricular ejection.

Waveform analysis involves assessing the arterial pressure waveform to ensure optimal IABP function. A well-timed IABP will show augmented diastolic pressure peaks and reduced systolic pressure, indicative of successful afterload reduction and increased coronary perfusion.

Nursing Care Priorities

Nursing care for patients with an IABP involves:

Hemodynamic Monitoring: Continuous monitoring of arterial blood pressure, heart rate, and IABP waveforms to ensure proper device timing and function.

Site Care: Regular inspection of the catheter insertion site for signs of infection, bleeding, or vascular complications.

Limb Assessment: Frequent checks of the limb distal to the insertion site for adequate perfusion, including pulses, temperature, color, and sensation, to detect any signs of limb ischemia early.

Patient Comfort and Safety: Management of patient discomfort related to the device, ensuring secure device fixation, and educating the patient and family about the IABP's role and function.

Complication Readiness: Being vigilant for potential complications such as thrombosis, embolism, balloon rupture, or displacement, and having protocols in place for immediate management.

Coordination of Care: Collaborating with the healthcare team for timely weaning and removal of the IABP as the patient's condition stabilizes or improves.

Effective nursing care and interdisciplinary collaboration are paramount in optimizing the therapeutic benefits of IABP therapy while minimizing the risks of complications, thereby improving outcomes for critically ill cardiac patients.

Implantable Cardioverter-Defibrillators (ICDs) are sophisticated devices designed to monitor heart rhythms and deliver life-saving therapies in the form of shocks or pacing to terminate dangerous arrhythmias, particularly ventricular tachycardia (VT) and ventricular fibrillation (VF). Understanding their indications, functionality, patient education requirements, post-implantation care, and the importance of device interrogation is crucial for healthcare providers and patients alike.

Indications

ICDs are primarily indicated for patients at high risk of sudden cardiac death due to ventricular arrhythmias. Key indications include:
1. **Primary Prevention**: In patients with a history of heart disease but no prior life-threatening arrhythmias, ICDs are implanted to prevent sudden cardiac death, especially in those with:
    - Reduced ejection fraction (EF ≤ 35%) due to prior myocardial infarction or non-ischemic cardiomyopathy.
    - Specific hereditary conditions predisposing to VT/VF, such as Long QT Syndrome, Brugada Syndrome, or Hypertrophic Cardiomyopathy.

2. **Secondary Prevention**: In patients who have survived a life-threatening arrhythmia, an ICD can prevent recurrence and sudden death. This includes survivors of cardiac arrest due to VT/VF not caused by a reversible condition.

Function

The ICD continuously monitors the heart rhythm. Upon detecting a malignant ventricular arrhythmia, it can:
- **Deliver Anti-tachycardia Pacing (ATP)**: A series of rapid pacing impulses to interrupt and terminate a tachyarrhythmia without the need for a shock.
- **Deliver a Defibrillation Shock**: If ATP is ineffective or the arrhythmia is too severe, the ICD delivers a high-energy shock to reset the heart's electrical activity and restore a normal rhythm.

Patient Education

Effective patient education is essential for individuals receiving an ICD:
- **Understanding the Device**: Patients should know how the ICD works, what to expect when it delivers therapy, and the importance of regular follow-up and device checks.
- **Activity Modifications**: While most activities can be resumed, patients may be advised to avoid activities that involve intense magnetic fields or could result in significant trauma to the device area.
- **Recognizing and Responding to Shocks**: Patients should know how to distinguish between the device's normal operations and emergencies requiring medical attention.
- **Lifestyle Considerations**: Discussing the impact on driving, travel, and exercise, and providing guidance on living with an ICD.

Post-Implantation Care

Following ICD implantation, care focuses on:
- **Wound Care**: Keeping the implant site clean and dry, monitoring for signs of infection.
- **Activity Restrictions**: Avoiding lifting or vigorous activity with the affected arm to prevent lead displacement.
- **Medication Management**: Adjusting or continuing medications for the underlying heart condition.

Device Interrogation

Regular device interrogation is a critical aspect of ICD management, involving:
- **Checking Device Function**: Assessing battery life, lead integrity, and ensuring the device is functioning within optimal parameters.
- **Evaluating Therapy History**: Reviewing the device's stored data on detected arrhythmias and delivered therapies to adjust settings if necessary and to inform clinical decisions.
- **Tailoring Therapy**: Adjusting device programming to minimize inappropriate shocks and optimize arrhythmia management based on the patient's clinical status and device data.

Proper management of ICD patients involves a multidisciplinary approach, ensuring that patients are well-informed about their device, receive appropriate follow-up care, and understand when to seek immediate medical attention, thereby enhancing their quality of life and clinical outcomes.

Pulmonary:

The lungs – our elegant bellows that fuel the body with every breath. Yet, like any complex system, they are vulnerable to disease. In this section, we'll dive into how common respiratory conditions unfold and the critical care interventions that can mean the difference between life and death.

Why Pulmonary Matters in Critical Care
Whether it's sudden respiratory failure or the slow decline of chronic lung disease, the ripple effects on the entire body are profound. Our ability to assess and act swiftly makes a huge impact on whether a patient overcomes the challenge or spirals into multi-system failure.

What We'll Cover in this Section
The Mechanics of It All: We'll refresh our understanding of how air moves in and out of the lungs, gas exchange works, and the intricate link between respiration and blood chemistry.
Image of lung anatomy
When Things Go Haywire:
COPD: The slow suffocation. We'll look at exacerbations and how to optimize treatment.
Pneumonia: Infection strikes! From diagnosis to targeted antibiotic choices, we'll cover it.
ARDS: A devastating inflammatory syndrome with unique management needs.
Pulmonary Embolism: When blood clots take a dangerous journey, we'll learn the risk factors and life-saving treatments.
Tools of the Trade: Mastering the art of interpreting blood gases, chest x-rays, and ventilator settings is non-negotiable in critical care.

Lifelines: Mechanical ventilation is intimidating. We'll break down the modes, when they're used, and how to troubleshoot problems.

This section is about empowering you to think critically – to connect the dots between a patient's labored breathing, their lab values, and the interventions that will give them the best chance to breathe easier again.

The respiratory system is intricately designed to facilitate the essential process of ventilation, ensuring oxygen delivery to the bloodstream and the removal of carbon dioxide from the body. Each component of the respiratory system plays a pivotal role in this process:

Trachea: Often referred to as the windpipe, the trachea serves as the main airway that conducts air in and out of the lungs. Its rigid structure, reinforced by cartilaginous rings, ensures it remains open, allowing free passage of air.

Bronchi: The trachea bifurcates into the right and left main bronchi, which enter the lungs and further branch into smaller bronchi. These conduits progressively decrease in size and cartilage content as they branch, directing air to each lung lobe.

Bronchioles: These are smaller, muscular airways that extend from the bronchi and branch into the lung's deeper tissues. Unlike the larger airways, bronchioles are devoid of cartilage and are capable of significant constriction and dilation, playing a key role in regulating airflow resistance.

Alveoli: At the terminal ends of the bronchioles lie the alveoli, tiny air sacs where gas exchange occurs. Surrounded by a network of capillaries, alveoli facilitate the diffusion of oxygen into the blood and the removal of carbon dioxide, thanks to their thin walls and vast surface area.

Diaphragm: This dome-shaped muscle forms the floor of the thoracic cavity and is crucial for breathing. During inhalation, the diaphragm contracts and flattens, increasing the thoracic cavity's volume and creating a negative pressure that draws air into the lungs.

Intercostal Muscles: Located between the ribs, these muscles assist in respiration by elevating the ribs during inhalation, which further expands the thoracic cavity. During forced exhalation, they help depress the ribs, decreasing the thoracic volume and aiding in expelling air from the lungs.

Together, these structures orchestrate the complex yet seamless process of ventilation, ensuring life-sustaining gas exchange is maintained efficiently with each breath.

Think of breathing as a beautifully choreographed dance between pressures, muscle power, and stretchy tissues. Let's break down the mechanical steps of inspiration and expiration:
The mechanics of ventilation involve a delicate interplay between pressure gradients, lung compliance, airway resistance, and the muscular actions of the diaphragm and intercostal muscles. This coordinated effort ensures effective inspiration and expiration, vital for gas exchange.

Inspiration
1. **Muscular Action**: Inspiration begins with the contraction of the diaphragm, which moves downward, and the external intercostal muscles, which elevate the ribs and sternum. This muscular action enlarges the thoracic cavity.
2. **Negative Intrathoracic Pressure**: The expansion of the thoracic cavity decreases the intrathoracic pressure (intrapleural pressure) below atmospheric pressure, creating a negative pressure gradient. This negative pressure is crucial as it draws air into the lungs to equalize the pressure.
3. **Lung Compliance**: Compliance refers to the lung's ability to expand in response to an applied pressure. High compliance means the lungs can easily expand when the intrathoracic pressure drops. Lung compliance is influenced by the elastic properties of lung tissue and the surface tension within the alveoli.
4. **Airway Resistance**: As air flows into the lungs, it encounters resistance primarily in the larger airways. During normal quiet breathing, this resistance is minimal. The rate of airflow is determined by the pressure gradient (between atmospheric pressure and intrathoracic pressure) and the resistance encountered.

Expiration
1. **Muscular Relaxation**: Expiration is mainly a passive process during quiet breathing, resulting from the relaxation of the diaphragm and the external intercostal muscles. The diaphragm returns to its dome shape, and the ribs move downward and inward under elastic recoil forces.
2. **Positive Intrathoracic Pressure**: The decrease in thoracic cavity volume increases the intrathoracic pressure above atmospheric pressure, creating a positive pressure gradient that drives air out of the lungs.
3. **Elastic Recoil**: The lungs' elastic recoil, due to the elastic fibers in lung tissue and alveolar surface tension, contributes to expelling air by returning the lungs to their pre-inspiration volume.
4. **Airway Resistance**: During expiration, especially forced expiration, airway resistance can increase due to the compression of airways. This is counteracted by the increased intrathoracic pressure which helps maintain airway patency.

Roles of the Diaphragm and Intercostal Muscles

The diaphragm and intercostal muscles are pivotal in generating the necessary changes in thoracic volume to create negative intrathoracic pressure for inspiration. The diaphragm's contraction accounts for about 75% of the air volume inhaled during quiet breathing, highlighting its critical role. The intercostal muscles assist by expanding the ribcage, further contributing to the decrease in intrathoracic pressure and facilitating air intake. The mechanics of ventilation are governed by the dynamic interactions between muscular actions, pressure gradients, lung compliance, and airway resistance. The diaphragm and intercostal muscles play central roles in modulating intrathoracic pressure to drive the rhythmic process of inspiration and expiration.

Gas diffusion across the alveolar-capillary membrane is a fundamental process in respiration, enabling the exchange of oxygen (O_2) and carbon dioxide (CO_2) between the alveoli and the blood in pulmonary capillaries. This process is governed by the principles of diffusion, where gases move from areas of higher concentration to areas of lower concentration until equilibrium is reached.

Alveolar-Capillary Interface
The alveolar-capillary membrane is a thin barrier that separates the air in the alveoli from the blood in the capillaries. It consists of the alveolar epithelium, the capillary endothelium, and their shared basement membrane. This membrane is remarkably thin (about 0.5 to 2.0 micrometers), facilitating efficient gas exchange.

Oxygen Diffusion
From Alveoli to Blood: Oxygen in the alveoli diffuses across the alveolar-capillary membrane into the blood because the partial pressure of oxygen (PaO_2) is typically higher in the alveoli than in the capillary blood.
Hemoglobin Binding: Once in the capillaries, oxygen binds to hemoglobin in red blood cells, forming oxyhemoglobin, which is transported throughout the body to deliver oxygen to tissues.
Carbon Dioxide Diffusion
From Blood to Alveoli: Carbon dioxide, produced as a waste product by cellular metabolism, is transported in the blood back to the lungs. It diffuses from the blood, where its partial pressure is higher, across the alveolar-capillary membrane into the alveoli, from where it is expelled during exhalation.
Transport Forms: CO_2 is carried in the blood in three main forms: dissolved in plasma, chemically bound to hemoglobin (as carbaminohemoglobin), and, most abundantly, as bicarbonate ions (HCO_3^-) formed from the reaction of CO_2 with water, catalyzed by the enzyme carbonic anhydrase.
Factors Influencing Gas Exchange
Partial Pressure Gradients: The difference in partial pressures of O_2 and CO_2 between alveolar air and capillary blood is the primary driving force for diffusion.
Surface Area: The extensive surface area of the alveoli (about 70 square meters in adults) facilitates ample gas exchange.
Membrane Thickness: Any increase in the thickness of the alveolar-capillary membrane, as seen in conditions like pulmonary fibrosis, can impede gas exchange.
Solubility and Molecular Weight of Gases: CO_2 is more soluble in blood than O_2 but has a similar diffusion rate due to its higher molecular weight.
This intricate process of gas diffusion ensures that oxygen is continually supplied to the body's tissues for metabolic needs while removing carbon dioxide, a metabolic waste product, thereby maintaining homeostasis and supporting cellular function.

Hemoglobin, a complex protein found in red blood cells, plays a crucial role in oxygen transport from the lungs to the body's tissues and the return transport of carbon dioxide. Its ability to bind, carry, and release oxygen is central to the respiratory function of blood.

Hemoglobin and Oxygen Binding
Structure: Hemoglobin is composed of four polypeptide chains, each with a heme group that contains an iron atom capable of binding one oxygen molecule. This structure allows each hemoglobin molecule to carry up to four oxygen molecules.
Oxygen Binding: Oxygen binds to the iron ions in the heme groups, forming oxyhemoglobin. This process occurs primarily in the pulmonary capillaries, where the oxygen partial pressure (PaO_2) is high.
Release to Tissues: As blood circulates and reaches systemic capillaries, where PaO_2 is lower, oxygen dissociates from hemoglobin and diffuses into tissues to meet metabolic demands.
Factors Influencing Oxygen Delivery
Several factors influence the efficiency of oxygen delivery to tissues:

Hemoglobin Concentration: The total amount of hemoglobin directly impacts the blood's oxygen-carrying capacity. Anemia (low hemoglobin levels) can significantly reduce oxygen delivery, while polycythemia (high hemoglobin levels) can increase it.

Partial Pressure of Oxygen (PaO_2): The gradient between the PaO_2 in blood and the tissues drives oxygen diffusion. Higher PaO_2 in arterial blood enhances oxygen loading, while lower PaO_2 in tissues facilitates unloading.

Oxygen-Hemoglobin Dissociation Curve: This sigmoidal curve describes the relationship between PaO_2 and hemoglobin saturation (SaO_2). Factors that shift this curve impact oxygen delivery:

Right Shift: Caused by increased CO_2 levels (Bohr effect), higher temperature, lower pH, and increased levels of 2,3-bisphosphoglycerate (2,3-BPG) in red blood cells. It indicates hemoglobin's reduced affinity for oxygen, facilitating oxygen release to tissues.
Left Shift: Results from decreased CO_2 levels, lower temperature, higher pH, and decreased 2,3-BPG levels, indicating increased oxygen affinity, which can hinder oxygen release to tissues.
Cardiac Output: The rate at which oxygenated blood is delivered to tissues also depends on cardiac output. Conditions affecting cardiac output, like heart failure or shock, can impair oxygen delivery despite adequate hemoglobin saturation.

Tissue Perfusion: Adequate capillary density and blood flow are essential for efficient oxygen delivery. Conditions that impair circulation, such as atherosclerosis or vasculitis, can restrict oxygen availability to tissues.

Understanding the mechanisms of hemoglobin's oxygen binding and transport, along with the factors influencing oxygen delivery, is essential for diagnosing and managing conditions related to impaired oxygenation and for optimizing patient care in both acute and chronic settings.

The oxygen-hemoglobin dissociation curve visualized above illustrates the sigmoidal relationship between the partial pressure of oxygen (PaO_2) and the percentage of hemoglobin saturation (SaO_2). This curve is pivotal for understanding how hemoglobin binds and releases oxygen under different physiological conditions.

Factors Shifting the Curve
pH (Bohr Effect):

Right Shift: A decrease in pH (acidosis) weakens hemoglobin's affinity for oxygen, facilitating oxygen release to tissues. This is crucial in active tissues where CO_2 production and lactic acid increase, lowering pH.
Left Shift: An increase in pH (alkalosis) strengthens hemoglobin's oxygen affinity, making oxygen release to tissues more difficult. This can occur in situations like hyperventilation, where CO_2 is excessively expelled.
Temperature:

Right Shift: Elevated temperatures, as seen in fever or hypermetabolism, decrease hemoglobin's oxygen affinity, enhancing oxygen delivery to meet increased metabolic demands.
Left Shift: Lower temperatures increase oxygen affinity, which can be observed in hypothermic conditions, potentially limiting oxygen availability to tissues.
2,3-Bisphosphoglycerate (2,3-DPG):

Right Shift: Increased levels of 2,3-DPG, which might occur in states of chronic hypoxia (e.g., high altitude, chronic lung disease), reduce hemoglobin's oxygen affinity, aiding in oxygen offloading to hypoxic tissues.
Left Shift: Decreased levels of 2,3-DPG enhance oxygen affinity, seen in conditions like transfusion of stored blood, where 2,3-DPG levels diminish over time.
Clinical Implications
Understanding these shifts is essential in clinical practice:

In conditions like chronic obstructive pulmonary disease (COPD) or heart failure, where tissue oxygen demand is high, a rightward shift in the curve helps unload oxygen more effectively at the tissue level. Conversely, in scenarios requiring improved oxygen loading in the lungs, such as certain lung diseases or environments with lower oxygen availability (high altitudes), a leftward shift might be temporarily beneficial.
Therapeutic interventions, such as oxygen therapy, transfusions, or adjustments in ventilation settings, can be guided by understanding these physiological principles to optimize oxygen delivery based on the patient's specific needs and underlying conditions.
This curve serves as a foundational concept in respiratory physiology, highlighting the dynamic nature of hemoglobin's oxygen-binding capacity and its adaptability to varying physiological and pathological states.

Arterial Blood Gas (ABG) analysis is a crucial diagnostic tool in assessing a patient's respiratory and metabolic status. A systematic approach to interpreting ABGs involves analyzing pH, partial pressures of carbon dioxide ($PaCO_2$) and oxygen (PaO_2), bicarbonate (HCO_3^-), and base excess/deficit. Here's how to navigate through an ABG report:
Step 1: Assess the pH
- **Normal Range**: 7.35 - 7.45
- **Interpretation**: A pH less than 7.35 indicates acidemia, whereas a pH greater than 7.45 signifies alkalemia. This initial step determines the primary process: acidosis or alkalosis.

Step 2: Examine $PaCO_2$
- **Normal Range**: 35 - 45 mmHg

- **Interpretation**: PaCO$_2$ reflects the respiratory component. A PaCO$_2$ above 45 mmHg suggests respiratory acidosis (hypoventilation), while a value below 35 mmHg indicates respiratory alkalosis (hyperventilation).

Step 3: Evaluate HCO$_3^-$
- **Normal Range**: 22 - 26 mEq/L
- **Interpretation**: Bicarbonate levels represent the metabolic component. Levels below 22 mEq/L suggest metabolic acidosis, while levels above 26 mEq/L point towards metabolic alkalosis.

Step 4: Consider PaO$_2$
- **Normal Range**: 75 - 100 mmHg
- **Interpretation**: PaO$_2$ assesses oxygenation status. Values below the normal range indicate hypoxemia, which could be due to various respiratory or circulatory causes.

Step 5: Check Base Excess/Deficit
- **Normal Range**: -2 to +2 mEq/L
- **Interpretation**: Base excess or deficit quantifies the metabolic component of the acid-base balance. A negative value indicates a base deficit (metabolic acidosis), while a positive value suggests a base excess (metabolic alkalosis).

Systematic Approach

1. **Determine the Primary Disorder**: Start with the pH to identify if the patient is in acidosis or alkalosis, then look at PaCO$_2$ and HCO$_3^-$ to ascertain if it's primarily respiratory or metabolic.
2. **Assess for Compensation**: The body attempts to compensate for acid-base imbalances. In respiratory disorders, the kidneys adjust HCO$_3^-$ levels, while in metabolic conditions, the lungs alter PaCO$_2$ through changes in ventilation.
3. **Evaluate the Degree of Compensation**: Full compensation occurs when the pH returns to normal, while partial compensation means the pH is still outside the normal range but the body is attempting to correct the imbalance.
4. **Consider Anion Gap**: For metabolic acidosis, calculate the anion gap ($[Na^+] - ([Cl^-] + [HCO_3^-])$) to differentiate between high-gap (e.g., lactic acidosis, ketoacidosis) and normal-gap acidosis.
5. **Oxygenation Status**: Always assess PaO$_2$ and oxygen saturation to gauge the patient's oxygenation efficiency, crucial for managing respiratory support.

Significance of Each Parameter

- **pH**: Indicates the overall acid-base status.
- **PaCO$_2$**: Reflects the adequacy of pulmonary ventilation and respiratory contribution to acid-base balance.
- **HCO$_3^-$**: Represents the renal response and the metabolic component of acid-base regulation.
- **PaO$_2$**: Assesses the lungs' ability to oxygenate the blood.
- **Base Excess/Deficit**: Provides insight into the metabolic component, indicating excess or deficiency of base in the blood.

ABG analysis is a powerful tool in clinical decision-making, providing insights into the patient's respiratory efficiency, metabolic status, and the body's compensatory responses to maintain acid-base equilibrium.

The body meticulously maintains acid-base balance through the respiratory and renal systems, ensuring the arterial blood pH stays within the narrow range of 7.35 to 7.45. Disturbances in this balance can lead to acid-base disorders, with compensatory mechanisms attempting to restore normalcy.

Respiratory and Renal Regulation of Acid-Base Balance

1. **Respiratory System**: Primarily regulates carbon dioxide (CO_2) levels, a major component of the body's acid load, through alterations in the rate and depth of breathing. An increase in CO_2 levels

stimulates the respiratory center to increase ventilation, expelling CO_2 and decreasing acidity. Conversely, a decrease in CO_2 slows down respiration, retaining CO_2 to increase acidity.
2. **Renal System**: Manages bicarbonate (HCO_3^-) and hydrogen ions (H^+) in the blood. The kidneys excrete or reabsorb HCO_3^- and secrete H^+ to regulate the body's metabolic component of acid-base balance. This process is slower than respiratory compensation but crucial for long-term pH regulation.

Compensatory Mechanisms

Compensation involves one system (respiratory or renal) attempting to correct an acid-base imbalance caused by a disturbance in the other system. Full compensation brings the pH back to normal, whereas partial compensation only partially corrects the pH.

Acid-Base Disturbances

Respiratory Acidosis
- **Causes**: Hypoventilation due to respiratory depression (drug overdose, neurological disorders), lung diseases (COPD, pneumonia), or airway obstruction.
- **Clinical Manifestations**: Headache, confusion, lethargy, and, in severe cases, coma.
- **Compensation**: Renal system increases HCO_3^- reabsorption and H^+ excretion to raise blood pH towards normal.

Respiratory Alkalosis
- **Causes**: Hyperventilation due to anxiety, pain, hypoxemia, or iatrogenic overventilation.
- **Clinical Manifestations**: Light-headedness, numbness, tingling of extremities, and tetany.
- **Compensation**: Renal system decreases HCO_3^- reabsorption, allowing more HCO_3^- to be excreted to lower blood pH.

Metabolic Acidosis
- **Causes**: Increased acid production (lactic acidosis, ketoacidosis), reduced HCO_3^- (diarrhea, renal tubular acidosis), or ingestion of acids (salicylate poisoning).
- **Clinical Manifestations**: Kussmaul respirations (deep, rapid breathing), lethargy, and confusion.
- **Compensation**: Respiratory system increases ventilation to expel CO_2, reducing acidity.

Metabolic Alkalosis
- **Causes**: Loss of gastric acid (vomiting, nasogastric suction), diuretic use, or excessive bicarbonate intake.
- **Clinical Manifestations**: Weakness, muscle cramps, hyperactive reflexes, and in severe cases, tetany.
- **Compensation**: Respiratory system decreases ventilation to retain CO_2, increasing acidity.

Understanding these acid-base disturbances and their compensatory mechanisms is essential for diagnosing and managing patients with electrolyte and pH imbalances. Treatment often involves addressing the underlying cause while supporting the affected compensatory system to restore acid-base equilibrium.

Respiratory failure, a critical condition where the respiratory system fails to maintain adequate gas exchange, can manifest as hypoxemia (Type 1) or hypercapnia (Type 2), each with distinct etiologies and clinical features.

Hypoxemic Respiratory Failure (Type 1)
Definition: Characterized by a PaO_2 (partial pressure of arterial oxygen) less than 60 mmHg with a normal or low $PaCO_2$ (partial pressure of arterial carbon dioxide). It indicates inadequate oxygenation of blood in the lungs.

Common Causes:
Ventilation-Perfusion (V/Q) Mismatch: The most common cause, where areas of the lung receive oxygen but not enough blood flow (e.g., pulmonary embolism) or receive blood flow but not enough oxygen (e.g., pneumonia, ARDS).
Diffusion Impairment: Conditions that thicken the alveolar-capillary membrane, such as interstitial lung disease, reducing oxygen transfer.
Right-to-Left Shunt: Blood bypasses the alveoli without gas exchange, seen in congenital heart diseases or severe intrapulmonary shunting (e.g., ARDS).
Low Ambient Oxygen: High altitudes where the inspired oxygen concentration is low.
Clinical Presentations: Patients often present with cyanosis, tachypnea, use of accessory muscles for breathing, confusion or agitation (due to hypoxia), and symptoms related to the underlying cause.

Hypercapnic Respiratory Failure (Type 2)
Definition: Characterized by a $PaCO_2$ greater than 45 mmHg, indicating inadequate CO_2 removal, with an accompanying acidemia (pH < 7.35).

Common Causes:
Alveolar Hypoventilation: Due to decreased respiratory drive (e.g., drug overdose affecting the central nervous system), neuromuscular disorders (e.g., amyotrophic lateral sclerosis, myasthenia gravis), or severe chest wall deformities.
Airway Obstruction: Chronic obstructive pulmonary disease (COPD) exacerbations, severe asthma, or conditions leading to upper airway obstruction.
Increased Dead Space Ventilation: Conditions like severe emphysema where a significant portion of each breath does not participate in gas exchange.
Clinical Presentations: Manifestations include dyspnea, morning headaches (due to elevated $PaCO_2$ during sleep), confusion or somnolence (due to CO_2 narcosis), and signs of right heart failure (cor pulmonale) in chronic cases.

Management Considerations
Hypoxemic Respiratory Failure: Management focuses on improving oxygenation, which may involve supplemental oxygen, mechanical ventilation in severe cases, and treating the underlying cause.

Hypercapnic Respiratory Failure: Treatment aims at enhancing alveolar ventilation, which might involve non-invasive ventilation (e.g., CPAP, BiPAP) or invasive mechanical ventilation, alongside addressing the precipitating factor.

Understanding the differences between hypoxemic and hypercapnic respiratory failure is crucial for appropriate diagnosis, management, and improving patient outcomes in these potentially life-threatening conditions.

Acute Respiratory Distress Syndrome (ARDS) is a severe form of acute lung injury characterized by diffuse alveolar damage, leading to increased pulmonary vascular permeability, severe hypoxemia, and bilateral pulmonary infiltrates. It's a critical condition associated with a high mortality rate, necessitating prompt recognition and management.
Pathophysiology of ARDS

ARDS results from a wide variety of direct or indirect insults to the lung, leading to an intense inflammatory response. This includes:
- **Inflammatory Cascade**: The inciting event triggers an overwhelming inflammatory response, releasing pro-inflammatory cytokines and attracting neutrophils to the lungs.
- **Increased Permeability**: Damage to the alveolar-capillary barrier causes leakage of protein-rich fluid into the alveoli, resulting in non-cardiogenic pulmonary edema.
- **Surfactant Dysfunction**: Injury to type II alveolar cells decreases surfactant production, increasing surface tension and leading to alveolar collapse (atelectasis).
- **Microvascular Thrombosis**: Coagulation cascade activation contributes to microvascular injury and thrombosis, further impairing gas exchange.
- **Fibroproliferation**: In later stages, fibroblast proliferation and extracellular matrix deposition can lead to pulmonary fibrosis, complicating recovery.

Berlin Definition Criteria

The Berlin Definition provides standardized diagnostic criteria for ARDS, focusing on timing, chest imaging, origin of edema, and the degree of hypoxemia:
1. **Timing**: Acute onset within one week of a known clinical insult or new/worsening respiratory symptoms.
2. **Chest Imaging**: Bilateral opacities on chest X-ray or CT scan not fully explained by effusions, lobar/lung collapse, or nodules.
3. **Origin of Edema**: Respiratory failure not fully explained by cardiac failure or fluid overload; objective assessment (e.g., echocardiography) needed if no risk factor is apparent.
4. **Oxygenation** (based on PaO_2/FiO_2 ratio with PEEP or CPAP $\geq$ 5 cm H_2O):
   - Mild ARDS: 200 mmHg < PaO_2/FiO_2 $\leq$ 300 mmHg
   - Moderate ARDS: 100 mmHg < PaO_2/FiO_2 $\leq$ 200 mmHg
   - Severe ARDS: PaO_2/FiO_2 $\leq$ 100 mmHg

Principles of ARDS Management

Lung-Protective Ventilation
- **Low Tidal Volume (VT)**: 4-8 mL/kg of predicted body weight to minimize volutrauma.
- **Limit Plateau Pressure**: $\leq$ 30 cm H_2O to reduce barotrauma risk.
- **PEEP**: Applied to prevent alveolar collapse, improve oxygenation, and reduce the FiO_2 needed to achieve adequate oxygenation.

Fluid Management
- **Conservative Strategy**: Aimed at minimizing fluid overload to reduce pulmonary edema while ensuring adequate organ perfusion and avoiding hypovolemia.

Prone Positioning
- **Improves Oxygenation**: Prone positioning for 12-16 hours per day can improve oxygenation by alleviating ventilation-perfusion mismatch and reducing lung compression by the heart and abdominal contents.

Other Considerations
- **Avoidance of Neuromuscular Blockade**: If possible, to minimize muscle weakness; may be used short-term for severe hypoxemia not responsive to other measures.
- **Management of Underlying Cause**: Identifying and treating the precipitating cause of ARDS is crucial.
- **Supportive Care**: Nutritional support, deep vein thrombosis prophylaxis, stress ulcer prophylaxis, and management of comorbidities.

ARDS management is complex and requires a multidisciplinary approach, with close monitoring and adjustment of therapeutic interventions based on the patient's evolving clinical status.

Mechanical ventilation is a lifesaving intervention used in patients who are unable to maintain adequate ventilation or oxygenation due to various respiratory conditions. Understanding the common modes of mechanical ventilation, including Assist Control (AC), Synchronized Intermittent Mandatory Ventilation (SIMV), and Pressure Support Ventilation (PSV), is crucial for optimizing patient care.

Assist Control Ventilation (AC)
- **Mechanism**: In AC mode, the ventilator delivers a set tidal volume (VT) or target pressure with each breath. The patient can initiate a breath, triggering the ventilator to deliver the preset VT or pressure, but if the patient does not initiate enough breaths, the ventilator will provide controlled breaths to ensure the minimum set respiratory rate is met.
- **Indications**: AC is often used in patients with acute respiratory failure who have a low drive to breathe or need full ventilatory support. It's beneficial for ensuring adequate minute ventilation and reducing the work of breathing.
- **Considerations**: Because the ventilator delivers full support with each patient-initiated breath, there's a risk of hyperventilation and respiratory alkalosis, especially if the patient's respiratory drive increases.

Synchronized Intermittent Mandatory Ventilation (SIMV)
- **Mechanism**: SIMV allows for a set number of mandatory breaths to be delivered by the ventilator at a preset VT or pressure, synchronized with the patient's spontaneous breathing efforts. Between these mandatory breaths, the patient can breathe spontaneously with or without additional pressure support.
- **Indications**: SIMV is useful for weaning patients from mechanical ventilation as it permits spontaneous breathing, allowing for the assessment of the patient's ability to breathe independently. It's also used in patients requiring long-term ventilation to maintain respiratory muscle function.
- **Considerations**: While SIMV can support the patient's spontaneous breathing efforts, it may also lead to increased work of breathing compared to AC, especially if inadequate pressure support is provided for spontaneous breaths.

Pressure Support Ventilation (PSV)
- **Mechanism**: PSV is a purely spontaneous mode where the ventilator provides a preset level of pressure support for each breath initiated by the patient, augmenting their tidal volume. There's no set respiratory rate; the patient controls the frequency and depth of breaths based on their respiratory drive and effort.
- **Indications**: PSV is commonly used during the weaning process from mechanical ventilation and for patients with a relatively intact respiratory drive but who require some assistance to overcome the work of breathing due to the endotracheal tube or disease pathology.
- **Considerations**: PSV requires the patient to have a stable respiratory drive and adequate respiratory muscle strength. Careful monitoring is needed to ensure the patient does not tire, leading to hypoventilation.

Key Differences
- **Control vs. Support**: AC provides full ventilatory support for each breath, whether initiated by the machine or the patient. SIMV offers a combination of controlled breaths and supported spontaneous breaths. PSV provides support only for spontaneous breaths initiated by the patient.

- **Patient Involvement**: AC and SIMV can control the minute ventilation entirely, making them suitable for patients with minimal respiratory effort. PSV requires active patient participation, making it more suitable for weaning and patients with some spontaneous breathing effort.
- **Flexibility**: SIMV offers flexibility in managing patients transitioning from full ventilatory support to spontaneous breathing, while PSV is more adaptable for patients in the later stages of weaning.

Selecting the appropriate mode of mechanical ventilation involves considering the patient's respiratory status, underlying condition, and goals of care, often requiring adjustments based on the patient's response and progress.

Essential ventilator settings are crucial in managing patients requiring mechanical ventilation. Adjustments to these settings are often made in response to the patient's clinical status and arterial blood gas (ABG) analysis to ensure optimal ventilation and oxygenation while minimizing the risk of ventilator-associated lung injury.

FiO_2 (Fraction of Inspired Oxygen)
- **Purpose**: FiO_2 determines the percentage of oxygen the patient receives and is adjusted to maintain adequate arterial oxygen saturation (SaO_2) and partial pressure of oxygen (PaO_2).
- **Typical Range**: 21% (room air) to 100%.
- **Adjustment**: Start with the lowest FiO_2 necessary to achieve target SaO_2 (usually >92%) or PaO_2 (>60 mmHg). Adjust based on ABG results and pulse oximetry, with the goal of using the minimum FiO_2 to avoid oxygen toxicity.

Tidal Volume (VT)
- **Purpose**: VT is the volume of gas delivered to the patient with each ventilator breath, crucial for adequate ventilation.
- **Typical Range**: 4-8 mL/kg of predicted body weight for lung-protective ventilation.
- **Adjustment**: Adjustments are made to prevent volutrauma and barotrauma while ensuring adequate CO_2 removal. In patients with ARDS or at risk of lung injury, lower end of the range is preferred. Adjust based on ABG analysis, particularly $PaCO_2$ levels and acid-base status.

Positive End-Expiratory Pressure (PEEP)
- **Purpose**: PEEP prevents alveolar collapse at the end of expiration, improves oxygenation, and increases functional residual capacity.
- **Typical Range**: 5-20 cm H_2O.
- **Adjustment**: Set initially at 5 cm H_2O and adjust upwards as needed to improve oxygenation (PaO_2 and SaO_2) without excessively increasing plateau pressure. Higher levels may be required in ARDS to maintain alveolar recruitment, but careful monitoring for hemodynamic compromise is necessary.

Respiratory Rate (RR)
- **Purpose**: RR is the number of breaths delivered by the ventilator per minute, important for adequate CO_2 removal.
- **Typical Range**: 12-20 breaths per minute.
- **Adjustment**: Adjust based on $PaCO_2$ and pH levels in ABG results. Increase RR to enhance CO_2 removal in the case of acidosis or decrease in alkalosis, ensuring that the patient does not experience breath stacking or auto-PEEP.

Monitoring and Adjustments

- **ABG Analysis**: Frequent ABG sampling is often necessary, especially after initial intubation or significant changes in ventilator settings, to assess the effectiveness of ventilation and oxygenation strategies.
- **Clinical Assessment**: Continuous monitoring of vital signs, ventilator waveforms, and the patient's comfort and synchrony with the ventilator is crucial. Look for signs of overdistension, inadequate ventilation, or hemodynamic instability.
- **Oxygenation Targets**: Aim for PaO_2 of 55-80 mmHg or SaO_2 of 88-95% to avoid hyperoxia while ensuring adequate tissue oxygenation.
- **Ventilation Targets**: Aim for a $PaCO_2$ that is normal or slightly elevated (35-45 mmHg) and a pH within the normal range (7.35-7.45), adjusting based on the patient's underlying condition and acid-base status.

Adjusting ventilator settings is a dynamic process that requires integration of ABG results, clinical judgment, and an understanding of the patient's underlying pulmonary pathology. The goal is to provide adequate support while minimizing potential harm from mechanical ventilation.

Weaning from mechanical ventilation is a critical phase in the management of patients requiring respiratory support. It involves gradually reducing and eventually removing ventilatory support as the patient's respiratory function improves. The process requires careful assessment of weaning readiness, implementation of weaning strategies, and monitoring for potential complications.

Assessment of Weaning Readiness
Before initiating weaning, the patient must be assessed for readiness, which involves evaluating several criteria:

Resolution or Improvement of Underlying Cause: The condition that necessitated mechanical ventilation should be resolved or significantly improved.
Stable Hemodynamics: The patient should have stable blood pressure and heart rate without excessive vasopressor support.
Adequate Oxygenation: Acceptable blood gas levels with PaO_2/FiO_2 > 150-200 mmHg on PEEP ≤ 5-8 cm H_2O and FiO_2 ≤ 0.4-0.5.
Adequate Ventilatory Capacity: Evidence of sufficient spontaneous breathing effort, indicated by a spontaneous respiratory rate of < 35 breaths/min and tidal volumes of 4-6 mL/kg of ideal body weight.
Consciousness and Ability to Protect Airway: The patient should be able to follow commands, have an intact cough reflex, and manage secretions.
Weaning Strategies
Once readiness is established, the weaning process can begin, typically following one of these strategies:

Spontaneous Breathing Trials (SBT): The most common method, involving placing the patient on minimal support (T-piece or CPAP mode with or without pressure support) for a trial period (30-120 minutes). Successful completion without signs of distress (increased respiratory rate, hypoxemia, tachycardia, hypertension, or agitation) suggests readiness for extubation.

Gradual Reduction of Support: In patients who fail initial SBTs or have prolonged ventilatory needs, gradual reduction in the level of ventilatory support (e.g., lowering pressure support levels or increasing intervals between mandatory breaths in SIMV mode) can be used.

Automated Weaning: Some modern ventilators offer automated weaning modes that continuously adjust support based on the patient's spontaneous breathing efforts and can facilitate the weaning process.

Monitoring and Complications
Monitoring: Continuous monitoring of respiratory rate, heart rate, blood pressure, oxygen saturation, and patient comfort is essential during weaning trials. Arterial blood gases (ABGs) may be checked before and after SBTs to assess gas exchange.

Complications: Potential complications during weaning include respiratory muscle fatigue, hypoxemia, hypercapnia, and respiratory acidosis. Psychological factors like anxiety and panic can also impede the process.

Extubation Criteria: Successful completion of an SBT, adequate cough and secretion management, and minimal oxygen requirements are prerequisites for extubation.

Post-Extubation Care: Monitoring in the immediate post-extubation period is crucial to detect early signs of respiratory distress, which may necessitate reintubation.

Weaning from mechanical ventilation is a dynamic and patient-specific process, requiring a multidisciplinary approach and close monitoring to ensure a smooth transition to spontaneous breathing and to minimize the risk of complications.

Acute exacerbations of Chronic Obstructive Pulmonary Disease (COPD) represent a significant worsening of the patient's respiratory symptoms beyond normal day-to-day variations, often necessitating additional treatment. Understanding the triggers and clinical manifestations of these exacerbations is essential for timely and effective management.

Triggers of COPD Exacerbations
Infections: The most common trigger, with viral upper respiratory infections accounting for a significant proportion, followed by bacterial infections. Pathogens like influenza, rhinovirus, and Streptococcus pneumoniae are frequent culprits.

Environmental Factors: Exposure to air pollutants, including tobacco smoke, indoor and outdoor pollution, and occupational dust and chemicals, can precipitate exacerbations.

Weather Changes: Extreme temperatures, high humidity, and sudden weather changes can exacerbate symptoms.

Non-Adherence to Treatment: Skipping maintenance medications can lead to worsening symptoms.

Comorbid Conditions: Conditions like congestive heart failure, pulmonary embolism, or pneumothorax can exacerbate or mimic COPD exacerbations.

Clinical Manifestations
The presentation of a COPD exacerbation can range from mild to life-threatening, with symptoms often developing over several days:

Increased Dyspnea: A noticeable and sustained increase in shortness of breath, often the primary complaint.

Increased Sputum Production: Changes in the volume, color, and consistency of sputum, often becoming more purulent due to infection.

Cough: An increase in cough frequency and intensity, which may be productive or non-productive.

Wheezing and Chest Tightness: Patients may report a sensation of chest constriction and audible wheezing, indicating airflow obstruction.

Hypoxemia: Decreased oxygen levels, which may manifest as cyanosis (bluish discoloration of the lips and fingernails) in severe cases.

Use of Accessory Muscles: In more severe exacerbations, patients may use neck and chest wall muscles to aid breathing, indicating respiratory distress.

Altered Mental Status: Confusion, lethargy, or somnolence in severe exacerbations, often due to hypercapnia (elevated CO_2 levels in the blood).

Prompt recognition of these signs and symptoms, combined with an understanding of potential triggers, is crucial for initiating appropriate treatment. Management often involves bronchodilators, corticosteroids, antibiotics (if a bacterial infection is suspected), supplemental oxygen, and in some cases, ventilatory support. Preventive measures, including vaccinations, smoking cessation, and avoidance of environmental irritants, play a key role in reducing the frequency and severity of exacerbations.

Acute exacerbations of Chronic Obstructive Pulmonary Disease (COPD) are episodes of worsening respiratory symptoms, particularly dyspnea, cough, and sputum production, that necessitate a change in regular medication. These exacerbations significantly impact health status, rates of hospitalization, and disease progression.

Triggers

Acute COPD exacerbations can be triggered by various factors, including:
1. **Infections**: Viral upper respiratory infections are the most common cause, followed by bacterial infections.
2. **Environmental Pollutants**: Air pollution, tobacco smoke, and occupational dusts and chemicals can exacerbate symptoms.
3. **Other Respiratory Conditions**: Coexisting conditions like asthma, pneumonia, or pulmonary embolism can trigger exacerbations.
4. **Non-Adherence to Treatment**: Inadequate use of maintenance medications can lead to worsening symptoms.
5. **Heart Failure**: Cardiovascular diseases, particularly heart failure, can exacerbate COPD symptoms due to fluid overload and reduced cardiac output.

Clinical Manifestations

During an exacerbation, patients may experience:
- **Increased Dyspnea**: More severe and frequent breathlessness than usual.
- **Increased Sputum Production**: Changes in the volume and color of sputum, often becoming more purulent.

- **Increased Cough**: More frequent and intense coughing episodes.
- **Wheezing and Chest Tightness**: Due to airway narrowing and inflammation.
- **Fatigue and Confusion**: Especially in severe exacerbations, due to hypoxia and hypercapnia.
- **Cyanosis**: In severe cases, indicating significant hypoxemia.

Evidence-Based Management

Bronchodilators
- **Short-Acting Beta$_2$ Agonists (SABAs)**: Such as albuterol, provide rapid relief by relaxing bronchial smooth muscles.
- **Short-Acting Muscarinic Antagonists (SAMAs)**: Ipratropium bromide can be added for additional bronchodilation.
- **Long-Acting Bronchodilators**: May be considered in certain cases to maintain airway dilation.

Corticosteroids
- **Systemic Corticosteroids**: Oral or intravenous corticosteroids, like prednisolone, reduce airway inflammation and improve symptoms. A short course (5-7 days) is usually sufficient.
- **Inhaled Corticosteroids (ICS)**: May be intensified during exacerbations in patients already on ICS/LABA combination therapy.

Antibiotics
- **Indications**: Recommended if there are signs of bacterial infection (increased sputum purulence, volume, or systemic symptoms like fever).
- **Choice of Antibiotics**: Depends on local guidelines, patient's exacerbation history, and risk factors for specific pathogens.

Non-Invasive Ventilation (NIV)
- **Indication**: For patients with acute respiratory failure not responding to initial medical therapy, characterized by worsening dyspnea, hypercapnia (PaCO$_2$ > 45 mmHg), and acidosis (pH < 7.35).
- **Benefits**: NIV can improve gas exchange, reduce work of breathing, and avoid the complications associated with endotracheal intubation.

Oxygen Therapy
- **Goal**: Maintain SpO$_2$ at 88-92% to avoid hypoxemia without causing hypercapnia due to oxygen-induced hypoventilation.

Additional Management Considerations
- **Pulmonary Rehabilitation**: May be initiated or resumed after stabilization to improve functional status.
- **Vaccinations**: Influenza and pneumococcal vaccinations to reduce the risk of future exacerbations.

Management of acute COPD exacerbations requires a multifaceted approach, tailored to the severity of the exacerbation and the patient's overall health status. Early intervention, appropriate use of pharmacotherapy, and supportive measures are key to improving outcomes and preventing future exacerbations.

Pneumonia, an infection of the lungs, presents in various forms, with Community-Acquired Pneumonia (CAP) and Hospital-Acquired Pneumonia (HAP) being two primary types. Understanding their differences, risk factors, diagnostic methods, and treatment strategies is crucial for effective management.

Community-Acquired Pneumonia (CAP)
- **Definition**: CAP is diagnosed in patients who present with pneumonia symptoms outside of the hospital setting or within 48 hours of hospital admission, without recent hospitalization or long-term care facility residence.

- **Risk Factors**: Include advanced age, smoking, chronic lung diseases (e.g., COPD), immunocompromised states, and comorbid conditions like diabetes or heart disease.
- **Diagnosis**:
    - **Clinical Presentation**: Symptoms include cough, fever, dyspnea, and pleuritic chest pain, often accompanied by sputum production.
    - **Chest Imaging**: Chest X-ray or CT scan showing infiltrates is essential for diagnosis. Imaging helps distinguish pneumonia from other causes of respiratory symptoms and assesses the extent and location of the infection.
    - **Laboratory Tests**: Blood cultures, sputum cultures, and antigen tests for specific pathogens can help identify the causative organism, though they're not always necessary for outpatient management.
- **Treatment**: Empiric antibiotic therapy is initiated based on severity, patient risk factors, and local microbial resistance patterns. Outpatient treatment may involve oral macrolides or doxycycline, while inpatient non-ICU treatment typically includes a respiratory fluoroquinolone or a combination of a beta-lactam plus a macrolide.

Hospital-Acquired Pneumonia (HAP)
- **Definition**: HAP occurs 48 hours or more after hospital admission, not incubating at the time of admission. Ventilator-Associated Pneumonia (VAP) is a subset, occurring in patients on mechanical ventilation.
- **Risk Factors**: Mechanical ventilation, prolonged hospital stay, underlying lung disease, immunosuppression, recent surgery, and the use of broad-spectrum antibiotics are significant risk factors.
- **Diagnosis**:
    - **Clinical Presentation**: Similar to CAP but occurs in the context of recent hospitalization. Fever, increased or new sputum production, and worsening oxygenation are common.
    - **Chest Imaging**: Essential for confirming the diagnosis, with infiltrates, consolidations, or other changes indicative of pneumonia.
    - **Microbiological Testing**: More critical than in CAP due to the risk of multi-drug resistant organisms. This includes respiratory secretions' cultures and susceptibility testing to guide antibiotic therapy.
- **Treatment**: Empiric therapy must consider the risk of multi-drug resistant pathogens. This often involves broader-spectrum antibiotics such as carbapenems, piperacillin/tazobactam, or cefepime, with adjustments based on culture results and antibiotic stewardship principles.

Key Differences
- **Setting and Timing**: CAP originates in the community, while HAP develops during hospitalization.
- **Risk Factors**: HAP patients often have more complex medical backgrounds and higher exposure to resistant pathogens.
- **Pathogens**: CAP commonly involves Streptococcus pneumoniae, Mycoplasma pneumoniae, and respiratory viruses. HAP may involve more resistant bacteria like MRSA or Pseudomonas aeruginosa.
- **Antibiotic Therapy**: Empiric treatment for CAP can be more straightforward, targeting common community pathogens. HAP treatment requires broader coverage initially, with de-escalation based on culture results.

Effective management of pneumonia, whether CAP or HAP, hinges on timely diagnosis, appropriate empirical antibiotic selection, and adjustments based on clinical response and microbiological findings.

Antibiotic selection in pneumonia is crucial and should be guided by the type of pneumonia, likely pathogens, local antibiotic resistance patterns, and individual patient factors. Supportive care measures play a significant role in managing symptoms and preventing complications.

Community-Acquired Pneumonia (CAP)
- **Antibiotic Selection**: Empirical therapy is based on the severity of the disease, comorbid conditions, and recent antibiotic use.
    - **Outpatients**: Macrolides (e.g., azithromycin) or doxycycline are typical first choices. Fluoroquinolones (e.g., levofloxacin) or amoxicillin-clavulanate may be alternatives, especially in patients with comorbidities or recent antibiotic use.
    - **Inpatients (Non-ICU)**: A beta-lactam antibiotic (e.g., ceftriaxone, ampicillin-sulbactam) plus a macrolide, or a monotherapy with a respiratory fluoroquinolone.
    - **Inpatients (ICU)**: A beta-lactam plus either azithromycin or a fluoroquinolone. Consider adding coverage for MRSA or Pseudomonas in patients with risk factors for these pathogens.

Hospital-Acquired Pneumonia (HAP) and Ventilator-Associated Pneumonia (VAP)
- **Antibiotic Selection**: Initial broad-spectrum coverage is recommended, tailored based on local microbiology and susceptibility patterns, patient risk factors for multi-drug resistant bacteria, and the severity of illness.
    - **Empiric Therapy**: May include carbapenems, piperacillin-tazobactam, cefepime, or a fluoroquinolone. Coverage for MRSA (e.g., vancomycin or linezolid) and Pseudomonas should be considered if risk factors are present.
    - **De-escalation**: Based on culture results and clinical response, antibiotics should be narrowed to target identified pathogens and minimize the development of resistance.

Supportive Care

Supportive measures are integral to the management of pneumonia, enhancing recovery and reducing the risk of complications:
- **Oxygen Therapy**: For hypoxemic patients to maintain $SpO_2 \geq 92\%$.
- **Hydration and Nutrition**: Adequate hydration helps in the clearance of respiratory secretions, while nutritional support is crucial for maintaining the body's immune function.
- **Fever and Pain Management**: Antipyretics (e.g., acetaminophen) can be used to manage fever and discomfort.
- **Pulmonary Hygiene**: Chest physiotherapy, incentive spirometry, and nebulized saline can assist in mobilizing secretions, especially in patients with productive coughs.
- **Respiratory Support**: Non-invasive ventilation (NIV) or mechanical ventilation may be necessary for patients with respiratory failure.
- **Prevention of Complications**: Deep vein thrombosis prophylaxis, stress ulcer prophylaxis, and measures to prevent pressure ulcers and nosocomial infections.

Monitoring and Follow-Up

Regular monitoring of clinical signs, oxygenation status, and response to treatment is essential, with adjustments made as needed. Follow-up chest imaging might be necessary for patients with slow or complicated recovery to assess for resolution or complications such as abscess formation or empyema. Effective pneumonia management combines appropriate antibiotic therapy tailored to the likely pathogens and individual patient risk factors with comprehensive supportive care to address symptoms, maintain vital functions, and prevent complications.

Pulmonary Embolism (PE) is a critical condition characterized by the obstruction of pulmonary arteries by thrombi, which usually originate from deep vein thrombosis (DVT) in the lower extremities. Understanding its pathophysiology, risk factors, and diagnostic approach is essential for timely management and prevention of complications.

Pathophysiology
Thrombus Formation: Most PEs are due to emboli from DVTs. The thrombus dislodges from its site of formation and travels through the venous system to the right side of the heart and then into the pulmonary circulation.

Obstruction and Impaired Gas Exchange: The embolus obstructs pulmonary blood flow, leading to impaired gas exchange, decreased oxygenation, and potential buildup of carbon dioxide. This can result in hypoxemia and respiratory distress.

Increased Pulmonary Vascular Resistance: The obstruction increases resistance to blood flow through the lungs, placing strain on the right ventricle (RV), which can lead to RV dysfunction or failure.

Release of Vasoactive Substances: The embolism triggers the release of vasoactive substances, causing further pulmonary vasoconstriction, exacerbating the increase in pulmonary vascular resistance and right ventricular strain.

Risk Factors (Virchow's Triad)
Virchow's triad describes three primary risk factors contributing to thrombus formation:

Venous Stasis: Conditions that slow blood flow in the veins, such as prolonged immobility (long flights, bed rest), paralysis, or heart failure, increase the risk of clot formation.

Endothelial Injury: Damage to the vessel wall, as seen in surgery, trauma, or intravenous catheterization, can initiate clot formation.

Hypercoagulability: Increased tendency of the blood to clot, which can be due to genetic conditions (Factor V Leiden, prothrombin gene mutation), malignancies, estrogen therapy, pregnancy, or certain medications.

Diagnostic Workup
Prompt and accurate diagnosis of PE is critical due to its potentially life-threatening nature:

Clinical Assessment: Symptoms can vary widely but often include sudden onset dyspnea, pleuritic chest pain, cough, and in severe cases, syncope. Signs include tachypnea, tachycardia, and hypoxemia.

D-dimer Test: Elevated levels suggest a hypercoagulable state and the presence of thrombus degradation products, common in PE. A normal D-dimer level can help rule out PE in low-risk patients.

Imaging:

Computed Tomography Pulmonary Angiography (CTPA): The gold standard for diagnosing PE, showing filling defects in the pulmonary arteries.

Ventilation-Perfusion (V/Q) Scan: Used in patients for whom CTPA is contraindicated. A mismatch between ventilation and perfusion suggests PE.
Ultrasound: Doppler ultrasound of the legs may identify DVT, supporting the diagnosis of PE.
Electrocardiogram (ECG): May show signs of right heart strain (S1Q3T3 pattern, right bundle branch block, or T-wave inversions in the right precordial leads), but these findings are not specific to PE.

Echocardiography: Useful in assessing RV function and detecting signs of RV strain, which can support the diagnosis and guide management in hemodynamically unstable patients.

The management of PE involves anticoagulation to prevent further clot formation, thrombolytic therapy in selected cases, and addressing underlying risk factors to prevent recurrence.

The treatment of pulmonary embolism (PE) is tiered according to the severity of the condition and the patient's overall health status. The primary goals are to stabilize the patient, prevent further thrombus formation, and, in certain cases, actively dissolve the existing clot. Here's an overview of the treatment strategies:

Anticoagulation
Initial Therapy: Immediate anticoagulation is crucial to prevent clot extension and new clot formation. Options include:

Low Molecular Weight Heparin (LMWH): Preferred for its ease of use, predictable pharmacokinetics, and lower risk of heparin-induced thrombocytopenia (HIT). Administered subcutaneously.
Unfractionated Heparin (UFH): Used in patients with severe renal impairment or when rapid reversibility is required. Requires intravenous administration and monitoring of activated partial thromboplastin time (aPTT).
Direct Oral Anticoagulants (DOACs): Rivaroxaban or apixaban can be used as initial therapy for PE in patients without severe renal impairment or significant drug-drug interactions.
Long-Term Anticoagulation: After initial stabilization, patients are typically transitioned to oral anticoagulants (e.g., warfarin, DOACs) for at least 3 to 6 months, depending on the risk of recurrence and underlying factors.

Thrombolytic Therapy
Indications: Reserved for patients with massive PE with hemodynamic instability (hypotension, shock) or those with a high risk of hemodynamic deterioration due to significant RV dysfunction and myocardial necrosis.

Agents: Alteplase is the most commonly used agent. It is administered intravenously and works by converting plasminogen to plasmin, leading to clot dissolution.

Considerations: Thrombolytics carry a significant risk of bleeding, including intracranial hemorrhage. Their use must be carefully weighed against the risk of bleeding.

Advanced Interventions
Catheter-Directed Thrombolysis: For selected high-risk patients or those with contraindications to systemic thrombolysis. A catheter is used to deliver thrombolytic agents directly to the clot site.

Surgical Embolectomy: Considered in life-threatening cases where thrombolysis is contraindicated or has failed, and in patients with massive clots causing severe hemodynamic compromise.

Percutaneous Mechanical Thrombectomy: An alternative to surgery in some centers, using devices to mechanically fragment and remove the clot.

Supportive Care and Other Considerations
Oxygen Therapy: To maintain adequate oxygen saturation, especially in hypoxemic patients.

Fluid Management: Cautious fluid administration to support blood pressure without exacerbating RV failure.

Hemodynamic Support: Use of inotropes (e.g., dobutamine) may be necessary for patients with significant RV dysfunction.

Prevention of Recurrence: Includes identifying and managing underlying risk factors, patient education on anticoagulant therapy, and, in certain cases, placement of an inferior vena cava (IVC) filter.

IVC Filter: Considered in patients who cannot receive anticoagulation due to bleeding risk or those with recurrent PE despite adequate anticoagulation.

The management of PE requires a multidisciplinary approach, tailoring treatment to the individual's risk profile, the severity of the embolism, and the presence of underlying conditions. Regular monitoring and follow-up are essential to adjust treatment as needed and to prevent recurrence.

Oxygen therapy is a crucial intervention for patients with hypoxemia, and selecting the appropriate delivery device is essential for effective treatment. Various devices offer different oxygen concentrations and flow rates, tailored to the patient's respiratory status and oxygen requirements.

Nasal Cannula
- **Mechanism**: Delivers oxygen directly into the nostrils.
- **Flow Rates**: Typically 1-6 liters per minute (L/min), providing approximately 24-44% oxygen.
- **Indications**: Suitable for patients requiring low to moderate supplemental oxygen with relatively stable respiration. Allows for eating, talking, and mobility.

Simple Face Mask
- **Mechanism**: Covers the nose and mouth, providing a reservoir of oxygen.
- **Flow Rates**: Minimum of 5 L/min to prevent rebreathing of CO_2, with oxygen delivery ranging from 35-60%.
- **Indications**: Used for short-term oxygen therapy in patients needing moderate oxygen supplementation. Not suitable for CO_2 retainers or patients requiring precise oxygen concentrations.

Venturi Mask
- **Mechanism**: Mixes oxygen with room air to deliver a precise, constant oxygen concentration; uses a system of valves and adaptors to control FiO_2.
- **Flow Rates**: Variable, with devices typically designed to deliver FiO_2 from 24-50%.
- **Indications**: Ideal for patients with chronic lung diseases (e.g., COPD) who require controlled oxygen therapy to avoid hypercapnia.

Non-Rebreather Mask
- **Mechanism**: Equipped with a reservoir bag and one-way valves to prevent room air and exhaled gas from diluting the oxygen concentration.
- **Flow Rates**: Requires a minimum flow of 10-15 L/min to maintain bag inflation, delivering up to 60-100% oxygen.
- **Indications**: For patients in acute respiratory distress requiring high concentrations of oxygen. It's a temporary measure, often used until a more definitive treatment (e.g., mechanical ventilation) can be initiated.

High-Flow Nasal Cannula (HFNC)
- **Mechanism**: Delivers heated, humidified oxygen at high flow rates through large-bore nasal prongs.
- **Flow Rates**: Can deliver flows up to 60 L/min, with adjustable FiO_2 up to 100%.
- **Indications**: Suitable for patients with acute hypoxemic respiratory failure, providing not only high-concentration oxygen but also some positive airway pressure, reducing work of breathing and improving alveolar ventilation.

Key Considerations
- **Patient Comfort and Tolerance**: Nasal cannulas and HFNC are generally more comfortable and better tolerated for long-term use compared to masks.
- **Need for Humidification**: High flow rates, especially with HFNC, require humidification to prevent mucosal drying and discomfort.
- **CO_2 Retention**: Patients at risk of hypercapnia (e.g., COPD patients) need careful monitoring, particularly with devices that deliver high FiO_2, as they may suppress the respiratory drive.
- **Emergency Situations**: Non-rebreather masks are often used in emergency settings requiring rapid oxygenation, while definitive airway management is being arranged.

Selecting the appropriate oxygen delivery device involves considering the patient's oxygenation goals, underlying respiratory condition, and the need for precise oxygen control, ensuring effective and safe oxygen therapy tailored to the individual's needs.

Oxygen titration is a critical aspect of respiratory management, aiming to provide sufficient oxygen to meet physiological needs while avoiding the detrimental effects of hyperoxia. The process involves adjusting the oxygen flow rate and delivery device based on the patient's saturation of peripheral oxygen (SpO_2) levels and clinical condition.

Principles of Oxygen Titration
Target SpO_2 Range: Establishing a target SpO_2 range is crucial for titration. For most patients, maintaining SpO_2 between 92-96% is appropriate. In certain conditions like chronic obstructive pulmonary disease (COPD) or in neonates, a lower target range (88-92%) may be preferred to avoid hypercapnia and oxidative stress.

Assessment and Monitoring: Continuous monitoring of SpO_2 using pulse oximetry, along with clinical assessment (mental status, respiratory rate, use of accessory muscles), provides the basis for titration decisions. Arterial blood gas (ABG) analysis may be needed for a more precise assessment in critically ill patients.

Incremental Adjustments: Oxygen flow should be adjusted incrementally, increasing to alleviate hypoxemia or decreasing to prevent hyperoxia, based on continuous SpO_2 monitoring and clinical response.

Device Selection: The choice of oxygen delivery device plays a significant role in titration. Devices with fixed oxygen concentrations (e.g., Venturi masks) allow for more precise control in patients at risk of hypercapnia, while high-flow systems like high-flow nasal cannula (HFNC) provide both high oxygen concentrations and positive airway pressure.

Avoiding Hyperoxia: Excessive oxygenation (SpO_2 > 96%) can lead to hyperoxia, associated with increased mortality, especially in acute conditions like myocardial infarction and stroke. Oxygen flow should be titrated down once SpO_2 exceeds the target range.

Special Populations: Particular attention is needed for patients with COPD, who may retain CO_2 in response to high oxygen levels, and for neonates, where strict control of oxygenation is crucial to avoid retinopathy of prematurity and other oxygen-related complications.

Clinical Considerations
Hypoxemic Events: During acute hypoxemic episodes, a temporary increase in oxygen flow may be necessary, followed by a gradual reduction as the patient stabilizes.

Weaning: As the patient's condition improves, a systematic approach to weaning off supplemental oxygen should be employed, reducing flow rates or stepping down to less intensive delivery devices while ensuring SpO_2 remains within the target range.

Patient Education: Educating patients and caregivers about the importance of SpO_2 monitoring, signs of inadequate oxygenation (increased dyspnea, confusion, cyanosis), and when to adjust oxygen flow or seek medical help is essential for long-term oxygen therapy at home.

Oxygen titration requires a careful balance between providing adequate oxygen to prevent hypoxemia and avoiding the risks associated with hyperoxia. It necessitates vigilance, regular assessment, and a patient-centered approach to ensure optimal outcomes.

Chest physiotherapy and airway clearance techniques are essential components in the management of patients with respiratory conditions that lead to increased mucus production and reduced mucus clearance, such as cystic fibrosis, chronic obstructive pulmonary disease (COPD), and bronchiectasis. These techniques aim to facilitate the removal of secretions from the airways, improving ventilation and reducing the risk of infection.

Postural Drainage
- **Principle**: Involves positioning the patient in various postures to use gravity to drain secretions from different lobes and segments of the lungs into the central airways, where they can be more easily coughed up.
- **Techniques**: The patient is positioned in specific ways that correspond to the lung segment being targeted. For example, to drain the apical segments of the upper lobes, the patient sits upright; to drain the basal segments of the lower lobes, the patient lies prone with the bed tilted so the feet are higher than the head.

- **Considerations**: Care must be taken with patients who have heart failure, severe hypertension, or other conditions where such positioning may be contraindicated.

Percussion
- **Principle**: Involves rhythmically clapping on the chest wall over the lung segment being treated, with the hand cupped, to mechanically dislodge secretions from the bronchial walls.
- **Application**: Performed in conjunction with postural drainage, targeting different lung segments based on the patient's position. Each segment is percussed for several minutes.
- **Considerations**: Should be avoided over areas with pain, recent surgery, fractures, or bruising.

Vibration
- **Principle**: Involves the use of manual or mechanical vibration on the chest wall during exhalation to increase the velocity of air expiration, helping to move secretions towards the central airways.
- **Technique**: Manual vibration is performed with flat hands, creating a fine shaking motion as the patient exhales. Mechanical vibration can be provided by devices specifically designed for this purpose.
- **Indications**: Used after percussion and during postural drainage to enhance mucus clearance.

Airway Clearance Devices

Several devices have been designed to assist with airway clearance, particularly for patients who require daily chest physiotherapy:

1. **Positive Expiratory Pressure (PEP) Devices**: The patient exhales through a device that creates back pressure, helping to keep airways open and mobilize secretions.
2. **Oscillatory PEP Devices**: Combine PEP with oscillations that help to dislodge mucus from the airway walls (e.g., Flutter device, Acapella).
3. **High-Frequency Chest Wall Oscillation (HFCWO) Vests**: Use an inflatable vest connected to a machine that provides high-frequency air pulses, creating chest wall oscillations to loosen and mobilize secretions.
4. **Intrapulmonary Percussive Ventilation (IPV)**: Delivers short bursts of air mixed with aerosolized medications directly into the lungs at high frequency, helping to loosen secretions and improve ventilation.

Considerations and Contraindications
- While these techniques are generally safe, certain conditions may contraindicate specific maneuvers (e.g., recent chest surgery, rib fractures, pneumothorax risk).
- Patient comfort, tolerance, and effectiveness of the technique should guide the choice of therapy.
- Proper training for caregivers and patients, especially for home use of devices, is essential to ensure safety and effectiveness.

Chest physiotherapy and airway clearance techniques are integral to the management of patients with conditions leading to impaired mucus clearance. Tailoring the approach to the individual's needs, capabilities, and underlying condition is key to maximizing the benefits of these therapies.

Chest physiotherapy and airway clearance techniques play a vital role in the management of critically ill patients, particularly those with conditions leading to increased mucus production or impaired mucus clearance. The indications for their use in critical care settings include:

Acute Respiratory Distress Syndrome (ARDS): In ARDS, where lung compliance is reduced, and the risk of atelectasis is high, airway clearance techniques can help improve ventilation and oxygenation by clearing secretions and re-expanding collapsed alveoli.

Pneumonia: Patients with pneumonia often have increased sputum production. Airway clearance can aid in the removal of infectious material and secretions, potentially reducing the risk of secondary infection or sepsis.

Chronic Obstructive Pulmonary Disease (COPD) Exacerbations: In COPD exacerbations, airway clearance can help manage increased sputum production, reduce airway obstruction, and improve lung function, which can be particularly beneficial in weaning from mechanical ventilation.

Cystic Fibrosis (CF): Although primarily managed in the outpatient setting, CF patients may require critical care for acute exacerbations. Airway clearance is fundamental in managing CF-related respiratory complications, helping to clear thick, tenacious secretions.

Bronchiectasis: In patients with bronchiectasis, airway clearance can help manage daily sputum production and prevent exacerbations that may lead to hospital or ICU admissions.

Neurological Conditions with Impaired Cough Reflex: Patients with neurological conditions that impair the ability to cough effectively (e.g., spinal cord injuries, neuromuscular disorders) can benefit from airway clearance techniques to prevent secretion buildup and respiratory complications.

Postoperative Care: Particularly after thoracic or upper abdominal surgery, airway clearance techniques can prevent postoperative complications such as atelectasis and pneumonia by encouraging deep breathing and clearing secretions.

Trauma Patients with Chest Injuries: In patients with rib fractures or other chest injuries, airway clearance techniques can help clear secretions when deep breathing and coughing are painful, reducing the risk of pneumonia.

Mechanically Ventilated Patients: In patients receiving long-term mechanical ventilation, airway clearance techniques can help prevent ventilator-associated pneumonia (VAP) by reducing the accumulation of secretions in the airways.

Immobility or Prolonged Bed Rest: Patients who are immobilized or on prolonged bed rest are at risk for secretion retention and atelectasis; airway clearance can help maintain pulmonary hygiene and prevent complications.

In critical care settings, the application of chest physiotherapy and airway clearance techniques must be carefully tailored to the individual's clinical status, with considerations for hemodynamic stability, oxygenation, and the presence of contraindications. Close monitoring during and after the application of these techniques is essential to ensure patient safety and therapeutic efficacy.

Renal/Gastrointestinal:

Think of the renal and gastrointestinal (GI) systems as your body's internal processing plant and waste management facility. When they malfunction, the ripple effects are swift and widespread. In this section, we'll delve into these systems and how critical care nurses save the day when they go awry.

Why Renal/GI Matters in Critical Care

- The Kidney Connection: Kidneys filter blood, maintain fluid balance, and are key regulators of electrolytes. Acute Kidney Injury (AKI) is a common critical care crisis, often a domino leading to multi-system problems.
- Gut Instincts: GI bleeding can be life-threatening, requiring rapid diagnosis and intervention. Nutrition in critically ill patients is complex – we'll explore the delicate balance between maintaining gut function and providing life-sustaining nutrients.
- It's All Connected: These systems don't operate in isolation. Kidney failure throws off electrolytes, impacting the heart and brain function. Gut problems affect fluid balance, which the kidneys must then manage.

What We'll Cover in this Section

- Kidney Fundamentals:
    - AKI: From recognizing the signs to understanding treatment strategies.
    - Electrolyte imbalances: How critical shifts in sodium, potassium, calcium, and more wreak havoc, and how we fix them.
    - Continuous Renal Replacement Therapy (CRRT): The lifesaving machine for when kidneys shut down.
- Gastrointestinal Tract:
    - GI Bleeding: Spotting the source, stopping the bleeding with both medications and endoscopic interventions.
    - Gut Protection: Strategies to prevent ulcers in critically ill patients.
    - Critical Nutrition: The enteral vs. parenteral debate, and managing the metabolic rollercoaster of critical illness.

Beyond the Textbook:

- Fluid Balance: It's an art form in critical care. We'll discuss the nuances of how and when to give (or restrict) fluids.
- Labs and Lines: Interpreting those strings of numbers on lab results to guide our actions.

This section will empower you to think critically – to link kidney function with heart function, gut health with overall recovery. It's about seeing the body as a dynamic, interconnected system where your interventions have profound consequences.

Acute Kidney Injury (AKI), previously known as acute renal failure, is a sudden episode of kidney failure or kidney damage that happens within a few hours or days. It causes waste products to build up in your blood and makes it hard for your kidneys to keep the right balance of fluid in your body. AKI can also affect other organs such as the brain, heart, and lungs. AKI is common in patients who are in the hospital, in intensive care units, and especially in older adults.

Definitions and Pathophysiology

AKI is characterized by a rapid decrease in renal function, leading to an accumulation of urea and other nitrogenous waste products in the blood. The pathophysiology of AKI can be categorized into three primary mechanisms:

1. **Prerenal AKI**: The most common form, caused by decreased renal perfusion due to volume depletion (e.g., hemorrhage, dehydration), cardiovascular failure, or decreased effective arterial blood volume as seen in sepsis or heart failure.
2. **Intrinsic (Intrarenal) AKI**: Results from direct damage to the renal parenchyma. Causes include acute tubular necrosis (ATN) due to ischemia or nephrotoxic agents, acute glomerulonephritis, acute interstitial nephritis, and vascular insults.
3. **Postrenal AKI**: Caused by obstruction of the urinary tract, leading to backpressure and kidney injury. Common causes include kidney stones, benign prostatic hyperplasia, and malignancies obstructing the urinary tract.

Staging and Diagnosis

The severity of AKI is commonly staged using three criteria: RIFLE, AKIN, and KDIGO, which help in identifying the severity and guiding management.

1. **RIFLE Criteria**:
    - **Risk**: Increase in serum creatinine ×1.5 or GFR decrease by >25%, or urine output <0.5 mL/kg/hr for 6 hours.
    - **Injury**: Increase in serum creatinine ×2 or GFR decrease by >50%, or urine output <0.5 mL/kg/hr for 12 hours.
    - **Failure**: Increase in serum creatinine ×3 or GFR decrease by >75%, or urine output <0.3 mL/kg/hr for 24 hours or anuria for 12 hours.
    - **Loss**: Persistent AKI or complete loss of kidney function for >4 weeks.
    - **End-Stage Renal Disease (ESRD)**: Complete loss of kidney function for >3 months.
2. **AKIN Criteria**:
    - Stages based on similar changes in serum creatinine and urine output as RIFLE but with modifications to the creatinine and timing criteria, emphasizing smaller changes within a 48-hour window.
3. **KDIGO Criteria**:
    - Combines and modifies RIFLE and AKIN criteria, defining stages of AKI based on increases in serum creatinine (1.5 times baseline within 7 days or increase by ≥0.3 mg/dL within 48 hours) and changes in urine output (<0.5 mL/kg/hr for 6-12 hours).

Management Implications

The staging of AKI is critical for determining the severity of kidney injury and guiding management, which includes:

- **Addressing the underlying cause**: Immediate intervention to manage the cause of AKI, such as fluid resuscitation for prerenal causes or relieving obstruction in postrenal AKI.
- **Supportive care**: Ensuring optimal fluid balance, electrolyte management, and hemodynamic support.
- **Avoidance of nephrotoxic agents**: Minimizing exposure to nephrotoxic medications and contrast agents.
- **Renal replacement therapy (RRT)**: In cases of severe AKI, dialysis or other forms of RRT may be required to support kidney function until recovery.

Patient Outcomes

The prognosis of AKI varies widely depending on the cause, severity, patient's overall health, and the timeliness and effectiveness of the management. While many patients recover renal function, AKI can lead to increased risk of chronic kidney disease (CKD), end-stage renal disease (ESRD), and increased mortality, particularly in severe cases or when associated with other organ failures.

AKI remains a significant challenge in clinical practice, requiring prompt recognition, an understanding of the underlying pathophysiology, and a multidisciplinary approach to management to optimize outcomes.

Electrolyte imbalances are common in clinical practice, particularly in patients with renal dysfunction, and can have significant physiological implications. Understanding the identification, clinical manifestations, and management strategies for key electrolyte imbalances is crucial for patient care.

Hyperkalemia
- **Identification**: Serum potassium >5.5 mEq/L.
- **Clinical Manifestations**: Muscle weakness, paralysis, cardiac arrhythmias, and, in severe cases, cardiac arrest.
- **Management**: Acute management includes calcium gluconate for cardioprotection, insulin with glucose to shift potassium intracellularly, and sodium bicarbonate if acidosis is present. Long-term management may involve sodium polystyrene sulfonate (Kayexalate) or loop diuretics to enhance potassium elimination.

Hyponatremia
- **Identification**: Serum sodium <135 mEq/L.
- **Clinical Manifestations**: Nausea, headache, confusion, seizures, and, in severe cases, coma.
- **Management**: Depends on the cause, volume status, and severity. Mild cases may require fluid restriction, whereas severe symptomatic hyponatremia might necessitate cautious hypertonic saline administration. The correction rate should not exceed 6-8 mEq/L in 24 hours to avoid osmotic demyelination syndrome.

Hypercalcemia
- **Identification**: Serum calcium >10.5 mg/dL.
- **Clinical Manifestations**: "Bones, stones, abdominal groans, and psychiatric overtones" - pain from osteoporosis and fractures, nephrolithiasis, nausea, vomiting, constipation, and altered mental status.
- **Management**: Hydration with isotonic saline, loop diuretics to increase calcium excretion, bisphosphonates, and in severe cases, calcitonin. The underlying cause (often malignancy or hyperparathyroidism) must be addressed.

Hypomagnesemia
- **Identification**: Serum magnesium <1.7 mg/dL.
- **Clinical Manifestations**: Neuromuscular irritability, tremors, seizures, arrhythmias, and hypokalemia and hypocalcemia that are resistant to treatment until magnesium is corrected.
- **Management**: Oral magnesium supplementation in mild cases, and intravenous magnesium sulfate in severe cases or when oral administration is not feasible.

Hypokalemia
- **Identification**: Serum potassium <3.5 mEq/L.
- **Clinical Manifestations**: Muscle weakness, cramps, arrhythmias, and, in severe cases, respiratory muscle weakness and paralysis.
- **Management**: Potassium supplementation, either orally for mild cases or intravenously for severe cases or when rapid replacement is needed. The underlying cause, often gastrointestinal loss or diuretic use, must be addressed.

Phosphorus Imbalances
- **Hypophosphatemia**: Serum phosphate <2.5 mg/dL, leading to muscle weakness, respiratory failure, hemolytic anemia, and neurological symptoms. Treated with oral or intravenous phosphate supplementation.

- **Hyperphosphatemia**: Serum phosphate >4.5 mg/dL, often due to renal failure, causing calcification in tissues and secondary hypocalcemia. Managed by reducing dietary phosphate intake, phosphate binders, and treating the underlying renal dysfunction.

Role of Renal Function and Strategies for Correction

Renal function is central to the regulation of electrolyte balance. Kidney impairment can lead to both retention (e.g., hyperkalemia, hyperphosphatemia) and excessive loss of electrolytes (e.g., hypokalemia, hypomagnesemia). Management strategies often involve:

- **Enhancing Renal Excretion**: Using loop or thiazide diuretics for hyperkalemia or hypercalcemia.
- **Limiting Intake**: Dietary restrictions for hyperkalemia, hyperphosphatemia, and hypercalcemia.
- **Renal Replacement Therapy**: Dialysis may be necessary in cases of severe imbalance or when renal function is significantly impaired.
- **Addressing Underlying Renal Dysfunction**: Optimizing the management of chronic kidney disease or acute kidney injury can help prevent and manage electrolyte disturbances.

Electrolyte imbalances require prompt recognition, a thorough understanding of the underlying pathophysiology, and tailored management strategies to correct the imbalance and address its root cause, especially in the context of renal dysfunction.

Continuous Renal Replacement Therapy (CRRT) is a form of dialysis used to provide renal support for critically ill patients with acute kidney injury (AKI), especially those who are hemodynamically unstable. CRRT is designed to mimic the kidneys' functions more gradually than intermittent hemodialysis, making it suitable for patients who might not tolerate the rapid fluid and electrolyte shifts of conventional dialysis.

Indications
CRRT is typically indicated in the following scenarios:

Hemodynamic Instability: Patients with AKI who cannot tolerate intermittent hemodialysis due to the risk of hypotension and other hemodynamic changes.
Fluid Overload: Particularly in the context of oliguria or anuria, where there is a need for precise fluid management.
Severe Azotemia: In the presence of high urea and creatinine levels that need gradual reduction.
Acute Brain Injury or Intracranial Hypertension: Where rapid shifts in osmolality need to be avoided.
Mechanisms and Modalities
CRRT can be delivered through various modalities, each with its mechanism of solute clearance:

Continuous Venovenous Hemofiltration (CVVH): Focuses on convection as the primary mechanism. Blood is driven through a filter, and hydrostatic pressure pushes water and solutes across the membrane in a process called ultrafiltration. Replacement fluid is added to the blood post-filter to replace the volume and maintain hemodynamic stability.

Continuous Venovenous Hemodialysis (CVVHD): Relies on diffusion as the primary mechanism. A concentration gradient across the dialysis membrane allows waste products to move from the blood to the dialysate. The dialysate flows counter-current to the blood, maximizing the gradient.

Continuous Venovenous Hemodiafiltration (CVVHDF): Combines both CVVH and CVVHD, utilizing both convection and diffusion for solute removal, offering efficient clearance of both small and larger molecules.

Solute Clearance Principles

Diffusion: Movement of solutes from an area of higher concentration (blood) to lower concentration (dialysate), effective for small molecules like urea.

Convection: Solvent drag, where solutes are carried with water across the membrane, effective for larger molecules.

Ultrafiltration: The movement of water across a semipermeable membrane driven by a transmembrane pressure gradient, facilitating fluid removal.

Nursing Considerations

Monitoring: Continuous monitoring of vital signs, CRRT machine settings, and alarms is crucial. Regular assessment of the vascular access site for signs of infection or thrombosis is necessary.

Anticoagulation: To prevent clotting within the circuit, anticoagulation is often required, with unfractionated heparin being the most common agent. Close monitoring of coagulation parameters (e.g., aPTT) is essential to adjust dosing and minimize bleeding risks.

Fluid Balance: Precise management of fluid removal and replacement is critical, with hourly assessments to ensure fluid goals are met without causing hemodynamic instability.

Complications: Nurses should be vigilant for complications such as hypotension, electrolyte imbalances, bleeding (related to anticoagulation), or filter clotting, and respond promptly.

Education and Communication: Providing information to the patient and family about the purpose and process of CRRT and maintaining clear communication with the multidisciplinary team for comprehensive care.

CRRT requires a collaborative, multidisciplinary approach, with skilled nursing care being pivotal in ensuring the safe and effective delivery of therapy. Understanding the intricacies of CRRT modalities, solute clearance mechanisms, and the meticulous management of fluid balance and anticoagulation are essential components of care for patients receiving CRRT.

Gastrointestinal (GI) bleeding is a common medical emergency that ranges from minor to life-threatening conditions. A structured approach to assessment and management is crucial for optimal outcomes.

Initial Assessment and Resuscitation

Stabilization: Initial management focuses on stabilizing the patient. Assess airway, breathing, and circulation (ABCs), and initiate resuscitation with intravenous fluids and, if necessary, blood products to maintain hemodynamic stability.

History and Physical Examination: Obtain a detailed history to identify potential sources of bleeding, previous GI issues, medication use (especially anticoagulants), and comorbid conditions. Physical examination should assess hemodynamic status, abdominal examination, and rectal examination to evaluate for potential sources of bleeding.

Differentiating Between Upper and Lower GI Bleeding

Upper GI Bleeding: Sources proximal to the ligament of Treitz, presenting as hematemesis (vomiting blood) or melena (black, tarry stools). Common causes include peptic ulcers, gastritis, esophageal varices, and Mallory-Weiss tears.

Lower GI Bleeding: Sources distal to the ligament of Treitz, presenting as hematochezia (bright red blood per rectum) or, less commonly, melena. Common causes include diverticulosis, angiodysplasia, colorectal cancer, and inflammatory bowel disease.

Diagnostic Workup
Laboratory Tests: Complete blood count, coagulation profile, blood type and screen, liver function tests, and renal function tests to assess the patient's baseline status and guide resuscitation.

Endoscopy:

Upper Endoscopy (EGD): The first-line investigation for suspected upper GI bleeding, ideally performed within 24 hours of presentation.
Colonoscopy: Indicated for lower GI bleeding once the upper source is excluded and the patient is hemodynamically stable.
Imaging:

CT Angiography: Useful in locating active bleeding if endoscopy is inconclusive or if the patient is unstable.
Tagged Red Blood Cell Scan: Can detect slow or intermittent bleeding when endoscopy is non-diagnostic.
Endoscopic and Radiologic Interventions
Endoscopic Therapy: Includes thermal coagulation, clipping, and banding of varices for upper GI bleeding, and similar modalities for accessible lower GI sources.

Radiologic Interventions: Angiographic embolization can be considered for active bleeding not amenable to endoscopic control, with a focus on preserving bowel viability.

Management Strategies
Proton Pump Inhibitors (PPIs): Initiated in cases of upper GI bleeding, especially with peptic ulcer disease, to reduce acid production and stabilize clot formation.

Variceal Bleeding Management: Includes vasoactive drugs (e.g., octreotide) and endoscopic variceal ligation or sclerotherapy. Consideration for transjugular intrahepatic portosystemic shunt (TIPS) in refractory cases.

Anticoagulation Reversal: In patients with GI bleeding on anticoagulation therapy, consider reversing the anticoagulant effect, balancing the risk of thrombosis with ongoing bleeding.

Prevention of Rebleeding: Includes risk stratification, treatment of underlying causes, and possibly long-term PPI therapy for peptic ulcer disease.

Nutritional Support: Early enteral nutrition, if possible, to support mucosal healing and patient recovery.

Nursing Considerations and Monitoring
Continuous monitoring of vital signs, input and output, hemoglobin levels, and coagulation parameters.

Ensuring patient comfort and providing education on the importance of notifying staff about new or worsening symptoms.
Post-procedure care for endoscopic or radiologic interventions, monitoring for complications such as perforation or post-embolization syndrome.
A multidisciplinary approach, involving gastroenterologists, surgeons, interventional radiologists, and critical care specialists, is often required to manage complex cases of GI bleeding effectively.

Nutrition plays a pivotal role in the management of critically ill patients, influencing recovery trajectories and outcomes. The choice between enteral nutrition (EN) and parenteral nutrition (PN) hinges on the patient's gastrointestinal function, clinical status, and specific nutritional requirements.

Enteral Nutrition (EN)
Indications:
- Preferred if the gastrointestinal (GI) tract is functional.
- Conditions like pancreatitis, postoperative states, and neurological or neuromuscular disorders impairing oral intake.

Benefits:
- Maintains gut integrity and function.
- Reduces the risk of infection compared to PN.
- Generally more physiological and cost-effective.

Risks and Complications:
- Aspiration pneumonia.
- Diarrhea or constipation.
- Tube displacement or blockage.

Metabolic Considerations:
- Overfeeding, particularly with high-carbohydrate formulas, can lead to hyperglycemia.
- Monitoring and adjusting electrolytes, especially in patients with renal or hepatic dysfunction.

Guidelines for Use:
- Initiate as soon as hemodynamically stable, typically within 24-48 hours of ICU admission.
- Start at a low rate, gradually increasing to meet full nutritional goals over 24-72 hours.
- Regularly assess gastric residual volumes (GRVs) to reduce the risk of aspiration, although recent guidelines suggest higher thresholds before adjusting EN.

Parenteral Nutrition (PN)
Indications:
- Used when the GI tract is not usable due to conditions like bowel obstruction, severe ileus, or short bowel syndrome.
- Considered when EN is contraindicated or fails to meet nutritional requirements.

Benefits:
- Provides nutritional support when EN is not possible.
- Allows precise control of nutrient composition and volume.

Risks and Complications:
- Increased risk of bloodstream infections.
- Liver dysfunction and fatty liver disease.
- Metabolic derangements, including hyperglycemia.

Metabolic Considerations:
- Careful monitoring of blood glucose levels, with insulin therapy as needed.
- Regular monitoring of liver enzymes and triglyceride levels.

Guidelines for Use:
- Reserved for patients who cannot tolerate or access EN after the initial days of critical illness.
- Initiate with cautious advancement to target rates, monitoring for refeeding syndrome in malnourished patients.
- Electrolyte, fluid, and micronutrient management are essential due to the risks of metabolic complications.

Monitoring and Complications
For Both EN and PN:
- Regular monitoring of nutritional status, electrolytes, fluid balance, and metabolic parameters is essential.
- Be vigilant for signs of refeeding syndrome, especially in severely malnourished patients, characterized by hypophosphatemia, hypokalemia, and hypomagnesemia.
- Adjustments may be needed based on renal and hepatic function, ongoing fluid losses, and changes in clinical status.

Choosing between EN and PN involves a careful assessment of the patient's GI function, risk of complications, and specific nutritional and metabolic needs. While EN is generally preferred for its physiological benefits and lower complication rates, PN is indispensable when the GI tract is not functional or accessible. A multidisciplinary approach, involving dietitians, physicians, and nursing staff, is crucial for optimizing nutritional support in critically ill patients, tailoring interventions to individual needs, and promptly addressing complications.

Musculoskeletal/Multisystem/Psychosocial:

Think of this section as the detective work of critical care. We'll explore hidden injuries, the mind-body connection in times of crisis, and the ripple effects a single problem can have on multiple bodily systems.

Why Musculoskeletal/Multisystem/Psychosocial Matters in Critical Care
- The Hidden Enemy: Compartment syndrome is a sneaky threat – miss the signs, and a patient can lose a limb. We'll learn how to recognize and treat this urgent situation.
- Beyond Single Organs: Critical illnesses don't play fair. We'll tackle multisystem disorders like sepsis, where early recognition and aggressive treatment across multiple fronts mean the difference between life and death.
- Shock States: When blood flow falters, organs starve. We'll break down the different types of shock (cardiogenic, hypovolemic, distributive) and the tailored interventions for each.
- The Power of the Mind: Anxiety, delirium, and the psychological toll of critical illness are just as real as physical insults. We'll discuss both supportive and pharmacological approaches.

What We'll Cover in this Section:
- Musculoskeletal:
    - Compartment Syndrome: Diagnosis and the dramatic relief of fasciotomy.
- Multisystem:
    - Sepsis: The body's war against infection – how it unfolds, how we stop it.
    - Shock States: Classification, signs, and management principles to reverse the course.
- Psychosocial:
    - Delirium: Recognizing it early is key. We'll cover assessment tools and management.
    - Supporting Families: Critical illness impacts loved ones too. We'll touch on communication strategies and resources.

Beyond the Facts:

- Interconnectedness: A failing heart burdens the kidneys, low blood pressure leads to brain fog. This section is about seeing the big picture.
- Prioritization: In a crisis, with multiple systems failing, what do we address first? We'll discuss a systematic approach.

This section empowers you to be proactive – to spot subtle cues, understand how problems cascade, and advocate for the whole patient, both physically and psychologically.

Compartment syndrome occurs when increased pressure within an enclosed muscle compartment in the body compromises blood flow and tissue viability. This condition is most commonly seen in the limbs but can occur in any muscle compartment. The pathophysiology involves a cascade of events leading to tissue ischemia, cell death, and potentially irreversible damage if not promptly treated.

Mechanisms of Increased Compartmental Pressure
Reduced Capillary Perfusion: Normal tissue perfusion relies on a delicate balance between capillary hydrostatic pressure and tissue pressure. When compartment pressure rises, it exceeds the capillary perfusion pressure, leading to capillary collapse and reduced blood flow. This diminishes oxygen and nutrient delivery to the tissues.

Venous Outflow Obstruction: Elevated compartmental pressure compresses veins, obstructing venous return. This venous congestion further elevates compartment pressure, creating a vicious cycle that exacerbates tissue ischemia.

Arterial Inflow Reduction: As compartment pressure continues to rise, it can eventually approach or surpass arterial pressure, leading to a significant reduction or cessation of arterial blood flow into the compartment. This acute reduction in arterial inflow severely limits oxygen delivery, accelerating tissue hypoxia and ischemia.

Ischemic Cascade: Ischemia triggers a cascade of metabolic changes within the tissues. Cells shift to anaerobic metabolism, producing lactic acid and other toxic metabolites, leading to acidosis. This acidic environment further damages cell membranes, causing the release of potassium and other intracellular components into the extracellular space, exacerbating edema and increasing compartmental pressure.

Microvascular Damage: Prolonged ischemia leads to endothelial damage and increased vascular permeability, contributing to edema and further elevating compartmental pressure. This microvascular damage also impairs the reperfusion of tissues once the pressure is relieved, potentially leading to reperfusion injury.

Myoneural Damage: Nerves and muscles within the compartment are particularly sensitive to ischemia. Prolonged ischemia can lead to irreversible muscle necrosis and nerve damage within hours. Muscle necrosis releases myoglobin, which can lead to renal failure, complicating the clinical scenario further.

Clinical Implications
The clinical manifestations of compartment syndrome, such as pain out of proportion to injury, pain on passive stretch of the muscles within the compartment, paresthesia, and decreased compartmental perfusion, reflect the underlying pathophysiology. Prompt diagnosis and intervention, typically via fasciotomy to relieve the pressure, are critical to restoring perfusion and preventing permanent tissue

damage. Failure to promptly address compartment syndrome can result in long-term functional impairment, muscle necrosis, limb loss, or systemic complications like renal failure due to myoglobinuria.

Compartment syndrome occurs when increased pressure within a closed anatomic space, usually one of the muscle compartments in the limbs, compromises blood flow and tissue viability. This condition can be acute, often due to trauma, or chronic, as seen in athletes.

Mechanisms Compromising Blood Flow and Tissue Viability
1. **Increased Compartmental Pressure**: Pressure within an anatomical compartment can increase due to swelling from trauma, bleeding, inflammation, or external compression. Each compartment is enclosed by fascia that does not easily expand, so any increase in volume within the compartment increases the pressure.
2. **Capillary Perfusion Pressure Reduction**: As the pressure within a compartment rises, it eventually exceeds the capillary perfusion pressure, leading to capillary collapse. This impedes the flow of oxygen and nutrients to the tissues.
3. **Ischemia**: The lack of blood flow results in ischemia of the muscle and nerve tissue within the compartment. Ischemia can lead to irreversible tissue damage within hours.
4. **Venous Outflow Obstruction**: Elevated compartmental pressure compresses veins, reducing venous return and leading to further vascular congestion and edema, which exacerbate the compartment pressure.
5. **Arterial Inflow Obstruction**: In severe cases, the pressure can obstruct arterial inflow, leading to a vicious cycle of worsening ischemia and edema.

Characteristic Signs and Symptoms ("6 Ps")
The classic signs and symptoms of acute compartment syndrome are summarized by the "6 Ps":
1. **Pain**: Out of proportion to what would be expected from the injury and not relieved by analgesics or elevation. Pain is often exacerbated by passive stretching of the muscles within the compartment.
2. **Pressure**: A feeling of tightness or fullness in the affected compartment.
3. **Paresthesia**: Tingling or burning sensations in the skin, indicating nerve involvement.
4. **Pallor**: The skin may appear pale due to reduced blood flow.
5. **Paralysis**: Loss of function in the affected limb or digits, which is a late and ominous sign indicating severe and possibly irreversible nerve and muscle damage.
6. **Pulselessness**: Absence of a pulse distal to the compartment, also a late sign, indicative of arterial occlusion. It's worth noting that pulses may be present in early or even in advanced cases due to collateral blood flow, making this an unreliable sign for early diagnosis.

Compartment Pressure Measurement
- **Invasive Monitoring**: The diagnosis of compartment syndrome can be confirmed by directly measuring the pressure within the compartment using a needle or catheter connected to a pressure transducer.
- **Diagnostic Thresholds**: An absolute compartment pressure of more than 30 mmHg, or a differential pressure (diastolic blood pressure minus compartment pressure) of less than 30 mmHg, is often used as a threshold for diagnosing compartment syndrome and considering fasciotomy.
- **Clinical Correlation**: Pressure measurements should be interpreted in the context of the overall clinical picture, as some patients may require intervention at lower pressures based on symptoms and clinical judgment.

Early recognition and diagnosis of compartment syndrome are critical to prevent irreversible damage to muscles and nerves. Clinical evaluation remains paramount, with compartment pressure measurement serving as an important diagnostic adjunct in ambiguous cases. Prompt surgical intervention, typically fasciotomy, is required to relieve the pressure and restore tissue perfusion.

Emergent management of compartment syndrome is critical to prevent irreversible damage to muscles, nerves, and other tissues within the affected compartment. The key to successful treatment is the timely recognition of symptoms and prompt surgical intervention. Here are the principles of emergent management for compartment syndrome:

Timely Diagnosis
- Early recognition of the signs and symptoms ("6 Ps") is crucial. Pain, particularly pain out of proportion to the injury and exacerbated by passive stretching of the muscles within the compartment, should raise suspicion.
- Invasive compartment pressure measurement can be instrumental in confirming the diagnosis, especially in cases where clinical signs are equivocal or in patients who are unconscious or unable to communicate.

Non-Surgical Interventions
While definitive treatment is surgical, certain non-surgical measures can be taken initially, provided they do not delay surgery:
- **Remove Constrictive Devices**: Casts, bandages, or any external compression should be removed immediately to relieve external pressure.
- **Limb Elevation**: The affected limb should be positioned at heart level to aid venous return without significantly affecting arterial pressure. However, elevation should not be excessive as it might reduce arterial perfusion.
- **Avoidance of Cold Therapy**: Although ice can reduce swelling, it can also exacerbate vasoconstriction and worsen compartmental perfusion.
- **Hemodynamic Support**: Ensuring adequate blood pressure to maintain perfusion to the affected compartment while preparing for surgery.

Surgical Intervention: Fasciotomy
- **Timeliness**: Fasciotomy is the definitive treatment for compartment syndrome and should be performed urgently, ideally within 6 hours of symptom onset, to prevent irreversible muscle and nerve damage.
- **Procedure**: The procedure involves making long incisions through the skin and fascia of the affected compartment to relieve pressure. The incisions may be left open (open fasciotomy) and covered with a sterile dressing to allow for continued swelling and subsequent evaluation. Closure or skin grafting can be performed later once the swelling has subsided.
- **Comprehensive Decompression**: All involved compartments must be adequately decompressed. In the case of the lower leg, for example, this might involve both the anterior and posterior compartments.

Postoperative Care
- **Wound Management**: After fasciotomy, careful wound management is required. The wound may be temporarily covered with a vacuum-assisted closure device or other temporary closure methods until definitive closure is possible.
- **Monitoring for Reperfusion Injury**: The restoration of blood flow can lead to reperfusion injury, characterized by swelling and further tissue damage. Continuous monitoring and management of compartment pressures are essential post-fasciotomy.
- **Physical Rehabilitation**: Early involvement of physical therapy is crucial for functional recovery, especially in patients with significant muscle injury.

Complication Prevention
- **Recognition and Education**: Healthcare providers should be educated about the risk factors and early signs of compartment syndrome, especially in postoperative patients or those with significant trauma.
- **Regular Assessments**: Frequent neurovascular checks should be part of the standard care for at-risk patients to facilitate early detection.

The prompt and effective management of compartment syndrome, centered around timely fasciotomy, is essential to prevent long-term disability. Multidisciplinary care, including surgery, critical care, nursing, and physical therapy, plays a pivotal role in the management and rehabilitation of these patients.

Sepsis and septic shock are critical conditions that represent severe ends of the spectrum of the body's response to infection. The latest definitions and criteria, known as Sepsis-3, were introduced by the Third International Consensus Definitions for Sepsis and Septic Shock in 2016, refining previous definitions to better align with clinical understanding and outcomes.

Sepsis-3 Definitions
Sepsis is defined as a life-threatening organ dysfunction caused by a dysregulated host response to infection. The emphasis is on the presence of infection leading to significant changes in organ function, moving away from the earlier focus on inflammation.

Operationalization of Organ Dysfunction: The Sepsis-3 definitions recommend using an increase of 2 or more points in the Sequential Organ Failure Assessment (SOFA) score to identify organ dysfunction. The SOFA score evaluates six organ systems (respiratory, coagulation, liver, cardiovascular, central nervous system, and renal), with higher scores indicating more severe organ dysfunction.
Septic Shock is a subset of sepsis in which underlying circulatory, cellular, and metabolic abnormalities are profound enough to substantially increase mortality. It is identified by two main criteria:

The need for vasopressor therapy to maintain a mean arterial pressure (MAP) of 65 mm Hg or greater.
A serum lactate level greater than 2 mmol/L (18 mg/dL) in the absence of hypovolemia after adequate fluid resuscitation.
Implications for Clinical Practice
The Sepsis-3 definitions have several implications for clinical practice:

Emphasis on Organ Dysfunction: The focus on organ dysfunction highlights the need for early recognition and management of organ impairment, which is crucial for improving outcomes in septic patients.

SOFA Score Utilization: The use of the SOFA score as a key component of the sepsis definition underscores the importance of comprehensive assessment of organ function in suspected sepsis cases. It helps clinicians quantify the severity of organ dysfunction and track changes over time.

Streamlining Identification: The simplification to sepsis and septic shock, without the previous categories of sepsis, severe sepsis, and septic shock, aims to streamline identification and management, focusing attention on the most critically ill patients.

Recognition of Septic Shock: The specific criteria for septic shock emphasize the critical nature of this condition and the need for aggressive management, including fluid resuscitation, vasopressors, and monitoring of lactate as a marker of tissue perfusion.

Clinical and Research Consistency: By providing clear, evidence-based definitions, Sepsis-3 aims to improve consistency in the diagnosis and management of sepsis and septic shock across different healthcare settings and in research studies.

Early Intervention: The definitions reinforce the importance of early recognition and intervention in the management of sepsis and septic shock, highlighting the need for rapid administration of antibiotics, source control, and supportive care to improve survival rates.

The Sepsis-3 definitions have been instrumental in refining the understanding and management of sepsis and septic shock, emphasizing the critical importance of early identification and aggressive treatment of these life-threatening conditions.

The pathophysiology of sepsis is complex, involving a dysregulated host response to infection that can lead to widespread inflammation, coagulation abnormalities, and multiple organ dysfunction syndrome (MODS). Understanding these mechanisms is crucial for managing sepsis and mitigating its severe consequences.

Dysregulated Inflammatory Response
Infection Initiation: Sepsis begins with an infection that triggers an immune response. Normally, this response is localized and controlled, aimed at eliminating the pathogen.

Cytokine Release: In sepsis, the detection of pathogens leads to an excessive and uncontrolled release of pro-inflammatory cytokines (e.g., TNF-α, IL-1, IL-6) and anti-inflammatory cytokines. This cytokine storm results in widespread inflammation.

Endothelial Activation and Permeability: The overwhelming inflammatory response leads to endothelial activation and increased vascular permeability, causing leakage of fluid into tissues, edema, and decreased effective circulating blood volume, contributing to hypotension and reduced tissue perfusion.

Coagulation Abnormalities
Tissue Factor Expression: The inflammatory response induces the expression of tissue factor on endothelial cells and monocytes, activating the extrinsic coagulation pathway and leading to thrombin generation.

Microvascular Thrombosis: Thrombin formation, along with suppression of anticoagulant pathways (e.g., antithrombin, protein C, and protein S pathways) and fibrinolysis inhibition, promotes widespread microvascular thrombosis. This contributes to organ ischemia and dysfunction.

Disseminated Intravascular Coagulation (DIC): In severe cases, the coagulation cascade's widespread activation can lead to DIC, characterized by systemic microthrombi formation and, paradoxically, an increased risk of bleeding due to consumption of coagulation factors and platelets.

Mechanisms of Organ Dysfunction
Hypoperfusion and Ischemia: The combination of hypotension, microvascular thrombosis, and increased vascular permeability leads to reduced blood flow and oxygen delivery to organs, resulting in ischemia and anaerobic metabolism.

Reperfusion Injury: If blood flow is restored, reperfusion injury can occur, characterized by oxidative stress, further endothelial damage, and inflammation, exacerbating tissue injury.

Mitochondrial Dysfunction: Sepsis can directly impair mitochondrial function, reducing ATP production and contributing to cellular injury and organ dysfunction.

Apoptosis: The dysregulated immune response in sepsis can also lead to increased apoptosis (programmed cell death), affecting immune cells and contributing to organ injury.

Immunosuppression: Over time, sepsis can lead to a state of immunosuppression, making patients more susceptible to secondary infections and complicating recovery.

The pathophysiology of sepsis involves a complex interplay between the host's immune response, coagulation system, and multiple organ systems. The dysregulated inflammatory response and coagulation abnormalities play central roles in the development of organ dysfunction. Understanding these mechanisms is essential for identifying therapeutic targets and improving outcomes in sepsis management.

Early recognition and timely intervention are critical in managing sepsis and septic shock, given their rapid progression and potentially fatal outcomes. The Surviving Sepsis Campaign guidelines emphasize the importance of treatment bundles to standardize care and improve patient outcomes.

Early Recognition

Key signs and symptoms prompting timely intervention include:
- **Systemic Inflammatory Response Syndrome (SIRS) Criteria**: While not specific to sepsis, the presence of two or more SIRS criteria (fever or hypothermia, tachycardia, tachypnea, or altered white blood cell count) in the context of a suspected or confirmed infection should raise suspicion.
- **Altered Mental Status**: Confusion or decreased alertness can be early signs of sepsis, particularly in the elderly.
- **Hypotension**: Systolic blood pressure less than 100 mmHg or a significant drop from the patient's baseline, not responsive to fluid resuscitation, may indicate septic shock.
- **Hypoperfusion or Organ Dysfunction**: Signs include oliguria, lactic acidosis, or abrupt changes in liver function tests, suggesting the need for immediate assessment and intervention.
- **Hyperthermia or Hypothermia**: Significant deviations in body temperature in the context of infection should prompt evaluation for sepsis.

Sepsis Treatment Bundles

The components of sepsis treatment bundles are designed to address the critical aspects of sepsis management within the first hours of recognition:
1. **Early Antibiotics**:
    - Rationale: Early administration of broad-spectrum antibiotics is crucial as it targets the underlying infection, which is the source of the septic response. Antibiotics should be administered within the first hour of recognizing sepsis or septic shock.
    - Selection: Antibiotic choice should cover all likely pathogens based on the infection source, local resistance patterns, and patient-specific factors.
2. **Fluid Resuscitation**:

- Rationale: Fluid resuscitation addresses hypovolemia and hypotension, aiming to restore tissue perfusion and organ function. It's a cornerstone in the initial management of sepsis-induced hypoperfusion and septic shock.
- Implementation: The guidelines recommend an initial rapid infusion of crystalloid fluids (30 mL/kg) for hypotension or lactate ≥4 mmol/L.
3. **Vasopressors**:
    - Rationale: If hypotension persists despite adequate fluid resuscitation, vasopressors are used to maintain mean arterial pressure (MAP) and ensure organ perfusion.
    - Choice: Norepinephrine is the first-choice vasopressor, with the addition of vasopressin or epinephrine as second-line agents if needed.
4. **Source Control**:
    - Rationale: Identifying and controlling the source of infection (e.g., drainage of an abscess, removal of infected devices, or debridement of infected tissue) is essential to mitigate the septic insult.
    - Timing: Source control measures should be implemented as soon as medically and logistically practical, ideally within the first 12 hours after diagnosis.
5. **Lactate Monitoring**:
    - Rationale: Serum lactate levels serve as a marker for tissue hypoperfusion. Elevated lactate levels (>2 mmol/L) indicate a need for aggressive resuscitation efforts.
    - Monitoring: Repeated lactate measurements can guide resuscitation efforts and provide prognostic information.

Implementing these treatment bundle components rapidly and effectively can significantly impact outcomes in sepsis and septic shock. The emphasis on early identification, antibiotic administration, hemodynamic support, and source control forms the foundation of sepsis management, aiming to reduce mortality and improve patient recovery.

Shock is a critical condition characterized by inadequate tissue perfusion and oxygen delivery, leading to cellular dysfunction and organ failure. It is classified into four main categories: hypovolemic, cardiogenic, obstructive, and distributive. Each category has distinct pathophysiological mechanisms and clinical features.

Hypovolemic Shock
- **Mechanism**: Caused by a significant loss of intravascular fluid volume, which can be due to hemorrhage (external or internal), dehydration, burns, or excessive diuresis.
- **Features**: Presents with signs of decreased preload, including rapid, thready pulse; low blood pressure; reduced jugular venous pressure; cool, clammy skin due to vasoconstriction; and oliguria. Patients may have a history of acute fluid loss or bleeding.
- **Management**: Focuses on fluid resuscitation with crystalloids, colloids, or blood products, depending on the cause of volume loss.

Cardiogenic Shock
- **Mechanism**: Results from the heart's inability to pump blood effectively due to intrinsic myocardial damage, which can be due to myocardial infarction, cardiomyopathies, or arrhythmias.
- **Features**: Characterized by signs of decreased cardiac output despite adequate intravascular volume, including hypotension, pulmonary congestion (manifesting as dyspnea, rales, or jugular venous distension), and signs of poor peripheral perfusion such as cool extremities and altered mental status.

- **Management**: Aims at improving cardiac function with inotropic agents, mechanical support devices (e.g., intra-aortic balloon pump), and addressing the underlying cardiac pathology.

Obstructive Shock
- **Mechanism**: Caused by a physical obstruction to blood flow in the cardiovascular circuit, leading to impaired cardiac filling or outflow. Common causes include tension pneumothorax, cardiac tamponade, and massive pulmonary embolism.
- **Features**: Presents with signs similar to cardiogenic shock but typically associated with specific clinical settings, such as severe chest pain, dyspnea, distended neck veins, and, in the case of tension pneumothorax, deviated trachea and hyperresonance on the affected side.
- **Management**: Involves rapidly relieving the obstruction, such as needle decompression for tension pneumothorax, pericardiocentesis for cardiac tamponade, or thrombolysis/anticoagulation for pulmonary embolism.

Distributive Shock
- **Mechanism**: Characterized by widespread vasodilation and increased vascular permeability, leading to relative hypovolemia and impaired tissue perfusion. Common causes include sepsis, anaphylaxis, and neurogenic shock.
- **Features**:
    - **Sepsis**: Presents with fever, tachycardia, hypotension, and signs of peripheral vasodilation such as warm, flushed skin.
    - **Anaphylaxis**: Rapid onset of hypotension, urticaria, angioedema, and severe bronchospasm following exposure to an allergen.
    - **Neurogenic**: Typically occurs after spinal cord injuries, leading to loss of sympathetic tone, resulting in vasodilation, bradycardia, and hypotension.
- **Management**: Focuses on treating the underlying cause, such as antibiotics for sepsis, epinephrine for anaphylaxis, and stabilization of the spinal cord injury for neurogenic shock. Vasopressors and intravenous fluids are used to support blood pressure and maintain tissue perfusion.

Understanding the different categories of shock and their distinct features is crucial for prompt diagnosis and targeted management, which is essential for improving outcomes in these critically ill patients.

Hemodynamic patterns in shock states involve alterations in preload, afterload, cardiac output, and systemic vascular resistance, varying significantly across the different types of shock. Understanding these alterations is key to diagnosing and managing each shock state effectively.

Hypovolemic Shock
- **Preload**: Decreased due to reduced intravascular volume, leading to diminished venous return to the heart.
- **Afterload**: Generally increased as a compensatory mechanism through systemic vasoconstriction, aiming to maintain blood pressure.
- **Cardiac Output**: Decreased as a result of reduced preload and stroke volume, despite compensatory increases in heart rate.
- **Systemic Vascular Resistance (SVR)**: Increased due to compensatory sympathetic activation and vasoconstriction in an attempt to maintain perfusion pressure to vital organs.

Cardiogenic Shock
- **Preload**: Often increased as a result of fluid backup due to the heart's inability to pump effectively, leading to venous congestion and pulmonary edema in left-sided heart failures.

- **Afterload**: Can be increased due to vasoconstriction; however, the heart's ability to overcome this afterload is compromised due to myocardial dysfunction.
- **Cardiac Output**: Significantly decreased due to impaired myocardial contractility.
- **SVR**: Often increased as a compensatory response to maintain blood pressure, further exacerbating cardiac workload and dysfunction.

Obstructive Shock
- **Preload**: Variable, but often decreased due to mechanical obstruction to venous return (e.g., cardiac tamponade) or ventricular filling (e.g., tension pneumothorax).
- **Afterload**: In the case of pulmonary embolism, afterload on the right ventricle is significantly increased due to obstruction in the pulmonary circulation.
- **Cardiac Output**: Decreased due to impaired ventricular filling or outflow obstruction.
- **SVR**: May increase as a compensatory mechanism, but this is often insufficient to overcome the reduced cardiac output.

Distributive Shock
- **Preload**: Decreased due to venous pooling and increased capillary leak, leading to relative hypovolemia.
- **Afterload**: Significantly decreased due to systemic vasodilation, which is a hallmark of distributive shock states like sepsis and anaphylaxis.
- **Cardiac Output**: Initially, cardiac output may be normal or increased due to reduced afterload and compensatory tachycardia. However, as the condition progresses, myocardial dysfunction can lead to decreased cardiac output.
- **SVR**: Markedly decreased due to widespread vasodilation, contributing to hypotension despite compensatory increases in heart rate.

Understanding these hemodynamic alterations provides a framework for the clinical assessment and management of shock. Monitoring parameters such as central venous pressure (CVP), pulmonary artery occlusion pressure (PAOP), cardiac output, and SVR, along with clinical signs and symptoms, aids in distinguishing between the types of shock and guiding targeted therapeutic interventions.

Management of shock involves both general resuscitative measures and specific interventions tailored to the underlying cause. Prompt recognition and treatment are crucial to improve outcomes.

General Principles
1. **Fluid Resuscitation**:
    - The initial step in most types of shock, especially hypovolemic and septic shock, to restore intravascular volume, enhance preload, and improve tissue perfusion.
    - Crystalloids are preferred for initial fluid resuscitation. Colloids or blood products may be considered based on the clinical scenario, such as significant hemorrhage.
    - Fluid resuscitation should be guided by hemodynamic response, including improvements in blood pressure, urine output, and other markers of end-organ perfusion.
2. **Vasopressors**:
    - Used to increase systemic vascular resistance (SVR) and blood pressure, particularly in septic, neurogenic, and anaphylactic shock when fluid resuscitation alone is insufficient.
    - Norepinephrine is often the first-choice vasopressor. Other agents, such as dopamine, vasopressin, or epinephrine, may be used based on specific clinical considerations and response to initial therapy.
3. **Inotropes**:

- Indicated in cardiogenic shock and other conditions with reduced cardiac contractility to improve cardiac output.
- Agents like dobutamine are commonly used to increase myocardial contractility without excessively increasing myocardial oxygen demand.

Specific Interventions

Hypovolemic Shock
- **Source Control**: Identifying and controlling the source of fluid loss, e.g., surgical intervention for hemorrhage or addressing the underlying cause of dehydration.
- **Volume Replacement**: Aggressive fluid resuscitation with isotonic crystalloids or blood products as indicated by the cause and extent of volume loss.

Cardiogenic Shock
- **Myocardial Perfusion**: Reperfusion strategies for myocardial infarction, such as percutaneous coronary intervention (PCI) or thrombolytic therapy.
- **Mechanical Support**: Intra-aortic balloon pump (IABP), left ventricular assist devices (LVADs), or extracorporeal membrane oxygenation (ECMO) as bridge therapy in severe cases.
- **Rate and Rhythm Control**: Management of arrhythmias that may contribute to or exacerbate shock.

Obstructive Shock
- **Relief of Obstruction**: Immediate interventions to relieve the physical obstruction, e.g., needle decompression for tension pneumothorax, pericardiocentesis for cardiac tamponade, or thrombolytic therapy for massive pulmonary embolism.

Distributive Shock
- **Sepsis**: Early administration of broad-spectrum antibiotics, source control (drainage of abscesses, removal of infected devices), and aggressive fluid resuscitation followed by vasopressors if needed.
- **Anaphylaxis**: Immediate administration of intramuscular epinephrine, antihistamines, and corticosteroids, along with airway management and fluid resuscitation.
- **Neurogenic**: Stabilization of the spine, if indicated, and the use of vasopressors to counteract the loss of sympathetic tone.

Monitoring and Supportive Care
- Continuous monitoring of hemodynamic parameters (blood pressure, heart rate, urine output, central venous pressure) and laboratory markers (lactate, base deficit) to guide therapy and assess response.
- Supportive care addressing oxygenation, ventilation, renal function, and metabolic needs is essential across all shock types.

Management strategies in shock should be dynamic, with adjustments made based on the patient's evolving clinical status and response to interventions. Early consultation with appropriate specialties, including surgery, cardiology, or critical care, can be crucial in managing complex cases.

Delirium, an acute state of confusion characterized by altered consciousness and impaired cognition, is a common and serious complication in critically ill patients, particularly those in the Intensive Care Unit (ICU). Understanding its risk factors and employing validated assessment tools are pivotal in its management.

Risk Factors for ICU Delirium

Delirium in the ICU is multifactorial, with both predisposing (baseline vulnerability) and precipitating (acute insults) factors contributing to its development:

Predisposing Factors:

Age: Advanced age is a significant risk factor for delirium.
Pre-existing Cognitive Impairment: Dementia or mild cognitive impairment increases delirium risk.
Comorbidities: Conditions such as hypertension, diabetes, and chronic kidney disease.
Polypharmacy: Especially the use of medications with anticholinergic properties, sedatives, and opioids.
Substance Abuse: History of alcohol or drug abuse.
Severity of Illness: Higher acuity of illness, as indicated by severity of illness scores.
Precipitating Factors:

Sedation: Especially the use of benzodiazepines and deep or prolonged sedation.
Mechanical Ventilation: Prolonged ventilation is associated with higher delirium rates.
Metabolic Derangements: Electrolyte imbalances, hypoxia, hypoglycemia, or renal and hepatic dysfunction.
Infection and Sepsis: Systemic infections and sepsis can precipitate delirium.
Environmental Factors: Lack of natural light, sleep disturbances, and sensory deprivation or overload in the ICU.

Assessment of ICU Delirium

The Confusion Assessment Method for the Intensive Care Unit (CAM-ICU) is a widely used, validated tool for the diagnosis of delirium in ICU patients, including those who are non-verbal or on mechanical ventilation. It assesses four key features:

Acute Change or Fluctuating Course of Mental Status: The hallmark of delirium, indicating a change from the patient's baseline or fluctuation over time.

Inattention: Difficulty focusing, maintaining, or shifting attention, assessed through tasks such as the "A" test or asking the patient to squeeze the examiner's hand upon hearing a specific letter in a string of letters.

Altered Level of Consciousness: Anything other than a normal level of alertness, ranging from hyperalert to stuporous.

Disorganized Thinking: Manifested by rambling or irrelevant conversation, unclear or illogical flow of ideas, or unpredictable switching of subjects.

For a diagnosis of delirium using CAM-ICU, both the first and second features must be present, along with either the third or fourth feature.

Importance of Early Identification and Management

Early identification of delirium using tools like CAM-ICU allows for timely interventions, which may include addressing modifiable risk factors, optimizing the environment to promote orientation and sleep, minimizing the use of deliriogenic medications, and considering pharmacologic treatment when necessary. Managing delirium effectively can improve patient outcomes, including reducing the length of

ICU stay, decreasing the duration of mechanical ventilation, and potentially improving long-term cognitive outcomes.

Effective management of delirium in critically ill patients involves a combination of non-pharmacological and, when necessary, pharmacological strategies. Emphasizing non-pharmacological interventions is crucial, as they are often effective in both prevention and treatment of delirium and carry fewer risks compared to pharmacological approaches.

Non-Pharmacological Interventions
Environmental Modifications:

Orientation Aids: Use clocks, calendars, and personal items to help maintain the patient's orientation to time, place, and person.
Lighting: Ensure exposure to natural light during the day and minimize light at night to help regulate circadian rhythms and promote sleep.
Noise Reduction: Minimize noise levels, use earplugs or white noise machines to improve sleep quality.
Sleep Hygiene:

Consistent Sleep Schedule: Encourage a regular sleep-wake cycle, even in an ICU setting.
Minimize Nighttime Disturbances: Cluster care activities to minimize awakenings and use medications that promote sleep continuity if needed.
Cognitive Engagement:

Reorientation: Regularly reorient the patient to their environment, the date, and the reason for their hospitalization.
Cognitive Stimulation: Engage the patient with conversation, music, reading, or other appropriate cognitive activities.
Early Mobilization:

Encourage physical activity and mobilization as soon as medically feasible to reduce the risk of delirium.
Family Involvement:

Involve family members in care when possible, as familiar voices and faces can be reorienting and comforting.
Minimizing Restraints:

Avoid physical restraints when possible, as they can increase agitation and disorientation.
Pharmacological Management
Pharmacological treatment should be considered when non-pharmacological measures are insufficient, particularly in patients with severe agitation that poses a risk to their safety or in refractory delirium cases.

Antipsychotics:

Typical and Atypical Antipsychotics: Agents like haloperidol, quetiapine, or olanzapine may be used, but with caution due to potential side effects, including QT prolongation with haloperidol.

Indications: Considered for severe agitation or when delirium symptoms are distressing to the patient and pose safety risks.
Monitoring: Regular assessment for efficacy and side effects is essential, with dosage adjustments as necessary.
Benzodiazepines:

Generally reserved for delirium associated with alcohol or benzodiazepine withdrawal, or when antipsychotics are contraindicated.
Use with caution due to the potential for respiratory depression and paradoxical agitation.
Alpha-2 Agonists:

Agents like dexmedetomidine may be beneficial in certain cases due to their sedative properties without significant respiratory depression, particularly in patients with delirium associated with mechanical ventilation.
Principles of Pharmacological Management
Start Low, Go Slow: Begin with the lowest effective dose and titrate cautiously.
Regular Reassessment: Continuously reassess the need for ongoing pharmacological treatment, aiming to discontinue as soon as clinically feasible.
Side Effect Monitoring: Be vigilant for potential adverse effects, including extrapyramidal symptoms with antipsychotics and oversedation or respiratory depression with benzodiazepines.
Multidisciplinary Approach: Involve a multidisciplinary team, including pharmacists and psychiatrists, to optimize delirium management.
Non-pharmacological strategies are the cornerstone of delirium management, focusing on modifiable risk factors, environmental adjustments, and supportive care. Pharmacological interventions are reserved for specific indications and should be used judiciously, with careful monitoring for efficacy and adverse effects.

The critical illness of a loved one exerts profound psychosocial effects on family members, impacting their emotional, psychological, and social well-being. The sudden and often unexpected nature of critical illness can thrust families into a maelstrom of stress, uncertainty, and grief, affecting each member uniquely yet pervasively.

Emotional and Psychological Impact
Anxiety and Fear: The uncertainty about the patient's prognosis and potential for sudden changes in clinical status can induce significant anxiety and fear among family members, often manifesting as constant worry, restlessness, or even panic attacks.

Depression: Witnessing a loved one in a critical state can lead to feelings of helplessness and despair, contributing to depressive symptoms such as persistent sadness, loss of interest in activities, and withdrawal from social interactions.

Stress and Burnout: The demands of navigating the healthcare system, making medical decisions, and the possibility of prolonged hospitalizations can lead to chronic stress and burnout, characterized by emotional exhaustion and decreased ability to cope with daily tasks.

Guilt: Family members may experience guilt over not having prevented the illness, decisions made regarding the patient's care, or balancing attention between the ill family member and other responsibilities.

Post-Traumatic Stress Disorder (PTSD): The traumatic experience of a loved one's critical illness can lead to PTSD in some family members, with symptoms including flashbacks, nightmares, and severe anxiety.

Social Impact
Altered Family Roles and Dynamics: Critical illness can disrupt established roles within the family, requiring members to adapt to new responsibilities, which can strain relationships and alter family dynamics.

Isolation: The time and emotional demands of having a loved one in the ICU can lead to social isolation, as family members may withdraw from their social networks, either due to lack of time, energy, or the perception that others may not understand their situation.

Financial Strain: The costs associated with critical care, including medical bills, lost income, and travel expenses, can lead to significant financial strain, further exacerbating stress and anxiety.

Impact on Children: Children may be particularly vulnerable to the psychosocial effects of a family member's critical illness, experiencing confusion, fear, and disruptions in their routine, which can affect their emotional and academic development.

Support Strategies
Providing comprehensive support to families of critically ill patients is essential and can include:

Clear and Compassionate Communication: Regular, honest, and empathetic communication about the patient's condition, treatment plans, and prognosis helps reduce uncertainty and fosters trust between healthcare providers and families.

Psychosocial Support: Access to counseling, support groups, and spiritual care services can offer much-needed emotional support and coping strategies for families.

Family Meetings: Regularly scheduled meetings with the healthcare team can help address concerns, involve family members in care decisions, and provide a structured forum for asking questions and receiving support.

Educational Resources: Providing information about the patient's condition, the ICU environment, and what to expect can help demystify the critical care process and empower families.

Encouraging Self-Care: Reminding family members to attend to their own health and well-being is crucial, as their ability to support their loved one depends on their own physical and emotional resilience.

The impact of a loved one's critical illness on family members is profound and multifaceted, necessitating a holistic approach to care that extends beyond the patient to include the entire family, acknowledging their emotional, psychological, and practical needs during this challenging time.

Effective communication and collaboration between healthcare providers and families of critically ill patients are paramount in ensuring high-quality care and supporting the decision-making process. These strategies not only foster trust and satisfaction but also help in aligning treatment goals with the patient's values and preferences.

Strategies for Effective Communication
Establish Rapport: Begin by building a relationship based on empathy and respect. Acknowledge the family's stress and anxiety, and introduce yourself and your role in the patient's care.

Regular Updates: Provide consistent and regular updates about the patient's condition, treatment plans, and any changes in their status. This helps to manage expectations and reduce uncertainty.

Clear and Understandable Language: Use language that is free of medical jargon to ensure that all family members can understand the information being conveyed.

Active Listening: Encourage family members to ask questions and express their concerns, and respond with active listening cues to demonstrate understanding and empathy.

Emotional Support: Recognize and address the emotional needs of family members, validating their feelings and providing reassurance when appropriate.

Shared Decision-Making
Involve Families Early: Engage family members in discussions about care preferences, goals, and treatment options early in the care process, especially for decisions regarding life-sustaining treatments.

Educate on Options and Outcomes: Clearly explain the potential benefits, risks, and outcomes of proposed treatments, ensuring that families have the information needed to make informed decisions.

Respect Cultural and Personal Values: Acknowledge and incorporate the patient's and family's cultural, religious, and personal values into the decision-making process.

Use Decision Aids: Utilize tools and resources, such as decision aids or informational brochures, to facilitate understanding and discussions about complex care decisions.

Collaborative Approach: Foster a collaborative environment where the healthcare team and family members work together to make decisions that align with the patient's wishes and best interests.

Involving Families in Care
Encourage Participation: Invite family members to be present during rounds or care planning meetings, where they can contribute insights into the patient's preferences and receive firsthand information from the care team.

Define Roles: Help family members identify how they can be involved in the patient's care, whether through providing comfort, assisting with feeding or personal care, or simply being present.

Flexible Visitation Policies: Implement visitation policies that are flexible and accommodate the needs of the patient and their family, recognizing the therapeutic value of family presence.

Support and Resources: Provide access to support services, such as social work, spiritual care, and patient advocacy, to assist families in navigating the healthcare system and accessing needed resources.

Discharge Planning: Involve family members in discharge planning to ensure a smooth transition from hospital to home or another care setting, including education on care needs, medications, and follow-up appointments.

Effective communication and collaboration are the cornerstones of family-centered care in critical illness, enhancing the care experience, supporting shared decision-making, and ensuring that care plans reflect the patient's values and goals.

Supporting families in the critical care setting involves providing access to a range of resources and support services designed to help them navigate the complexities of critical illness, cope with stress and emotional burdens, and participate effectively in the care of their loved ones. Available resources include:

Support Groups
- **Peer Support Groups**: Offer families the opportunity to connect with others experiencing similar challenges, share experiences, and receive emotional support in a group setting. These groups may be condition-specific (e.g., for families of patients with traumatic brain injuries or cancer) or general to critical illness.
- **Online Support Communities**: Digital platforms and social media groups can provide accessible support for family members who may not be able to attend in-person meetings, offering a space to share resources, advice, and emotional support.

Counseling Services
- **Psychological Counseling**: Professional counseling services, including psychologists and psychiatrists, can assist family members in dealing with complex emotions, stress, and potential mental health issues arising from their loved one's critical illness.
- **Social Work Services**: Social workers in the hospital can provide counseling, help families navigate healthcare and insurance systems, and connect them with community resources for additional support.

Spiritual Care
- **Chaplains and Spiritual Advisors**: Offer spiritual support tailored to the family's religious beliefs and spiritual needs, providing comfort, prayer, rituals, and guidance through spiritual distress.

Educational Resources
- **Patient Education Materials**: Brochures, pamphlets, and digital content explaining the critical care environment, common procedures, and what to expect can help demystify the ICU experience for families.
- **Condition-Specific Information**: Detailed information about the patient's specific condition, treatment options, and prognosis can help families make informed decisions and prepare for the future.

Financial and Legal Assistance
- **Financial Counseling**: Services to help families understand medical bills, navigate insurance claims, and explore options for financial assistance to mitigate the economic impact of prolonged critical illness.
- **Legal Aid**: Access to legal advice for issues such as advanced directives, power of attorney, and guardianship can be crucial for families facing complex decisions regarding their loved one's care.

Health and Well-being Programs
- **Well-being Workshops**: Programs focusing on stress management, mindfulness, and self-care can equip family members with strategies to maintain their well-being while supporting their critically ill loved one.
- **Fitness and Relaxation Areas**: Access to hospital facilities such as gardens, meditation rooms, or fitness centers can provide necessary breaks and stress relief for families.

Communication Tools
- **Care Coordination Platforms**: Digital tools and applications that facilitate communication between the healthcare team and family members, providing updates on the patient's status, care plans, and scheduling family meetings.

Advocacy and Navigation Services
- **Patient Advocates**: Professionals who assist families in understanding their rights, mediating concerns with healthcare providers, and ensuring that the patient's and family's voices are heard in care decisions.

Providing comprehensive resources and support for families in the critical care setting is essential for their well-being, enabling them to be effective partners in care and advocates for their loved ones. Tailoring support to meet the diverse needs of families can enhance their resilience and capacity to navigate the challenges of critical illness.

Professional Aspects of Critical Care Nursing:

Think of this section as your guide to thriving, not just surviving, in the demanding world of critical care nursing. We'll discuss the ethical dilemmas, the importance of continuous learning, and how to build both the professional skills and resilience needed for a fulfilling career.

Why This Matters:
- Critical Care is Intense: Witnessing suffering, life-and-death decisions within complex cases... it takes a toll. This section is about equipping you with tools to navigate that intensity.
- It's Not Just About Medical Knowledge: This job calls for strong communication, advocacy skills, and a commitment to lifelong learning as the field evolves.
- Finding Your Voice: Critical care isn't for the faint of heart. We'll explore how to build a sustainable, rewarding career in this specialized area.

What We'll Cover
- Ethics at the Bedside:
    - Analyzing complex dilemmas where there's no easy answer – end-of-life decisions, working with difficult families, navigating cultural differences.
    - Frameworks for ethical decision-making to guide your actions.
- Professional Growth:
    - The importance of certifications, conferences, and mentorship to continually improve your practice.
    - Embracing leadership, potentially moving into roles in education or management.
- The Resilience Factor:
    - Burnout is real! We'll discuss self-care, setting boundaries, and finding support systems to help you weather the storms of critical care.
    - De-escalation: Strategies for handling intense patient and family interactions.

Beyond the Textbook

- Teamwork is Everything: This isn't a solo mission. We'll look at building effective interdisciplinary relationships.
- The Power of Advocacy: Speaking up for your patients and their needs.

This section is about empowering you to not just be a great critical care nurse, but to build a career that is sustainable, ethical, and deeply fulfilling for the long-term.

Ethical dilemmas in critical care are complex situations where the right course of action is unclear, often involving conflicting values, beliefs, or principles. These dilemmas are particularly prevalent in critical care settings due to the severity of illnesses, the urgency of decisions required, and the high stakes involved in terms of patient outcomes. Here are some common ethical dilemmas encountered in critical care:

End-of-Life Decisions
- **Withdrawal or Withholding of Life-Sustaining Treatments**: Deciding when to initiate or discontinue treatments such as mechanical ventilation, dialysis, or artificial nutrition and hydration, especially when the likelihood of recovery is low or the treatment may prolong suffering.
- **Do-Not-Resuscitate (DNR) Orders**: Determining when and how to respect a patient's wishes or the family's wishes regarding resuscitation efforts in the event of cardiac or respiratory arrest, especially when these wishes are not clearly documented or communicated.
- **Palliative Care vs. Aggressive Treatment**: Balancing the decision to focus on comfort and quality of life through palliative care versus continuing aggressive interventions in the hope of prolonging life, even if the chances of meaningful recovery are slim.

Resource Allocation
- **Scarce Resource Allocation**: Making decisions about the allocation of limited resources, such as ICU beds, ventilators, or donor organs, particularly during crises like pandemics or natural disasters. This includes deciding who receives care when not all patients can be accommodated.
- **Cost Considerations**: Navigating situations where the cost of medical interventions may impose a significant burden on the patient, family, or healthcare system, potentially influencing decisions about which treatments to pursue.

Patient Autonomy and Informed Consent
- **Surrogate Decision-Making**: Respecting the autonomy of patients who cannot make decisions for themselves by working with surrogate decision-makers, often family members, who may have different views about the desired level of care.
- **Informed Consent in Urgent Situations**: Obtaining informed consent for procedures or treatments in emergencies when the patient is incapacitated, and the decision must be made swiftly, possibly without the opportunity to discuss it thoroughly with the patient or family.

Conflicts Between Care Team Members and Families
- **Disagreements Over Treatment Plans**: Situations where the healthcare team and family members (or between family members themselves) disagree on the best course of action, such as opting for aggressive treatment versus focusing on comfort measures.
- **Cultural and Religious Considerations**: Navigating care decisions that are influenced by cultural or religious beliefs that may conflict with standard medical practices or recommendations, such as refusing certain treatments or blood transfusions.

Privacy and Confidentiality
- **Sharing Sensitive Information**: Ensuring patient privacy and confidentiality while also communicating necessary information to family members and involved healthcare professionals,

particularly in situations where the patient's wishes about information sharing are not known or documented.

Addressing these ethical dilemmas requires a multidisciplinary approach, involving open communication, ethical reasoning, and often the consultation of hospital ethics committees. The goal is to make decisions that are in the best interest of the patient, respect the wishes of the patient and their family, and are aligned with ethical principles such as autonomy, beneficence, non-maleficence, and justice.

Ethical decision-making frameworks provide structured approaches to navigate the complex and often morally ambiguous dilemmas encountered in critical care. These models help healthcare professionals weigh competing values and principles to arrive at decisions that are ethically justifiable. Here are several key ethical decision-making models and their application in critical care scenarios:

Principlism
- **Framework**: Based on four primary ethical principles: autonomy (respect for the patient's right to make their own decisions), beneficence (doing what is best for the patient), non-maleficence (avoiding harm to the patient), and justice (fair distribution of healthcare resources).
- **Application**: In critical care, principlism can guide decisions such as withdrawing life-sustaining treatment by balancing respect for patient autonomy (honoring advance directives or surrogate decisions), with beneficence and non-maleficence (assessing whether continued treatment is in the patient's best interest or merely prolongs suffering).

Consequentialism (Utilitarianism)
- **Framework**: Focuses on the outcomes of actions, suggesting that the ethically correct choice is the one that maximizes overall good or minimizes harm.
- **Application**: In scenarios like resource allocation during a pandemic, consequentialism would advocate for maximizing the overall benefit to the greatest number of patients, such as prioritizing the allocation of ventilators to those with the best prognosis for recovery and quality of life.

Deontological Ethics (Duty-Based Ethics)
- **Framework**: Emphasizes the importance of moral rules and duties, suggesting that some actions are inherently right or wrong, regardless of their consequences.
- **Application**: In critical care, a deontological approach might insist on always telling the truth to patients and families about prognoses and treatment options, upholding the duty of honesty, even if the information may cause distress.

Virtue Ethics
- **Framework**: Focuses on the character and virtues of the moral agent (e.g., healthcare provider) rather than on ethical duties or consequences alone. It emphasizes traits like compassion, empathy, and courage.
- **Application**: When dealing with end-of-life care, a healthcare provider guided by virtue ethics would focus on empathy and compassion, ensuring that discussions about palliative care options support the patient's and family's emotional and spiritual needs, in addition to their physical care.

Care Ethics
- **Framework**: Centers on the importance of interpersonal relationships and care as a guiding ethical consideration, emphasizing the context of care relationships and the role of emotions in ethical decision-making.

- **Application**: In managing a long-term critically ill patient, care ethics would prioritize the nurturing aspects of care, advocating for decisions that strengthen the patient-caregiver relationship, support family involvement, and address the holistic needs of the patient.

Casuistry (Case-Based Reasoning)
- **Framework**: Involves the analysis of individual cases in detail, drawing on analogies with previously resolved cases to guide decision-making in new, similar situations.
- **Application**: In complex ethical dilemmas, such as deciding on the appropriateness of experimental treatments, casuistry would involve comparing the current scenario to past cases with similar ethical issues, using precedent to guide the decision-making process.

Each of these ethical frameworks offers valuable perspectives for addressing the multifaceted ethical dilemmas in critical care. Often, a combination of these approaches, tailored to the specific context and individuals involved, is necessary to navigate ethical decisions in a way that is both principled and compassionate. Engaging in multidisciplinary discussions, including ethics consultations when available, can further enrich the decision-making process by incorporating diverse viewpoints and expertise.

The role of the critical care nurse as a patient advocate is multifaceted and vital to ensuring the delivery of high-quality, ethical, and patient-centered care. Nurses often serve as the primary liaison between patients, their families, and the rest of the healthcare team, placing them in a unique position to advocate for the patient's needs, preferences, and rights. Here's how critical care nurses embody the role of patient advocate:

Navigating Conflicts
- **Mediating Communication**: Nurses frequently mediate conflicts that may arise between patients, families, and healthcare providers by facilitating open, honest, and compassionate communication. They help clarify misunderstandings and ensure that all voices are heard.
- **Ethical Dilemmas**: Nurses are often at the forefront of identifying and addressing ethical dilemmas, such as disagreements over treatment plans. They can help initiate ethics consultations and ensure that discussions are aligned with ethical principles and the patient's values.
- **Interdisciplinary Collaboration**: Critical care nurses work closely with an interdisciplinary team and can advocate for reconsideration or modification of care plans that may not align with the patient's needs or wishes.

Upholding Patient Rights
- **Informed Consent**: Nurses play a key role in ensuring that patients or their surrogates are fully informed about their care options, understanding the risks, benefits, and alternatives to proposed treatments, thereby supporting the process of informed consent.
- **Confidentiality and Privacy**: Maintaining the patient's confidentiality and privacy is a fundamental aspect of advocacy, with nurses ensuring that sensitive information is protected and shared only with authorized individuals.
- **Respecting Wishes**: Advocacy involves honoring the patient's advance directives and end-of-life care preferences, ensuring that care aligns with the patient's expressed wishes, including DNR orders and preferences regarding life-sustaining treatments.

Promoting Patient-Centered Care
- **Holistic Care**: Nurses advocate for holistic care that addresses not just the physical aspects of the patient's condition but also their psychological, social, and spiritual needs, recognizing the patient as a whole person.

- **Empowerment**: Empowering patients and families by providing education about the patient's condition, care processes, and self-care strategies is a form of advocacy that enables patients to participate actively in their care.
- **Supporting Family Involvement**: Advocating for the involvement of family members in the care process, including decision-making and care planning, reinforces the importance of the patient's support system in their recovery and well-being.

Addressing Healthcare Disparities
- Nurses advocate for equitable care by recognizing and addressing healthcare disparities that may affect their patients. This includes advocating for vulnerable populations and working to ensure that all patients receive high-quality and culturally competent care.

The critical care nurse's role as an advocate is integral to safeguarding the interests and dignity of patients during some of their most vulnerable moments. By navigating conflicts, upholding patient rights, and promoting patient-centered care, nurses ensure that the healthcare system remains responsive to the individual needs of each patient, thereby upholding the highest standards of care and ethics in critical care settings.

Interdisciplinary collaboration is paramount in critical care settings, where the complexity of patient care demands expertise from various healthcare disciplines. Effective communication and teamwork among physicians, nurses, respiratory therapists, pharmacists, and other healthcare professionals are crucial for ensuring comprehensive, cohesive, and high-quality patient care. Here's why interdisciplinary collaboration is essential and strategies to foster such an environment:

Importance of Interdisciplinary Collaboration
Comprehensive Care: Patients in critical care often have multifaceted needs that require the specialized knowledge and skills of different healthcare disciplines. Collaboration ensures that all aspects of patient care are addressed, from medical and nursing care to respiratory support and medication management.

Improved Patient Outcomes: Studies have shown that effective interdisciplinary teamwork can lead to better patient outcomes, including reduced mortality rates, shorter lengths of stay in the ICU, and fewer complications.

Enhanced Decision-Making: Collaborative teams bring diverse perspectives and expertise to the decision-making process, leading to more informed and nuanced clinical decisions that consider all aspects of patient care.

Increased Job Satisfaction: A collaborative work environment can lead to higher job satisfaction among team members, reducing burnout and turnover rates, which are particularly high in high-stress environments like the ICU.

Strategies for Fostering a Collaborative Environment
Regular Multidisciplinary Rounds: Conducting regular rounds with the entire care team facilitates open discussion about each patient's status, care plan, and challenges. This ensures that all team members are informed and can contribute their expertise.

Clear Communication Channels: Establishing clear and open channels of communication is essential. This can be facilitated by using shared electronic health records, communication tools, and setting up regular team meetings.

Defined Roles and Responsibilities: Clearly defining the roles and responsibilities of each team member can prevent overlap and ensure that all aspects of patient care are covered. Understanding each other's scopes of practice fosters mutual respect and trust.

Conflict Resolution Mechanisms: Establishing protocols for resolving conflicts constructively is crucial in preventing misunderstandings and ensuring that disagreements do not negatively impact patient care.

Continuing Education and Team-Building Activities: Providing opportunities for team members to learn from each other through interdisciplinary education sessions and team-building activities can enhance team cohesion and understanding.

Leadership Support: Leadership plays a crucial role in fostering a collaborative culture by setting expectations for teamwork, providing necessary resources, and modeling collaborative behavior.

Patient and Family Involvement: Including patients and their families in care discussions when appropriate can provide valuable insights and ensure that care plans align with patient values and preferences.

Recognition and Appreciation: Recognizing and appreciating the contributions of all team members can reinforce the value of each discipline's contributions to patient care.

Effective interdisciplinary collaboration in critical care settings is not only about pooling expertise but also about creating a culture of mutual respect, continuous learning, and shared goals. By implementing strategies that promote open communication, define roles, and encourage teamwork, critical care teams can enhance their ability to provide the best possible care for their patients.

Communication with Patients and Families
Effective communication in the critical care setting is fundamental to providing high-quality care, facilitating shared decision-making, and offering emotional support. Here are some best practices:

Clarity and Simplicity: Use clear, straightforward language when explaining complex medical information. Avoid medical jargon and ensure that explanations are accessible to those without a medical background.

Active Listening: Show genuine interest in the patient's and family's concerns and questions. Active listening involves nodding, maintaining eye contact, and repeating back what you've heard to confirm understanding.

Empathy and Compassion: Approach conversations with empathy, acknowledging the stress, fear, and uncertainty that patients and families may be experiencing. A compassionate approach can help build trust and rapport.

Regular Updates: Provide regular and consistent updates about the patient's condition, treatment plans, and any changes in their status. Consistency helps manage expectations and reduces anxiety.

Shared Decision-Making: Involve patients and families in care decisions by presenting options, explaining the benefits and risks of each, and considering the patient's values and preferences. Shared decision-making empowers patients and families and fosters a sense of control.

Visual Aids: Utilize diagrams, models, or other visual aids to help explain complex concepts, making the information more digestible and easier to understand.

Emotional Support: Recognize and address the emotional needs of patients and families. Offer resources such as counseling, support groups, or spiritual care services when appropriate.

Documentation: Document key conversations, decisions made, and any consent obtained in the patient's medical record to ensure continuity of care and communication among the healthcare team.

Conflict Resolution
Conflicts in the critical care unit can arise from emotional stress, communication breakdowns, or disagreements over treatment plans. Here are techniques for conflict resolution and de-escalation:

Stay Calm: Maintain a calm and composed demeanor, even in the face of anger or hostility. Your calmness can help de-escalate tensions.

Acknowledge Emotions: Recognize and validate the emotions being expressed. Acknowledging feelings can help diffuse anger and open the door to more rational discussions.

Seek to Understand: Ask open-ended questions to understand the root cause of the conflict. Understanding the underlying concerns or misunderstandings can guide the resolution process.

Find Common Ground: Identify shared goals and values, such as the patient's well-being, to reframe the conversation around common objectives.

Offer Solutions: Once the concerns are understood, work collaboratively to explore possible solutions or compromises. Be flexible and creative in problem-solving.

Set Boundaries: Clearly communicate what is and isn't possible within the constraints of medical ethics, hospital policy, and patient safety.

Use Mediators: In situations where conflicts cannot be resolved directly, consider involving a neutral third party, such as a hospital mediator or ethics committee, to facilitate discussion.

Follow-Up: After a resolution is reached, follow up to ensure that the agreed-upon actions are implemented and that the underlying issues have been adequately addressed.

Effective communication and conflict resolution are critical skills in the high-stakes environment of critical care. By employing these strategies, healthcare professionals can foster a collaborative, supportive atmosphere that prioritizes the well-being of patients and their families.

Mentorship and Preceptorship
Mentorship and preceptorship play pivotal roles in the professional development of critical care nurses, facilitating the transition from novice to expert practitioners.
- **Mentorship**: Involves a supportive, long-term relationship between an experienced nurse (mentor) and a less experienced nurse (mentee). Mentors provide guidance, support, and

knowledge sharing, not only about clinical skills but also about navigating the complexities of the healthcare environment, career development, and work-life balance.
- **Preceptorship**: Typically a more structured and time-limited relationship focusing on specific learning objectives and the acquisition of clinical skills. Preceptors work closely with new nurses or nursing students during their clinical rotations, offering direct supervision, teaching, and feedback in the clinical setting.

Both roles are essential for fostering clinical competence, confidence, and professional growth, ensuring that new nurses are well-prepared to meet the challenges of critical care nursing.

Evidence-Based Practice

The incorporation of evidence-based practice (EBP) is crucial in critical care nursing to ensure that patient care is grounded in the best available evidence, leading to improved patient outcomes.

- **Importance**: EBP integrates clinical expertise, patient values, and the best research evidence into the decision-making process for patient care. In the dynamic environment of critical care, where patients' conditions can change rapidly, EBP provides a framework for making informed clinical decisions.
- **Strategies for Implementation**:
  - **Education and Training**: Providing nurses with training in EBP principles, including how to formulate clinical questions, search for and appraise evidence, and apply findings to practice.
  - **Access to Resources**: Ensuring that nurses have access to databases, journals, and other resources to find relevant research.
  - **Interdisciplinary Collaboration**: Working with other healthcare professionals, such as physicians and pharmacists, to review and integrate evidence into care protocols and guidelines.
  - **Quality Improvement Projects**: Encouraging nurses to lead or participate in quality improvement initiatives that address clinical questions or issues, applying EBP findings to improve care processes and outcomes.

Leadership in Critical Care

Leadership within critical care nursing encompasses a range of qualities and skills that extend beyond clinical expertise to include team management, advocacy, ethical decision-making, and the promotion of quality improvement.

- **Team Management**: Effective leaders foster a collaborative team environment, clearly communicate expectations, and support team members in achieving shared goals. They are skilled in conflict resolution and creating a positive work culture that promotes learning and excellence.
- **Advocacy**: Critical care nurses often advocate for their patients, ensuring that care decisions align with patients' wishes and best interests. They also advocate for their colleagues and the nursing profession, contributing to policy discussions and professional organizations.
- **Quality Improvement**: Leaders in critical care nursing are committed to continuous improvement, utilizing EBP to identify areas for improvement, implementing changes, and evaluating outcomes. They encourage innovation and the adoption of best practices to enhance patient care and safety.
- **Professional Development**: Leaders mentor and develop others, recognizing the importance of succession planning and the ongoing professional growth of their team members.

Leadership in critical care nursing is about inspiring and empowering others, advocating for patients and the profession, and driving improvements in patient care. It requires a commitment to lifelong learning, ethical practice, and a vision for excellence in the challenging and rewarding field of critical care.

Practice Questions:

Welcome to the practice test section of the PCCN Exam Prep Study Guide. This section is designed to reinforce your understanding of the critical care nursing concepts covered throughout this guide and to prepare you for the types of questions you'll encounter on the PCCN exam. The questions are crafted to reflect the exam's format and difficulty level, covering various topics essential to progressive and critical care nursing.

Each question in this section is followed immediately by the correct answer and a detailed rationale. This format is chosen to provide immediate feedback, enhancing your learning and retention of the material. By understanding not just the correct answer but also the reasoning behind it, you can deepen your grasp of the underlying principles and how they apply to real-world clinical scenarios. This immediate reinforcement aids in identifying knowledge gaps, strengthening critical thinking skills, and building confidence in your clinical judgment.

As you work through these practice questions, take the time to reflect on each rationale, even for questions you answer correctly. This approach will help solidify your knowledge base, refine your test-taking strategies, and better prepare you for the PCCN examination. Remember, practice is key to success, and this section is a valuable tool in your exam preparation journey. Let's begin.

1. A patient in cardiogenic shock has cool, clammy extremities and declining urine output. Which intervention would be the priority?
a. Administer IV fluids
b. Initiate a dopamine infusion
c. Elevate the head of the bed
d. Obtain a STAT 12-lead EKG

Answer: b. Initiate a dopamine infusion. Explanation: Cardiogenic shock is characterized by inadequate cardiac output. Inotropes like dopamine improve heart contractility, addressing the core problem and potentially improving perfusion to vital organs.

2. A patient with an acute anterior wall MI develops hypotension and tachycardia. Bedside echocardiogram reveals decreased left ventricular function. Which hemodynamic profile would be most consistent with this presentation?
a. High preload, low afterload, low cardiac output
b. Low preload, high afterload, low cardiac output
c. High preload, high afterload, high cardiac output
d. Normal preload, high afterload, low cardiac output

Answer: b. Low preload, high afterload, low cardiac output. Explanation: Acute MI, especially involving the anterior wall, can lead to cardiogenic shock. This presents with low output due to damaged heart muscle (low preload), and the body's compensatory vasoconstriction increases afterload.

3. A patient admitted with heart failure has a pulmonary artery catheter in place. Which measurement most directly reflects left ventricular preload?
a. Pulmonary artery wedge pressure (PAWP)
b. Central venous pressure (CVP)
c. Systemic vascular resistance (SVR)
d. Cardiac output (CO)

Answer: a. Pulmonary artery wedge pressure (PAWP). Explanation: The PAWP closely approximates left atrial pressure, which in turn reflects pressure within the left ventricle at the end of diastole (preload).

4. You're caring for a patient in septic shock on multiple vasoactive medications. Despite aggressive therapy, the patient's mean arterial pressure (MAP) remains low. Which additional intervention might have the most significant impact on MAP?
a. Albumin infusion
b. Packed red blood cell transfusion
c. Initiating continuous renal replacement therapy (CRRT)
d. Increasing the vasopressor dose

Answer: d. Increasing the vasopressor dose. Explanation: While fluids or blood products might be needed, the core problem in refractory septic shock is inadequate vascular tone. Increasing vasopressor support directly targets this issue to raise the MAP.

5. A patient with chronic atrial fibrillation is admitted for elective cardioversion. Prior to the procedure, which medication is essential to reduce the risk of thromboembolic events?
a. Aspirin
b. Intravenous heparin
c. Warfarin (Coumadin)
d. Beta-blocker

Answer: c. Warfarin (Coumadin). Explanation: Extended periods of atrial fibrillation carry a high risk of clot formation. Warfarin (or a similar oral anticoagulant) for several weeks pre-cardioversion is crucial to reduce embolic risk during and after the procedure.

6. A post-cardiac surgery patient experiences a sudden drop in blood pressure, muffled heart sounds, and jugular venous distention. Which immediate intervention is the priority?
a. Initiate inotropic support
b. Fluid bolus
c. Pericardiocentesis

d. Chest x-ray

Answer: c. Pericardiocentesis. Explanation: This clinical picture is highly suggestive of cardiac tamponade, a life-threatening emergency. Pericardiocentesis to remove accumulated fluid and relieve pressure on the heart is the immediate lifesaving intervention.

7. A patient with NSTEMI has ongoing chest pain despite nitrates and heparin. ECG shows new ST-segment depressions. Which medication would be the most appropriate addition to their therapy?
a. Beta-blocker
b. Glycoprotein IIb/IIIa inhibitor
c. Calcium channel blocker
d. ACE inhibitor

Answer: b. Glycoprotein IIb/IIIa inhibitor. Explanation: Ongoing chest pain and dynamic ECG changes suggest possible progression of the NSTEMI. Glycoprotein IIb/IIIa inhibitors block platelet aggregation, reducing the risk of clot formation and acute coronary occlusion.

8. A patient with heart failure is prescribed spironolactone. Which lab value should the nurse monitor most closely after initiating this medication?
a. Sodium
b. Potassium
c. Magnesium
d. Creatinine

Answer: b. Potassium. Explanation: Spironolactone is a potassium-sparing diuretic, meaning it can increase potassium levels. Hyperkalemia is a dangerous potential side effect requiring close monitoring.

9. A patient with infective endocarditis develops acute worsening of shortness of breath. On exam, a new murmur is heard. Which complication is most likely?
a. Septic emboli to the lungs
b. Myocardial infarction
c. Valve leaflet rupture
d. Abscess formation

Answer: c. Valve leaflet rupture. Explanation: Endocarditis can damage heart valves. Acute valvular dysfunction with a new murmur suggests rupture, leading to severe heart failure and pulmonary congestion.

10. A patient is brought to the ED with severe chest pain. ECG reveals ST-segment elevation in leads II, III, and AVF. Which coronary artery occlusion is most likely responsible?
a. Left anterior descending (LAD)

b. Circumflex artery
c. Right coronary artery (RCA)
d. Left main coronary artery

Answer: c. Right coronary artery (RCA). Explanation: Inferior wall infarctions (detected in leads II, III, and AVF) are typically due to RCA occlusion.

11. A patient with known severe aortic stenosis presents with fatigue and exertional shortness of breath. Which physical exam finding would further support the diagnosis of decompensated heart failure?
a. Hepatomegaly
b. New diastolic murmur
c. Elevated jugular venous pressure (JVP)
d. S3 gallop

Answer: d. S3 gallop. Explanation: While all options could be present in decompensated heart failure, an S3 is a classic sign of volume overload and ventricular dysfunction, common in worsening aortic stenosis.

12. A patient with a history of chronic heart failure is presenting with worsening dyspnea, orthopnea, and bilateral ankle edema. Which of the following findings would most likely indicate acute decompensated heart failure exacerbation?
a. Decreased B-type natriuretic peptide (BNP) levels
b. Pulmonary crackles and jugular venous distension
c. Improved exercise tolerance
d. Decreased central venous pressure

Answer: b. Pulmonary crackles and jugular venous distension. Explanation: Pulmonary crackles and jugular venous distension are classic physical examination findings in acute decompensated heart failure, indicating fluid overload and increased central venous pressure, common in exacerbations of heart failure.

13. In assessing a patient with suspected acute coronary syndrome, which of the following ECG changes would most specifically suggest an ongoing myocardial infarction?
a. T-wave inversions in leads I and aVL
b. ST-segment elevations in consecutive leads
c. Sinus tachycardia
d. PR-segment depression

Answer: b. ST-segment elevations in consecutive leads. Explanation: ST-segment elevations in consecutive leads on an ECG are highly indicative of an ongoing myocardial infarction, reflecting acute injury to the myocardium in the territory supplied by the affected coronary artery.

14. During a stress test, a patient develops hypotension with increasing workload. This finding most likely suggests:
a. Normal cardiovascular response to exercise
b. Left ventricular outflow tract obstruction
c. Significant coronary artery disease
d. Vasovagal response

Answer: c. Significant coronary artery disease. Explanation: Hypotension during a stress test, rather than the expected increase in blood pressure with exercise, is an ominous sign that suggests significant left main coronary artery disease or severe multivessel coronary artery disease, indicating inadequate myocardial perfusion during increased demand.

15. For a patient presenting with acute pericarditis, which of the following clinical features is least consistent with the diagnosis?
a. Pericardial friction rub
b. Pulsus paradoxus
c. Elevation of the ST segment in all ECG leads
d. Pleuritic chest pain relieved by sitting up and leaning forward

Answer: b. Pulsus paradoxus. Explanation: Pulsus paradoxus, an exaggerated decrease in systolic blood pressure during inspiration, is more characteristic of cardiac tamponade than acute pericarditis. The other options are classic findings in acute pericarditis.

16. A 55-year-old male with a history of hypertension and diabetes presents with sudden onset of severe chest pain radiating to his back. The pain is tearing in nature. Which of the following is the most likely diagnosis?
a. Acute myocardial infarction
b. Aortic dissection
c. Pulmonary embolism
d. Esophageal rupture

Answer: b. Aortic dissection. Explanation: The sudden onset of severe, tearing chest pain radiating to the back is highly suggestive of an aortic dissection, especially in a patient with risk factors such as hypertension and diabetes.

17. In evaluating a patient with primary hypertension, which of the following would be considered a secondary cause of hypertension?
a. Obesity
b. Renal artery stenosis
c. High sodium intake
d. Sedentary lifestyle

Answer: b. Renal artery stenosis. Explanation: Renal artery stenosis is a condition that can lead to secondary hypertension due to reduced kidney blood flow and subsequent activation of the renin-angiotensin-aldosterone system, unlike the other options which are primary risk factors for essential hypertension.

18. A patient undergoing cardiac catheterization shows a pressure gradient across the mitral valve. This finding is most indicative of:
a. Mitral valve prolapse
b. Mitral regurgitation
c. Mitral stenosis
d. Aortic regurgitation

Answer: c. Mitral stenosis. Explanation: A pressure gradient across the mitral valve, detected during cardiac catheterization, is indicative of mitral stenosis, as this condition obstructs blood flow from the left atrium to the left ventricle, creating a pressure difference.

19. For a patient with a mechanical heart valve, which of the following anticoagulation strategies is most appropriate to prevent thromboembolism?
a. Aspirin therapy alone
b. Warfarin with a target INR of 2.5-3.5
c. Direct oral anticoagulants (DOACs) like rivaroxaban
d. Clopidogrel and aspirin

Answer: b. Warfarin with a target INR of 2.5-3.5. Explanation: Patients with mechanical heart valves require lifelong anticoagulation with warfarin, with a target INR typically between 2.5 and 3.5, to prevent valve thrombosis and thromboembolism, as DOACs are not recommended for this indication.

20. A patient with heart failure is prescribed a beta-blocker. Which of the following is a primary reason for this medication in heart failure management?
a. Immediate increase in cardiac output
b. Reduction of heart rate and myocardial oxygen demand
c. Direct vasodilation of the coronary arteries
d. Increase in sodium and water excretion

Answer: b. Reduction of heart rate and myocardial oxygen demand. Explanation: In heart failure management, beta-blockers are used primarily to reduce heart rate and myocardial oxygen demand, thereby improving myocardial efficiency and reducing the detrimental effects of chronic sympathetic stimulation on the heart.

21. A 70-year-old woman with atrial fibrillation and a CHA2DS2-VASc score of 4 is being evaluated for stroke prevention. Which of the following is the most appropriate anticoagulation strategy?
a. Aspirin therapy alone
b. Aspirin and clopidogrel
c. Warfarin with a target INR of 2-3
d. No anticoagulation needed

Answer: c. Warfarin with a target INR of 2-3. Explanation: For patients with atrial fibrillation and a CHA2DS2-VASc score of 2 or higher, anticoagulation with warfarin (target INR 2-3) or a direct oral anticoagulant (DOAC) is recommended to prevent stroke, with aspirin alone or no anticoagulation being inappropriate choices due to the high stroke risk.

22. A patient with a history of COPD is admitted for shortness of breath and increased sputum production. Despite receiving antibiotics and bronchodilators, their respiratory status worsens. Which intervention would be the most appropriate next step?
a. Initiate high-flow nasal cannula oxygen therapy
b. Begin non-invasive positive pressure ventilation (NIPPV)
c. Obtain a STAT chest CT scan
d. Intubate and initiate mechanical ventilation

Answer: b. Begin non-invasive positive pressure ventilation (NIPPV). Explanation: This patient is showing signs of an acute COPD exacerbation that's not responding to initial therapy. NIPPV provides ventilatory support without invasive intubation, reducing work of breathing and potentially preventing respiratory collapse.

23. You're interpreting an arterial blood gas (ABG) for a patient with respiratory distress. Results are: pH 7.25, PaCO2 60 mmHg, HCO3 24 mEq/L. Which acid-base disturbance is present?
a. Respiratory acidosis
b. Respiratory alkalosis
c. Metabolic acidosis
d. Metabolic alkalosis

Answer: a. Respiratory acidosis. Explanation: The low pH and elevated PaCO2 indicate a primary respiratory acidosis. The HCO3 is normal, indicating no metabolic compensation at this time.

24. A patient with ARDS is on mechanical ventilation with high PEEP and FiO2 requirements. Which assessment finding would be most concerning for a potential complication related to these settings?
a. Decreased urine output
b. New-onset hypotension
c. Crackles audible throughout all lung fields
d. Elevated liver enzymes

Answer: b. New-onset hypotension. Explanation: High levels of PEEP can decrease venous return to the heart, leading to decreased preload and hypotension. This requires close monitoring and potential interventions like fluid boluses.

25. A patient is intubated for acute respiratory failure. Their ventilator is set on volume control mode with a tidal volume of 500mL. During your assessment, you note the patient's peak inspiratory pressure (PIP) has increased significantly. What is your priority action?
a. Increase the set tidal volume

b. Administer a bronchodilator
c. Suction the patient's airway
d. Auscultate the patient's lungs bilaterally

Answer: d. Auscultate the patient's lungs bilaterally. Explanation: A sudden rise in PIP suggests decreased lung compliance or airway obstruction. Auscultating breath sounds is crucial to identify potential causes like a pneumothorax, tube displacement, or secretions.

26. A patient with pneumonia has thick, tenacious secretions that are difficult to clear. Which intervention would be most effective to improve secretion mobilization?
a. Aggressive chest percussion therapy
b. Administering IV fluids
c. Increasing the FiO2 on the ventilator
d. Providing nebulized hypertonic saline

Answer: d. Providing nebulized hypertonic saline. Explanation: Hypertonic saline helps to loosen thick mucus by increasing hydration, facilitating easier clearance and improving airway patency.

27. A patient is receiving mechanical ventilation in the SIMV mode (synchronized intermittent mandatory ventilation). You notice the patient's spontaneous respiratory rate is 35 breaths/minute. What adjustment would be most appropriate?
a. Decrease the set FiO2
b. Initiate a sedative medication
c. Increase the set SIMV rate
d. Switch the ventilator mode to pressure support

Answer: c. Increase the set SIMV rate. Explanation: A high spontaneous respiratory rate suggests the patient is working too hard. Increasing the SIMV rate provides more mandatory breaths, offloading the patient's respiratory effort.

28. A patient with status asthmaticus is not responding adequately to bronchodilators and steroids. Which additional therapy might be considered?
a. Intravenous magnesium sulfate
b. Heliox (helium-oxygen mixture)
c. Prone positioning
d. Nitric oxide

Answer: b. Heliox (helium-oxygen mixture). Explanation: In severe airway obstruction, Heliox lowers airway resistance due to its lower density, improving ventilation and reducing work of breathing.

29. You receive a patient post-thoracentesis. Which of the following findings would require immediate notification of the physician?
a. Slight oxygen desaturation that resolves quickly
b. Persistent cough
c. Discomfort at the procedure site
d. Blood pressure 10 mmHg below baseline

Answer: d. Blood pressure 10 mmHg below baseline. Explanation: A drop in blood pressure after thoracentesis could suggest a complication like bleeding or re-expansion pulmonary edema, necessitating urgent evaluation.

30. A chest x-ray report for a ventilated patient describes "diffuse bilateral infiltrates with air bronchograms". Which condition is most consistent with these findings?
a. Pulmonary embolism
b. Acute Respiratory Distress Syndrome (ARDS)
c. Cardiogenic pulmonary edema
d. Atelectasis

Answer: b. Acute Respiratory Distress Syndrome (ARDS). Explanation: The classic radiographic pattern of ARDS is diffuse "ground-glass" opacities and air bronchograms, representing widespread inflammation and fluid buildup in the alveoli.

31. A patient with septic shock develops respiratory distress, and a new chest x-ray reveals bilateral pulmonary infiltrates. The patient's PaO2/FiO2 ratio is 150. How would you classify this patient's acute lung injury?
a. No acute lung injury
b. Mild ARDS
c. Moderate ARDS
d. Severe ARDS

Answer: b. Mild ARDS. Explanation: The Berlin Criteria for ARDS use the PaO2/FiO2 ratio: Mild (200-300), Moderate (100-200), Severe (<100). This patient falls into the mild category.

32. A progressive care nurse is assessing a patient with chronic obstructive pulmonary disease (COPD) who is on oxygen therapy. The patient's current oxygen saturation is 88%. Which of the following actions is most appropriate?
a. Increase the oxygen flow rate significantly to achieve saturation above 92%
b. Maintain the current oxygen flow rate, as this is an acceptable target for COPD patients
c. Immediately intubate the patient due to severe hypoxemia
d. Switch to high-flow nasal cannula at the same oxygen percentage

Answer: b. Maintain the current oxygen flow rate, as this is an acceptable target for COPD patients. Explanation: For COPD patients, maintaining an oxygen saturation between 88-92% is recommended to avoid oxygen-induced hypercapnia, which can result from suppressing the hypoxic drive.

33. In managing a patient with acute respiratory distress syndrome (ARDS), which ventilator setting adjustment is most appropriate to improve oxygenation?
a. Increase tidal volume to 10 mL/kg
b. Apply positive end-expiratory pressure (PEEP) to prevent alveolar collapse
c. Decrease the inspiratory flow rate to prolong the inspiratory phase
d. Switch to an inverse ratio ventilation strategy

Answer: b. Apply positive end-expiratory pressure (PEEP) to prevent alveolar collapse. Explanation: In ARDS, applying PEEP is crucial for preventing alveolar collapse at the end of expiration, thus improving oxygenation by increasing functional residual capacity.

34. A patient with a pulmonary embolism is hemodynamically unstable. What is the most immediate and appropriate intervention?
a. Start anticoagulation with unfractionated heparin
b. Administer thrombolytic therapy, if there are no contraindications
c. Schedule the patient for a pulmonary embolectomy
d. Initiate a high-dose corticosteroid regimen

Answer: b. Administer thrombolytic therapy, if there are no contraindications. Explanation: For hemodynamically unstable patients with pulmonary embolism, thrombolytic therapy is indicated to rapidly dissolve the clot, improving hemodynamics, provided there are no contraindications to its use.

35. In evaluating a patient with suspected tension pneumothorax, which clinical finding is most indicative of this condition?
a. Bilateral wheezing on auscultation
b. Hyperresonance and diminished breath sounds on one side
c. Pulsus paradoxus and muffled heart sounds
d. Sudden onset of central chest pain radiating to the shoulder

Answer: b. Hyperresonance and diminished breath sounds on one side. Explanation: Hyperresonance and diminished or absent breath sounds on the affected side are classic signs of tension pneumothorax, caused by trapped air in the pleural space that compresses lung tissue.

36. A patient with asthma is experiencing an acute exacerbation. Which medication should be administered first?
a. Oral corticosteroids
b. A short-acting beta-2 agonist via a nebulizer
c. A long-acting muscarinic antagonist
d. Intravenous magnesium sulfate

Answer: b. A short-acting beta-2 agonist via a nebulizer. Explanation: The first-line treatment for an acute asthma exacerbation is a short-acting beta-2 agonist, such as albuterol, administered via nebulizer or metered-dose inhaler for immediate bronchodilation.

37. For a patient with interstitial lung disease, which pulmonary function test pattern is most characteristic?
a. Obstructive pattern with decreased FEV1/FVC ratio
b. Restrictive pattern with reduced total lung capacity
c. Mixed pattern with both obstructive and restrictive features
d. Normal spirometry with reduced diffusion capacity

Answer: b. Restrictive pattern with reduced total lung capacity. Explanation: Interstitial lung disease typically presents with a restrictive pattern on pulmonary function testing, characterized by reduced total lung capacity due to stiffness of the lung parenchyma.

38. A patient is suspected of having a pleural effusion. Which diagnostic method is most definitive for identifying and characterizing the effusion?
a. Chest X-ray in upright position
b. Lateral decubitus chest X-ray
c. Thoracentesis with pleural fluid analysis
d. Pulmonary function tests

Answer: c. Thoracentesis with pleural fluid analysis. Explanation: Thoracentesis, followed by pleural fluid analysis, is the most definitive way to identify and characterize a pleural effusion, allowing for determination of its nature (transudative vs. exudative) and potential causes.

39. In a patient with cystic fibrosis, which intervention is crucial for managing thick pulmonary secretions?
a. High-dose ibuprofen therapy
b. Airway clearance techniques and inhaled mucolytics
c. Long-term oxygen therapy
d. Continuous positive airway pressure (CPAP) during sleep

Answer: b. Airway clearance techniques and inhaled mucolytics. Explanation: In cystic fibrosis, managing thick pulmonary secretions is crucial and is effectively achieved through airway clearance techniques (e.g., chest physiotherapy) and the use of inhaled mucolytics to thin the secretions.

40. When assessing a patient with sarcoidosis, which finding would be consistent with the diagnosis?
a. Positive tuberculin skin test
b. Bilateral hilar lymphadenopathy on chest imaging
c. Elevated serum alpha-1 antitrypsin levels
d. Nail clubbing and cyanosis

Answer: b. Bilateral hilar lymphadenopathy on chest imaging. Explanation: Bilateral hilar lymphadenopathy is a hallmark finding in sarcoidosis, often detected on chest imaging and consistent with the granulomatous inflammation typical of the disease.

41. A patient with a tracheostomy is experiencing difficulty with secretion clearance. Which intervention is most effective for mobilizing secretions?
a. Increasing the frequency of tracheal suctioning
b. Administering hypertonic saline nebulization prior to suctioning
c. Reducing the humidity of the inhaled air
d. Elevating the head of the bed to 45 degrees

Answer: b. Administering hypertonic saline nebulization prior to suctioning. Explanation: Hypertonic saline nebulization can help mobilize secretions by hydrating and thinning them, making it easier to clear the airways through suctioning, especially in tracheostomized patients.

42. A patient with acute kidney injury (AKI) has a potassium level of 6.2 mEq/L. ECG shows peaked T-waves. Which treatment would be the most immediate priority?
a. Oral sodium polystyrene sulfonate (Kayexalate)
b. Initiate hemodialysis
c. Administer IV calcium gluconate
d. 10 units of regular insulin with D50 IV push

Answer: c. Administer IV calcium gluconate. Explanation: Hyperkalemia with ECG changes is a critical emergency. Calcium gluconate helps stabilize the cardiac membrane, temporarily counteracting the effects of potassium on the heart. Other treatments can take longer to lower potassium levels.

43. A patient with septic shock is started on continuous renal replacement therapy (CRRT). Which complication should the nurse most closely monitor for during the initial hours of therapy?
a. Hypernatremia
b. Electrolyte imbalances
c. Hyperglycemia
d. Air embolism

Answer: b. Electrolyte imbalances. Explanation: CRRT can cause rapid shifts in electrolytes like potassium, calcium, and phosphorus, especially early in treatment. Close monitoring and frequent lab draws are essential.

44. A patient with cirrhosis and ascites is admitted for possible spontaneous bacterial peritonitis (SBP). Which of the following diagnostic findings would be most consistent with this diagnosis?
a. Serum albumin level <2.5 g/dL
b. Abdominal fluid showing elevated protein
c. Abdominal fluid neutrophil count >250 cells/mm3

d. Positive blood cultures

Answer: c. Abdominal fluid neutrophil count >250 cells/mm3. Explanation: SBP is diagnosed based on paracentesis results. A neutrophil count above 250 cells/mm3, even without positive cultures, is highly suggestive of infection.

45. A patient with acute pancreatitis has worsening abdominal pain and tachycardia. Lab results show a decreasing calcium level. Which intervention is crucial?
a. Aggressive IV fluid administration
b. Calcium replacement
c. Initiate broad-spectrum antibiotics
d. Administer IV glucagon

Answer: b. Calcium replacement. Explanation: Hypocalcemia is a complication of severe pancreatitis. Calcium binds to fats released from pancreatic inflammation. Replacement is crucial, as low calcium exacerbates pain and can lead to arrhythmias.

46. A patient is started on total parenteral nutrition (TPN) due to severe GI dysfunction. Which monitoring parameter is the highest priority during the first 24 hours?
a. Liver function tests
b. Blood glucose levels
c. Triglyceride levels
d. Serum potassium

Answer: b. Blood glucose levels. Explanation: TPN solutions are high in dextrose. Patients are at risk for hyperglycemia, especially initially, requiring frequent blood sugar checks and potential insulin adjustments.

47. A patient presents with severe diarrhea, abdominal cramping, and fever. Stool testing is positive for Clostridium difficile toxin. Which treatment would be the first-line therapy?
a. Intravenous vancomycin
b. Intravenous metronidazole
c. Oral vancomycin
d. Probiotics

Answer: c. Oral vancomycin. Explanation: For mild to moderate C. difficile infections, oral vancomycin is the recommended initial treatment. IV metronidazole is typically reserved for severe cases or if oral therapy isn't tolerated.

48. A patient with active upper GI bleeding undergoes endoscopic evaluation. A bleeding ulcer is treated with epinephrine injection and cauterization. Which post-procedure order is essential to prevent re-bleeding?
a. Clear liquid diet for 24 hours

b. Sucralfate suspension
c. Nasogastric tube placement
d. Proton pump inhibitor (PPI) therapy

Answer: d. Proton pump inhibitor (PPI) therapy. Explanation: PPIs reduce gastric acid production, creating an environment conducive to healing and minimizing re-bleeding risk after endoscopic hemostasis.

49. You receive a patient admitted for an intentional overdose of acetaminophen (Tylenol). Which lab value is the most urgent to obtain?
a. Aspartate aminotransferase (AST) and alanine aminotransferase (ALT)
b. Serum acetaminophen level
c. Complete blood count (CBC)
d. Arterial blood gas (ABG)

Answer: b. Serum acetaminophen level. Explanation: To determine the need for N-acetylcysteine (NAC), the antidote for Tylenol toxicity, the acetaminophen level must be plotted against time on a nomogram. Liver enzymes may not be elevated early on.

50. A patient with Crohn's disease experiences a flare-up with bloody diarrhea and abdominal pain. Which medication class would likely be contraindicated during an acute flare?
a. Antibiotics
b. Corticosteroids
c. Biologics (anti-TNF agents)
d. Non-steroidal anti-inflammatories (NSAIDs)

Answer: d. Non-steroidal anti-inflammatories (NSAIDs). Explanation: NSAIDs can exacerbate GI inflammation and bleeding, worsening symptoms in inflammatory bowel disease patients. They should be avoided, especially during active flares.

51. A patient post-liver transplant is on immunosuppressive therapy. Which dietary restriction is most important to educate the patient about?
a. Avoiding raw fruits and vegetables
b. Limiting sodium intake
c. Choosing low-fat foods
d. Avoiding grapefruit juice

Answer: d. Avoiding grapefruit juice. Explanation: Grapefruit interacts with many medications, including immunosuppressants. It can increase drug levels significantly, leading to potential toxicity.

52. In a patient with acute pancreatitis, which laboratory finding is most indicative of severe disease?

a. Serum amylase three times the upper limit of normal
b. Elevated serum lipase level
c. Hypocalcemia
d. Elevated alanine aminotransferase (ALT)

Answer: c. Hypocalcemia. Explanation: Hypocalcemia in the context of acute pancreatitis is indicative of severe disease, likely due to fat saponification and systemic inflammation. While elevated amylase and lipase are diagnostic, they do not correlate well with severity.

53. A patient with end-stage renal disease on hemodialysis presents with a serum potassium level of 6.5 mEq/L. What is the most immediate intervention?
a. Increase dietary potassium intake
b. Administer sodium polystyrene sulfonate orally
c. Start intravenous insulin and glucose
d. Schedule an additional hemodialysis session

Answer: c. Start intravenous insulin and glucose. Explanation: In the case of severe hyperkalemia, especially with ECG changes, the immediate intervention is intravenous insulin and glucose to shift potassium intracellularly, temporarily reducing serum levels.

54. For a patient presenting with hepatic encephalopathy, which treatment option is most appropriate to reduce ammonia levels?
a. Lactulose
b. Propranolol
c. Vitamin K
d. Ursodeoxycholic acid

Answer: a. Lactulose. Explanation: Lactulose is used in hepatic encephalopathy to reduce ammonia levels by acidifying colonic contents and promoting ammonia excretion.

55. In assessing a patient with suspected bowel obstruction, which imaging modality is most informative for initial evaluation?
a. Abdominal ultrasound
b. Plain abdominal radiography
c. CT scan of the abdomen and pelvis with contrast
d. MRI of the abdomen

Answer: b. Plain abdominal radiography. Explanation: Plain abdominal radiographs are a valuable initial tool in the assessment of bowel obstruction, showing air-fluid levels and dilated loops of bowel, guiding further diagnostic steps.

56. A patient with chronic kidney disease has a phosphate level of 5.8 mg/dL. Which dietary modification is most appropriate?
a. Increase intake of dairy products
b. Limit foods high in phosphate, such as processed meats and sodas
c. Increase protein intake
d. Decrease calcium intake

Answer: b. Limit foods high in phosphate, such as processed meats and sodas. Explanation: In chronic kidney disease, dietary phosphate restriction is crucial to manage hyperphosphatemia and prevent secondary hyperparathyroidism and bone disease.

57. A 60-year-old patient with cirrhosis is noted to have ascites. Which pathophysiological mechanism primarily contributes to ascites formation in cirrhosis?
a. Increased hydrostatic pressure in the hepatic sinusoids
b. Decreased aldosterone breakdown by the liver
c. Hypoalbuminemia leading to decreased oncotic pressure
d. Increased hepatic lymph production

Answer: c. Hypoalbuminemia leading to decreased oncotic pressure. Explanation: Ascites in cirrhosis is primarily due to portal hypertension and hypoalbuminemia, which decreases the oncotic pressure, leading to fluid accumulation in the peritoneal cavity.

58. In managing a patient with acute kidney injury (AKI) and oliguria, which fluid management strategy is preferred?
a. Liberal fluid administration to ensure adequate hydration
b. Careful fluid balance with restriction to prevent volume overload
c. High-dose diuretics to force diuresis
d. Immediate initiation of renal replacement therapy

Answer: b. Careful fluid balance with restriction to prevent volume overload. Explanation: In AKI with oliguria, careful management of fluid balance is essential to prevent volume overload while avoiding dehydration, with fluid restriction often necessary depending on the patient's volume status.

59. A patient with gastroesophageal reflux disease (GERD) is not responding to proton pump inhibitors. Which additional diagnostic test is most appropriate to evaluate the severity of GERD?
a. Upper gastrointestinal series
b. 24-hour esophageal pH monitoring
c. Abdominal ultrasound
d. Gastric emptying study

Answer: b. 24-hour esophageal pH monitoring. Explanation: In patients with GERD not responding to treatment, 24-hour esophageal pH monitoring is the gold standard for assessing the severity of acid reflux and correlating symptoms with acid exposure.

60. For a patient with ulcerative colitis experiencing a moderate flare, which therapeutic option is most appropriate?
a. Systemic corticosteroids
b. Oral 5-aminosalicylic acid (5-ASA) compounds
c. Antibiotic therapy
d. Immediate colectomy

Answer: a. Systemic corticosteroids. Explanation: For moderate to severe flares of ulcerative colitis, systemic corticosteroids are often required to achieve remission, with 5-ASA compounds typically used for milder disease and maintenance of remission.

61. In evaluating a patient with acute cholecystitis, which finding on ultrasound is most indicative of the diagnosis?
a. Gallbladder wall thickening >3mm
b. Presence of gallstones alone
c. Dilated common bile duct
d. Pericholecystic fluid

Answer: a. Gallbladder wall thickening >3mm. Explanation: Gallbladder wall thickening greater than 3mm in the context of appropriate clinical symptoms is highly suggestive of acute cholecystitis, especially when associated with gallstones and pericholecystic fluid.

62. A patient in the ICU develops new-onset confusion and agitation. Which assessment finding would point towards delirium rather than a primary neurological event?
a. Focal weakness on one side of the body
b. Fluctuating level of consciousness
c. Positive Babinski reflex
d. Pupillary asymmetry

Answer: b. Fluctuating level of consciousness. Explanation: Delirium is marked by acute changes in mental status, often with waxing and waning alertness. Focal neurological deficits or pupillary changes suggest a structural brain problem.

63. You're caring for a patient with increased intracranial pressure (ICP). Which intervention would likely be contraindicated?
a. Elevating the head of the bed to 30 degrees
b. Administering IV mannitol
c. Maintaining PEEP at 10 cmH2O on the ventilator
d. Frequent neurological assessments

Answer: c. Maintaining PEEP at 10 cmH2O on the ventilator. Explanation: High levels of PEEP can increase intrathoracic pressure, impeding venous return from the brain and potentially worsening ICP.

64. A patient with a suspected subarachnoid hemorrhage undergoes a CT scan, which is negative. What is the next essential step in diagnosis?
a. Magnetic resonance imaging (MRI)
b. Electroencephalogram (EEG)
c. Lumbar puncture
d. Cerebral angiogram

Answer: c. Lumbar puncture. Explanation: If a CT scan is negative but suspicion for subarachnoid hemorrhage remains high, a lumbar puncture is needed to look for blood or xanthochromia (yellowish discoloration) in the cerebrospinal fluid.

65. A patient with myasthenia gravis experiences a sudden worsening of their muscle weakness. Which medication is most appropriate for rapid symptom improvement?
a. Oral pyridostigmine (Mestinon)
b. Intravenous immunoglobulin (IVIG)
c. Prednisone
d. Atropine

Answer: b. Intravenous immunoglobulin (IVIG). Explanation: In a myasthenic crisis, IVIG works quickly to block pathogenic antibodies. Pyridostigmine takes longer, and prednisone is for longer-term management. Atropine is used for side effects of cholinesterase inhibitors, not for crisis management.

66. A patient is admitted with a diagnosis of Guillain-Barré syndrome. Which assessment finding would require immediate intervention?
a. Ascending paralysis
b. Decreased deep tendon reflexes
c. New-onset dysphagia
d. Numbness and tingling in the extremities

Answer: c. New-onset dysphagia. Explanation: Dysphagia suggests cranial nerve involvement and puts the patient at risk for aspiration. Ascending paralysis, decreased reflexes, and paresthesias are expected findings in Guillain-Barré.

67. You're assessing a patient's Glasgow Coma Scale (GCS) score. They open their eyes to verbal command, are confused but conversant, and follow motor commands. What is their total GCS score?
a. 11
b. 12
c. 13

d. 14

Answer: d. 14. Explanation: This patient scores a 4 for eye-opening, 4 for verbal response, and 6 for motor response, totaling a GCS of 14.

68. A patient with a traumatic brain injury is being monitored for signs of brain herniation. Which change in pupillary response would be most concerning?
a. Pupils become pinpoint
b. One pupil becomes dilated and non-reactive
c. Both pupils are briskly reactive to light
d. Pupils are sluggishly reactive to light

Answer: b. One pupil becomes dilated and non-reactive. Explanation: Unilateral pupillary dilation and non-reactivity indicate compression of the oculomotor nerve (cranial nerve III), a classic sign of impending herniation.

69. A patient is diagnosed with status epilepticus. After administering a benzodiazepine, which medication class is typically the next line of treatment?
a. Anticholinergics
b. Calcium channel blockers
c. Opioid analgesics
d. Anticonvulsants (phenytoin, levetiracetam, etc.)

Answer: d. Anticonvulsants (phenytoin, levetiracetam, etc.). Explanation: If seizures don't stop with benzodiazepines, a loading dose of a long-acting anticonvulsant is needed to achieve seizure control.

70. A patient post-stroke has difficulty with coordination and balance on their left side. This finding suggests a stroke affecting which brain region?
a. Frontal lobe
b. Brainstem
c. Cerebellum
d. Parietal lobe

Answer: c. Cerebellum. Explanation: The cerebellum is responsible for coordination and balance. Strokes in this area lead to ataxia.

71. A patient presents with sudden onset of severe headache, vomiting, and neck stiffness. Which diagnostic test is the most urgent priority?
a. Non-contrast CT scan of the head
b. MRI of the brain and cervical spine
c. Lumbar puncture

d. Complete blood count (CBC)

Answer: a. Non-contrast CT scan of the head. Explanation: These symptoms raise suspicion for a life-threatening bleed like a subarachnoid hemorrhage. A rapid CT scan is needed to rule this out before proceeding with other tests like lumbar puncture, which could be dangerous in the setting of increased intracranial pressure.

72. In a patient presenting with acute ischemic stroke symptoms, which of the following interventions is most critical within the first 4.5 hours of symptom onset?
a. Administration of oral aspirin
b. Initiation of therapeutic hypothermia
c. Intravenous thrombolysis with recombinant tissue plasminogen activator (rt-PA)
d. Immediate anticoagulation with warfarin

Answer: c. Intravenous thrombolysis with recombinant tissue plasminogen activator (rt-PA). Explanation: For eligible patients presenting with acute ischemic stroke, intravenous rt-PA is recommended within 4.5 hours of symptom onset to dissolve the blood clot and restore blood flow to the affected part of the brain, significantly improving outcomes.

73. A 65-year-old male with a history of hypertension and diabetes mellitus presents with sudden onset of right-sided weakness and aphasia. His CT scan shows no hemorrhage. The patient's NIH Stroke Scale score is 18. Which of the following is the most appropriate next step?
a. Immediate administration of intravenous rt-PA
b. Wait for MRI results before any intervention
c. Start antiplatelet therapy with clopidogrel
d. Proceed with mechanical thrombectomy

Answer: d. Proceed with mechanical thrombectomy. Explanation: Given the severity of the patient's symptoms as indicated by an NIH Stroke Scale score of 18, and the absence of hemorrhage on CT, mechanical thrombectomy is indicated as it can be beneficial for patients with large vessel occlusions presenting within 6 to 24 hours of symptom onset.

74. For a patient diagnosed with Bell's palsy, which of the following treatments is recommended within 72 hours of symptom onset for the best chance of full recovery?
a. High-dose antiviral therapy
b. Corticosteroids
c. Calcium channel blockers
d. Acupuncture

Answer: b. Corticosteroids. Explanation: Early treatment with corticosteroids within 72 hours of symptom onset has been shown to significantly increase the likelihood of full recovery in patients with Bell's palsy by reducing inflammation and swelling of the facial nerve.

75. A patient with multiple sclerosis (MS) reports increased fatigue, muscle weakness, and blurred vision during periods of high temperature. Which of the following terms best describes this phenomenon?
a. Uhthoff's phenomenon
b. Lhermitte's sign
c. Charcot's triad
d. Romberg's sign

Answer: a. Uhthoff's phenomenon. Explanation: Uhthoff's phenomenon is the worsening of neurologic symptoms in MS patients due to increased body temperature, commonly observed during exercise, hot weather, or fever.

76. In assessing a patient with suspected Guillain-Barré syndrome (GBS), which of the following cerebrospinal fluid (CSF) findings is characteristic of the condition?
a. Elevated protein with normal white cell count
b. Neutrophilic pleocytosis
c. Decreased glucose level
d. Elevated IgG index

Answer: a. Elevated protein with normal white cell count. Explanation: A key diagnostic feature of Guillain-Barré syndrome is an elevated CSF protein level with a normal white blood cell count, known as albuminocytologic dissociation, reflecting the demyelinating nature of the disease.

77. A 55-year-old woman with a history of migraine headaches presents with a new type of headache that is brief, unilateral, and accompanied by ipsilateral lacrimation and nasal congestion. Which of the following headache disorders is most consistent with her presentation?
a. Cluster headache
b. Tension-type headache
c. Chronic migraine
d. Temporal arteritis

Answer: a. Cluster headache. Explanation: The description of brief, unilateral headaches with autonomic symptoms such as lacrimation and nasal congestion is characteristic of cluster headaches, which are part of the trigeminal autonomic cephalalgias.

78. In a patient with Parkinson's disease, which of the following medications directly replaces dopamine in the brain?
a. Carbidopa
b. Levodopa
c. Selegiline
d. Amantadine

Answer: b. Levodopa. Explanation: Levodopa is a precursor to dopamine that can cross the blood-brain barrier and is then converted to dopamine within the brain, directly supplementing the decreased dopamine levels characteristic of Parkinson's disease.

79. A patient presents with sudden onset of severe headache, described as "the worst headache of my life," followed by a brief loss of consciousness. On examination, neck stiffness is noted. Which diagnostic test is most appropriate to confirm the suspected diagnosis?
a. MRI of the brain
b. CT scan of the head without contrast
c. Lumbar puncture for CSF analysis
d. Electroencephalogram (EEG)

Answer: b. CT scan of the head without contrast. Explanation: The clinical presentation is suggestive of a subarachnoid hemorrhage, and a non-contrast CT scan of the head is the most appropriate initial test to confirm the diagnosis, as it can rapidly detect blood in the subarachnoid space.

80. In evaluating a patient for Alzheimer's disease, which of the following findings on neuropsychological testing would most likely be observed?
a. Predominant frontal lobe dysfunction
b. Impaired short-term memory and difficulty with word-finding
c. Isolated calculation difficulties
d. Marked visuospatial impairment without memory loss

Answer: b. Impaired short-term memory and difficulty with word-finding. Explanation: Alzheimer's disease typically presents with impaired short-term memory and language difficulties, such as aphasia, which are key findings on neuropsychological testing.

81. A patient with a recent history of viral infection presents with asymmetric weakness of the lower extremities, absent deep tendon reflexes, and sensory disturbances. Which of the following is the most likely diagnosis?
a. Amyotrophic lateral sclerosis (ALS)
b. Acute inflammatory demyelinating polyradiculoneuropathy (AIDP), a variant of Guillain-Barré syndrome
c. Multiple sclerosis (MS)
d. Myasthenia gravis (MG)

Answer: b. Acute inflammatory demyelinating polyradiculoneuropathy (AIDP), a variant of Guillain-Barré syndrome. Explanation: The clinical presentation of asymmetric lower extremity weakness, absent reflexes, and sensory changes following a viral infection is characteristic of AIDP, the most common variant of Guillain-Barré syndrome, which involves immune-mediated demyelination of peripheral nerves.

82. A patient with type 1 diabetes presents with confusion, sweating, and palpitations. The bedside glucose reading is 50 mg/dL. Which of the following is the most appropriate initial treatment?
a. 25 grams of intravenous dextrose

b. Subcutaneous insulin
c. Oral glucose gel
d. 100 mL of 0.9% saline infusion

Answer: a. 25 grams of intravenous dextrose. Explanation: In a conscious patient with hypoglycemia, oral carbohydrates are preferred, but in cases of severe hypoglycemia or if the patient is confused or unable to swallow, intravenous dextrose is the fastest and most effective way to raise blood glucose levels.

83. In a patient with Graves' disease, which of the following findings would you expect on physical examination?
a. Bradycardia
b. Pretibial myxedema
c. Hyporeflexia
d. Cold intolerance

Answer: b. Pretibial myxedema. Explanation: Pretibial myxedema is a characteristic finding in Graves' disease, an autoimmune hyperthyroid condition. It presents as thickened, erythematous, and indurated skin on the anterior aspect of the lower legs.

84. A 60-year-old male with a history of chronic kidney disease presents with fatigue, pallor, and a hemoglobin level of 8.5 g/dL. Which of the following is the most likely cause of his anemia?
a. Vitamin B12 deficiency
b. Hemolysis
c. Iron deficiency
d. Erythropoietin deficiency

Answer: d. Erythropoietin deficiency. Explanation: Chronic kidney disease commonly leads to anemia primarily due to erythropoietin deficiency, as the kidneys are responsible for the production of erythropoietin, which stimulates red blood cell production in the bone marrow.

85. A patient with no prior history of diabetes presents with polyuria, polydipsia, and unexplained weight loss. Blood glucose is 320 mg/dL and HbA1c is 12%. Which of the following is the most likely diagnosis?
a. Type 1 diabetes
b. Type 2 diabetes
c. Gestational diabetes
d. Diabetes insipidus

Answer: b. Type 2 diabetes. Explanation: The presentation of polyuria, polydipsia, significant hyperglycemia, and elevated HbA1c in an adult patient with no prior history of diabetes is most suggestive of type 2 diabetes.

86. A 45-year-old woman presents with fatigue, constipation, and depression. Laboratory tests reveal high TSH and low free T4. Which of the following is the most appropriate treatment?
a. Methimazole
b. Levothyroxine
c. Radioactive iodine therapy
d. Prednisone

Answer: b. Levothyroxine. Explanation: The patient's symptoms and lab results are indicative of hypothyroidism, which is treated with levothyroxine, a synthetic form of the thyroid hormone thyroxine (T4).

87. A patient with a known history of polycythemia vera presents with itching after showers and a ruddy complexion. Which of the following interventions is most effective in reducing thrombotic complications in this patient?
a. Hydroxyurea
b. Aspirin
c. Phlebotomy
d. Interferon-alpha

Answer: c. Phlebotomy. Explanation: Phlebotomy is a primary treatment for polycythemia vera, aimed at reducing the hematocrit to normal levels to decrease blood viscosity and the risk of thrombosis.

88. In a patient with suspected acute adrenal crisis, which of the following laboratory findings is most indicative of this condition?
a. Hyperkalemia and hyponatremia
b. Hypernatremia and hypokalemia
c. Hypocalcemia and hyperphosphatemia
d. Hypercalcemia and hypophosphatemia

Answer: a. Hyperkalemia and hyponatremia. Explanation: Acute adrenal crisis results in cortisol deficiency, leading to hyponatremia and hyperkalemia due to the loss of cortisol's effect on renal sodium and potassium handling.

89. A patient with Addison's disease is most at risk for developing which of the following during periods of stress or illness?
a. Thyrotoxic crisis
b. Diabetic ketoacidosis
c. Acute adrenal crisis
d. Hyperosmolar hyperglycemic state

Answer: c. Acute adrenal crisis. Explanation: Patients with Addison's disease (primary adrenal insufficiency) have inadequate cortisol production, placing them at risk for acute adrenal crisis during stress or illness, necessitating stress-dose steroids.

90. A 35-year-old female with a history of systemic lupus erythematosus presents with thrombocytopenia and recurrent fetal loss. Which of the following antibodies is most likely to be positive?
a. Anti-Smith
b. Anti-double-stranded DNA
c. Antiphospholipid
d. Anti-Jo1

Answer: c. Antiphospholipid. Explanation: The presence of antiphospholipid antibodies is associated with thrombocytopenia and recurrent fetal loss, especially in patients with autoimmune disorders like systemic lupus erythematosus.

91. In evaluating a patient for hemochromatosis, which of the following genetic tests would confirm the diagnosis?
a. HFE gene mutation analysis
b. Karyotyping for Philadelphia chromosome
c. JAK2 V617F mutation analysis
d. BRCA1 and BRCA2 gene mutation analysis

Answer: a. HFE gene mutation analysis. Explanation: Hereditary hemochromatosis is most commonly caused by mutations in the HFE gene, particularly C282Y and H63D mutations, making HFE gene mutation analysis the confirmatory test for diagnosis.

92. A patient with newly diagnosed Type 1 diabetes mellitus arrives in the ED confused, lethargic, and with fruity-smelling breath. Arterial blood gas (ABG) shows a pH of 7.20. Which is the most likely diagnosis?
a. Hypoglycemic coma
b. Diabetic ketoacidosis (DKA)
c. Hyperosmolar hyperglycemic state (HHS)
d. Alcoholic ketoacidosis

Answer: b. Diabetic ketoacidosis (DKA). Explanation: The low pH indicates acidosis, and the fruity breath suggests ketones. This presentation, in the context of new-onset Type 1 diabetes, is classic for DKA. Hypoglycemia wouldn't cause acidosis, and HHS is more common in Type 2 diabetes.

93. You're caring for a patient in DKA receiving an insulin infusion. Their potassium level drops from 4.5 mEq/L to 3.0 mEq/L despite ongoing potassium supplementation. What's the most appropriate next step?
a. Stop the insulin infusion.
b. Increase the rate of potassium replacement.
c. Obtain an electrocardiogram (ECG).
d. Recheck the potassium level in 30 minutes.

Answer: c. Obtain an electrocardiogram (ECG). Explanation: Potassium shifts intracellularly as DKA is treated, sometimes masking true hypokalemia. ECG changes are the most reliable indicator of dangerously low potassium. Increasing potassium without assessing cardiac effects is risky.

94. A patient with sepsis has a platelet count of 25,000/mm3 and oozing blood from IV sites. Which intervention is the priority?
a. Administer fresh frozen plasma (FFP).
b. Initiate a heparin infusion.
c. Prepare for platelet transfusion.
d. Assess for signs of active bleeding.

Answer: c. Prepare for platelet transfusion. Explanation: Severe thrombocytopenia (<50,000/mm3) with active bleeding warrants platelet transfusion. FFP is for coagulopathy, not low platelets. Heparin is contraindicated with active bleeding. Further assessment is needed, but transfusions are likely urgent.

95. A patient admitted for sickle cell crisis is experiencing severe pain. Which medication class would be an important component of their pain management plan?
a. Opioids
b. Benzodiazepines
c. Non-steroidal anti-inflammatories (NSAIDs)
d. Antibiotics

Answer: a. Opioids. Explanation: Sickle cell crises involve severe pain often requiring strong analgesics like opioids. NSAIDs can worsen renal function, which is already a concern in these patients. Benzodiazepines might help with anxiety, but don't address the primary pain. Antibiotics are for infection, not pain control.

96. A patient with pancytopenia undergoes a bone marrow biopsy. Results show hypercellular bone marrow with >20% blast cells. Which diagnosis is most likely?
a. Aplastic anemia
b. Iron deficiency anemia
c. Acute leukemia
d. Myelodysplastic syndrome

Answer: c. Acute leukemia. Explanation: Blast cells are immature blood cells. A high percentage in the bone marrow is the hallmark of acute leukemia. Aplastic anemia shows hypocellular marrow, and iron deficiency affects red cell production, not all cell lines.

97. A patient with a history of atrial fibrillation on warfarin (Coumadin) presents with acute confusion and weakness. Their INR is 5.5. Which treatment is indicated?
a. Vitamin K
b. Fresh frozen plasma (FFP)
c. Protamine sulfate

d. Heparin

Answer: a. Vitamin K. Explanation: Vitamin K slowly reverses the effects of warfarin. FFP is for active bleeding or urgent procedures in the setting of an elevated INR. Protamine sulfate reverses heparin, and heparin would worsen the situation.

98. A patient with chronic anemia is found to have a very low reticulocyte count. Which of the following is the most likely explanation?
a. Iron deficiency
b. Hemolysis
c. Bone marrow suppression
d. Vitamin B12 deficiency

Answer: c. Bone marrow suppression. Explanation: Reticulocytes are immature red blood cells. A low count suggests the bone marrow isn't producing enough cells. Iron deficiency and hemolysis would show increased reticulocytes as the marrow tries to compensate.

99. A patient develops a fever and chills a few hours after receiving a blood transfusion. What is the first priority action?
a. Administer acetaminophen (Tylenol).
b. Stop the transfusion.
c. Send blood cultures.
d. Obtain a urine sample.

Answer: b. Stop the transfusion. Explanation: Fever and chills suggest a possible transfusion reaction. Stopping the infusion is the immediate priority to prevent further exposure. Other actions are important but secondary.

100. A postoperative patient with deep vein thrombosis (DVT) is started on a heparin drip. Which lab value is most important to monitor during heparin therapy?
a. Partial thromboplastin time (PTT)
b. Prothrombin time (PT)
c. Platelet count
d. Hemoglobin and hematocrit

Answer: a. Partial thromboplastin time (PTT). Explanation: The PTT measures the effectiveness of heparin, with a therapeutic goal range typically 1.5-2.5 times the normal value. PT monitors warfarin therapy, and platelets and H&H assess for bleeding risks.

101. A patient with hypothyroidism is prescribed levothyroxine. Which counseling point is essential for this patient?
a. Take the medication with food to avoid stomach upset.

b. It may take several weeks to notice symptom improvement.
c. Expect to lose weight rapidly after starting the medication.
d. Stop the medication immediately if you experience palpitations.

Answer: b. It may take several weeks to notice symptom improvement. Explanation: Levothyroxine works by replacing deficient thyroid hormone, and it takes time to restore normal levels. It's important to set realistic expectations for patients. The medication should be taken on an empty stomach, weight loss is gradual, and any side effects warrant discussion with the prescriber, not abrupt cessation.

102. A patient with acute decompensated heart failure has a pulmonary artery catheter in place. Which measurement most directly correlates with left ventricular preload?
a. Cardiac Output (CO)
b. Systemic Vascular Resistance (SVR)
c. Pulmonary Artery Wedge Pressure (PAWP)
d. Right Atrial Pressure (RAP)/ Central Venous Pressure (CVP)

Answer: c. Pulmonary Artery Wedge Pressure (PAWP). Explanation: The PAWP closely approximates pressure within the left atrium, which reflects the pressure at the end of diastole in the left ventricle (preload).

103. A patient in cardiogenic shock has cool extremities, low urine output, and a blood pressure of 80/50 mmHg. Their SVR is calculated at 1800 dynes*sec/cm-5. Which intervention would be most appropriate?
a. Volume expansion with crystalloids
b. Dobutamine infusion
c. Norepinephrine infusion
d. Intra-aortic balloon pump (IABP)

Answer: c. Norepinephrine infusion. Explanation: The patient is hypotensive with a very high SVR, indicating severe vasoconstriction. Norepinephrine increases blood pressure through both vasoconstriction and some cardiac inotropy. Fluids alone may be insufficient, dobutamine primarily improves contractility, and IABP is for mechanical support.

104. You're titrating a vasodilator drip for a patient with severe hypertension. Which hemodynamic change would suggest the medication is effective?
a. Increased cardiac output
b. Decreased central venous pressure (CVP)
c. Decreased systemic vascular resistance (SVR)
d. Increased pulmonary artery wedge pressure (PAWP)

Answer: c. Decreased systemic vascular resistance (SVR). Explanation: Vasodilators work by decreasing afterload, and this effect is directly measured by the SVR. Changes in CO, CVP, or PAWP may occur indirectly but aren't the primary target of vasodilators.

105. A patient with septic shock has been on multiple vasopressors, but their mean arterial pressure (MAP) remains low. Which additional hemodynamic parameter might give insight into their poor response?
a. Mixed venous oxygen saturation (ScvO2)
b. Pulmonary artery occlusion pressure (PAOP)
c. Ejection fraction (EF) on echocardiogram
d. Serum lactate level

Answer: a. Mixed venous oxygen saturation (ScvO2). Explanation: A low ScvO2 suggests inadequate oxygen delivery to tissues despite interventions. This could indicate a need to optimize cardiac output or consider blood transfusions, rather than simply escalating vasopressors further.

106. A patient with a myocardial infarction develops a new systolic murmur and hypotension. Pulmonary artery catheter readings show a significant increase in PAWP. Which complication is most likely?
a. Ventricular septal defect
b. Acute mitral regurgitation
c. Right ventricular failure
d. Cardiac tamponade

Answer: b. Acute mitral regurgitation. Explanation: Sudden onset of severe mitral regurgitation can cause a spike in PAWP due to backflow into the left atrium, with subsequent pulmonary congestion and decreased cardiac output.

107. A patient is being weaned from a milrinone infusion. Which assessment finding would be most concerning for decreased cardiac contractility?
a. Increase in heart rate
b. Decrease in blood pressure
c. New-onset atrial fibrillation
d. Widening of the QRS complex

Answer: b. Decrease in blood pressure. Explanation: Milrinone is an inotrope, meaning it directly improves contractility. A drop in blood pressure during weaning suggests insufficient cardiac force without the medication. Increased HR and arrhythmias are potential side effects but less directly tied to contractility.

108. You are interpreting cardiac output (CO) data obtained via thermodilution on a patient with a pulmonary artery catheter. Which factor could lead to a falsely low calculated CO?
a. Tricuspid regurgitation
b. Mitral stenosis
c. Hyperthermia
d. Rapid infusion of warm saline

Answer: a. Tricuspid regurgitation. Explanation: Thermodilution measures right-sided CO. Tricuspid regurgitation leaks blood back into the atrium, leading to underestimation of true output from the right ventricle.

109. A patient's ScvO2 drops from 70% to 55%. Which of the following changes could be responsible?
a. Significant blood loss
b. Improvement in pulmonary edema
c. Increased cardiac output
d. Resolution of sepsis

Answer: a. Significant blood loss. Explanation: ScvO2 reflects oxygen balance – supply vs. demand. Blood loss decreases oxygen-carrying capacity, thus lowering the ScvO2. The other options would likely improve oxygenation and thus increase the ScvO2.

110. A patient with cardiogenic shock has a cardiac index (CI) of 1.8 L/min/m2 (normal range 2.5-4). Which intervention would likely be the most beneficial?
a. Packed red blood cell transfusion
b. Aggressive diuresis
c. Dobutamine infusion
d. Nitroprusside infusion

Answer: c. Dobutamine infusion. Explanation: A low cardiac index indicates poor cardiac output. Dobutamine's inotropic effect would directly address this. Transfusions are for low oxygen-carrying capacity, diuresis could worsen hypoperfusion, and vasodilators would further drop blood pressure.

111. A patient with a PA catheter has the following readings: CVP 15 mmHg, PAWP 20 mmHg. Which condition is most consistent with these findings?
a. Hypovolemia
b. Cardiogenic shock
c. Left ventricular failure
d. Right ventricular failure

Answer: c. Left ventricular failure. Explanation: Elevated PAWP reflects back pressure from the left heart. A high CVP can be seen in both right and left failure, making it less specific. Hypovolemia would present with low filling pressures.

112. In a patient with acute decompensated heart failure, which hemodynamic parameter is most indicative of left ventricular failure?
a. Decreased central venous pressure (CVP)
b. Increased pulmonary capillary wedge pressure (PCWP)
c. Decreased systemic vascular resistance (SVR)
d. Increased cardiac output (CO)

Answer: b. Increased pulmonary capillary wedge pressure (PCWP). Explanation: PCWP is an indirect measure of left atrial pressure and is elevated in left ventricular failure, reflecting increased pressure and congestion in the pulmonary circulation due to the heart's inability to effectively pump blood.

113. A patient with septic shock is receiving aggressive fluid resuscitation. Which of the following outcomes indicates adequate fluid resuscitation has been achieved?
a. Central venous pressure (CVP) > 12 mmHg
b. Urine output > 0.5 mL/kg/hr
c. Mean arterial pressure (MAP) < 65 mmHg
d. Increased lactate levels

Answer: b. Urine output > 0.5 mL/kg/hr. Explanation: Adequate fluid resuscitation in septic shock is indicated by improved organ perfusion, with urine output > 0.5 mL/kg/hr being a key marker of renal perfusion and therefore, adequate systemic perfusion.

114. In assessing a patient for fluid responsiveness, which dynamic parameter is most useful?
a. Pulmonary artery pressure
b. Stroke volume variation (SVV)
c. Central venous pressure (CVP)
d. Mean arterial pressure (MAP)

Answer: b. Stroke volume variation (SVV). Explanation: SVV, measured during mechanical ventilation, is a dynamic parameter that helps predict fluid responsiveness. Significant variations indicate that the patient is likely to respond to fluid administration with an increase in stroke volume.

115. A patient with cardiogenic shock has a Swan-Ganz catheter in place. Which finding is most consistent with this condition?
a. Low cardiac output and low pulmonary capillary wedge pressure
b. High cardiac output and high systemic vascular resistance
c. Low cardiac output and high pulmonary capillary wedge pressure
d. High cardiac output and low central venous pressure

Answer: c. Low cardiac output and high pulmonary capillary wedge pressure. Explanation: Cardiogenic shock is characterized by inadequate cardiac output due to myocardial dysfunction, with elevated pulmonary capillary wedge pressure indicating left ventricular failure.

116. For a patient with acute respiratory distress syndrome (ARDS) and hemodynamic instability, which ventilatory strategy could potentially worsen hemodynamics?
a. Low tidal volume ventilation
b. Application of high positive end-expiratory pressure (PEEP)

c. Prone positioning
d. Use of inhaled pulmonary vasodilators

Answer: b. Application of high positive end-expiratory pressure (PEEP). Explanation: While PEEP is beneficial for oxygenation in ARDS, excessive PEEP can increase intrathoracic pressure, leading to decreased venous return and compromised cardiac output, potentially worsening hemodynamics.

117. In evaluating a patient with suspected constrictive pericarditis, which hemodynamic pattern is most suggestive of the diagnosis?
a. Equalization of diastolic pressures in all four cardiac chambers
b. Elevated left ventricular end-diastolic pressure with normal right-sided pressures
c. Marked elevation of pulmonary artery systolic pressure
d. Isolated elevation of central venous pressure

Answer: a. Equalization of diastolic pressures in all four cardiac chambers. Explanation: Constrictive pericarditis restricts diastolic filling of the heart, leading to equalization of diastolic pressures across all cardiac chambers, a hallmark of the condition.

118. A patient undergoing major surgery develops significant blood loss. Which hemodynamic change is most immediately observed?
a. Increased systemic vascular resistance (SVR)
b. Decreased central venous pressure (CVP)
c. Increased cardiac output (CO)
d. Increased left ventricular stroke work index (LVSWI)

Answer: b. Decreased central venous pressure (CVP). Explanation: Significant blood loss leads to decreased venous return and preload, resulting in an immediate drop in CVP, reflecting the reduced blood volume.

119. In managing a patient with hypovolemic shock, which of the following is the priority intervention?
a. Vasopressor administration
b. Rapid crystalloid fluid resuscitation
c. Immediate initiation of inotropic support
d. Application of noninvasive positive pressure ventilation

Answer: b. Rapid crystalloid fluid resuscitation. Explanation: The priority in hypovolemic shock is to restore intravascular volume. Rapid administration of crystalloid fluids is the initial step to increase preload and improve tissue perfusion.

120. A patient with a pulmonary artery catheter in place has the following readings: CVP 8 mmHg, PCWP 26 mmHg, cardiac output 4.2 L/min. These findings are most consistent with:

a. Right ventricular failure
b. Left ventricular failure
c. Volume overload
d. Septic shock

Answer: b. Left ventricular failure. Explanation: The elevated PCWP with a relatively normal CVP suggests left ventricular failure, as PCWP is an indirect marker of left atrial pressure and is elevated when the left ventricle is unable to effectively pump blood, leading to pulmonary congestion.

121. In a patient with traumatic brain injury, which hemodynamic goal is critical to ensure adequate cerebral perfusion?
a. Maintaining central venous pressure (CVP) > 12 mmHg
b. Ensuring mean arterial pressure (MAP) > 80 mmHg
c. Keeping pulmonary artery wedge pressure (PAWP) < 15 mmHg
d. Limiting cardiac output to reduce intracranial pressure

Answer: b. Ensuring mean arterial pressure (MAP) > 80 mmHg. Explanation: In the setting of traumatic brain injury, maintaining an adequate MAP is crucial to ensure sufficient cerebral perfusion pressure (CPP) and prevent secondary ischemic brain injury.

122. To calculate systemic vascular resistance (SVR), which of the following sets of hemodynamic data is essential?
a. Cardiac output (CO), central venous pressure (CVP), and pulmonary artery wedge pressure (PAWP)
b. Mean arterial pressure (MAP), central venous pressure (CVP), and cardiac output (CO)
c. Pulmonary artery systolic pressure (PASP) and diastolic pressure (PADP)
d. Stroke volume (SV) and heart rate (HR)

Answer: b. Mean arterial pressure (MAP), central venous pressure (CVP), and cardiac output (CO). Explanation: SVR is calculated using the formula SVR = (MAP - CVP) / CO × 80. MAP provides the average pressure driving blood through the systemic circulation, CVP represents the back pressure from the venous system, and CO is the volume of blood being pumped by the heart per minute.

123. In a patient with septic shock, you would expect the SVR to be:
a. Significantly elevated due to increased afterload
b. Decreased due to systemic vasodilation
c. Unchanged from baseline levels
d. Variable, with no predictable pattern

Answer: b. Decreased due to systemic vasodilation. Explanation: Septic shock is characterized by widespread systemic vasodilation due to the release of inflammatory mediators, leading to a decrease in SVR.

124. Which intervention is most likely to increase SVR in a patient with low afterload?
a. Intravenous fluids
b. Vasodilator therapy
c. Beta-blockers
d. Vasopressor therapy

Answer: d. Vasopressor therapy. Explanation: Vasopressors, such as norepinephrine or phenylephrine, increase SVR by causing vasoconstriction, thereby increasing afterload.

125. A patient with acute heart failure is noted to have a high SVR. Which of the following medications would be most appropriate to reduce SVR and afterload?
a. Dopamine
b. Nitroglycerin
c. Dobutamine
d. Norepinephrine

Answer: b. Nitroglycerin. Explanation: Nitroglycerin is a vasodilator that reduces SVR and afterload, making it beneficial in the management of acute heart failure where high afterload is compromising cardiac output.

126. In calculating SVR, why is it necessary to subtract central venous pressure (CVP) from mean arterial pressure (MAP)?
a. To account for the pressure gradient across the systemic circulation
b. To isolate the contribution of the right heart to afterload
c. To correct for variations in intrathoracic pressure
d. To adjust for the effects of pulmonary vascular resistance

Answer: a. To account for the pressure gradient across the systemic circulation. Explanation: SVR calculation requires subtracting CVP from MAP to determine the true pressure gradient driving blood through the systemic vascular bed, which is the force the left ventricle must overcome (afterload).

127. In a patient with high afterload, which echocardiographic finding is commonly observed?
a. Increased left ventricular ejection fraction
b. Hypokinesis of the left ventricular wall
c. Reduced left ventricular end-diastolic volume
d. Left ventricular hypertrophy

Answer: d. Left ventricular hypertrophy. Explanation: Chronic high afterload, as seen in hypertension, can lead to left ventricular hypertrophy as the heart muscle compensates for the increased resistance it must pump against.

128. How does aortic stenosis affect systemic vascular resistance (SVR)?

a. SVR decreases to compensate for the increased left ventricular afterload
b. SVR increases due to the reduced cardiac output
c. SVR remains unchanged as it is primarily determined by peripheral vessels
d. SVR initially decreases but then increases as the disease progresses

Answer: b. SVR increases due to the reduced cardiac output. Explanation: Aortic stenosis increases left ventricular afterload directly. The body may compensate by increasing SVR to maintain blood pressure in the face of reduced cardiac output.

129. In the context of cardiogenic shock, why might SVR be elevated?
a. As a compensatory mechanism to maintain systemic blood pressure
b. Due to decreased sympathetic nervous system activity
c. As a direct result of increased cardiac output
d. Due to the administration of exogenous vasodilators

Answer: a. As a compensatory mechanism to maintain systemic blood pressure. Explanation: In cardiogenic shock, SVR often increases as a compensatory mechanism via sympathetic nervous system activation to maintain systemic blood pressure despite reduced cardiac output.

130. Which parameter, when increased, indicates improved contractility but potentially increased afterload?
a. Decreased ejection fraction
b. Increased stroke volume
c. Increased left ventricular end-diastolic pressure
d. Increased systemic vascular resistance

Answer: d. Increased systemic vascular resistance. Explanation: Increased SVR reflects increased afterload, which can indicate improved contractility as the heart works harder to overcome the resistance; however, persistently high SVR can be detrimental and lead to worsening cardiac function.

131. In treating a patient with distributive shock, the goal of therapy to normalize SVR involves:
a. Fluid resuscitation to increase preload
b. Administration of inotropic agents to enhance contractility
c. Use of vasopressors to increase vascular tone
d. Application of non-invasive ventilation to improve oxygenation

Answer: c. Use of vasopressors to increase vascular tone. Explanation: In distributive shock, characterized by pathologically low SVR due to vasodilation (e.g., septic shock), the therapeutic goal includes the use of vasopressors to increase vascular tone and normalize SVR.

132. A progressive care nurse is monitoring a patient with suspected fluid overload. Which clinical finding is most indicative of increased central venous pressure (CVP)?
a. Bradycardia
b. Hypertension
c. Jugular venous distension
d. Peripheral edema

Answer: c. Jugular venous distension. Explanation: Jugular venous distension is a key clinical indicator of increased central venous pressure, reflecting fluid overload or heart failure. While peripheral edema might also suggest fluid overload, it is not as directly related to CVP as jugular venous distension. Bradycardia and hypertension can be associated with various cardiac conditions but are not specific indicators of increased CVP.

133. In evaluating preload in a patient with acute heart failure, which parameter would provide the most accurate assessment?
a. Blood urea nitrogen (BUN) levels
b. Central venous pressure (CVP)
c. Arterial blood gas (ABG) analysis
d. Serum creatinine levels

Answer: b. Central venous pressure (CVP). Explanation: CVP is a direct measure of the blood volume in the venous system and right atrium, making it a critical parameter for assessing preload, especially in patients with heart conditions such as acute heart failure. BUN and serum creatinine are indicators of renal function, and ABG analysis provides information on respiratory and metabolic status but not directly on preload.

134. A patient with septic shock is receiving fluid resuscitation. The nurse knows that the goal of managing preload in this condition is to:
a. Minimize fluid administration to avoid pulmonary edema
b. Aggressively increase fluid volume to ensure adequate perfusion
c. Balance fluid administration to optimize stroke volume
d. Prioritize vasopressors over fluid administration to maintain systemic vascular resistance

Answer: c. Balance fluid administration to optimize stroke volume. Explanation: In septic shock, managing preload involves careful fluid administration to optimize stroke volume without causing fluid overload, which can lead to pulmonary edema. Aggressive fluid administration or minimization alone might not achieve this balance, and while vasopressors are important for maintaining vascular tone, they are adjunctive to fluid resuscitation in septic shock management.

135. During an assessment, a nurse notes that a patient's central venous pressure (CVP) reading is lower than expected. Which intervention is most appropriate to increase preload and improve hemodynamic stability?
a. Administer a loop diuretic
b. Initiate vasodilator therapy
c. Increase the rate of IV fluid administration
d. Elevate the patient's legs

Answer: c. Increase the rate of IV fluid administration. Explanation: A low CVP indicates reduced preload, often requiring increased IV fluid administration to enhance venous return and cardiac output. Elevating the patient's legs can transiently increase venous return but is not as effective as fluid administration for sustained improvement. Loop diuretics and vasodilators would further decrease preload, contrary to the desired effect.

136. In a patient with cardiogenic shock, the nurse expects the central venous pressure (CVP) to be:
a. Significantly decreased due to hypovolemia
b. Elevated, reflecting fluid back-up due to left ventricular dysfunction
c. Unchanged, as cardiogenic shock does not affect preload
d. Variable, depending solely on the patient's hydration status

Answer: b. Elevated, reflecting fluid back-up due to left ventricular dysfunction. Explanation: In cardiogenic shock, left ventricular dysfunction leads to fluid back-up in the lungs and increased venous pressure, often reflected as elevated CVP. This condition is not primarily related to hypovolemia or hydration status, and preload is directly affected by the impaired cardiac function.

137. When assessing a patient for signs of increased preload, which symptom would the nurse prioritize?
a. Dry mucous membranes
b. Orthopnea
c. Decreased urine output
d. Cool extremities

Answer: b. Orthopnea. Explanation: Orthopnea, or difficulty breathing when lying flat, is a key symptom of heart failure and increased preload, as it indicates fluid accumulation in the pulmonary system. Dry mucous membranes might suggest dehydration, decreased urine output could indicate renal dysfunction, and cool extremities might be associated with peripheral vascular disease or shock, but these are not direct indicators of preload status.

138. In managing a patient with right ventricular failure, the nurse understands that monitoring CVP is crucial because:
a. It directly reflects left ventricular function
b. It indicates the efficiency of gas exchange in the lungs
c. It provides insight into the filling pressure of the right ventricle
d. It determines the need for antiarrhythmic medications

Answer: c. It provides insight into the filling pressure of the right ventricle. Explanation: In right ventricular failure, CVP is a critical parameter as it reflects the pressure in the right atrium and ventricle, indicating how well the right side of the heart is filling and functioning. CVP is not a direct measure of left ventricular function, gas exchange, or a determinant for antiarrhythmic medication use.

139. A progressive care nurse is caring for a patient with hypovolemic shock. Which of the following interventions is essential to improve the patient's preload?
a. Administering beta-blockers
b. Fluid resuscitation with isotonic solutions
c. Providing supplemental oxygen
d. Starting an insulin infusion

Answer: b. Fluid resuscitation with isotonic solutions. Explanation: In hypovolemic shock, the primary issue is inadequate circulating volume, so fluid resuscitation with isotonic solutions is essential to increase preload and restore tissue perfusion. Beta-blockers, supplemental oxygen, and insulin infusion might be part of the broader management but do not directly address the need to increase preload.

140. A patient with chronic heart failure is being monitored for preload to guide therapy. Which assessment finding would suggest effective management of preload?
a. Persistent cough and wheezing
b. Decreased jugular venous pressure
c. Increased orthopnea and paroxysmal nocturnal dyspnea
d. Weight gain and ankle swelling

Answer: b. Decreased jugular venous pressure. Explanation: Effective management of preload in heart failure aims to reduce fluid congestion; thus, decreased jugular venous pressure would indicate reduced venous return to the heart and improved fluid status. Persistent cough, wheezing, orthopnea, and paroxysmal nocturnal dyspnea are symptoms of fluid overload, and weight gain and ankle swelling suggest peripheral edema, both of which would indicate inadequate management of preload.

141. A progressive care nurse is evaluating the effectiveness of interventions aimed at optimizing preload in a patient with acute decompensated heart failure. Which parameter would be most indicative of successful preload optimization?
a. Increased heart rate
b. Decreased central venous pressure (CVP)
c. Increased systolic blood pressure
d. Decreased urine output

Answer: b. Decreased central venous pressure (CVP). Explanation: In the context of acute decompensated heart failure, successful preload optimization would lead to decreased CVP, indicating reduced fluid congestion and improved cardiac function. Increased heart rate, systolic blood pressure, or decreased urine output are not direct indicators of preload optimization and could be associated with various other clinical conditions or therapeutic interventions.

142. When interpreting data from a pulmonary artery (PA) catheter, which measurement is most directly indicative of left ventricular end-diastolic pressure (LVEDP)?
a. Central venous pressure (CVP)
b. Pulmonary artery systolic pressure (PASP)

c. Pulmonary artery diastolic pressure (PADP)
d. Pulmonary capillary wedge pressure (PCWP)

Answer: d. Pulmonary capillary wedge pressure (PCWP). Explanation: PCWP is obtained by inflating the balloon at the tip of the PA catheter, which occludes a branch of the pulmonary artery, reflecting pressures backward into the left atrium, serving as an indirect measure of LVEDP, especially useful in assessing left ventricular function and fluid status.

143. In a critically ill patient, a continuous ScvO2 of 75% suggests:
a. Adequate tissue oxygenation and perfusion
b. Impaired cardiac output and potential hypoperfusion
c. The need for immediate blood transfusion
d. Excessive oxygen delivery relative to consumption

Answer: a. Adequate tissue oxygenation and perfusion. Explanation: ScvO2, or central venous oxygen saturation, reflects the balance between oxygen delivery and consumption. A value of 75% is generally considered within normal range, suggesting adequate tissue oxygenation and perfusion.

144. A PA catheter reveals a cardiac output (CO) of 4 L/min and a cardiac index (CI) of 2.2 L/min/m² in a 70 kg patient. What does this indicate?
a. Normal cardiac function
b. High cardiac output state
c. Low cardiac output state
d. Direct measure of right ventricular function

Answer: c. Low cardiac output state. Explanation: Cardiac index (CI) is a more precise measure of cardiac function as it relates CO to body surface area. A CI of 2.2 L/min/m² is below the normal range (2.5-4.0 L/min/m²), indicating a low cardiac output state, which may signify impaired cardiac function.

145. During PA catheterization, an elevated mean pulmonary artery pressure (MPAP) is noted. This finding is most consistent with:
a. Left ventricular failure
b. Hypovolemia
c. Pulmonary embolism
d. Vasodilatory shock

Answer: c. Pulmonary embolism. Explanation: An elevated MPAP can be indicative of pulmonary hypertension, which may result from various conditions including pulmonary embolism, a blockage in one of the pulmonary arteries in the lungs, often leading to increased pulmonary vascular resistance and pressure.

146. A decrease in ScvO2 below normal levels could be caused by all of the following EXCEPT:
a. Increased oxygen consumption (e.g., due to fever or shivering)
b. Decreased cardiac output
c. Increased hemoglobin concentration
d. Impaired oxygen delivery

Answer: c. Increased hemoglobin concentration. Explanation: While increased hemoglobin concentration can improve oxygen-carrying capacity, a decrease in ScvO2 typically reflects either increased oxygen consumption, decreased cardiac output, or impaired oxygen delivery, not changes in hemoglobin concentration alone.

147. In using a PA catheter, the thermodilution method for measuring cardiac output involves:
a. Injection of a cold saline solution into the right atrium
b. Direct measurement of blood flow through the pulmonary artery
c. Use of a Doppler signal to calculate flow
d. Continuous measurement of arterial blood pressure

Answer: a. Injection of a cold saline solution into the right atrium. Explanation: The thermodilution method for measuring cardiac output with a PA catheter involves injecting a known amount of cold saline solution into the right atrium and measuring the temperature change downstream in the pulmonary artery, allowing calculation of cardiac output based on the change in temperature over time.

148. A patient with a PA catheter has a PCWP of 28 mmHg. This finding most likely indicates:
a. Right ventricular failure
b. Volume depletion
c. Left ventricular failure or fluid overload
d. Normal pulmonary artery pressure

Answer: c. Left ventricular failure or fluid overload. Explanation: An elevated PCWP (>18 mmHg) suggests elevated left atrial pressures, which can be due to left ventricular failure, mitral valve disease, or fluid overload, indicating a need for interventions to reduce preload and improve ventricular function.

149. When analyzing hemodynamic data from a PA catheter, which parameter best reflects the contractility of the heart?
a. Cardiac output (CO)
b. Systemic vascular resistance (SVR)
c. Stroke volume variation (SVV)
d. Pulmonary vascular resistance (PVR)

Answer: a. Cardiac output (CO). Explanation: While CO is influenced by preload, afterload, and heart rate, it is also a reflection of the heart's contractility, with changes in CO (in the absence of significant preload or afterload changes) suggesting changes in the heart's contractile function.

150. A PA catheter measurement shows a CVP of 15 mmHg in a patient with shortness of breath and edema. This suggests:
a. Left-sided heart failure
b. Right-sided heart failure or volume overload
c. Pulmonary arterial hypertension
d. Acute respiratory distress syndrome (ARDS)

Answer: b. Right-sided heart failure or volume overload. Explanation: An elevated CVP (>8 mmHg) can indicate right-sided heart failure or volume overload, reflecting increased pressure in the right atrium and venous system, often associated with clinical signs such as edema.

151. In a patient being monitored with ScvO2, a sudden drop in ScvO2 value would most likely indicate:
a. A sudden improvement in oxygen delivery
b. A reduction in oxygen consumption
c. A decrease in cardiac output or hemoglobin, or an increase in oxygen demand
d. An error in the ScvO2 monitoring equipment

Answer: c. A decrease in cardiac output or hemoglobin, or an increase in oxygen demand. Explanation: A sudden drop in ScvO2 typically indicates a mismatch between oxygen delivery and consumption, often due to decreased cardiac output, reduced hemoglobin levels, or increased oxygen demand, necessitating further assessment and intervention.

152. A progressive care nurse is monitoring a patient who has been started on dobutamine for low cardiac output syndrome post-cardiac surgery. Which of the following parameters is most directly indicative of improved contractility due to the medication?
a. Decreased heart rate
b. Increased urine output
c. Narrowed pulse pressure
d. Elevated central venous pressure (CVP)

Answer: b. Increased urine output. Explanation: Dobutamine is an inotropic agent that increases myocardial contractility, which can lead to improved cardiac output. Increased urine output is a clinical indicator of improved renal perfusion secondary to increased cardiac output. Decreased heart rate and narrowed pulse pressure are not direct indicators of improved contractility, and elevated CVP might indicate fluid overload, not necessarily improved contractility.

153. During the administration of inotropic therapy with milrinone in a patient with heart failure, which of the following assessments is crucial for evaluating the effectiveness of the treatment?
a. Daily weight and fluid intake/output balance
b. Capillary refill and peripheral temperature
c. Blood urea nitrogen (BUN) and creatinine levels
d. Arterial blood gas (ABG) analysis

Answer: a. Daily weight and fluid intake/output balance. Explanation: Milrinone, a phosphodiesterase inhibitor, has positive inotropic and vasodilatory effects. Monitoring daily weight and fluid balance is essential to assess the effectiveness of therapy in reducing fluid overload, a common issue in heart failure. While BUN and creatinine levels, capillary refill, and ABG analysis provide valuable information, they do not directly assess the effectiveness of inotropic therapy on cardiac output and fluid status.

154. In evaluating a patient's response to inotropic support, which echocardiographic finding would most directly indicate improved left ventricular contractility?
a. Increased ejection fraction
b. Decreased left atrial size
c. Reduced mitral valve regurgitation
d. Diminished aortic valve insufficiency

Answer: a. Increased ejection fraction. Explanation: Ejection fraction (EF) is a direct measurement of ventricular contractility and cardiac performance. An increase in EF following inotropic support indicates improved left ventricular contractility. While decreased left atrial size, reduced mitral valve regurgitation, and diminished aortic valve insufficiency may occur secondary to improved cardiac function, they are not direct measures of contractility.

155. When assessing a patient for potential inotropic support, which laboratory value provides critical information regarding the patient's baseline myocardial function?
a. Serum electrolytes
b. Liver function tests
c. Brain Natriuretic Peptide (BNP)
d. Complete blood count (CBC)

Answer: c. Brain Natriuretic Peptide (BNP). Explanation: BNP is released in response to ventricular volume expansion and pressure overload, which are often present in heart failure. Elevated levels of BNP serve as a biomarker for cardiac dysfunction, providing crucial baseline information before initiating inotropic support. Serum electrolytes, liver function tests, and CBC are important but do not directly reflect myocardial function.

156. A patient on inotropic support with digoxin presents with new-onset visual disturbances, including seeing yellow halos around lights. Which of the following actions is most appropriate?
a. Increase the dose of digoxin to achieve therapeutic levels
b. Evaluate serum digoxin levels and electrolytes, particularly potassium
c. Administer a diuretic to reduce fluid overload
d. Perform a carotid massage to decrease heart rate

Answer: b. Evaluate serum digoxin levels and electrolytes, particularly potassium. Explanation: Visual disturbances, such as seeing yellow halos, are signs of digoxin toxicity. It's crucial to evaluate serum digoxin levels and electrolytes, as hypokalemia can exacerbate toxicity. Increasing the digoxin dose would likely worsen toxicity, diuretics may alter electrolyte balance further, and carotid massage is not indicated in this scenario.

157. For a patient receiving inotropic therapy with epinephrine due to cardiogenic shock, which vital sign change requires immediate intervention?
a. Heart rate increase from 80 to 100 bpm
b. Blood pressure increase from 90/60 mmHg to 110/70 mmHg
c. Respiratory rate increase from 18 to 22 breaths per minute
d. Temperature increase from 98.6°F to 99.2°F

Answer: a. Heart rate increase from 80 to 100 bpm. Explanation: While epinephrine increases contractility and cardiac output, it can also significantly increase heart rate. A rapid increase in heart rate can exacerbate myocardial oxygen demand and potentially worsen the patient's condition. The other vital sign changes are relatively benign and expected in the context of recovery from cardiogenic shock.

158. In a patient with dilated cardiomyopathy receiving dopamine for low cardiac output, which hemodynamic parameter best indicates a positive response to the therapy?
a. Decrease in systemic vascular resistance (SVR)
b. Increase in pulmonary capillary wedge pressure (PCWP)
c. Increase in stroke volume (SV)
d. Decrease in heart rate (HR)

Answer: c. Increase in stroke volume (SV). Explanation: In patients with dilated cardiomyopathy, an increase in stroke volume following dopamine administration indicates improved cardiac contractility and output, which is the therapeutic goal of inotropic support. A decrease in SVR may also be observed due to dopamine's vasodilatory effects at low doses, but an increase in SV is a more direct indicator of improved myocardial performance.

159. Assessing a patient on levosimendan for acute decompensated heart failure, which clinical sign would suggest a favorable therapeutic response?
a. Reduction in jugular venous distension
b. Prolongation of QT interval on ECG
c. Increase in peripheral edema
d. Development of sinus tachycardia

Answer: a. Reduction in jugular venous distension. Explanation: Levosimendan enhances myocardial contractility without significantly increasing myocardial oxygen demand. A reduction in jugular venous distension indicates decreased central venous pressure and improved cardiac function. Prolongation of QT interval, increased peripheral edema, and sinus tachycardia are potential adverse effects or signs of worsening heart failure, not therapeutic responses.

160. When initiating inotropic support for a patient with septic shock and myocardial depression, which parameter is most critical for guiding therapy titration?

a. Mean arterial pressure (MAP)
b. Central venous oxygen saturation (ScvO2)
c. Lactate levels
d. Urine output

Answer: b. Central venous oxygen saturation (ScvO2). Explanation: In septic shock with myocardial depression, ScvO2 is a key parameter for assessing tissue oxygenation and guiding the titration of inotropic support. While maintaining adequate MAP is important, ScvO2 provides direct insight into the balance between oxygen delivery and consumption, crucial for optimizing cardiac function and tissue perfusion. Lactate levels and urine output are important but secondary to the immediate need to stabilize hemodynamics and oxygen delivery.

161. Cardiac output (CO) is calculated by multiplying which two parameters?
a. Heart rate (HR) and systemic vascular resistance (SVR)
b. Heart rate (HR) and stroke volume (SV)
c. Stroke volume (SV) and central venous pressure (CVP)
d. Central venous pressure (CVP) and systemic vascular resistance (SVR)

Answer: b. Heart rate (HR) and stroke volume (SV). Explanation: Cardiac output is the volume of blood the heart pumps per minute and is calculated by multiplying the heart rate (number of heartbeats per minute) by the stroke volume (the amount of blood pumped by the left ventricle with each heartbeat).

162. Which determinant of cardiac output is primarily affected by myocardial contractility?
a. Preload
b. Afterload
c. Stroke volume
d. Heart rate

Answer: c. Stroke volume. Explanation: Stroke volume is influenced by myocardial contractility (the force of cardiac muscle contraction), preload (the volume of blood in the ventricles at the end of diastole), and afterload (the resistance the left ventricle must overcome to circulate blood). Of these, myocardial contractility has a direct impact on stroke volume.

163. A patient's cardiac output is noted to be low. Which intervention would most directly improve cardiac output by increasing stroke volume?
a. Administering a beta-blocker
b. Fluid resuscitation
c. Increasing the rate of a pacemaker
d. Administering a vasodilator

Answer: b. Fluid resuscitation. Explanation: Fluid resuscitation increases preload, which can enhance stroke volume and thus cardiac output according to Starling's law, up to an optimal point of myocardial fiber stretch.

164. In a patient with heart failure, which medication would be most beneficial to improve cardiac output by decreasing afterload?
a. Digoxin
b. Furosemide
c. Enalapril
d. Metoprolol

Answer: c. Enalapril. Explanation: Enalapril, an ACE inhibitor, reduces afterload by causing vasodilation, which decreases the resistance against which the heart must pump, thereby potentially improving cardiac output.

165. For a patient with a normal heart rate but decreased cardiac output, which of the following would be the most appropriate initial assessment?
a. Evaluation of systemic vascular resistance
b. Measurement of heart rate variability
c. Assessment of stroke volume and preload
d. Monitoring of diastolic blood pressure

Answer: c. Assessment of stroke volume and preload. Explanation: In the setting of a normal heart rate, a decrease in cardiac output is likely due to a reduction in stroke volume, which could be related to issues with preload, afterload, or contractility. Assessing stroke volume and preload can provide insights into the underlying cause.

166. A patient with cardiogenic shock is receiving inotropic support. The primary goal of this therapy is to:
a. Increase heart rate
b. Decrease preload
c. Improve myocardial contractility
d. Reduce afterload

Answer: c. Improve myocardial contractility. Explanation: Inotropic agents are used to enhance myocardial contractility, thereby increasing stroke volume and cardiac output, which is crucial in the management of cardiogenic shock.

167. In the context of hemodynamic monitoring, how would an increase in afterload affect cardiac output, assuming other factors remain constant?
a. Increase cardiac output by increasing stroke volume
b. Decrease cardiac output due to increased myocardial workload
c. Have no effect on cardiac output
d. Increase cardiac output by increasing heart rate

Answer: b. Decrease cardiac output due to increased myocardial workload. Explanation: An increase in afterload increases the resistance the heart must work against to eject blood, which can decrease stroke volume and thus cardiac output if the heart cannot compensate.

168. When considering interventions to optimize cardiac output, which strategy is least likely to be effective in isolation for a patient with hypovolemic shock?
a. Aggressive fluid resuscitation
b. Administering high-dose vasopressors
c. Using inotropic agents to improve contractility
d. Applying non-invasive ventilation to reduce preload

Answer: b. Administering high-dose vasopressors. Explanation: In hypovolemic shock, the primary issue is insufficient circulating volume. While vasopressors can improve vascular tone and organ perfusion pressure, they do not address the fundamental problem of volume deficit and may not be effective in isolation without adequate fluid resuscitation.

169. For a patient undergoing major surgery, which parameter should be closely monitored to assess for potential decreases in cardiac output?
a. Arterial blood gases
b. Central venous pressure (CVP)
c. Pulmonary artery wedge pressure (PAWP)
d. Urine output

Answer: d. Urine output. Explanation: Urine output is a practical, non-invasive indicator of organ perfusion and can reflect changes in cardiac output. A decrease in urine output may indicate reduced renal perfusion due to decreased cardiac output.

170. In a patient with acute pulmonary edema, the immediate use of which medication would most likely improve cardiac output by reducing preload?
a. Dobutamine
b. Amiodarone
c. Nitroglycerin
d. Dopamine

Answer: c. Nitroglycerin. Explanation: Nitroglycerin is a venodilator that can reduce preload by decreasing venous return to the heart, which can help reduce pulmonary congestion and improve cardiac output in the setting of acute pulmonary edema.

171. A patient with a history of heart failure presents with palpitations. The ECG shows a narrow QRS complex tachycardia with a heart rate of 160 bpm and no visible P waves. What is the most likely diagnosis?
a. Atrial fibrillation
b. Atrial flutter
c. Supraventricular tachycardia (SVT)

d. Ventricular tachycardia

Answer: c. Supraventricular tachycardia (SVT). Explanation: SVT is characterized by a narrow QRS complex and a very rapid heart rate, often without visible P waves due to the rapid rate. Atrial fibrillation would show an irregularly irregular rhythm, atrial flutter would typically show flutter waves, and ventricular tachycardia would have a wide QRS complex.

172. During a 12-lead ECG interpretation, you notice a sawtooth pattern in the inferior leads. The patient's heart rate is 250 bpm. What arrhythmia does this pattern suggest?
a. Ventricular fibrillation
b. Atrial flutter
c. First-degree AV block
d. Multifocal atrial tachycardia

Answer: b. Atrial flutter. Explanation: The sawtooth pattern, known as "flutter waves," is characteristic of atrial flutter, especially noticeable in the inferior leads (II, III, aVF) at a rapid rate, typically around 250-350 bpm.

173. A 55-year-old man with a history of ischemic heart disease presents with a wide QRS tachycardia at a rate of 120 bpm. The QRS duration is 140 ms. What is the most appropriate initial management?
a. Immediate synchronized cardioversion
b. Administration of IV adenosine
c. Application of a transcutaneous pacemaker
d. Intravenous amiodarone infusion

Answer: d. Intravenous amiodarone infusion. Explanation: Wide QRS tachycardia, especially in the context of ischemic heart disease, is likely ventricular tachycardia. Amiodarone is effective for both ventricular and supraventricular arrhythmias and is safe to use before confirming the exact type of arrhythmia. Adenosine is typically used for narrow complex tachycardias, and immediate cardioversion is reserved for hemodynamically unstable patients.

174. A patient is diagnosed with atrial fibrillation with a rapid ventricular response. Which of the following medications is most effective for rate control in this patient?
a. Digoxin
b. Ibutilide
c. Diltiazem
d. Flecainide

Answer: c. Diltiazem. Explanation: Diltiazem, a calcium channel blocker, is effective for rate control in atrial fibrillation with a rapid ventricular response by slowing AV nodal conduction. Digoxin is also used for rate control but is less effective in acute settings. Ibutilide is a Class III antiarrhythmic used for chemical cardioversion, and flecainide is a Class IC antiarrhythmic used in patients without structural heart disease.

175. In a patient with symptomatic bradycardia due to sinus node dysfunction, which of the following is the most appropriate next step?
a. Administration of atropine
b. Implantation of a permanent pacemaker
c. Observation and serial ECGs
d. IV beta-blocker therapy

Answer: b. Implantation of a permanent pacemaker. Explanation: Symptomatic bradycardia, especially due to sinus node dysfunction, often requires a permanent pacemaker for definitive management. Atropine can be used temporarily in acute settings, but it's not a long-term solution.

176. A patient with no known heart disease comes to the ER complaining of sudden onset palpitations. The ECG shows a regular narrow complex tachycardia with a heart rate of 180 bpm. Vagal maneuvers were unsuccessful. What is the next best step?
a. Oral beta-blocker
b. IV adenosine
c. IV amiodarone
d. Direct current cardioversion

Answer: b. IV adenosine. Explanation: In cases of stable, narrow complex tachycardia unresponsive to vagal maneuvers, IV adenosine is the next best step as it can help diagnose and potentially terminate reentrant supraventricular tachycardias.

177. A patient on telemetry suddenly develops a wide complex tachycardia at 150 bpm. The patient is hemodynamically stable but reports feeling lightheaded. What is the first-line treatment?
a. IV lidocaine
b. Synchronized cardioversion
c. IV procainamide
d. Observation

Answer: c. IV procainamide. Explanation: For hemodynamically stable patients with wide complex tachycardia, IV procainamide is a suitable first-line treatment. Lidocaine is an alternative but less preferred. Synchronized cardioversion is reserved for unstable patients.

178. An ECG from a stable patient shows a regular rhythm with a rate of 70 bpm, a normal QRS duration, but with a PR interval of 220 ms. What does this indicate?
a. Normal sinus rhythm
b. First-degree AV block
c. Second-degree AV block, Mobitz type I
d. Third-degree AV block

Answer: b. First-degree AV block. Explanation: A PR interval longer than 200 ms indicates a first-degree AV block, which is characterized by delayed conduction through the AV node but with each atrial impulse eventually conducted to the ventricles.

179. A patient's ECG shows irregularly irregular rhythm with absent P waves and varying QRS complexes. What is the most likely diagnosis?
a. Atrial fibrillation
b. Ventricular fibrillation
c. Atrial flutter
d. Premature ventricular contractions

Answer: a. Atrial fibrillation. Explanation: An irregularly irregular rhythm without distinct P waves is indicative of atrial fibrillation, characterized by chaotic atrial activity leading to irregular ventricular response.

180. A 68-year-old patient with chronic atrial fibrillation is scheduled for elective surgery. Which of the following strategies is most appropriate for stroke prevention in this patient?
a. Discontinue anticoagulation therapy one week before surgery
b. Continue warfarin with INR in the therapeutic range
c. Bridging with low molecular weight heparin
d. No anticoagulation is needed due to the elective nature of the surgery

Answer: c. Bridging with low molecular weight heparin. Explanation: For patients at high risk of thromboembolism, such as those with atrial fibrillation, bridging anticoagulation with low molecular weight heparin is recommended when warfarin is held before surgery. This strategy minimizes the time the patient is not anticoagulated, reducing the risk of stroke.

181. In a patient with newly diagnosed atrial fibrillation (AF), which of the following is the most appropriate initial step to prevent thromboembolic events?
a. Immediate cardioversion
b. Administration of an intravenous beta-blocker
c. Initiation of anticoagulation therapy
d. Implantation of a pacemaker

Answer: c. Initiation of anticoagulation therapy. Explanation: For patients with AF, particularly those at higher risk for stroke based on risk factors (e.g., CHA2DS2-VASc score), initiation of anticoagulation therapy is crucial to reduce the risk of thromboembolic events, as AF increases the risk of stroke due to the formation of clots in the poorly contracting atria.

182. When considering rate control in a patient with AF, which of the following medications is preferred to decrease ventricular response?
a. Digoxin

b. Amiodarone
c. Diltiazem
d. Furosemide

Answer: c. Diltiazem. Explanation: Diltiazem, a calcium channel blocker, is effective for rate control in AF by slowing down the atrioventricular (AV) node conduction, thereby reducing the ventricular response rate, especially in patients without significant heart failure.

183. A 70-year-old patient with AF and a history of hypertension and diabetes presents for evaluation. Which scoring system is most appropriate to assess stroke risk in this patient?
a. TIMI score
b. CHA2DS2-VASc score
c. GRACE score
d. HAS-BLED score

Answer: b. CHA2DS2-VASc score. Explanation: The CHA2DS2-VASc score is specifically designed to assess stroke risk in patients with AF, taking into account factors such as age, sex, and comorbid conditions like hypertension and diabetes.

184. In a patient with persistent AF, which intervention is most likely to restore sinus rhythm?
a. Long-term beta-blocker therapy
b. Electrical cardioversion
c. High-dose diuretic therapy
d. Lifestyle modifications alone

Answer: b. Electrical cardioversion. Explanation: Electrical cardioversion is a procedure used to restore sinus rhythm in patients with persistent AF, particularly when rate control and anticoagulation have been addressed and in the absence of contraindications to restoring sinus rhythm.

185. For a patient with AF and rapid ventricular rate not controlled by medication, which procedure is indicated to maintain rate control?
a. Percutaneous coronary intervention (PCI)
b. AV node ablation and pacemaker insertion
c. Left atrial appendage closure
d. Pulmonary vein isolation

Answer: b. AV node ablation and pacemaker insertion. Explanation: AV node ablation, followed by pacemaker insertion, is an option for patients with AF when the ventricular rate cannot be controlled with medication alone, effectively preventing rapid impulses from reaching the ventricles.

186. In managing a patient with AF and congestive heart failure, which medication is most appropriate to improve cardiac function and control heart rate?
a. Digoxin
b. Ibuprofen
c. Atorvastatin
d. Aspirin

Answer: a. Digoxin. Explanation: Digoxin is beneficial in patients with AF and congestive heart failure as it can help control the heart rate and has a positive inotropic effect, thereby improving cardiac function.

187. Which anticoagulant is preferred for a patient with AF and chronic kidney disease (CKD)?
a. Warfarin with careful INR monitoring
b. Unfractionated heparin
c. High-dose aspirin
d. Direct oral anticoagulants without dose adjustment

Answer: a. Warfarin with careful INR monitoring. Explanation: In patients with AF and CKD, warfarin is often preferred, with careful INR monitoring due to the risk of altered pharmacokinetics and pharmacodynamics of direct oral anticoagulants in CKD.

188. For a patient with AF and a high risk of stroke, which of the following non-pharmacological interventions could be considered to reduce stroke risk?
a. Daily aspirin therapy
b. Regular aerobic exercise
c. Left atrial appendage closure device implantation
d. Increased dietary potassium intake

Answer: c. Left atrial appendage closure device implantation. Explanation: For patients with AF at high risk of stroke who are unsuitable for long-term anticoagulation, left atrial appendage closure device implantation can be considered to reduce stroke risk by preventing clot formation in the left atrial appendage.

189. In evaluating a patient with AF, which imaging modality is most useful for assessing left atrial size and function?
a. Chest X-ray
b. Transthoracic echocardiogram (TTE)
c. Computed tomography (CT) scan of the chest
d. Magnetic resonance imaging (MRI) of the brain

Answer: b. Transthoracic echocardiogram (TTE). Explanation: TTE is the imaging modality of choice for evaluating left atrial size and function in patients with AF, as it provides detailed images of the heart's structure and function, including the atria.

190. When considering rhythm control in a patient with newly diagnosed AF, which factor is most important in deciding between pharmacological and non-pharmacological strategies?
a. Patient age
b. Duration of AF
c. Presence of valvular disease
d. Patient preference and lifestyle

Answer: b. Duration of AF. Explanation: The duration of AF is a critical factor in deciding between rhythm control strategies; early in the course of AF, pharmacological rhythm control may be effective, but in longer-standing AF, non-pharmacological strategies such as ablation may be more appropriate.

191. A 32-year-old patient presents with a sudden onset of palpitations. The ECG demonstrates a regular, narrow QRS complex tachycardia with a heart rate of 180 bpm. No P waves are visible before the QRS complexes. Which of the following is the most likely diagnosis?
a. Atrial fibrillation
b. Atrioventricular nodal reentrant tachycardia (AVNRT)
c. Atrial flutter
d. Ventricular tachycardia

Answer: b. Atrioventricular nodal reentrant tachycardia (AVNRT). Explanation: AVNRT is characterized by sudden onset and termination of regular, narrow QRS complex tachycardia, often without visible P waves or with P waves that appear just after the QRS complex due to retrograde atrial activation.

192. During an episode of supraventricular tachycardia (SVT), a patient undergoes an electrophysiological study. The study reveals a reentrant circuit involving an accessory pathway. Which of the following conditions is most consistent with this finding?
a. AVNRT
b. Atrioventricular reciprocating tachycardia (AVRT)
c. Sinus tachycardia
d. Junctional tachycardia

Answer: b. Atrioventricular reciprocating tachycardia (AVRT). Explanation: AVRT involves a reentrant circuit that includes an accessory pathway outside the AV node, commonly seen in conditions like Wolff-Parkinson-White syndrome.

193. A patient with known Wolff-Parkinson-White (WPW) syndrome presents with palpitations. The ECG shows a wide complex tachycardia with a pre-excited atrial fibrillation. Which of the following is the most appropriate initial management?
a. IV adenosine
b. IV verapamil
c. Direct current cardioversion
d. Oral beta-blockers

Answer: c. Direct current cardioversion. Explanation: In cases of pre-excited atrial fibrillation in WPW syndrome with hemodynamic instability, immediate direct current cardioversion is recommended. Agents like adenosine and verapamil are contraindicated as they may facilitate anterograde conduction through the accessory pathway.

194. In a patient diagnosed with AVNRT, which of the following maneuvers is most likely to terminate the tachycardia?
a. Valsalva maneuver
b. Rapid squatting
c. Hyperventilation
d. Arm immersion in cold water

Answer: a. Valsalva maneuver. Explanation: The Valsalva maneuver increases intrathoracic pressure and stimulates the vagus nerve, which can interrupt the reentrant circuit in AVNRT, terminating the tachycardia.

195. A patient with SVT is responsive to adenosine. Which of the following mechanisms best explains adenosine's effectiveness in terminating the tachycardia?
a. Calcium channel blockade
b. Potassium channel activation
c. Sodium channel inhibition
d. AV nodal temporary block

Answer: d. AV nodal temporary block. Explanation: Adenosine works by temporarily blocking AV nodal conduction, interrupting reentrant circuits involving the AV node, such as in AVNRT, thereby terminating the tachycardia.

196. During an SVT episode, the ECG shows a short RP interval followed by a delta wave in the QRS complex. Which of the following is the most likely diagnosis?
a. AVNRT
b. Orthodromic AVRT
c. Antidromic AVRT
d. Sinus tachycardia with first-degree AV block

Answer: b. Orthodromic AVRT. Explanation: Orthodromic AVRT involves antegrade conduction through the AV node and retrograde conduction through an accessory pathway, often presenting with a short RP interval but without a delta wave; the delta wave description might be misleading here. This scenario typically occurs in the setting of WPW syndrome during an SVT episode.

197. A patient undergoing electrophysiological testing for SVT is found to have dual AV nodal pathways. Which type of SVT is most directly associated with this finding?
a. AVNRT

b. AVRT
c. Sinus node reentry tachycardia
d. Focal atrial tachycardia

Answer: a. AVNRT. Explanation: Dual AV nodal pathways are a hallmark of AVNRT, where the reentrant circuit involves fast and slow pathways within the AV node.

198. In a patient with SVT, which of the following ECG findings suggests the presence of an accessory pathway?
a. Prolonged QT interval
b. Slurred upstroke in the QRS complex (delta wave)
c. Inverted P waves in leads II, III, and aVF
d. PR interval greater than 200 ms

Answer: b. Slurred upstroke in the QRS complex (delta wave). Explanation: A delta wave, which represents pre-excitation of the ventricles through an accessory pathway, is a key ECG finding suggestive of conditions like WPW syndrome, associated with AVRT.

199. A healthcare provider is attempting to differentiate between AVNRT and AVRT in a patient with SVT. Which of the following characteristics is more indicative of AVRT?
a. Inducibility with atrial pacing
b. Presence of a delta wave during sinus rhythm
c. Termination with carotid sinus massage
d. Initiation with premature atrial contractions

Answer: b. Presence of a delta wave during sinus rhythm. Explanation: The presence of a delta wave during sinus rhythm suggests pre-excitation of the ventricles through an accessory pathway, which is characteristic of AVRT, especially in the context of WPW syndrome.

200. A patient with recurrent SVT episodes is scheduled for radiofrequency catheter ablation. The target of the ablation is likely to be:
a. The sinus node
b. An accessory pathway
c. The AV node
d. The bundle of His

Answer: b. An accessory pathway. Explanation: Radiofrequency catheter ablation for SVT, especially in cases of AVRT associated with WPW syndrome, often targets the accessory pathway to interrupt the reentrant circuit and prevent recurrence.

201. In the event of ventricular fibrillation (VF), which immediate action is recommended according to the Advanced Cardiac Life Support (ACLS) guidelines?
a. Administer high-dose amiodarone IV
b. Perform synchronized cardioversion
c. Initiate high-quality cardiopulmonary resuscitation (CPR) and defibrillation
d. Provide immediate IV bolus of normal saline

Answer: c. Initiate high-quality cardiopulmonary resuscitation (CPR) and defibrillation. Explanation: The initial management of VF according to ACLS guidelines involves immediate initiation of high-quality CPR, with rapid defibrillation being a critical component, as early defibrillation is the most important factor in survival from VF.

202. Which of the following is a common cause of ventricular fibrillation in the acute setting?
a. Hypothyroidism
b. Digitalis toxicity
c. Acute myocardial infarction
d. Chronic atrial fibrillation

Answer: c. Acute myocardial infarction. Explanation: Acute myocardial infarction is a common cause of ventricular fibrillation due to ischemia-induced electrical instability in the ventricular myocardium, making it prone to arrhythmias.

203. After successful defibrillation of VF, which medication is most appropriate for preventing recurrence?
a. Intravenous diltiazem
b. Oral warfarin
c. Intravenous amiodarone
d. Subcutaneous insulin

Answer: c. Intravenous amiodarone. Explanation: Amiodarone is often used after successful defibrillation for VF to prevent recurrence, as it stabilizes the cardiac membrane and has antiarrhythmic properties that are effective in treating and preventing ventricular arrhythmias.

204. In a patient with VF, which ECG characteristic is most indicative of the arrhythmia?
a. Regular narrow complexes
b. Sawtooth flutter waves
c. Irregularly irregular rhythm
d. Chaotic and irregular baseline without discernible QRS complexes

Answer: d. Chaotic and irregular baseline without discernible QRS complexes. Explanation: VF is characterized on the ECG by a chaotic and irregular electrical activity, with a lack of identifiable QRS complexes, P waves, or T waves, reflecting the disorganized electrical activity in the ventricles.

205. For a patient with known coronary artery disease, which intervention has been shown to reduce the risk of sudden cardiac death and VF?
a. Routine administration of oral calcium channel blockers
b. Implantation of a cardioverter-defibrillator (ICD)
c. Lifetime administration of intravenous heparin
d. Daily therapeutic phlebotomy

Answer: b. Implantation of a cardioverter-defibrillator (ICD). Explanation: In patients at high risk for sudden cardiac death, such as those with significant coronary artery disease, implantation of an ICD has been shown to reduce the risk of sudden death by providing immediate therapy for life-threatening arrhythmias like VF.

206. In the setting of VF, which factor most significantly influences the likelihood of successful defibrillation?
a. Duration of VF before defibrillation attempt
b. Ambient temperature at the time of defibrillation
c. The patient's age
d. The presence of a witnessed collapse

Answer: a. Duration of VF before defibrillation attempt. Explanation: The likelihood of successful defibrillation decreases with the duration of VF; early defibrillation, ideally within the first few minutes after the onset of VF, significantly increases the chances of successful resuscitation.

207. Which electrolyte disturbance is most commonly associated with the development of VF?
a. Hypercalcemia
b. Hypokalemia
c. Hyperphosphatemia
d. Hypermagnesemia

Answer: b. Hypokalemia. Explanation: Hypokalemia can lead to various cardiac arrhythmias, including VF, by altering the electrical stability of cardiac cells, making the myocardium more susceptible to arrhythmias.

208. In a patient resuscitated from VF, which therapeutic strategy is beneficial in improving neurological outcomes?
a. Immediate induction of hyperthermia
b. Therapeutic hypothermia or targeted temperature management
c. High-dose steroid administration
d. Rapid infusion of glucose-containing solutions

Answer: b. Therapeutic hypothermia or targeted temperature management. Explanation: Therapeutic hypothermia or targeted temperature management has been shown to improve neurological outcomes in comatose survivors of cardiac arrest, including those resuscitated from VF, by reducing metabolic demand and the effects of reperfusion injury.

209. During CPR for VF, which adjunct may be considered to optimize perfusion when manual compressions are not effective?
a. Intra-aortic balloon pump (IABP)
b. Mechanical CPR device
c. Left ventricular assist device (LVAD)
d. Percutaneous coronary intervention (PCI)

Answer: b. Mechanical CPR device. Explanation: When high-quality manual chest compressions are challenging or ineffective, a mechanical CPR device can provide consistent and effective compressions, potentially optimizing perfusion during resuscitation efforts for VF.

210. In the post-resuscitation care of a patient who experienced VF, which assessment is crucial for identifying potential reversible causes?
a. Comprehensive metabolic panel
b. 12-lead electrocardiogram (ECG) and cardiac enzymes
c. Full-body computed tomography (CT) scan
d. Immediate lumbar puncture

Answer: b. 12-lead electrocardiogram (ECG) and cardiac enzymes. Explanation: A 12-lead ECG and cardiac enzymes are crucial in the post-resuscitation period to assess for acute myocardial infarction or ischemia, which are common reversible causes of VF, guiding further management and interventions.

211. A 62-year-old patient with a history of coronary artery disease presents with palpitations. The ECG shows a wide QRS complex at a rate of 160 bpm with a regular rhythm. The patient is alert and oriented but reports mild chest discomfort. Which of the following is the most appropriate initial management?
a. Immediate synchronized cardioversion
b. High-flow oxygen and IV amiodarone
c. Observation and telemetry monitoring
d. Vagal maneuvers

Answer: b. High-flow oxygen and IV amiodarone. Explanation: In a hemodynamically stable patient with ventricular tachycardia and mild symptoms, the administration of IV amiodarone along with high-flow oxygen is appropriate to attempt chemical cardioversion and stabilization. Synchronized cardioversion is reserved for unstable patients, while observation and vagal maneuvers are not appropriate for ventricular tachycardia.

212. In the ER, a patient with ventricular tachycardia becomes hypotensive, diaphoretic, and increasingly lethargic. The next step in management should be:
a. Administration of IV lidocaine
b. Immediate synchronized cardioversion
c. Increase the dose of IV amiodarone
d. Initiation of transcutaneous pacing

Answer: b. Immediate synchronized cardioversion. Explanation: A patient with ventricular tachycardia who becomes hemodynamically unstable (evidenced by hypotension, diaphoresis, altered mental status) requires immediate synchronized cardioversion to restore a stable rhythm and improve hemodynamics.

213. A patient diagnosed with ventricular tachycardia has a blood pressure of 110/70 mmHg, heart rate of 150 bpm, and is experiencing slight shortness of breath. What does this scenario describe?
a. Stable ventricular tachycardia
b. Unstable ventricular tachycardia
c. Ventricular fibrillation
d. Supraventricular tachycardia with aberrancy

Answer: a. Stable ventricular tachycardia. Explanation: Stable ventricular tachycardia is characterized by the presence of a wide QRS complex tachycardia with maintained blood pressure and mild to no symptoms, allowing for time to attempt medical management before considering more invasive interventions.

214. A patient with stable ventricular tachycardia is refractory to IV amiodarone. Which of the following is the most appropriate next step?
a. Oral beta-blockers
b. Electrical cardioversion
c. IV magnesium sulfate
d. Catheter ablation

Answer: b. Electrical cardioversion. Explanation: If a patient with ventricular tachycardia is refractory to initial medical therapy like amiodarone and remains stable, electrical cardioversion may be considered to convert the rhythm, especially if the VT is causing discomfort or any hemodynamic compromise.

215. During a code blue for ventricular tachycardia, what is the initial dose of epinephrine if the patient is pulseless?
a. 1 mg IV push
b. 0.5 mg IV push
c. 2 mg IV push
d. 5 mg IV push

Answer: a. 1 mg IV push. Explanation: In the Advanced Cardiac Life Support (ACLS) protocol for pulseless ventricular tachycardia, the initial recommended dose of epinephrine is 1 mg IV push, repeated every 3-5 minutes.

216. A patient with ventricular tachycardia has a QT interval of 520 ms on the ECG. Which medication should be avoided?
a. Amiodarone
b. Sotalol

c. Lidocaine
d. Procainamide

Answer: b. Sotalol. Explanation: Sotalol, a Class III antiarrhythmic, can prolong the QT interval and should be avoided in patients with already prolonged QT intervals to prevent the risk of torsades de pointes.

217. A patient with a history of ventricular tachycardia is on chronic amiodarone therapy. What is an important long-term side effect to monitor for in this patient?
a. Hepatotoxicity
b. Hyperkalemia
c. Hypothyroidism
d. Leukopenia

Answer: c. Hypothyroidism. Explanation: Amiodarone has several long-term side effects, including thyroid dysfunction (both hypo- and hyperthyroidism), making regular thyroid function tests important in patients on chronic therapy.

218. In a patient with ventricular tachycardia, which of the following findings on echocardiogram would suggest a structural cause for the arrhythmia?
a. Left ventricular ejection fraction of 55%
b. Mild mitral regurgitation
c. Left ventricular hypertrophy
d. Dilated right atrium

Answer: c. Left ventricular hypertrophy. Explanation: Structural heart changes such as left ventricular hypertrophy can predispose patients to ventricular arrhythmias, including ventricular tachycardia, by creating a substrate for reentrant circuits or increased automaticity.

219. A patient with ventricular tachycardia and a history of myocardial infarction is scheduled for an electrophysiology study (EPS). What is the primary purpose of this study?
a. To assess the need for anticoagulation
b. To evaluate the risk of future heart failure
c. To identify the origin of the arrhythmia for possible ablation
d. To determine the need for coronary artery bypass grafting

Answer: c. To identify the origin of the arrhythmia for possible ablation. Explanation: An EPS in the context of ventricular tachycardia, especially post-myocardial infarction, is primarily performed to map the arrhythmia's origin and assess the feasibility of catheter ablation as a treatment to prevent recurrence.

220. A patient presents with ventricular tachycardia and an implanted cardioverter-defibrillator (ICD) that has fired multiple times in the last 24 hours. What is the most appropriate management for this patient?

a. Immediate device removal
b. Beta-blocker therapy adjustment
c. Sedation and observation
d. Hospital admission for monitoring and potential ICD reprogramming

Answer: d. Hospital admission for monitoring and potential ICD reprogramming. Explanation: Frequent ICD firings may indicate inadequate control of the underlying arrhythmia or device malfunction. Hospital admission allows for continuous monitoring, assessment of the arrhythmia, and potential reprogramming of the device to better manage the patient's condition.

221. A patient presents with a regular rhythm, heart rate of 75 bpm, and a prolonged PR interval on ECG. Each QRS complex is preceded by a P wave. Which type of heart block does this describe?
a. First-degree AV block
b. Second-degree Mobitz type I (Wenckebach) AV block
c. Second-degree Mobitz type II AV block
d. Third-degree (complete) AV block

Answer: a. First-degree AV block. Explanation: In first-degree AV block, there is a delay in the conduction between the atria and ventricles, evidenced by a prolonged PR interval (>0.20 seconds) on the ECG, but each P wave is followed by a QRS complex, indicating that all atrial impulses are conducted to the ventricles.

222. A patient's ECG shows progressively lengthening PR intervals until a QRS complex is dropped. What is the most likely diagnosis?
a. First-degree AV block
b. Second-degree Mobitz type I (Wenckebach) AV block
c. Second-degree Mobitz type II AV block
d. Third-degree (complete) AV block

Answer: b. Second-degree Mobitz type I (Wenckebach) AV block. Explanation: The Wenckebach phenomenon is characterized by progressive lengthening of the PR interval on consecutive beats until a beat is dropped (a P wave not followed by a QRS complex), indicative of a Mobitz type I second-degree AV block.

223. In a patient with a fixed PR interval and intermittent non-conducted P waves, what is the most likely type of heart block?
a. First-degree AV block
b. Second-degree Mobitz type I (Wenckebach) AV block
c. Second-degree Mobitz type II AV block
d. Third-degree (complete) AV block

Answer: c. Second-degree Mobitz type II AV block. Explanation: Mobitz type II second-degree AV block is characterized by a fixed PR interval with occasional P waves not followed by QRS complexes, without progressive PR interval lengthening.

224. A patient's ECG shows no relationship between P waves and QRS complexes, with P waves and QRS complexes appearing at their own independent rates. What does this indicate?
a. First-degree AV block
b. Second-degree Mobitz type I (Wenckebach) AV block
c. Second-degree Mobitz type II AV block
d. Third-degree (complete) AV block

Answer: d. Third-degree (complete) AV block. Explanation: In third-degree (complete) AV block, there is complete dissociation between atrial and ventricular activities. The atria and ventricles beat independently of each other, as seen by P waves and QRS complexes occurring at different rates without coordination.

225. A patient with chest pain and palpitations shows a regular but slow QRS rhythm and more P waves than QRS complexes on ECG. What is the most likely diagnosis?
a. First-degree AV block
b. Second-degree Mobitz type I (Wenckebach) AV block
c. Second-degree Mobitz type II AV block
d. Third-degree (complete) AV block

Answer: d. Third-degree (complete) AV block. Explanation: The presence of more P waves than QRS complexes, with the two showing no relation, points toward a third-degree AV block, where atrial impulses fail to conduct to the ventricles, leading to independent and usually slower ventricular rhythm.

226. In the management of third-degree AV block, what is the immediate treatment of choice for a hemodynamically unstable patient?
a. Oral beta-blockers
b. Transcutaneous pacing
c. High-dose diuretic therapy
d. Intravenous fluid bolus

Answer: b. Transcutaneous pacing. Explanation: For hemodynamically unstable patients with third-degree AV block, immediate transcutaneous pacing is indicated to maintain an adequate heart rate and cardiac output until more definitive therapy (like a permanent pacemaker) can be established.

227. A patient with a history of myocardial infarction presents with dizziness and fatigue. The ECG shows a regular atrial rate of 100 bpm and a slower, regular ventricular rate. P waves do not consistently precede QRS complexes. Which intervention is most appropriate?
a. Await spontaneous resolution
b. Immediate cardioversion

c. Evaluation for pacemaker placement
d. Intravenous beta-blocker administration

Answer: c. Evaluation for pacemaker placement. Explanation: The described ECG findings suggest a higher-degree AV block, possibly type II or III, particularly in the setting of post-myocardial infarction, which could require pacemaker placement to ensure reliable ventricular pacing and prevent symptomatic bradycardia.

228. During a routine check-up, a patient's ECG reveals a constant PR interval prolongation but no missed beats. The patient is asymptomatic. What is the most likely course of action?
a. Start antiarrhythmic medication immediately
b. Schedule for pacemaker implantation
c. Regular monitoring and patient education
d. Immediate hospitalization for cardiac monitoring

Answer: c. Regular monitoring and patient education. Explanation: In asymptomatic first-degree AV block, where there is a constant prolongation of the PR interval without missed beats, the recommended approach is regular monitoring and patient education without immediate intervention unless symptoms develop.

229. A patient presents with an irregular rhythm, and the ECG shows some P waves followed by a QRS complex and some not, without a consistent pattern. What type of block is indicated?
a. First-degree AV block
b. Second-degree Mobitz type I (Wenckebach) AV block
c. Second-degree Mobitz type II AV block
d. Advanced second-degree AV block

Answer: d. Advanced second-degree AV block. Explanation: An advanced second-degree AV block (also known as high-grade AV block) is suggested by an irregular rhythm where only some P waves are followed by QRS complexes without a consistent pattern, indicating multiple consecutive non-conducted atrial impulses.

230. In a patient with known second-degree Mobitz type I AV block, which symptom would indicate progression to a more serious block and necessitate immediate intervention?
a. Occasional palpitations
b. Mild fatigue
c. Syncope
d. Intermittent shortness of breath

Answer: c. Syncope. Explanation: Syncope in the context of a known heart block suggests a significant drop in cardiac output, likely due to progression to a higher degree of block, and necessitates immediate evaluation for advanced interventions, such as pacing.

231. During a code blue, a patient is found to be in asystole. What is the first line of treatment according to ACLS guidelines?
a. Immediate intubation
b. Intravenous amiodarone
c. High-quality CPR and epinephrine
d. Defibrillation with 200 joules

Answer: c. High-quality CPR and epinephrine. Explanation: For asystole, ACLS guidelines recommend immediate initiation of high-quality CPR followed by administration of epinephrine as soon as possible. Defibrillation is not indicated for asystole, and while securing the airway is important, it should not supersede the initiation of CPR and epinephrine administration.

232. A patient in ventricular fibrillation (VF) undergoes the first shock with an automated external defibrillator (AED). The VF persists on the subsequent rhythm check. What is the next immediate step?
a. Administer a second shock immediately
b. Start an amiodarone infusion
c. Resume high-quality CPR for 2 minutes
d. Give IV epinephrine

Answer: c. Resume high-quality CPR for 2 minutes. Explanation: After a defibrillation attempt, if VF persists, the next step is to resume high-quality CPR for 2 minutes before repeating the rhythm check and considering additional interventions, including further defibrillation, epinephrine, and antiarrhythmic medications.

233. In the case of pulseless electrical activity (PEA), which of the following is a crucial part of the management strategy?
a. Rapid sequence intubation
b. Immediate defibrillation
c. High-quality CPR and search for reversible causes
d. Intravenous calcium administration

Answer: c. High-quality CPR and search for reversible causes. Explanation: Management of PEA focuses on providing high-quality CPR and rapidly identifying and treating any reversible causes (e.g., the H's and T's like hypovolemia, hypoxia, hydrogen ion (acidosis), hyper-/hypokalemia, hypothermia, tension pneumothorax, tamponade, toxins, thrombosis (pulmonary or coronary)).

234. A patient is experiencing supraventricular tachycardia (SVT) with hemodynamic instability. What is the most appropriate intervention?
a. Vagal maneuvers
b. Intravenous adenosine
c. Synchronized cardioversion
d. Beta-blocker administration

Answer: c. Synchronized cardioversion. Explanation: For SVT with hemodynamic instability, immediate synchronized cardioversion is recommended to restore sinus rhythm and stabilize the patient. While vagal maneuvers and adenosine are first-line for stable SVT, they are not appropriate for hemodynamically unstable patients.

235. During ACLS, a patient with a witnessed shockable rhythm (VF/pulseless VT) arrest receives epinephrine. How often should this drug be administered?
a. Every 2 minutes
b. Every 3-5 minutes
c. Every 5-10 minutes
d. Only once during resuscitation

Answer: b. Every 3-5 minutes. Explanation: According to ACLS guidelines, epinephrine should be administered every 3-5 minutes during cardiac arrest management for a patient in a shockable rhythm (VF/pulseless VT).

236. A patient is suspected of having a tension pneumothorax during ACLS. What is the most appropriate immediate intervention?
a. Needle decompression
b. High-flow oxygen therapy
c. Bilateral chest tube insertion
d. Immediate intubation

Answer: a. Needle decompression. Explanation: Immediate needle decompression is the recommended intervention for a suspected tension pneumothorax during resuscitation, particularly if it is causing hemodynamic instability, followed by definitive care such as chest tube placement.

237. For a patient in stable VT with a pulse, which medication is considered first-line treatment according to ACLS guidelines?
a. Intravenous amiodarone
b. Intravenous lidocaine
c. Oral beta-blockers
d. Synchronized cardioversion

Answer: a. Intravenous amiodarone. Explanation: For a patient in stable VT with a pulse, ACLS guidelines recommend amiodarone as the first-line antiarrhythmic medication. Synchronized cardioversion may be considered if medication is ineffective and the patient becomes unstable.

238. In ACLS, what is the recommended dosage of amiodarone for a patient in VF/pulseless VT after the first defibrillation?
a. 150 mg IV push
b. 300 mg IV push
c. 450 mg IV push

d. 600 mg IV push

Answer: b. 300 mg IV push. Explanation: The initial recommended dose of amiodarone for VF/pulseless VT after the first defibrillation is 300 mg IV push, followed by one repeat dose of 150 mg if needed.

239. When encountering a patient with bradycardia and poor perfusion, despite adequate oxygenation and ventilation, which drug is recommended?
a. Atropine
b. Dopamine infusion
c. Epinephrine infusion
d. Both b and c

Answer: d. Both b and c. Explanation: For bradycardia with poor perfusion not responsive to atropine, ACLS guidelines recommend starting an infusion of either dopamine or epinephrine as a temporizing measure to improve heart rate and perfusion until the underlying cause can be addressed or pacing can be initiated.

240. A patient with a known history of chronic obstructive pulmonary disease (COPD) goes into cardiac arrest. After return of spontaneous circulation (ROSC), which of the following is the most appropriate to manage potential hypercapnic respiratory failure?
a. Non-invasive ventilation
b. High-dose corticosteroids
c. Immediate intubation and mechanical ventilation
d. Oxygen via nasal cannula at 2 L/min

Answer: c. Immediate intubation and mechanical ventilation. Explanation: For a patient with COPD who achieves ROSC but is at risk of hypercapnic respiratory failure, immediate intubation and mechanical ventilation may be necessary to ensure adequate ventilation and oxygenation, and to manage potential CO2 retention.

241. On an ECG, a sawtooth pattern of atrial activity is noted, especially visible in leads II, III, and aVF. What is the most likely diagnosis?
a. Atrial fibrillation
b. Atrial flutter
c. Ventricular tachycardia
d. Sinus bradycardia

Answer: b. Atrial flutter. Explanation: Atrial flutter is characterized by a "sawtooth" pattern of regular atrial activity called flutter waves, particularly noticeable in the inferior leads (II, III, and aVF), indicative of the rapid atrial rates typically associated with this arrhythmia.

242. A 12-lead ECG shows ST-segment elevation in leads V1 through V4. Which area of the heart is most likely affected?
a. Inferior wall
b. Lateral wall
c. Anterior wall
d. Posterior wall

Answer: c. Anterior wall. Explanation: ST-segment elevation in leads V1 through V4 is indicative of an anterior wall myocardial infarction, which involves the left anterior descending (LAD) artery territory of the heart.

243. An ECG demonstrates a PR interval that progressively lengthens until a QRS complex is dropped. This pattern then repeats. What is this pattern called?
a. First-degree AV block
b. Second-degree Mobitz type I (Wenckebach) AV block
c. Second-degree Mobitz type II AV block
d. Third-degree (complete) AV block

Answer: b. Second-degree Mobitz type I (Wenckebach) AV block. Explanation: This pattern of progressive PR interval lengthening until a beat is dropped, followed by the pattern repeating, is characteristic of a Wenckebach or Mobitz type I second-degree AV block.

244. In the context of acute chest pain, which ECG finding is most immediately concerning for ongoing myocardial ischemia?
a. Peaked T waves
b. ST-segment depression
c. U waves
d. Q waves

Answer: b. ST-segment depression. Explanation: ST-segment depression is a critical finding in the context of acute chest pain, as it can indicate ongoing myocardial ischemia, necessitating urgent assessment and intervention.

245. A patient's ECG shows regular R-R intervals, but with varying P wave morphologies. What does this suggest?
a. Sinus rhythm
b. Multifocal atrial tachycardia (MAT)
c. Ventricular fibrillation
d. Atrial fibrillation

Answer: b. Multifocal atrial tachycardia (MAT). Explanation: MAT is characterized by at least three different P wave morphologies in the same ECG lead, reflecting multiple ectopic atrial pacemaker activities, while maintaining regular R-R intervals.

246. On an ECG, a wide QRS complex (>0.12 seconds) that precedes each T wave without a visible P wave is observed. What is the most likely rhythm?
a. Ventricular tachycardia
b. Supraventricular tachycardia with aberrant conduction
c. Complete heart block
d. Premature ventricular contraction (PVC)

Answer: a. Ventricular tachycardia. Explanation: A wide QRS complex rhythm without preceding P waves, especially if the rate is fast and the pattern is sustained, is indicative of ventricular tachycardia, originating below the AV node.

247. A patient presents with an ECG that shows irregularly irregular rhythm with no discernible P waves. What is the most likely diagnosis?
a. Sinus arrhythmia
b. Atrial flutter
c. Atrial fibrillation
d. Ventricular fibrillation

Answer: c. Atrial fibrillation. Explanation: Atrial fibrillation is characterized by an irregularly irregular rhythm and the absence of distinct P waves, due to the chaotic atrial activity that overrides normal sinus rhythm.

248. An ECG reveals elevated ST segments in leads II, III, and aVF. This pattern suggests ischemia in which region of the heart?
a. Anterior wall
b. Lateral wall
c. Inferior wall
d. Posterior wall

Answer: c. Inferior wall. Explanation: ST-segment elevation in leads II, III, and aVF indicates an inferior wall myocardial infarction, typically involving the right coronary artery (RCA) territory.

249. A patient's ECG shows a PR interval consistently greater than 0.20 seconds, but each P wave is followed by a QRS complex. What is the diagnosis?
a. First-degree AV block
b. Second-degree Mobitz type I (Wenckebach) AV block
c. Second-degree Mobitz type II AV block
d. Third-degree (complete) AV block

Answer: a. First-degree AV block. Explanation: A consistent PR interval prolongation greater than 0.20 seconds, with each P wave followed by a QRS complex, is indicative of a first-degree AV block, reflecting delayed conduction through the AV node.

250. In identifying left ventricular hypertrophy (LVH) on an ECG, which criteria are commonly used?
a. Presence of Q waves in leads V1-V3
b. ST-segment elevation in leads I and aVL
c. Increased amplitude of R waves in left precordial leads and deep S waves in right precordial leads
d. Peaked T waves in leads II, III, and aVF

Answer: c. Increased amplitude of R waves in left precordial leads and deep S waves in right precordial leads. Explanation: Criteria for LVH often include increased amplitude of R waves in left precordial leads (V5-V6) and deep S waves in right precordial leads (V1-V2), reflecting increased left ventricular muscle mass.

251. In a systematic approach to a critically ill patient, which of the following is the first priority?
a. Airway assessment and management
b. Circulation with hemorrhage control
c. Disability assessment (neurological status)
d. Exposure and environmental control

Answer: a. Airway assessment and management. Explanation: The primary step in a systematic approach, especially in critical care, is ensuring a patent airway. This is crucial as it precedes all other interventions; without a secure airway, oxygenation and ventilation could be compromised, leading to rapid deterioration.

252. When evaluating a patient's breathing in a systematic approach, what is an essential aspect to assess?
a. Skin color and temperature
b. Capillary refill time
c. Breath sounds and respiratory effort
d. Pupil response

Answer: c. Breath sounds and respiratory effort. Explanation: In assessing breathing, evaluating the quality of breath sounds (e.g., presence of wheezing, crackles) and the effort involved in breathing (e.g., use of accessory muscles, presence of retractions) is critical to identifying respiratory distress or failure and guiding appropriate interventions.

253. During the 'Circulation' assessment of a critically ill patient, which of the following is crucial to evaluate?
a. Blood pressure and heart rate
b. Glasgow Coma Scale score
c. Urinary output
d. Pupil size and reactivity

Answer: a. Blood pressure and heart rate. Explanation: Circulation assessment focuses on hemodynamic stability, which includes monitoring blood pressure and heart rate to detect signs of shock or cardiac compromise, guiding fluid and pharmacologic therapy.

254. In the context of 'Disability' during a systematic assessment, what does checking the Glasgow Coma Scale (GCS) help determine?
a. The patient's hydration status
b. The need for immediate intubation
c. The patient's neurological function
d. The patient's pain level

Answer: c. The patient's neurological function. Explanation: The GCS is a quick, practical, and standardized system for assessing the degree of consciousness impairment in the critically ill and is particularly useful in evaluating the neurological status as part of the 'Disability' component of a systematic approach.

255. When performing the 'Exposure' step in a systematic approach to patient assessment, why is it important to also consider 'Environmental control'?
a. To ensure patient privacy during examination
b. To prevent hypothermia by controlling the environment
c. To assess the patient's ability to respond to verbal commands
d. To facilitate the administration of medications

Answer: b. To prevent hypothermia by controlling the environment. Explanation: Full exposure is necessary for a thorough assessment, but it can lead to heat loss and hypothermia, especially in critical settings. Environmental control, such as warming the room and using blankets, helps prevent this while still allowing for complete patient evaluation.

256. In a systematic review, after 'Airway' and 'Breathing' have been assessed, what is the NEXT best step when you suspect internal bleeding in a patient?
a. Immediate surgical intervention
b. Rapid fluid resuscitation and blood transfusion as needed
c. Administration of broad-spectrum antibiotics
d. Immediate chest X-ray

Answer: b. Rapid fluid resuscitation and blood transfusion as needed. Explanation: Following 'Airway' and 'Breathing,' 'Circulation' assessment is crucial, especially if internal bleeding is suspected. Fluid resuscitation and blood transfusion are key to restoring circulating volume and perfusion.

257. During the 'Airway' assessment of a trauma patient, you notice gurgling sounds. What is the most appropriate immediate action?
a. Administer high-flow oxygen via a non-rebreather mask
b. Initiate rapid sequence intubation
c. Suction the airway
d. Perform a cricothyroidotomy

Answer: c. Suction the airway. Explanation: Gurgling indicates the presence of fluid or secretions in the airway. Immediate suctioning is necessary to clear the airway, which can then be followed by further assessment and interventions such as oxygenation or advanced airway management if required.

258. In assessing 'Circulation' with hemorrhage control, which of the following signs would indicate the need for immediate intervention due to significant blood loss?
a. Heart rate of 90 bpm
b. Warm, dry skin
c. Systolic blood pressure of 100 mmHg
d. Cool, clammy skin, and tachycardia

Answer: d. Cool, clammy skin, and tachycardia. Explanation: Cool, clammy skin and tachycardia are compensatory mechanisms in response to hypovolemia from significant blood loss, indicating the need for immediate fluid resuscitation and efforts to control hemorrhage.

259. In the 'Disability' assessment of a systematic approach, what is the significance of assessing pupil size and reaction?
a. To determine the patient's visual acuity
b. To evaluate for potential spinal cord injury
c. To assess for changes in intracranial pressure
d. To gauge the patient's hydration status

Answer: c. To assess for changes in intracranial pressure. Explanation: Pupil size and reaction are assessed as part of neurological evaluation because changes can indicate alterations in intracranial pressure, which is critical for early detection of conditions such as brain injury or stroke.

260. When assessing a patient with suspected sepsis, which component of the systematic approach is most critical to address immediately?
a. Ensuring adequate ventilation
b. Fluid resuscitation and starting empirical antibiotics
c. Checking blood glucose levels
d. Administering analgesics for pain

Answer: b. Fluid resuscitation and starting empirical antibiotics. Explanation: In sepsis, rapid fluid resuscitation to maintain perfusion and starting broad-spectrum antibiotics are crucial interventions to address the systemic inflammatory response and potential source of infection, aligning with the 'Circulation' component of the systematic approach.

261. On an ECG, which finding is indicative of left ventricular hypertrophy (LVH)?
a. QRS duration less than 0.12 seconds

b. ST-segment elevation in leads I and aVL
c. S wave depth in V1 plus R wave height in V5 or V6 greater than 35 mm
d. Presence of Q waves in leads II, III, and aVF

Answer: c. S wave depth in V1 plus R wave height in V5 or V6 greater than 35 mm. Explanation: One of the criteria for diagnosing LVH on an ECG is the Sokolow-Lyon index, where the S wave depth in lead V1 plus the R wave height in lead V5 or V6 exceeds 35 mm, indicating increased left ventricular muscle mass.

262. Which ECG pattern suggests right ventricular hypertrophy (RVH)?
a. Tall R waves in leads I and aVL
b. Deep S waves in leads V5 and V6
c. Tall R waves in lead V1 and deep S waves in lead V5 or V6
d. ST-segment depression and T wave inversion in leads V1 to V3

Answer: c. Tall R waves in lead V1 and deep S waves in lead V5 or V6. Explanation: RVH is suggested by tall R waves in lead V1 and deep S waves in leads V5 or V6, reflecting the increased muscle mass of the right ventricle.

263. In identifying atrial enlargement on an ECG, what indicates left atrial enlargement?
a. Peaked P waves in leads II, III, and aVF
b. Biphasic P wave in lead V1 with a terminal negative portion wider than 1 mm and deeper than 1 mm
c. P wave duration less than 0.12 seconds
d. Constantly inverted P waves in leads I and aVL

Answer: b. Biphasic P wave in lead V1 with a terminal negative portion wider than 1 mm and deeper than 1 mm. Explanation: Left atrial enlargement is often suggested by a biphasic P wave in lead V1, where the terminal negative portion of the P wave is wider than 1 mm and deeper than 1 mm, reflecting delayed left atrial depolarization.

264. What ECG feature is typical of right atrial enlargement (RAE)?
a. P wave duration greater than 0.12 seconds in lead II
b. Peaked P waves in leads II, III, and aVF with amplitude greater than 2.5 mm
c. Notched P waves in leads I and aVL
d. P wave inversion in lead V1

Answer: b. Peaked P waves in leads II, III, and aVF with amplitude greater than 2.5 mm. Explanation: Right atrial enlargement is characterized by peaked P waves (P pulmonale) in the inferior leads (II, III, aVF) with an amplitude greater than 2.5 mm, indicating increased right atrial depolarization force.

265. In the context of hypertensive heart disease, which ECG finding is most commonly associated?
a. Left bundle branch block (LBBB)
b. LVH with strain pattern, characterized by ST depression and T wave inversion in the left precordial leads

c. Right bundle branch block (RBBB)
d. Pathological Q waves in leads V1 to V3

Answer: b. LVH with strain pattern, characterized by ST depression and T wave inversion in the left precordial leads. Explanation: Hypertensive heart disease often leads to LVH, which may present on the ECG with a strain pattern consisting of ST depression and asymmetric T wave inversion in the left precordial leads, indicative of subendocardial ischemia.

266. How does mitral valve disease typically manifest on an ECG?
a. Shortened PR interval and widened QRS complex
b. Left atrial enlargement and possible LVH
c. Tall, peaked T waves in the right precordial leads
d. Predominant R wave progression in the chest leads

Answer: b. Left atrial enlargement and possible LVH. Explanation: Mitral valve disease, such as mitral stenosis or regurgitation, often leads to left atrial enlargement due to increased pressure and volume load, which may be accompanied by signs of LVH as the disease progresses.

267. What ECG change is indicative of chronic pulmonary disease, such as chronic obstructive pulmonary disease (COPD)?
a. Clockwise rotation, right axis deviation, and possible P pulmonale
b. Left axis deviation and QRS prolongation
c. Delta waves and shortened PR interval
d. Increased R wave progression across the chest leads

Answer: a. Clockwise rotation, right axis deviation, and possible P pulmonale. Explanation: Chronic pulmonary diseases, including COPD, may lead to clockwise rotation of the heart, right axis deviation due to right ventricular hypertrophy, and tall peaked P waves in the inferior leads (P pulmonale), reflecting right atrial enlargement.

268. In a patient with aortic stenosis, what ECG findings might you expect?
a. LVH, often with a strain pattern, and occasionally left atrial enlargement
b. Isolated right axis deviation without other significant changes
c. Prominent U waves and QT interval prolongation
d. Diffuse ST-segment elevations and PR depressions

Answer: a. LVH, often with a strain pattern, and occasionally left atrial enlargement. Explanation: Aortic stenosis leads to pressure overload of the left ventricle, resulting in LVH that can be identified on the ECG by increased voltage in the left-sided leads and a strain pattern. Left atrial enlargement may also occur due to increased left ventricular end-diastolic pressure.

269. For a patient with suspected hypertrophic cardiomyopathy, which ECG pattern is most suggestive?
a. Deep, narrow Q waves in the lateral and inferior leads
b. Short PR interval with wide QRS complexes
c. Sawtooth flutter waves in the inferior leads
d. Sinus bradycardia with intermittent atrial ectopic beats

Answer: a. Deep, narrow Q waves in the lateral and inferior leads. Explanation: Hypertrophic cardiomyopathy often presents with deep, narrow Q waves in the lateral (I, aVL, V5, V6) and inferior leads (II, III, aVF), which can be mistaken for infarction Q waves. These are due to the septal hypertrophy and abnormal septal depolarization associated with the disease.

270. A 58-year-old male with a history of hypertension presents to the emergency department with chest pain. Which ECG change most specifically suggests the presence of myocardial ischemia?
a. Peaked T waves
b. ST-segment elevation
c. QRS widening
d. PR interval prolongation

Answer: b. ST-segment elevation. Explanation: ST-segment elevation is a specific sign of acute myocardial infarction and indicates transmural ischemia. It is a critical finding that necessitates immediate intervention, typically reperfusion therapy.

271. In evaluating a patient for myocardial infarction (MI), which biomarker is most indicative of cardiac injury when elevated?
a. Creatinine kinase-MB (CK-MB)
b. Myoglobin
c. Troponin
d. Aspartate aminotransferase (AST)

Answer: c. Troponin. Explanation: Troponin is the most sensitive and specific biomarker for myocardial injury. It rises within hours of an MI and remains elevated for up to two weeks, making it an essential marker for diagnosing acute and recent MIs.

272. A patient complains of sudden onset of severe chest pain radiating to the left arm. The pain is not relieved by rest or nitroglycerin. This presentation is most suggestive of:
a. Stable angina
b. Unstable angina
c. Acute myocardial infarction
d. Pericarditis

Answer: c. Acute myocardial infarction. Explanation: The characteristics of the pain, including its severity, radiation, and lack of relief with rest or nitroglycerin, suggest an acute myocardial infarction rather than stable angina, unstable angina, or pericarditis.

273. On an ECG, pathological Q waves are indicative of:
a. Early repolarization
b. Hyperkalemia
c. Myocardial infarction
d. Left ventricular hypertrophy

Answer: c. Myocardial infarction. Explanation: Pathological Q waves are a sign of previous myocardial infarction and indicate necrosis. They are typically seen in the leads overlying the infarcted area and persist indefinitely.

274. A patient's ECG shows ST-segment depression and T-wave inversion in leads II, III, and aVF. These findings are most consistent with ischemia in which area of the heart?
a. Anterior wall
b. Lateral wall
c. Inferior wall
d. Septal area

Answer: c. Inferior wall. Explanation: ST-segment depression and T-wave inversion in leads II, III, and aVF suggest ischemia in the inferior wall of the heart, which is typically supplied by the right coronary artery.

275. During a stress test, a patient develops horizontal ST-segment depression of 2 mm in leads V4-V6. This finding most likely represents:
a. Normal physiologic response to exercise
b. Left ventricular hypertrophy
c. Subendocardial ischemia
d. Right bundle branch block

Answer: c. Subendocardial ischemia. Explanation: Horizontal or downsloping ST-segment depression during a stress test, particularly ≥1 mm, is indicative of subendocardial ischemia, suggesting the presence of significant coronary artery disease.

276. A 65-year-old woman with a history of diabetes mellitus presents with epigastric discomfort and nausea. Considering her risk factors and atypical presentation, which diagnostic test is most crucial for identifying myocardial ischemia?
a. Abdominal ultrasound
b. Troponin levels
c. Upper endoscopy
d. Thyroid function tests

Answer: b. Troponin levels. Explanation: In patients with diabetes, myocardial ischemia may present atypically, such as epigastric discomfort. Troponin levels are crucial for identifying myocardial injury in such atypical presentations.

277. An ECG from a patient with chest pain reveals ST-segment elevations in leads V1-V4. This pattern suggests an infarction in which part of the heart?
a. Posterior wall
b. Anterior wall
c. Inferior wall
d. Lateral wall

Answer: b. Anterior wall. Explanation: ST-segment elevations in precordial leads V1-V4 are indicative of an anterior wall myocardial infarction, typically associated with occlusion of the left anterior descending artery.

278. In the context of myocardial infarction, "referred pain" to the jaw and left arm is explained by:
a. The proximity of the heart to the left arm and jaw
b. Shared neural pathways between the heart and these areas
c. The intensity of the myocardial infarction
d. Peripheral neuropathy common in these patients

Answer: b. Shared neural pathways between the heart and these areas. Explanation: Referred pain during myocardial infarction to areas like the jaw and left arm occurs due to shared neural pathways in the spinal cord between the visceral nerves from the heart and the somatic nerves from these areas.

279. A patient with suspected myocardial infarction has clear lung sounds, jugular venous distension, and hypotension. These findings suggest:
a. Left-sided heart failure
b. Right-sided heart failure
c. Pulmonary embolism
d. Acute pericarditis

Answer: b. Right-sided heart failure. Explanation: In the setting of myocardial infarction, clear lung sounds with jugular venous distension and hypotension suggest right-sided heart failure, possibly due to infarction of the right ventricle or significant ischemia affecting its function.

280. A 58-year-old male patient presents with dyspnea on exertion and fatigue. Echocardiography reveals a left ventricular ejection fraction (LVEF) of 35%. Based on this information, how would this patient's heart failure be classified?
a. Heart failure with preserved ejection fraction (HFpEF)
b. Heart failure with reduced ejection fraction (HFrEF)
c. Heart failure with mid-range ejection fraction (HFmrEF)

d. Heart failure with improved ejection fraction (HFimpEF)

Answer: b. Heart failure with reduced ejection fraction (HFrEF). Explanation: HFrEF is characterized by an LVEF of less than 40%. The patient's symptoms of dyspnea on exertion and fatigue, coupled with an LVEF of 35%, align with the diagnostic criteria for HFrEF.

281. A patient with heart failure reports no limitations in physical activity and no symptoms with ordinary exertion. According to the New York Heart Association (NYHA) functional classification, this patient would be classified as:
a. Class I
b. Class II
c. Class III
d. Class IV

Answer: a. Class I. Explanation: NYHA Class I refers to patients with cardiac disease but without resulting limitations of physical activity. Ordinary physical activity does not cause undue fatigue, palpitation, dyspnea, or anginal pain in these patients.

282. In assessing a patient with heart failure, an echocardiogram shows an LVEF of 55% with signs of diastolic dysfunction. This patient's condition is best described as:
a. Heart failure with preserved ejection fraction (HFpEF)
b. Heart failure with reduced ejection fraction (HFrEF)
c. Heart failure with mid-range ejection fraction (HFmrEF)
d. Acute decompensated heart failure (ADHF)

Answer: a. Heart failure with preserved ejection fraction (HFpEF). Explanation: HFpEF is characterized by symptoms of heart failure with a normal or near-normal ejection fraction (≥50%) and evidence of diastolic dysfunction, which matches the described echocardiographic findings.

283. A 65-year-old patient with heart failure experiences marked limitation of physical activity due to symptoms, even during less-than-ordinary activity, but is comfortable at rest. According to the NYHA classification, this patient is in:
a. Class I
b. Class II
c. Class III
d. Class IV

Answer: c. Class III. Explanation: NYHA Class III describes patients with heart failure who have marked limitation of physical activity. They are comfortable at rest but less-than-ordinary activity causes fatigue, palpitation, dyspnea, or anginal pain.

284. A patient with heart failure has an LVEF of 45%, with symptoms of heart failure and evidence of cardiac remodeling on echocardiography. This patient's heart failure would be categorized as:
a. Heart failure with preserved ejection fraction (HFpEF)
b. Heart failure with reduced ejection fraction (HFrEF)
c. Heart failure with mid-range ejection fraction (HFmrEF)
d. Acute decompensated heart failure (ADHF)

Answer: c. Heart failure with mid-range ejection fraction (HFmrEF). Explanation: HFmrEF is defined by an LVEF of 41% to 49%, with symptoms of heart failure and evidence of cardiac remodeling or diastolic dysfunction, fitting the patient's described condition.

285. A patient with heart failure is unable to perform any physical activity without discomfort and experiences symptoms of heart failure even at rest. According to the NYHA functional classification, this patient would be classified as:
a. Class I
b. Class II
c. Class III
d. Class IV

Answer: d. Class IV. Explanation: NYHA Class IV is characterized by patients with heart failure who are unable to carry on any physical activity without discomfort. Symptoms of heart failure are present even at rest, indicating severe limitations.

286. In a patient with heart failure and an LVEF of 38%, which therapeutic approach is most appropriate based on the classification of heart failure?
a. Optimization of blood pressure control only
b. Use of ACE inhibitors, beta-blockers, and aldosterone antagonists
c. Diuretics only, to manage fluid overload
d. Atrial septostomy to reduce left atrial pressure

Answer: b. Use of ACE inhibitors, beta-blockers, and aldosterone antagonists. Explanation: In patients with HFrEF (LVEF < 40%), guideline-directed medical therapy includes ACE inhibitors (or ARBs if ACE inhibitors are not tolerated), beta-blockers, and aldosterone antagonists to improve survival and reduce heart failure symptoms.

287. A patient with heart failure is comfortable at rest but ordinary physical activity results in fatigue, palpitation, or dyspnea. This patient's NYHA classification is:
a. Class I
b. Class II
c. Class III
d. Class IV

Answer: b. Class II. Explanation: NYHA Class II describes patients with heart failure who are comfortable at rest but ordinary physical activity results in symptoms such as fatigue, palpitation, dyspnea, or anginal pain, indicating slight limitations in physical activity.

288. For a patient with heart failure who initially presented with an LVEF of 30% but improved to 50% after treatment, which term best describes their current heart failure status?
a. Heart failure with preserved ejection fraction (HFpEF)
b. Heart failure with reduced ejection fraction (HFrEF)
c. Heart failure with recovered ejection fraction (HFrecEF)
d. Heart failure with mid-range ejection fraction (HFmrEF)

Answer: c. Heart failure with recovered ejection fraction (HFrecEF). Explanation: HFrecEF refers to patients who previously had HFrEF but whose LVEF has improved to >40% following treatment, indicating significant improvement in left ventricular function.

289. In a patient with heart failure symptoms and an LVEF of 60%, but with significant diastolic dysfunction and elevated natriuretic peptides, the most accurate classification is:
a. Heart failure with preserved ejection fraction (HFpEF)
b. Heart failure with reduced ejection fraction (HFrEF)
c. Heart failure with mid-range ejection fraction (HFmrEF)
d. Acute decompensated heart failure (ADHF)

Answer: a. Heart failure with preserved ejection fraction (HFpEF). Explanation: HFpEF is characterized by heart failure symptoms with preserved ejection fraction (LVEF ≥ 50%), significant diastolic dysfunction, and often elevated natriuretic peptides, aligning with the patient's presentation.

290. In evaluating a patient with heart failure, an echocardiogram reveals a left ventricular ejection fraction (LVEF) of 35%. This finding is most consistent with:
a. High-output heart failure
b. Heart failure with preserved ejection fraction (HFpEF)
c. Heart failure with reduced ejection fraction (HFrEF)
d. Restrictive cardiomyopathy

Answer: c. Heart failure with reduced ejection fraction (HFrEF). Explanation: An LVEF of 35% indicates a reduced ejection fraction, characteristic of HFrEF, where the heart's ability to pump blood is diminished. HFpEF involves a preserved ejection fraction typically >50%, while high-output heart failure and restrictive cardiomyopathy present with different echocardiographic findings.

291. A 70-year-old patient with chronic heart failure reports increasing dyspnea on exertion and ankle swelling. The most appropriate adjustment to their medication regimen would be:
a. Decrease beta-blocker dosage
b. Initiate or increase a loop diuretic

c. Add a calcium channel blocker
d. Increase angiotensin-converting enzyme (ACE) inhibitor to maximum dose

Answer: b. Initiate or increase a loop diuretic. Explanation: Increasing symptoms of congestion, such as dyspnea and edema, suggest volume overload, which is best managed by initiating or increasing the dose of a loop diuretic to reduce fluid retention. Beta-blockers and ACE inhibitors are foundational in HFrEF management but are not primarily used for acute decongestion. Calcium channel blockers are generally avoided in HFrEF due to negative inotropic effects.

292. In heart failure, the mechanism of action of beta-blockers such as carvedilol includes:
a. Direct vasodilation of coronary arteries
b. Increase in heart rate to improve cardiac output
c. Inhibition of renin release and sympathetic nervous system activity
d. Increase in sodium and water excretion

Answer: c. Inhibition of renin release and sympathetic nervous system activity. Explanation: Beta-blockers work in heart failure primarily by blocking the harmful effects of excessive sympathetic nervous system stimulation, including reducing heart rate and blood pressure, which decreases the heart's workload and oxygen demand. They do not directly cause vasodilation of coronary arteries or increase heart rate and have minimal direct effects on renal sodium and water excretion.

293. A patient with heart failure is prescribed spironolactone. The primary rationale for this medication is to:
a. Improve cardiac contractility
b. Reduce preload through venodilation
c. Block the effects of aldosterone in the renin-angiotensin-aldosterone system (RAAS)
d. Provide direct renal vasodilation

Answer: c. Block the effects of aldosterone in the renin-angiotensin-aldosterone system (RAAS). Explanation: Spironolactone is an aldosterone antagonist that works by blocking the effects of aldosterone in the RAAS, leading to diuresis and natriuresis, and preventing fibrosis and remodeling of the heart, which are beneficial in heart failure management.

294. A 60-year-old patient with heart failure and atrial fibrillation has a CHA_2DS_2-VASc score of 3. The most appropriate anticoagulation therapy would be:
a. Aspirin
b. Warfarin with a target INR of 2-3
c. Dabigatran
d. No anticoagulation is necessary

Answer: c. Dabigatran. Explanation: For patients with heart failure and atrial fibrillation, particularly with a CHA_2DS_2-VASc score of 2 or higher, direct oral anticoagulants (DOACs) like dabigatran are preferred over warfarin for stroke prevention due to their favorable risk-benefit profile, unless contraindicated.

295. In a patient with advanced heart failure, the presence of Cheyne-Stokes respiration indicates:
a. An imminent respiratory arrest
b. A stable phase of chronic heart failure
c. Periods of apnea alternating with periods of tachypnea, reflecting poor cerebral perfusion
d. A compensatory mechanism to correct metabolic alkalosis

Answer: c. Periods of apnea alternating with periods of tachypnea, reflecting poor cerebral perfusion. Explanation: Cheyne-Stokes respiration, characterized by periodic breathing with alternating apnea and hyperpnea, is often seen in advanced heart failure due to poor cerebral perfusion and feedback delay in the respiratory center.

296. B-type natriuretic peptide (BNP) levels are elevated in a patient with dyspnea. This finding is most suggestive of:
a. Pneumonia
b. Pulmonary embolism
c. Heart failure
d. Chronic obstructive pulmonary disease (COPD)

Answer: c. Heart failure. Explanation: Elevated BNP levels are indicative of heart failure, as BNP is released in response to ventricular volume expansion and pressure overload. While dyspnea can be a symptom of various conditions, elevated BNP specifically suggests a cardiac cause.

297. A patient with heart failure is noted to have worsening renal function after starting enalapril. This effect is most likely due to:
a. Direct nephrotoxicity of enalapril
b. Reduction in afferent arteriolar tone leading to decreased glomerular filtration rate
c. Intrarenal accumulation of angiotensin II
d. Hyperkalemia-induced tubular dysfunction

Answer: b. Reduction in afferent arteriolar tone leading to decreased glomerular filtration rate. Explanation: ACE inhibitors like enalapril can lead to a reduction in glomerular filtration rate (GFR) by dilating efferent arterioles and decreasing intraglomerular pressure, especially in patients with pre-existing renal insufficiency or those on diuretics, not due to direct nephrotoxicity or intrarenal angiotensin II accumulation.

298. The use of Ivabradine in a patient with heart failure is specifically indicated to:
a. Increase cardiac output by enhancing myocardial contractility
b. Reduce heart rate in patients who are in sinus rhythm with a heart rate ≥70 bpm and on maximally tolerated beta-blocker therapy
c. Act as a direct vasodilator to decrease afterload
d. Increase renal blood flow and promote diuresis

Answer: b. Reduce heart rate in patients who are in sinus rhythm with a heart rate ≥70 bpm and on maximally tolerated beta-blocker therapy. Explanation: Ivabradine selectively inhibits the If (funny) current in the sinoatrial node, leading to heart rate reduction without affecting myocardial contractility or blood pressure, indicated for patients with heart failure who are in sinus rhythm with a high heart rate despite beta-blocker therapy.

299. In assessing jugular venous pressure (JVP) in a patient with heart failure, which finding is indicative of elevated right atrial pressure?
a. A JVP of 2 cm above the sternal angle
b. A JVP that collapses on inspiration
c. Kussmaul's sign
d. A pulsatile liver

Answer: c. Kussmaul's sign.

300. A patient with chronic heart failure is started on an ACE inhibitor. What is the primary benefit of this medication in heart failure management?
a. Increase heart rate to improve cardiac output
b. Vasoconstriction to increase blood pressure
c. Reduction of preload and afterload through vasodilation
d. Direct increase in myocardial contractility

Answer: c. Reduction of preload and afterload through vasodilation. Explanation: ACE inhibitors are beneficial in heart failure management primarily due to their ability to cause vasodilation, which reduces both preload and afterload, thereby decreasing the work the heart has to do and improving cardiac output and symptoms.

301. When prescribing a beta-blocker for a patient with heart failure, which of the following effects is most desirable?
a. Positive inotropic effect
b. Chronotropic effect to increase heart rate
c. Reduction of sympathetic nervous system activity
d. Immediate improvement in ejection fraction

Answer: c. Reduction of sympathetic nervous system activity. Explanation: Beta-blockers are beneficial in heart failure by reducing the sympathetic nervous system activity on the heart, leading to decreased heart rate and myocardial demand, and over time can improve cardiac function and ejection fraction.

302. A patient with hypertension and diabetes is prescribed an angiotensin receptor blocker (ARB). This medication class is particularly chosen for its ability to:
a. Increase renal potassium excretion
b. Provide renal protection by reducing glomerular filtration pressure

c. Directly stimulate insulin secretion
d. Increase peripheral vascular resistance

Answer: b. Provide renal protection by reducing glomerular filtration pressure. Explanation: ARBs are often chosen for patients with hypertension and diabetes for their renal protective effects, particularly in reducing glomerular filtration pressure, which helps in preserving kidney function over time.

303. A patient with acute decompensated heart failure is administered intravenous loop diuretics. The immediate effect expected from this intervention is:
a. Increase in venous return to the heart
b. Reduction of systemic vascular resistance
c. Rapid reduction in blood volume to decrease pulmonary congestion
d. Stimulation of the parasympathetic nervous system to decrease heart rate

Answer: c. Rapid reduction in blood volume to decrease pulmonary congestion. Explanation: The administration of intravenous loop diuretics in acute decompensated heart failure primarily aims to achieve a rapid reduction in blood volume, leading to decreased pulmonary congestion and relief from symptoms of fluid overload.

304. In managing a patient with stable ischemic heart disease, beta-blockers are indicated to:
a. Increase myocardial oxygen demand by increasing contractility
b. Reduce myocardial oxygen demand by decreasing heart rate and contractility
c. Cause peripheral vasodilation to reduce afterload
d. Directly dilate coronary arteries

Answer: b. Reduce myocardial oxygen demand by decreasing heart rate and contractility. Explanation: Beta-blockers are used in stable ischemic heart disease to reduce myocardial oxygen demand by decreasing heart rate and myocardial contractility, which helps in managing angina symptoms and improving cardiac efficiency.

305. For a patient with recurrent calcium oxalate kidney stones and hypertension, which type of diuretic would be most appropriate to avoid?
a. Loop diuretics
b. Thiazide diuretics
c. Potassium-sparing diuretics
d. Osmotic diuretics

Answer: b. Thiazide diuretics. Explanation: Thiazide diuretics are generally avoided in patients with calcium oxalate kidney stones because they can increase calcium reabsorption in the renal tubules, potentially leading to an increased risk of stone formation.

306. In the context of acute myocardial infarction, ACE inhibitors are initiated early to:

a. Immediately relieve chest pain
b. Prevent arrhythmias associated with myocardial infarction
c. Limit ventricular remodeling and prevent heart failure
d. Increase platelet aggregation to prevent further clot formation

Answer: c. Limit ventricular remodeling and prevent heart failure. Explanation: Early initiation of ACE inhibitors after acute myocardial infarction helps in limiting ventricular remodeling, a process that can lead to dilation of the ventricles and heart failure, thereby improving long-term outcomes.

307. A patient with asthma requiring hypertension management should be cautioned against which class of medication due to potential exacerbation of asthma?
a. ACE inhibitors
b. Beta-blockers
c. Calcium channel blockers
d. Angiotensin receptor blockers

Answer: b. Beta-blockers. Explanation: Beta-blockers can potentially exacerbate asthma by causing bronchoconstriction and should be used with caution or avoided in patients with asthma. Selective beta-1 blockers are generally safer but still require careful consideration.

308. When considering diuretic therapy for a patient with heart failure and significant renal impairment, which diuretic class is preferred for its efficacy in reduced glomerular filtration rate conditions?
a. Thiazide diuretics
b. Loop diuretics
c. Potassium-sparing diuretics
d. Carbonic anhydrase inhibitors

Answer: b. Loop diuretics. Explanation: Loop diuretics are more effective in patients with heart failure and significant renal impairment due to their ability to act at the loop of Henle, where they can still exert their diuretic effect even when glomerular filtration rate is reduced.

309. In the management of heart failure, spironolactone, a potassium-sparing diuretic, is used primarily for its ability to:
a. Block aldosterone receptors and reduce myocardial fibrosis
b. Increase natriuresis and control hypertension
c. Act as a potent diuretic to relieve pulmonary congestion
d. Directly improve myocardial contractility

Answer: a. Block aldosterone receptors and reduce myocardial fibrosis. Explanation: Spironolactone, an aldosterone antagonist, is used in heart failure management for its ability to block aldosterone receptors, which helps in reducing myocardial fibrosis and remodeling, thereby providing long-term benefits in heart failure management.

310. In a patient presenting with chest pain and ST-segment elevation on the ECG, what is the most urgent initial management step?
a. Oral administration of a statin
b. Immediate percutaneous coronary intervention (PCI)
c. Initiation of oral beta-blocker therapy
d. Sublingual nitroglycerin administration

Answer: b. Immediate percutaneous coronary intervention (PCI). Explanation: In the setting of ST-segment elevation myocardial infarction (STEMI), the most urgent initial management is reperfusion therapy, with primary percutaneous coronary intervention (PCI) being the preferred method if it can be performed in a timely manner (ideally within 90 minutes of first medical contact).

311. For a patient diagnosed with NSTEMI, which medication is essential to initiate as part of the acute management?
a. Intravenous nitroglycerin
b. Dual antiplatelet therapy
c. High-dose diuretic
d. Immediate full-dose anticoagulation with warfarin

Answer: b. Dual antiplatelet therapy. Explanation: Dual antiplatelet therapy, typically aspirin and a P2Y12 inhibitor, is crucial in the management of NSTEMI to prevent further thrombosis and improve outcomes.

312. In a patient with STEMI, what is the recommended time frame for PCI from the first medical contact?
a. Within 12 hours
b. Within 2 hours
c. Within 90 minutes
d. Within 24 hours

Answer: c. Within 90 minutes. Explanation: The recommended time frame for performing primary PCI in a patient with STEMI is within 90 minutes of first medical contact, as early revascularization is associated with improved survival and outcomes.

313. Which of the following findings on an ECG would differentiate STEMI from NSTEMI?
a. T-wave inversion
b. ST-segment depression
c. Pathological Q waves
d. ST-segment elevation

Answer: d. ST-segment elevation. Explanation: ST-segment elevation on an ECG is indicative of STEMI, which involves full-thickness myocardial infarction, whereas NSTEMI typically involves partial-thickness infarction and may show ST-segment depression, T-wave inversion, or even normal ECG in some cases.

314. In the management of acute coronary syndrome (ACS), what is the role of beta-blockers within the first 24 hours?
a. Contraindicated in all patients
b. Indicated in all patients, regardless of hemodynamic status
c. Administered to patients without signs of heart failure or shock
d. Reserved for patients with tachyarrhythmias only

Answer: c. Administered to patients without signs of heart failure or shock. Explanation: Beta-blockers should be initiated within the first 24 hours in patients with ACS who do not have signs of heart failure, evidence of a low-output state, increased risk for cardiogenic shock, or other contraindications to beta-blocker therapy.

315. For a patient with STEMI, unable to undergo PCI within the recommended time frame, what is the alternative reperfusion strategy?
a. Fibrinolytic therapy, if no contraindications
b. Immediate coronary artery bypass graft surgery
c. Delayed PCI beyond 12 hours
d. Therapeutic hypothermia

Answer: a. Fibrinolytic therapy, if no contraindications. Explanation: If primary PCI cannot be performed within the recommended time frame for a patient with STEMI and there are no contraindications, fibrinolytic therapy should be administered as soon as possible, ideally within 30 minutes of hospital arrival.

316. In distinguishing between STEMI and NSTEMI, which biomarker is most commonly elevated in both conditions?
a. C-reactive protein (CRP)
b. Cardiac troponins
c. Rheumatoid factor (RF)
d. Erythrocyte sedimentation rate (ESR)

Answer: b. Cardiac troponins. Explanation: Cardiac troponins are sensitive and specific biomarkers for myocardial injury and are elevated in both STEMI and NSTEMI, aiding in the diagnosis of acute myocardial infarction.

317. In a patient with suspected NSTEMI and a high risk of adverse events, what is the recommended invasive strategy timing?
a. Immediate PCI within 2 hours
b. Early invasive strategy within 24 hours
c. Invasive strategy only upon recurrence of symptoms
d. Elective invasive strategy after 72 hours

Answer: b. Early invasive strategy within 24 hours. Explanation: For patients with NSTEMI, particularly those at high risk of adverse events, an early invasive strategy (angiography and revascularization as indicated) within 24 hours is recommended to improve outcomes.

318. For ongoing management of a patient post-ACS, which medication class has been shown to reduce the risk of recurrent events and improve survival?
a. Calcium channel blockers
b. Long-acting nitrates
c. Statins
d. Thiazide diuretics

Answer: c. Statins. Explanation: Statins are a cornerstone in the secondary prevention of ACS, reducing the risk of recurrent events and improving survival by lowering cholesterol levels and stabilizing atherosclerotic plaques.

319. In managing an acute exacerbation of COPD, which initial pharmacological intervention is most appropriate?
a. High-dose corticosteroids intravenously
b. Nebulized short-acting beta-agonists
c. Oral antibiotics as first-line treatment
d. Long-acting muscarinic antagonists

Answer: b. Nebulized short-acting beta-agonists. Explanation: For acute exacerbations of COPD, nebulized short-acting beta-agonists (e.g., albuterol) are often the first-line pharmacological treatment to provide rapid bronchodilation and relief of bronchospasm.

320. A patient with acute asthma exacerbation presents with wheezing and shortness of breath. What is the most effective initial treatment?
a. Oral corticosteroids
b. Nebulized ipratropium bromide
c. High-dose inhaled corticosteroids
d. Nebulized short-acting beta-agonists combined with anticholinergics

Answer: d. Nebulized short-acting beta-agonists combined with anticholinergics. Explanation: In acute asthma exacerbations, the combination of nebulized short-acting beta-agonists (e.g., albuterol) with anticholinergics (e.g., ipratropium) is effective in providing rapid relief from airway constriction and bronchospasm.

321. During a severe exacerbation of heart failure, a patient presents with pulmonary edema. What is the most immediate action?
a. Administration of an oral ACE inhibitor
b. Intravenous loop diuretics
c. Initiation of a beta-blocker regimen

d. Oral administration of a thiazide diuretic

Answer: b. Intravenous loop diuretics. Explanation: In the case of acute decompensated heart failure presenting with pulmonary edema, intravenous loop diuretics (e.g., furosemide) are the immediate treatment to rapidly reduce fluid overload and relieve pulmonary congestion.

322. A patient with chronic heart failure experiences a sudden exacerbation. After stabilizing the patient, what medication adjustment might be considered to prevent future exacerbations?
a. Discontinuation of beta-blockers to prevent bradycardia
b. Reduction in diuretic dosage to avoid renal impairment
c. Introduction or optimization of ACE inhibitors or ARBs
d. Increase in calcium channel blockers to improve cardiac output

Answer: c. Introduction or optimization of ACE inhibitors or ARBs. Explanation: In patients with chronic heart failure, ACE inhibitors or ARBs are cornerstone therapies that reduce afterload and prevent adverse remodeling, thereby potentially reducing the risk of future exacerbations.

323. For a diabetic patient experiencing a hypoglycemic episode, what is the most rapid initial intervention to elevate blood glucose levels?
a. Subcutaneous insulin
b. Oral glucose tablet or gel
c. Intravenous glucagon
d. Complex carbohydrates

Answer: b. Oral glucose tablet or gel. Explanation: For conscious patients experiencing hypoglycemia, oral glucose in the form of tablets, gel, or juice is the quickest method to raise blood glucose levels. Intravenous glucagon is reserved for unconscious patients or those unable to swallow.

324. In the management of an acute exacerbation of ulcerative colitis, which medication is typically used for induction of remission?
a. Oral 5-aminosalicylic acid (5-ASA) agents
b. Systemic corticosteroids
c. Antibiotics as first-line therapy
d. Long-term immunosuppressants

Answer: b. Systemic corticosteroids. Explanation: For acute exacerbations of ulcerative colitis, systemic corticosteroids are often used initially to induce remission due to their potent anti-inflammatory effects. 5-ASA agents are more commonly used for maintenance of remission.

325. In a patient with acute gout attack, what is the preferred initial treatment to reduce inflammation and pain?

a. Long-term allopurinol therapy
b. High-dose aspirin
c. Nonsteroidal anti-inflammatory drugs (NSAIDs)
d. Chronic corticosteroid therapy

Answer: c. Nonsteroidal anti-inflammatory drugs (NSAIDs). Explanation: NSAIDs are the first-line treatment for acute gout attacks due to their rapid anti-inflammatory and analgesic effects. Aspirin is avoided as it can alter uric acid levels, and allopurinol is used for long-term management, not acute attacks.

326. A patient with an acute exacerbation of multiple sclerosis (MS) presents with new neurological symptoms. What is the standard initial treatment?
a. Plasma exchange
b. High-dose intravenous corticosteroids
c. Initiation of interferon-beta therapy
d. Oral muscle relaxants

Answer: b. High-dose intravenous corticosteroids. Explanation: High-dose intravenous corticosteroids, such as methylprednisolone, are the standard treatment for acute exacerbations of MS to reduce inflammation and potentially shorten the duration of the exacerbation.

327. For a patient with acute kidney injury (AKI) secondary to dehydration, what is the most critical initial intervention?
a. Immediate start of renal replacement therapy
b. Administration of a loop diuretic to increase urine output
c. Fluid resuscitation with isotonic saline
d. High-dose dopamine infusion to improve renal perfusion

Answer: c. Fluid resuscitation with isotonic saline. Explanation: In cases of AKI caused by dehydration, the most critical initial step is fluid resuscitation with isotonic saline to restore intravascular volume and renal perfusion, potentially reversing the AKI.

328. A patient with a history of chronic obstructive pulmonary disease (COPD) presents with an acute exacerbation characterized by increased dyspnea, wheezing, and productive cough. What is the preferred initial pharmacological treatment?
a. Antibiotics as a first-line treatment
b. Systemic corticosteroids and short-acting bronchodilators
c. Theophylline intravenously
d. Long-term oxygen therapy initiation

Answer: b. Systemic corticosteroids and short-acting bronchodilators. Explanation: The initial management of an acute COPD exacerbation typically involves systemic corticosteroids to reduce airway inflammation and short-acting bronchodilators (beta-agonists and anticholinergics) for immediate relief of bronchoconstriction and wheezing.

329. In a patient with septic shock, which hemodynamic change is most characteristic?
a. High systemic vascular resistance (SVR) with low cardiac output
b. Low SVR with high cardiac output
c. High pulmonary capillary wedge pressure (PCWP) with low SVR
d. Low cardiac output with high central venous pressure (CVP)

Answer: b. Low SVR with high cardiac output. Explanation: Septic shock is characterized by systemic vasodilation due to the release of inflammatory mediators, leading to low SVR. Despite the vasodilation, cardiac output may be normal or high initially due to compensatory mechanisms.

330. A 45-year-old male presents with hypotension, tachycardia, and cold, clammy skin following a significant blood loss from trauma. Which type of shock is most likely?
a. Cardiogenic shock
b. Hypovolemic shock
c. Septic shock
d. Neurogenic shock

Answer: b. Hypovolemic shock. Explanation: Hypovolemic shock occurs due to significant fluid or blood loss, leading to inadequate circulating volume, evident in this patient with a history of trauma and signs of poor perfusion.

331. In cardiogenic shock, what is the primary dysfunction?
a. Loss of vascular tone leading to systemic vasodilation
b. Inadequate circulating blood volume
c. Pump failure of the heart leading to inadequate cardiac output
d. Obstruction to blood flow due to a pulmonary embolism

Answer: c. Pump failure of the heart leading to inadequate cardiac output. Explanation: Cardiogenic shock is primarily caused by the heart's inability to pump blood effectively, leading to inadequate cardiac output and tissue perfusion, despite sufficient intravascular volume.

332. Which intervention is most critical in the initial management of a patient with anaphylactic shock?
a. Intravenous fluid resuscitation
b. Immediate administration of intramuscular epinephrine
c. Broad-spectrum antibiotics
d. High-dose corticosteroids

Answer: b. Immediate administration of intramuscular epinephrine. Explanation: In anaphylactic shock, the most critical and life-saving intervention is the immediate administration of intramuscular epinephrine, which counteracts the severe allergic reaction and systemic vasodilation.

333. In neurogenic shock, resulting from a spinal cord injury, which hemodynamic pattern is typically observed?
a. High SVR with bradycardia
b. Low SVR with tachycardia
c. Low SVR with bradycardia
d. High CVP with low cardiac output

Answer: c. Low SVR with bradycardia. Explanation: Neurogenic shock, due to spinal cord injury, is characterized by loss of sympathetic tone, leading to vasodilation (low SVR) and, frequently, bradycardia due to unopposed parasympathetic activity.

334. In a patient with obstructive shock caused by a tension pneumothorax, which finding would be most immediate on physical examination?
a. Bilateral wheezing
b. Distended neck veins and tracheal deviation
c. Muffled heart sounds
d. Pulsus paradoxus

Answer: b. Distended neck veins and tracheal deviation. Explanation: Obstructive shock from tension pneumothorax is characterized by increased intrathoracic pressure, leading to distended neck veins and potentially tracheal deviation away from the side of the pneumothorax.

335. A patient in shock has warm, flushed skin, and a bounding pulse with a rapid rate. Which type of shock should be suspected?
a. Cardiogenic shock
b. Septic shock
c. Hypovolemic shock
d. Neurogenic shock

Answer: b. Septic shock. Explanation: The warm, flushed skin and bounding pulse, despite hypotension, are characteristic of the hyperdynamic phase of septic shock, where there is systemic vasodilation and increased cardiac output.

336. In treating cardiogenic shock, why is it important to avoid aggressive fluid resuscitation?
a. It can decrease SVR and worsen shock
b. It may lead to pulmonary edema and worsen gas exchange
c. It can cause rapid electrolyte shifts and arrhythmias
d. It increases the risk of anaphylactic reactions

Answer: b. It may lead to pulmonary edema and worsen gas exchange. Explanation: In cardiogenic shock, the heart's pumping ability is compromised, and aggressive fluid resuscitation can exacerbate pulmonary congestion and edema, further impairing gas exchange and cardiac function.

337. For a patient with distributive shock secondary to sepsis, which combined therapeutic approach is most effective?
a. Antibiotics and vasodilators
b. Vasopressors and inotropic support
c. Corticosteroids and anti-inflammatory medications
d. Antibiotics, fluid resuscitation, and vasopressors

Answer: d. Antibiotics, fluid resuscitation, and vasopressors. Explanation: In septic shock, the cornerstone of therapy includes early administration of broad-spectrum antibiotics, adequate fluid resuscitation to restore intravascular volume, and vasopressors to counteract vasodilation and maintain perfusion pressure.

338. Identifying the underlying cause is a crucial step in the management of shock. In a patient with sudden onset of shock symptoms following a bee sting, which underlying cause is most likely?
a. Cardiogenic shock due to myocardial infarction
b. Hypovolemic shock due to internal bleeding
c. Anaphylactic shock due to allergic reaction
d. Septic shock due to infection

Answer: c. Anaphylactic shock due to allergic reaction. Explanation: Anaphylactic shock is a severe, life-threatening allergic reaction, and in the context of a recent bee sting, it is the most likely cause of shock, characterized by systemic vasodilation, increased vascular permeability, and airway compromise.

339. A 72-year-old patient presents with signs of shock after sustaining a large burn. The patient's skin is warm and flushed. Which type of shock is most likely?
a. Hypovolemic
b. Cardiogenic
c. Distributive
d. Obstructive

Answer: c. Distributive. Explanation: Distributive shock, seen in conditions like sepsis, anaphylaxis, and neurogenic shock, is characterized by vasodilation and increased vascular permeability. In the case of a large burn, septic shock (a type of distributive shock) can occur, presenting with warm and flushed skin due to vasodilation.

340. A patient in the ICU develops sudden onset of hypotension, distended neck veins, and muffled heart sounds after a central line placement. What type of shock should be suspected?
a. Hypovolemic

b. Cardiogenic
c. Distributive
d. Obstructive

Answer: d. Obstructive. Explanation: The presentation is indicative of cardiac tamponade, which is a form of obstructive shock. It occurs due to the accumulation of fluid in the pericardial space, impeding ventricular filling and leading to decreased cardiac output.

341. Following a severe gastrointestinal bleed, a patient presents with cool, clammy skin, rapid thready pulse, and hypotension. This presentation is indicative of which type of shock?
a. Hypovolemic
b. Cardiogenic
c. Distributive
d. Obstructive

Answer: a. Hypovolemic. Explanation: Hypovolemic shock occurs due to significant fluid loss, leading to decreased intravascular volume, reduced venous return, and consequently diminished cardiac output. The symptoms described are classic for hypovolemic shock following acute blood loss.

342. A patient with a history of myocardial infarction now presents with pulmonary edema, increased central venous pressure (CVP), and hypotension. Which shock classification does this scenario best fit?
a. Hypovolemic
b. Cardiogenic
c. Distributive
d. Obstructive

Answer: b. Cardiogenic. Explanation: Cardiogenic shock is characterized by the heart's inability to pump blood effectively, often due to myocardial damage, as seen in myocardial infarction. The resultant backup of fluid into the pulmonary system (pulmonary edema) and increased CVP, along with systemic hypotension, are indicative of cardiogenic shock.

343. During an anaphylactic reaction, a patient develops widespread vasodilation, increased capillary permeability, and subsequent hypotension. This reaction is typical of which shock category?
a. Hypovolemic
b. Cardiogenic
c. Distributive
d. Obstructive

Answer: c. Distributive. Explanation: Anaphylactic shock is a type of distributive shock characterized by systemic vasodilation and increased capillary permeability due to a severe allergic reaction, leading to relative hypovolemia and circulatory collapse.

344. A patient with a pulmonary embolism presents with sudden onset shortness of breath, chest pain, and hypotension. Which type of shock is most consistent with this presentation?
a. Hypovolemic
b. Cardiogenic
c. Distributive
d. Obstructive

Answer: d. Obstructive. Explanation: Pulmonary embolism can lead to obstructive shock by obstructing pulmonary circulation, which impedes blood flow from the right side of the heart to the lungs, causing a decrease in left ventricular preload and subsequent cardiac output.

345. In a patient with severe dehydration due to vomiting and diarrhea, the expected type of shock would be:
a. Hypovolemic
b. Cardiogenic
c. Distributive
d. Obstructive

Answer: a. Hypovolemic. Explanation: Severe dehydration from vomiting and diarrhea can lead to significant fluid loss, resulting in hypovolemic shock due to reduced circulating blood volume.

346. A patient presents with shock symptoms following a severe spinal cord injury. The likely mechanism involves disruption of sympathetic tone, leading to vasodilation. This scenario describes which shock type?
a. Hypovolemic
b. Cardiogenic
c. Distributive
d. Obstructive

Answer: c. Distributive. Explanation: Neurogenic shock, a subtype of distributive shock, can occur after a severe spinal cord injury due to the loss of sympathetic tone, leading to unopposed parasympathetic activity, vasodilation, and decreased systemic vascular resistance.

347. A patient with end-stage heart failure develops worsening symptoms of shock with a reduced ejection fraction and signs of organ hypoperfusion. This scenario is characteristic of:
a. Hypovolemic
b. Cardiogenic
c. Distributive
d. Obstructive

Answer: b. Cardiogenic. Explanation: In patients with end-stage heart failure, worsening cardiac function can lead to cardiogenic shock, where the heart's diminished ejection fraction results in inadequate systemic perfusion and organ hypoperfusion.

348. A patient experiences shock after a tension pneumothorax, characterized by hypotension, absent breath sounds on one side, and jugular vein distention. This presentation is typical of which shock type?
a. Hypovolemic
b. Cardiogenic
c. Distributive
d. Obstructive

Answer: d. Obstructive. Explanation: Tension pneumothorax can cause obstructive shock by increasing intrathoracic pressure, which impairs venous return to the heart and decreases cardiac output, leading to the observed clinical signs.

349. In a patient with septic shock, which hemodynamic pattern is typically observed?
a. High cardiac output and high systemic vascular resistance
b. Low cardiac output and high systemic vascular resistance
c. High cardiac output and low systemic vascular resistance
d. Low cardiac output and low systemic vascular resistance

Answer: c. High cardiac output and low systemic vascular resistance. Explanation: Septic shock is characterized by a distributive shock pattern, where systemic vascular resistance is low due to widespread vasodilation from inflammatory mediators, and cardiac output is often high in an attempt to maintain perfusion.

350. A patient presents with cardiogenic shock following a large anterior myocardial infarction. What hemodynamic changes are most likely?
a. Increased preload, decreased afterload, and increased cardiac output
b. Decreased preload, increased afterload, and decreased cardiac output
c. Increased preload, increased afterload, and decreased cardiac output
d. Decreased preload, decreased afterload, and increased cardiac output

Answer: c. Increased preload, increased afterload, and decreased cardiac output. Explanation: Cardiogenic shock results from the heart's inability to pump effectively, often due to myocardial damage, leading to decreased cardiac output. Compensatory mechanisms may increase preload and afterload in an attempt to maintain cardiac output, further stressing the failing heart.

351. During an episode of acute hypovolemic shock, what hemodynamic changes are expected?
a. Increased cardiac output, decreased central venous pressure (CVP), increased systemic vascular resistance (SVR)
b. Decreased cardiac output, decreased CVP, increased SVR
c. Increased cardiac output, increased CVP, decreased SVR
d. Decreased cardiac output, increased CVP, decreased SVR

Answer: b. Decreased cardiac output, decreased CVP, increased SVR. Explanation: Hypovolemic shock, caused by a significant loss of intravascular volume, leads to decreased preload (reflected by decreased CVP), decreased cardiac output, and compensatory increased SVR as the body attempts to maintain blood pressure.

352. In a patient with obstructive shock due to a massive pulmonary embolism, which hemodynamic pattern is most likely?
a. High cardiac output, low pulmonary artery pressure, low SVR
b. Low cardiac output, high pulmonary artery pressure, high SVR
c. High cardiac output, high pulmonary artery pressure, low SVR
d. Low cardiac output, low pulmonary artery pressure, high SVR

Answer: b. Low cardiac output, high pulmonary artery pressure, high SVR. Explanation: Obstructive shock, such as that caused by a massive pulmonary embolism, leads to increased afterload due to obstruction of the pulmonary artery, resulting in high pulmonary artery pressure, low cardiac output due to impaired right ventricular ejection, and increased SVR as a compensatory mechanism.

353. A patient with advanced heart failure exhibits a reduced ejection fraction, elevated pulmonary capillary wedge pressure (PCWP), and reduced systemic blood pressure. This pattern suggests:
a. Preload dependency with adequate afterload reduction
b. High output failure with vasodilatory shock
c. Low output failure with high afterload
d. Right ventricular failure with normal left ventricular function

Answer: c. Low output failure with high afterload. Explanation: Advanced heart failure typically presents with low cardiac output due to impaired myocardial function (reduced ejection fraction), high filling pressures (elevated PCWP indicating high preload), and high afterload, contributing to reduced systemic blood pressure and perfusion.

354. In a patient with neurogenic shock following a spinal cord injury, what hemodynamic findings are typically observed?
a. Normal cardiac output, increased SVR, bradycardia
b. Decreased cardiac output, decreased SVR, hypotension
c. Increased cardiac output, decreased SVR, tachycardia
d. Decreased cardiac output, increased SVR, hypertension

Answer: b. Decreased cardiac output, decreased SVR, hypotension. Explanation: Neurogenic shock, resulting from spinal cord injury, is characterized by loss of sympathetic tone, leading to decreased SVR (vasodilation), decreased cardiac output due to impaired venous return and bradycardia, and resultant hypotension.

355. A patient with tamponade physiology presents with hypotension, jugular venous distension, and muffled heart sounds. Hemodynamically, you would expect:
a. Elevated CVP, decreased SVR, and decreased cardiac output
b. Decreased CVP, increased SVR, and increased cardiac output
c. Elevated CVP, increased SVR, and decreased cardiac output
d. Decreased CVP, decreased SVR, and decreased cardiac output

Answer: c. Elevated CVP, increased SVR, and decreased cardiac output. Explanation: Cardiac tamponade leads to increased intrapericardial pressure, which elevates CVP due to impaired venous return. The body compensates with increased SVR to maintain blood pressure, but cardiac output remains decreased due to the heart's impaired filling and pumping ability.

356. In the early stages of septic shock, what hemodynamic pattern is commonly observed?
a. Hyperdynamic state with high cardiac output and low SVR
b. Hypodynamic state with low cardiac output and high SVR
c. Hyperdynamic state with high cardiac output and high SVR
d. Hypodynamic state with low cardiac output and low SVR

Answer: a. Hyperdynamic state with high cardiac output and low SVR. Explanation: Early septic shock often presents as a hyperdynamic state characterized by high cardiac output due to increased metabolic demands and low SVR due to systemic vasodilation driven by inflammatory mediators.

357. A patient undergoing massive fluid resuscitation for burn injuries is at risk for developing which type of shock?
a. Hypovolemic due to ongoing fluid losses
b. Cardiogenic due to fluid overload and myocardial stress
c. Distributive due to systemic inflammatory response
d. Obstructive due to abdominal compartment syndrome

Answer: b. Cardiogenic due to fluid overload and myocardial stress. Explanation: Massive fluid resuscitation, especially in burn patients, can lead to fluid overload, increasing myocardial stress and potentially precipitating cardiogenic shock, particularly in patients with pre-existing heart disease or when resuscitation exceeds compensatory mechanisms.

358. In a patient with acute liver failure and ascites, which hemodynamic changes are most likely?
a. Low cardiac output, high SVR, high CVP
b. High cardiac output, low SVR, low CVP
c. Low cardiac output, low SVR, high CVP
d. High cardiac output, high SVR, low CVP

Answer: b. High cardiac output, low SVR, low CVP. Explanation: Acute liver failure can lead to a distributive shock-like state with systemic vasodilation (low SVR) due to circulating vasodilators, often accompanied by high cardiac output as a compensatory mechanism, and low CVP due to fluid shifts into the peritoneal cavity (ascites).

359. For a patient with acute pulmonary edema secondary to heart failure, which intervention is most appropriate?
a. Administration of high-flow oxygen and non-invasive positive pressure ventilation (NIPPV)
b. Immediate initiation of high-dose corticosteroids
c. Scheduled diuretics as outpatient therapy
d. Initiation of long-term anticoagulation therapy

Answer: a. Administration of high-flow oxygen and non-invasive positive pressure ventilation (NIPPV). Explanation: In acute pulmonary edema, particularly when secondary to heart failure, the immediate goals are to improve oxygenation and reduce the work of breathing. High-flow oxygen and NIPPV, such as CPAP or BiPAP, are effective interventions to achieve these goals by improving gas exchange and reducing preload and afterload on the heart.

360. In the management of a patient with cardiogenic shock post-myocardial infarction, which of the following is a priority intervention?
a. Rapid volume expansion with isotonic saline
b. Administration of inotropic agents to support cardiac output
c. Immediate anticoagulation with heparin
d. Therapeutic hypothermia to reduce metabolic demand

Answer: b. Administration of inotropic agents to support cardiac output. Explanation: In cardiogenic shock, especially post-myocardial infarction, the primary issue is the reduced ability of the heart to pump effectively. Inotropic agents such as dobutamine can increase cardiac contractility and support cardiac output, addressing the root cause of the shock state.

361. For a patient experiencing anaphylactic shock after a bee sting, which immediate intervention is most critical?
a. Oral antihistamines
b. Intramuscular epinephrine
c. Intravenous corticosteroids
d. High-dose intravenous antibiotics

Answer: b. Intramuscular epinephrine. Explanation: In anaphylactic shock, the most critical and life-saving intervention is the immediate administration of intramuscular epinephrine. Epinephrine counteracts the widespread vasodilation, increased vascular permeability, and bronchoconstriction characteristic of severe allergic reactions.

362. In managing a patient with septic shock, what initial fluid therapy is recommended?
a. Administration of 500 mL of crystalloid fluids as a rapid bolus
b. Slow infusion of 5% dextrose in water
c. Rapid administration of at least 30 mL/kg of crystalloid fluids
d. Immediate blood transfusion regardless of hemoglobin levels

Answer: c. Rapid administration of at least 30 mL/kg of crystalloid fluids. Explanation: The initial management of septic shock includes the rapid administration of fluids to counteract hypotension and improve tissue perfusion. The recommendation is for at least 30 mL/kg of crystalloid fluids to be administered rapidly to restore circulating volume.

363. For a patient with neurogenic shock following a spinal cord injury, which pharmacological intervention is typically required to manage hypotension?
a. Beta-blockers to control heart rate
b. Vasopressors to maintain adequate blood pressure
c. Diuretics to manage fluid overload
d. Calcium channel blockers to reduce vascular resistance

Answer: b. Vasopressors to maintain adequate blood pressure. Explanation: Neurogenic shock is characterized by the loss of sympathetic tone, leading to vasodilation and hypotension. Vasopressors are required to increase vascular tone and maintain adequate blood pressure in the absence of sympathetic control.

364. In a burn victim with hypovolemic shock due to extensive fluid loss through burned skin, which fluid replacement strategy is most appropriate?
a. Lactated Ringer's solution based on the Parkland formula
b. Immediate blood transfusion to replace lost red blood cells
c. Colloid solutions exclusively to restore oncotic pressure
d. Normal saline boluses guided solely by urine output

Answer: a. Lactated Ringer's solution based on the Parkland formula. Explanation: In burn patients, fluid resuscitation is critical to address hypovolemic shock. The Parkland formula provides a guideline for fluid resuscitation using lactated Ringer's solution, taking into account the extent of the burns and the patient's body weight to estimate fluid needs in the first 24 hours.

365. For the management of obstructive shock due to a tension pneumothorax, which intervention is most immediately required?
a. Broad-spectrum antibiotics
b. Needle decompression followed by chest tube placement
c. High-dose loop diuretics
d. Intravenous beta-blockers

Answer: b. Needle decompression followed by chest tube placement. Explanation: Obstructive shock from a tension pneumothorax requires immediate intervention to relieve the pressure on the heart and lungs. Needle decompression, followed by definitive management with chest tube placement, is essential to restore hemodynamic stability.

366. In treating hypovolemic shock secondary to gastrointestinal bleeding, which of the following is a key component of management?
a. Early initiation of beta-blocker therapy
b. Rapid crystalloid fluid resuscitation and blood product transfusion if indicated
c. Immediate administration of high-dose proton pump inhibitors
d. Vasopressor support as the initial step

Answer: b. Rapid crystalloid fluid resuscitation and blood product transfusion if indicated. Explanation: In hypovolemic shock due to acute blood loss, such as from gastrointestinal bleeding, the priority is to restore intravascular volume. This is achieved through rapid crystalloid fluid resuscitation and, if necessary, transfusion of blood products based on hemodynamic status and hemoglobin levels.

367. For a patient in shock with suspected adrenal insufficiency, which therapeutic intervention is crucial?
a. Immediate insulin therapy to manage hyperglycemia
b. High-dose intravenous corticosteroids
c. Oral thyroid hormone replacement
d. Continuous renal replacement therapy

Answer: b. High-dose intravenous corticosteroids. Explanation: In shock that is suspected to be due to adrenal insufficiency, administration of high-dose intravenous corticosteroids is crucial to replace the deficient adrenal hormones and improve hemodynamic stability.

368. In the context of cardiogenic shock, why is it important to carefully monitor fluid administration?
a. Fluid overload can precipitate acute respiratory distress syndrome (ARDS)
b. Excessive fluid can exacerbate left ventricular dysfunction, leading to pulmonary edema
c. Rapid fluid administration can lead to reperfusion injury
d. Fluids can dilute circulating catecholamines, reducing their effectiveness

Answer: b. Excessive fluid can exacerbate left ventricular dysfunction, leading to pulmonary edema. Explanation: In cardiogenic shock, the heart's pumping ability is compromised. Excessive fluid administration can further burden the heart, potentially worsening left ventricular dysfunction and leading to pulmonary edema, thus careful fluid management is essential.

369. Which clinical finding is most suggestive of cardiac tamponade in a patient with a pericardial effusion?
a. Bilateral leg swelling
b. Pulsus paradoxus greater than 10 mmHg
c. A high-pitched, blowing diastolic murmur
d. Widened pulse pressure

Answer: b. Pulsus paradoxus greater than 10 mmHg. Explanation: Pulsus paradoxus, defined as an exaggerated decrease in systolic blood pressure (>10 mmHg) during inspiration, is a hallmark sign of cardiac tamponade. This occurs due to the impaired filling of the right ventricle during inspiration, leading to a significant drop in left ventricular stroke volume and consequently systolic blood pressure.

370. A patient presents with Beck's triad (distant heart sounds, jugular venous distension, and hypotension). This triad is indicative of which condition?
a. Acute myocardial infarction
b. Aortic dissection
c. Cardiac tamponade
d. Pulmonary embolism

Answer: c. Cardiac tamponade. Explanation: Beck's triad is classically associated with cardiac tamponade and reflects the effects of increased intrapericardial pressure on the heart and venous system, leading to decreased cardiac output and venous congestion.

371. In assessing a patient for pulsus paradoxus, which method is most accurate?
a. Observing for a decrease in pulse amplitude during inspiration
b. Measuring the difference in systolic blood pressure between inspiration and expiration
c. Noting changes in jugular venous pressure with respiration
d. Assessing heart rate variability with respiratory cycles

Answer: b. Measuring the difference in systolic blood pressure between inspiration and expiration. Explanation: Pulsus paradoxus is quantitatively assessed by measuring the decrease in systolic blood pressure during inspiration compared to expiration, with a difference greater than 10 mmHg being significant and suggestive of cardiac tamponade.

372. A patient with suspected cardiac tamponade exhibits Kussmaul's sign. This sign is characterized by:
a. A decrease in jugular venous pressure on inspiration
b. An increase in jugular venous pressure on inspiration
c. A decrease in diastolic blood pressure by more than 10 mmHg during inspiration
d. An inspiratory silence in heart sounds

Answer: b. An increase in jugular venous pressure on inspiration. Explanation: Kussmaul's sign, which is an increase in jugular venous pressure during inspiration, is not typically associated with cardiac tamponade but can be observed in some cases. It is more commonly seen in conditions like constrictive pericarditis but indicates impaired right heart filling which can also occur in tamponade.

373. In the context of cardiac tamponade, electrical alternans on the ECG is characterized by:
a. Alternating QRS complex amplitudes from beat to beat
b. A constant PR interval with varying QRS complex widths
c. Regular alteration in the P wave morphology
d. Cyclic changes in the ST segment and T wave

Answer: a. Alternating QRS complex amplitudes from beat to beat. Explanation: Electrical alternans, defined as alternating amplitudes of the QRS complexes on an ECG, is suggestive of cardiac tamponade. It reflects the swinging motion of the heart within a large pericardial effusion, affecting the electrical vectors detected by the ECG.

374. During a bedside echocardiogram for a hypotensive patient, which finding would be most suggestive of cardiac tamponade?
a. Left ventricular hypertrophy
b. Right ventricular diastolic collapse
c. Mitral valve prolapse
d. Aortic root dilation

Answer: b. Right ventricular diastolic collapse. Explanation: Right ventricular diastolic collapse is a key echocardiographic sign of cardiac tamponade, indicating that the increased pericardial pressure is impeding the filling of the right ventricle during diastole.

375. A patient with cardiac tamponade is likely to exhibit which hemodynamic pattern on invasive monitoring?
a. Decreased cardiac output, increased systemic vascular resistance
b. Increased cardiac output, decreased pulmonary capillary wedge pressure
c. Decreased cardiac output, decreased systemic vascular resistance
d. Increased cardiac output, increased central venous pressure

Answer: a. Decreased cardiac output, increased systemic vascular resistance. Explanation: Cardiac tamponade typically leads to decreased cardiac output due to impaired ventricular filling, with compensatory increases in systemic vascular resistance as the body attempts to maintain blood pressure.

376. In managing a patient with acute cardiac tamponade, which intervention is considered definitive?
a. High-dose loop diuretics
b. Emergency pericardiocentesis
c. Intravenous beta-blockers
d. Administration of inotropic agents

Answer: b. Emergency pericardiocentesis. Explanation: Emergency pericardiocentesis, the removal of fluid from the pericardial space using a needle, is the definitive treatment for acute cardiac tamponade to relieve the pressure on the heart and restore normal hemodynamics.

377. When considering the diagnosis of cardiac tamponade, which clinical scenario would be most consistent with this condition?
a. A patient with chest trauma presents with hypotension, clear lung fields, and elevated jugular venous pressure.
b. A patient with a history of hypertension presents with a sudden onset of severe chest pain radiating to the back.
c. A patient with chronic renal failure presents with dyspnea on exertion and bilateral leg edema.

d. A patient with a recent upper respiratory infection presents with sharp, pleuritic chest pain that improves when sitting up.

Answer: a. A patient with chest trauma presents with hypotension, clear lung fields, and elevated jugular venous pressure. Explanation: This scenario suggests cardiac tamponade, especially following chest trauma, where hypotension (due to decreased cardiac output), clear lung fields (indicating the absence of heart failure), and elevated jugular venous pressure (reflecting increased intrapericardial pressure) are classic findings.

378. What is the primary mechanism by which an Intra-Aortic Balloon Pump (IABP) provides hemodynamic support?
a. Continuous infusion of inotropic drugs into the aorta
b. Mechanical squeezing of the heart to improve ejection
c. Augmentation of diastolic pressure and afterload reduction
d. Replacement of the heart's pumping function with a mechanical device

Answer: c. Augmentation of diastolic pressure and afterload reduction. Explanation: The IABP works by inflating during diastole to increase diastolic pressure, which improves coronary artery perfusion, and deflating just before systole to reduce afterload, which decreases the work of the heart and improves cardiac output.

379. In which clinical scenario is the use of an IABP most appropriate?
a. Refractory hypertension
b. Cardiogenic shock following acute myocardial infarction
c. Primary prevention of heart failure in high-risk patients
d. Chronic stable angina without left ventricular dysfunction

Answer: b. Cardiogenic shock following acute myocardial infarction. Explanation: The IABP is commonly used in cardiogenic shock following acute myocardial infarction to temporarily support cardiac function by increasing myocardial oxygen supply and decreasing oxygen demand until definitive treatment can be administered.

380. Which statement best describes the operational principle of Ventricular Assist Devices (VADs)?
a. VADs directly compress the heart muscle to enhance contraction.
b. VADs rhythmically inflate and deflate to mimic the cardiac cycle.
c. VADs mechanically pump blood, supplementing or replacing the function of one or both ventricles.
d. VADs use electrical stimulation to enhance the heart's natural contractions.

Answer: c. VADs mechanically pump blood, supplementing or replacing the function of one or both ventricles. Explanation: VADs are mechanical pumps that assist or take over the pumping function of the ventricles by drawing blood from the ventricles and delivering it to the aorta or pulmonary artery, thus supporting circulation in patients with severe heart failure.

381. What is a key benefit of using an IABP in patients with acute myocardial ischemia?

a. Permanent correction of the underlying coronary artery disease
b. Immediate restoration of normal cardiac rhythm
c. Enhanced myocardial oxygen supply through increased diastolic pressure
d. Immediate and complete offloading of the left ventricle

Answer: c. Enhanced myocardial oxygen supply through increased diastolic pressure. Explanation: The IABP enhances myocardial oxygen supply by augmenting diastolic pressure, which increases coronary blood flow, providing temporary support to ischemic myocardium.

382. When considering a patient for VAD implantation, what is a critical factor to evaluate?
a. Ability to perform daily vigorous exercise
b. Adequate renal and hepatic function
c. Absence of all comorbid conditions
d. History of previous cardiac surgeries

Answer: b. Adequate renal and hepatic function. Explanation: Before VAD implantation, it is critical to assess the patient's renal and hepatic function among other factors, as these organs' function can significantly impact the patient's ability to tolerate the device and the surgery, and their overall prognosis.

383. How does an IABP affect myocardial oxygen demand?
a. Increases demand by increasing afterload
b. Decreases demand by reducing afterload through diastolic augmentation
c. Has no effect on myocardial oxygen demand
d. Increases demand by augmenting systolic pressure

Answer: b. Decreases demand by reducing afterload through diastolic augmentation. Explanation: The IABP decreases myocardial oxygen demand by reducing afterload through its mechanism of deflating just before systole, which decreases the resistance against which the heart must pump.

384. In the context of heart failure management, what is a primary indication for VAD implantation?
a. As a bridge to myocardial recovery in acute heart failure
b. As a permanent solution in all patients with end-stage heart failure
c. In patients with mild heart failure as a preventive measure
d. As destination therapy in patients who are not candidates for heart transplantation

Answer: d. As destination therapy in patients who are not candidates for heart transplantation. Explanation: VADs are used as destination therapy in patients with end-stage heart failure who are not candidates for heart transplantation, providing long-term support to improve quality of life and survival.

385. What is the impact of IABP therapy on renal perfusion in the setting of cardiogenic shock?

a. Worsens renal perfusion by increasing renal vascular resistance
b. No significant effect on renal perfusion
c. Improves renal perfusion by enhancing overall hemodynamics
d. Directly improves renal function by mechanical effects on the kidneys

Answer: c. Improves renal perfusion by enhancing overall hemodynamics. Explanation: IABP therapy can improve renal perfusion indirectly by enhancing overall hemodynamics, including increased cardiac output and improved systemic blood flow, which in turn can lead to better renal blood flow.

386. Which patient monitoring parameter is essential during IABP therapy to ensure proper timing of balloon inflation and deflation?
a. Continuous renal function tests
b. Intra-aortic pressure waveforms
c. Daily echocardiograms
d. Serial liver function tests

Answer: b. Intra-aortic pressure waveforms. Explanation: Continuous monitoring of intra-aortic pressure waveforms is essential during IABP therapy to ensure proper timing of balloon inflation (during diastole) and deflation (just before systole), which is critical for the device's effectiveness and the patient's safety.

387. A patient with COPD is experiencing increased work of breathing. Which respiratory mechanics change is most responsible for this symptom?
a. Decreased tidal volume
b. Increased airway resistance
c. Decreased respiratory rate
d. Increased lung compliance

Answer: b. Increased airway resistance. Explanation: In COPD, the primary issue leading to increased work of breathing is increased airway resistance due to chronic inflammation, mucus production, and structural changes in the airways. This resistance makes it harder for air to move in and out of the lungs, thereby increasing the effort required to breathe.

388. A patient is diagnosed with restrictive lung disease. Which characteristic change in respiratory mechanics is typically observed?
a. Increased lung compliance
b. Decreased lung compliance
c. Increased airway resistance
d. Decreased airway resistance

Answer: b. Decreased lung compliance. Explanation: Restrictive lung diseases are characterized by decreased lung compliance due to stiffening of the lung tissue, making it more difficult for the lungs to expand during inhalation. This stiffness can result from fibrosis, inflammation, or other alterations in lung parenchyma.

389. During mechanical ventilation, a sudden increase in peak airway pressures is noted. What is the most likely cause?
a. Endotracheal tube displacement
b. Pneumothorax
c. Decreased lung compliance
d. Bronchospasm

Answer: d. Bronchospasm. Explanation: A sudden increase in peak airway pressures during mechanical ventilation can indicate bronchospasm, which increases airway resistance. This resistance to airflow can significantly raise the pressure needed to deliver a set tidal volume.

390. In a patient with acute respiratory distress syndrome (ARDS), which finding is most consistent with the underlying pathophysiology?
a. Increased lung compliance
b. Decreased lung compliance
c. Unchanged airway resistance
d. Decreased functional residual capacity (FRC)

Answer: b. Decreased lung compliance. Explanation: ARDS is characterized by diffuse alveolar damage leading to significant inflammation, pulmonary edema, and fibrosis, resulting in decreased lung compliance. The lungs become stiff and difficult to ventilate, a hallmark of ARDS pathophysiology.

391. A patient presents with a history of asthma. During an exacerbation, which change in respiratory mechanics is expected?
a. Decreased lung compliance
b. Increased lung compliance
c. Increased airway resistance
d. Decreased airway resistance

Answer: c. Increased airway resistance. Explanation: Asthma exacerbations are marked by bronchoconstriction, inflammation, and increased mucus production, all of which contribute to increased airway resistance. This resistance makes it more difficult for air to flow through the bronchial tubes, leading to symptoms like wheezing and shortness of breath.

392. In evaluating a patient with pulmonary fibrosis, what alteration in respiratory mechanics is most anticipated?
a. Increased tidal volume
b. Decreased lung compliance
c. Increased functional residual capacity (FRC)

d. Decreased airway resistance

Answer: b. Decreased lung compliance. Explanation: Pulmonary fibrosis leads to the thickening and scarring of lung tissue, resulting in decreased lung compliance. The stiff lung tissue requires more effort to expand during inhalation, reducing lung volumes and capacities.

393. During a spirometry test, a patient with emphysema is likely to show:
a. Decreased forced expiratory volume in 1 second (FEV1)/Forced vital capacity (FVC) ratio
b. Increased peak expiratory flow rate (PEFR)
c. Decreased residual volume
d. Increased lung compliance

Answer: a. Decreased forced expiratory volume in 1 second (FEV1)/Forced vital capacity (FVC) ratio. Explanation: Emphysema, a type of COPD, is characterized by the destruction of alveolar walls and loss of elastic recoil, leading to air trapping. This results in a decreased FEV1/FVC ratio on spirometry, indicative of obstructive lung disease.

394. A mechanically ventilated patient exhibits a sudden decrease in compliance. What could be the immediate clinical implication of this finding?
a. The need to decrease tidal volume
b. The possibility of acute pneumothorax
c. The need to increase respiratory rate
d. The development of pulmonary embolism

Answer: b. The possibility of acute pneumothorax. Explanation: A sudden decrease in lung compliance in a mechanically ventilated patient could indicate the development of an acute pneumothorax, where air accumulates in the pleural space, increasing intrathoracic pressure and significantly reducing lung compliance.

395. In a patient with a flail chest injury, what abnormal respiratory mechanics are typically observed?
a. Paradoxical chest wall movement
b. Decreased airway resistance
c. Increased lung compliance
d. Uniform chest expansion during inspiration

Answer: a. Paradoxical chest wall movement. Explanation: Flail chest results from multiple rib fractures, leading to a segment of the chest wall that moves paradoxically (inward during inspiration and outward during expiration), significantly impairing ventilation efficiency and gas exchange.

396. A patient with neuromuscular disease exhibits a reduced forced vital capacity (FVC). This reduction is primarily due to:
a. Increased airway resistance

b. Decreased airway resistance
c. Decreased lung compliance
d. Reduced respiratory muscle strength

Answer: d. Reduced respiratory muscle strength. Explanation: In patients with neuromuscular diseases, the primary issue leading to reduced FVC is the diminished strength of respiratory muscles, which impairs the ability to generate adequate ventilation pressure, affecting lung volumes and capacities.

397. What is the primary driving force for air movement into the lungs during normal quiet breathing?
a. Positive pressure from the environment
b. Negative intrapleural pressure created by diaphragmatic contraction
c. Positive intrapulmonary pressure generated by the respiratory muscles
d. Active transport mechanisms in the alveolar walls

Answer: b. Negative intrapleural pressure created by diaphragmatic contraction. Explanation: During normal quiet breathing, the primary driving force for air movement into the lungs is the creation of negative intrapleural pressure, which results from the contraction of the diaphragm. This negative pressure relative to atmospheric pressure causes air to flow into the lungs.

398. In mechanical ventilation, what does the term "peak inspiratory pressure" (PIP) refer to?
a. The highest level of positive pressure in the airways at the end of spontaneous inhalation
b. The maximum pressure the ventilator generates to overcome airway resistance and lung compliance during inhalation
c. The steady pressure maintained in the airways during the expiratory phase
d. The pressure applied to ensure alveolar recruitment during the inspiratory hold

Answer: b. The maximum pressure the ventilator generates to overcome airway resistance and lung compliance during inhalation. Explanation: Peak inspiratory pressure (PIP) in mechanical ventilation refers to the maximum level of positive pressure reached in the airways during inhalation. This pressure is necessary to overcome airway resistance and the elastic recoil of the lungs to deliver the set tidal volume.

399. How does airway resistance impact ventilation?
a. Increased airway resistance decreases the rate of air flow into the lungs
b. Decreased airway resistance increases the pressure gradient required for ventilation
c. Increased airway resistance enhances alveolar gas exchange
d. Decreased airway resistance leads to reduced oxygen delivery to the alveoli

Answer: a. Increased airway resistance decreases the rate of air flow into the lungs. Explanation: Airway resistance is a critical factor in determining the ease of airflow into and out of the lungs. Increased airway resistance, as seen in conditions like asthma or chronic obstructive pulmonary disease (COPD), impedes airflow, making ventilation more difficult and less efficient.

400. What role does the pressure gradient between the atmosphere and the alveoli play in ventilation?
a. It determines the diffusion capacity of the alveolar membrane
b. It directly influences the oxygen-carrying capacity of hemoglobin
c. It is the driving force for air movement during the respiratory cycle
d. It regulates the rate of carbon dioxide elimination from the blood

Answer: c. It is the driving force for air movement during the respiratory cycle. Explanation: The pressure gradient between the atmosphere and the alveoli is the fundamental driving force for air movement during the respiratory cycle. Air moves from areas of higher pressure to areas of lower pressure, facilitating inhalation and exhalation based on the changes in alveolar and atmospheric pressures.

401. In the context of mechanical ventilation, what effect does an increase in airway resistance have on the patient's breathing effort?
a. It decreases the work of breathing by reducing the pressure needed for inhalation
b. It increases the work of breathing due to higher pressures required to maintain airflow
c. It has no significant effect on the work of breathing as it is compensated by the ventilator
d. It reduces the tidal volume without affecting the breathing effort

Answer: b. It increases the work of breathing due to higher pressures required to maintain airflow. Explanation: An increase in airway resistance, such as from bronchospasm or mucous plugging, elevates the pressures needed to maintain adequate airflow during mechanical ventilation. This results in an increased work of breathing for the patient, even if the ventilator is providing support, making the breathing effort more strenuous.

402. What is the primary determinant of airway resistance in the bronchial tree?
a. The length of the airways
b. The radius of the bronchioles
c. The viscosity of the inspired air
d. The surface tension of the alveoli

Answer: b. The radius of the bronchioles. Explanation: According to Poiseuille's law, the primary determinant of airway resistance in the bronchial tree is the radius of the airways, particularly the bronchioles. Even small changes in the radius can significantly impact airway resistance, with resistance inversely proportional to the fourth power of the radius.

403. During mechanical ventilation, how does positive end-expiratory pressure (PEEP) affect oxygenation?
a. By increasing airway resistance and thus improving alveolar ventilation
b. By decreasing the functional residual capacity and increasing shunt
c. By preventing alveolar collapse and improving functional residual capacity
d. By increasing the pressure gradient for oxygen diffusion into the blood

Answer: c. By preventing alveolar collapse and improving functional residual capacity. Explanation: PEEP is used in mechanical ventilation to maintain positive pressure in the lungs at the end of expiration. This prevents alveolar collapse (atelectasis), maintains a higher functional residual capacity, and improves oxygenation by ensuring better alveolar gas exchange.

404. What is the impact of high tidal volumes on lung injury during mechanical ventilation?
a. High tidal volumes are protective against ventilator-induced lung injury
b. High tidal volumes can lead to alveolar overdistension and barotrauma
c. High tidal volumes decrease airway resistance and improve compliance
d. High tidal volumes enhance oxygenation by increasing the diffusion gradient

Answer: b. High tidal volumes can lead to alveolar overdistension and barotrauma. Explanation: The use of high tidal volumes in mechanical ventilation can lead to overdistension of alveoli, contributing to ventilator-induced lung injury (VILI), characterized by barotrauma, volutrauma, and the exacerbation of acute lung injury.

405. How does the body compensate for increased airway resistance in conditions like asthma?
a. By decreasing respiratory rate to reduce airflow demand
b. By increasing inspiratory muscle effort to generate higher negative intrathoracic pressure
c. By reducing tidal volume to minimize airway stretch
d. By increasing oxygen extraction at the tissue level to reduce ventilatory needs

Answer: b. By increasing inspiratory muscle effort to generate higher negative intrathoracic pressure. Explanation: In response to increased airway resistance, as seen in conditions like asthma, the body compensates by increasing the effort of inspiratory muscles. This generates a higher negative intrathoracic pressure to overcome the resistance and maintain adequate ventilation.

406. What is the significance of the compliance-pressure curve in mechanical ventilation?
a. It determines the optimal PEEP level to avoid alveolar collapse
b. It indicates the patient's ability to initiate spontaneous breaths
c. It reflects the efficiency of gas exchange across the alveolar membrane
d. It predicts the likelihood of developing pulmonary hypertension

Answer: a. It determines the optimal PEEP level to avoid alveolar collapse. Explanation: The compliance-pressure curve, particularly the lower inflection point, helps in determining the optimal level of PEEP in mechanical ventilation. Setting PEEP above this point can prevent alveolar collapse at the end of expiration, improving oxygenation and reducing the risk of ventilator-induced lung injury.

407. During normal quiet breathing, the primary muscle responsible for inhalation is the:
a. External intercostal muscles
b. Diaphragm
c. Internal intercostal muscles

d. Sternocleidomastoid

Answer: b. Diaphragm. Explanation: The diaphragm is the primary muscle of respiration during quiet breathing. It contracts and moves downward, increasing the thoracic cavity's volume and decreasing intrathoracic pressure, leading to air inflow into the lungs.

408. In a patient with diaphragmatic paralysis, which compensatory mechanism is most commonly observed during respiration?
a. Increased use of accessory neck muscles
b. Decreased tidal volume with increased respiratory rate
c. Abdominal paradox during inspiration
d. Enhanced activity of the internal intercostal muscles

Answer: a. Increased use of accessory neck muscles. Explanation: In cases of diaphragmatic paralysis, patients often compensate by using accessory muscles of respiration, including the neck muscles (such as sternocleidomastoid), to aid in inhalation when the diaphragm's function is compromised.

409. During forced expiration, such as in coughing or heavy exercise, which muscles become more actively involved?
a. Diaphragm and external intercostal muscles
b. Internal intercostal muscles and abdominal muscles
c. Scalene muscles and pectoralis minor
d. Diaphragm and scalene muscles

Answer: b. Internal intercostal muscles and abdominal muscles. Explanation: During forced expiration, the internal intercostal muscles and abdominal muscles contract to decrease the thoracic cavity's volume by pulling the ribs downward and compressing the abdominal contents upwards against the diaphragm, respectively, increasing the intrathoracic pressure and forcing air out of the lungs.

410. In a patient with severe COPD, how might the role of the diaphragm change due to the disease's progression?
a. The diaphragm becomes more dome-shaped, increasing its efficiency
b. The diaphragm flattens, leading to reduced inspiratory capacity
c. The diaphragm's contraction strength increases, compensating for airway resistance
d. The diaphragm relies more on the intercostal muscles for inhalation

Answer: b. The diaphragm flattens, leading to reduced inspiratory capacity. Explanation: In severe COPD, hyperinflation of the lungs can lead to a flattened diaphragm. This altered shape reduces the diaphragm's mechanical advantage and efficiency in generating negative intrathoracic pressure, thereby decreasing inspiratory capacity.

411. Which of the following best describes the action of the external intercostal muscles during normal quiet breathing?

a. They contract during expiration to pull the ribs downward
b. They relax during inspiration, allowing the ribs to move inward
c. They contract during inspiration, elevating the ribs and expanding the thoracic cavity
d. They remain passive throughout the respiratory cycle

Answer: c. They contract during inspiration, elevating the ribs and expanding the thoracic cavity. Explanation: The external intercostal muscles contract during inspiration, pulling the ribs upward and outward, which increases the thoracic cavity's volume and aids in reducing intrathoracic pressure to facilitate air inflow into the lungs.

412. In a patient with flail chest following trauma, how does the movement of the diaphragm and intercostal muscles change during respiration?
a. The diaphragm moves upwards during inspiration
b. Paradoxical movement of the affected chest wall segment occurs
c. The external intercostal muscles become inactive
d. The diaphragm remains stationary throughout the respiratory cycle

Answer: b. Paradoxical movement of the affected chest wall segment occurs. Explanation: In flail chest, multiple adjacent ribs are fractured in multiple places, leading to a segment of the chest wall that moves paradoxically (inward during inspiration and outward during expiration), contrary to normal chest wall movement, which can severely impair ventilation.

413. During a maximal inspiration effort, which muscle action is least involved in expanding the thoracic cavity?
a. Contraction of the diaphragm
b. Contraction of the external intercostal muscles
c. Contraction of accessory muscles like the sternocleidomastoid
d. Contraction of the internal intercostal muscles

Answer: d. Contraction of the internal intercostal muscles. Explanation: During maximal inspiration, the internal intercostal muscles are not primarily involved in expanding the thoracic cavity. Instead, the diaphragm, external intercostal muscles, and accessory muscles (such as the sternocleidomastoid and scalenes) actively contract to maximize thoracic expansion.

414. How does the diaphragm move during inspiration in a healthy individual?
a. It contracts and moves upward, decreasing thoracic volume
b. It relaxes and curves upwards, increasing thoracic pressure
c. It contracts and flattens downward, increasing thoracic volume
d. It remains stationary while the rib cage expands

Answer: c. It contracts and flattens downward, increasing thoracic volume. Explanation: During inspiration, the diaphragm contracts and moves downward, flattening its dome shape, which increases the thoracic cavity's volume and decreases intrathoracic pressure, facilitating air inflow into the lungs.

415. In assessing a patient's breathing pattern, you observe a significant inward movement of the abdomen during inspiration. This finding is known as:
a. Hoover's sign
b. Kussmaul's respiration
c. Cheyne-Stokes respiration
d. Abdominal paradox

Answer: d. Abdominal paradox. Explanation: Abdominal paradox is observed when the abdomen moves inward during inspiration, contrary to the normal outward movement. This can indicate diaphragmatic dysfunction or fatigue, where the diaphragm is unable to contract effectively.

416. What is the impact of abdominal surgery on diaphragmatic function and respiratory mechanics?
a. Increased diaphragmatic movement due to reduced abdominal content pressure
b. Decreased diaphragmatic movement due to pain and splinting
c. Unchanged diaphragmatic function as it is not influenced by abdominal processes
d. Enhanced efficiency of the diaphragm due to reduced intra-abdominal volume

Answer: b. Decreased diaphragmatic movement due to pain and splinting. Explanation: After abdominal surgery, patients often experience pain that leads to splinting and reduced movement of the diaphragm. This can impair diaphragmatic function and reduce the efficiency of respiratory mechanics, contributing to shallow breathing and increased risk of postoperative pulmonary complications.

417. What shift in the oxygen-hemoglobin dissociation curve would be expected in a patient with respiratory alkalosis?
a. Rightward shift, indicating increased oxygen affinity
b. Leftward shift, indicating increased oxygen affinity
c. Rightward shift, indicating decreased oxygen affinity
d. No significant shift, as pH changes do not affect the curve

Answer: b. Leftward shift, indicating increased oxygen affinity. Explanation: Respiratory alkalosis, characterized by a higher pH (lower hydrogen ion concentration), leads to a leftward shift in the oxygen-hemoglobin dissociation curve. This shift increases hemoglobin's affinity for oxygen, making it less likely to release oxygen to the tissues.

418. In a patient with chronic obstructive pulmonary disease (COPD), how might the oxygen-hemoglobin dissociation curve be affected during an exacerbation?
a. Leftward shift due to decreased carbon dioxide levels
b. Rightward shift due to increased carbon dioxide levels
c. Leftward shift due to increased oxygen levels
d. Rightward shift due to decreased oxygen levels

Answer: b. Rightward shift due to increased carbon dioxide levels. Explanation: During a COPD exacerbation, carbon dioxide levels may rise, leading to respiratory acidosis. This results in a rightward shift of the oxygen-hemoglobin dissociation curve, decreasing hemoglobin's affinity for oxygen and facilitating oxygen release to the tissues.

419. How does an increase in body temperature affect the oxygen-hemoglobin dissociation curve?
a. Causes a leftward shift, increasing oxygen affinity
b. Causes a rightward shift, decreasing oxygen affinity
c. Results in an upward shift, increasing hemoglobin saturation
d. Results in a downward shift, decreasing hemoglobin saturation

Answer: b. Causes a rightward shift, decreasing oxygen affinity. Explanation: An increase in body temperature leads to a rightward shift in the oxygen-hemoglobin dissociation curve. This shift decreases hemoglobin's affinity for oxygen, enhancing oxygen unloading to the tissues where it is needed most, such as in metabolically active or inflamed areas.

420. What effect does fetal hemoglobin (HbF) have on the oxygen-hemoglobin dissociation curve compared to adult hemoglobin (HbA)?
a. Rightward shift, indicating lower oxygen affinity
b. Leftward shift, indicating higher oxygen affinity
c. No shift, but a higher P50 value, indicating lower oxygen affinity
d. No shift, but a lower P50 value, indicating higher oxygen affinity

Answer: b. Leftward shift, indicating higher oxygen affinity. Explanation: Fetal hemoglobin (HbF) has a higher oxygen affinity than adult hemoglobin (HbA), which is represented by a leftward shift in the oxygen-hemoglobin dissociation curve. This higher affinity facilitates the transfer of oxygen from the mother's hemoglobin to the fetus.

421. In the setting of acute anemia, how does the oxygen-hemoglobin dissociation curve aid in maintaining tissue oxygenation?
a. Leftward shift to increase hemoglobin's oxygen affinity
b. Rightward shift to enhance oxygen unloading to tissues
c. Upward shift to increase hemoglobin saturation at lower oxygen levels
d. Downward shift to decrease hemoglobin saturation at higher oxygen levels

Answer: b. Rightward shift to enhance oxygen unloading to tissues. Explanation: In response to acute anemia, physiological adaptations may include a rightward shift in the oxygen-hemoglobin dissociation curve, which decreases hemoglobin's oxygen affinity and facilitates oxygen unloading to the tissues, helping to compensate for the reduced oxygen-carrying capacity.

422. How does 2,3-Bisphosphoglycerate (2,3-BPG) concentration affect the oxygen-hemoglobin dissociation curve in patients residing at high altitudes?
a. Decreased 2,3-BPG leads to a leftward shift
b. Increased 2,3-BPG leads to a leftward shift

c. Decreased 2,3-BPG leads to a rightward shift
d. Increased 2,3-BPG leads to a rightward shift

Answer: d. Increased 2,3-BPG leads to a rightward shift. Explanation: High altitude adaptation involves increased 2,3-BPG concentrations in red blood cells, which bind to hemoglobin and decrease its oxygen affinity. This results in a rightward shift of the oxygen-hemoglobin dissociation curve, facilitating oxygen unloading to tissues under conditions of low ambient oxygen.

423. In a patient with carbon monoxide poisoning, how is the oxygen-hemoglobin dissociation curve affected?
a. Leftward shift due to carbon monoxide's higher affinity for hemoglobin
b. Rightward shift due to carbon monoxide's lower affinity for hemoglobin
c. Upward shift, increasing the hemoglobin saturation with oxygen
d. Downward shift, decreasing the hemoglobin saturation with oxygen

Answer: a. Leftward shift due to carbon monoxide's higher affinity for hemoglobin. Explanation: Carbon monoxide (CO) binds to hemoglobin with much greater affinity than oxygen, leading to a leftward shift in the oxygen-hemoglobin dissociation curve. This shift reflects the increased affinity of hemoglobin for oxygen in the presence of CO, but it also means that less oxygen is available to be unloaded to tissues, contributing to tissue hypoxia.

424. What impact does metabolic acidosis have on the oxygen-hemoglobin dissociation curve?
a. Leftward shift, indicating increased oxygen affinity
b. Rightward shift, indicating decreased oxygen affinity
c. No significant shift, but an increase in hemoglobin saturation
d. No significant shift, but a decrease in hemoglobin saturation

Answer: b. Rightward shift, indicating decreased oxygen affinity. Explanation: Metabolic acidosis, characterized by a decrease in blood pH, leads to a rightward shift in the oxygen-hemoglobin dissociation curve. This shift decreases hemoglobin's affinity for oxygen, promoting oxygen unloading to the tissues, which is beneficial in states of acidosis where tissue oxygen demand is increased.

425. During vigorous exercise, how does the oxygen-hemoglobin dissociation curve facilitate increased oxygen delivery to active muscles?
a. By shifting leftward, increasing oxygen affinity
b. By shifting rightward, decreasing oxygen affinity
c. By remaining unchanged, maintaining baseline oxygen delivery
d. By shifting upward, increasing the maximum oxygen saturation

Answer: b. By shifting rightward, decreasing oxygen affinity. Explanation: During vigorous exercise, local factors such as increased carbon dioxide, temperature, and decreased pH in active muscles cause a rightward shift in the oxygen-hemoglobin dissociation curve. This shift decreases hemoglobin's affinity for oxygen, enhancing oxygen unloading to meet the heightened metabolic demands of active tissues.

426. In patients with chronic renal failure, how might the oxygen-hemoglobin dissociation curve be altered?
a. Leftward shift due to decreased production of 2,3-BPG
b. Rightward shift due to increased production of 2,3-BPG
c. Leftward shift due to accumulation of acidic metabolites
d. Rightward shift due to accumulation of acidic metabolites

Answer: d. Rightward shift due to accumulation of acidic metabolites. Explanation: Chronic renal failure can lead to metabolic acidosis due to the accumulation of acidic metabolites, which can cause a rightward shift in the oxygen-hemoglobin dissociation curve.

427. What is the primary driving force for oxygen to move from the alveoli into the capillary blood?
a. The concentration gradient of oxygen between the alveoli and capillaries
b. Active transport mechanisms within the alveolar walls
c. The hydrostatic pressure in the pulmonary capillaries
d. The osmotic pressure difference between the alveolar air and blood

Answer: a. The concentration gradient of oxygen between the alveoli and capillaries. Explanation: The primary driving force for oxygen to move from the alveoli into the capillary blood is the concentration gradient (partial pressure difference) of oxygen between the alveoli (higher concentration) and the capillaries (lower concentration). This passive diffusion process does not require energy.

428. In a patient with chronic obstructive pulmonary disease (COPD), how does the disease process typically affect gas exchange?
a. By increasing the diffusion capacity of the alveoli
b. By reducing airway resistance and improving airflow
c. By causing mismatched ventilation-perfusion (V/Q) ratios
d. By increasing the oxygen-carrying capacity of hemoglobin

Answer: c. By causing mismatched ventilation-perfusion (V/Q) ratios. Explanation: COPD typically leads to areas of the lung with poor ventilation relative to perfusion, causing mismatched ventilation-perfusion (V/Q) ratios. This mismatch can lead to inadequate oxygenation of blood and retention of carbon dioxide, impairing gas exchange.

429. What is the effect of high altitude on oxygenation and how is it compensated?
a. High altitude decreases atmospheric oxygen pressure, compensated by increased hemoglobin affinity for oxygen
b. High altitude increases atmospheric oxygen pressure, compensated by hyperventilation
c. High altitude decreases atmospheric oxygen pressure, compensated by hyperventilation and increased red blood cell production
d. High altitude increases atmospheric carbon dioxide pressure, compensated by increased breathing rate

Answer: c. High altitude decreases atmospheric oxygen pressure, compensated by hyperventilation and increased red blood cell production. Explanation: High altitude leads to decreased atmospheric oxygen pressure, reducing the partial pressure of oxygen in the alveoli. Compensation includes hyperventilation to increase oxygen uptake and erythropoiesis to increase the oxygen-carrying capacity of the blood.

430. In the context of acute respiratory distress syndrome (ARDS), what mechanism primarily contributes to impaired gas exchange?
a. Increased capillary hydrostatic pressure leading to alveolar flooding
b. Destruction of the alveolar-capillary membrane
c. Formation of intrapulmonary shunts due to alveolar collapse and fluid-filled alveoli
d. Hyperinflation of alveoli leading to decreased surface area for gas exchange

Answer: c. Formation of intrapulmonary shunts due to alveolar collapse and fluid-filled alveoli. Explanation: In ARDS, impaired gas exchange is primarily due to the formation of intrapulmonary shunts, where blood passes through the lungs without being oxygenated due to alveolar collapse and fluid-filled alveoli, resulting from inflammatory processes and increased permeability of the alveolar-capillary barrier.

431. How does carbon dioxide removal differ from oxygen uptake in the lungs?
a. CO_2 is actively transported out of the blood, while O_2 diffusion is passive
b. CO_2 removal is less efficient than O_2 uptake due to lower solubility in blood
c. CO_2 is more soluble in blood and diffuses more readily across the alveolar-capillary membrane than O_2
d. CO_2 requires a carrier molecule for diffusion, whereas O_2 diffuses freely

Answer: c. CO_2 is more soluble in blood and diffuses more readily across the alveolar-capillary membrane than O_2. Explanation: Carbon dioxide is more soluble in blood than oxygen and diffuses more readily across the alveolar-capillary membrane. This higher solubility allows for efficient removal of CO_2 from the blood, even in areas with impaired ventilation-perfusion ratios.

432. What role does the Haldane effect play in gas exchange within the lungs?
a. It enhances oxygen unloading in tissues by increasing hemoglobin's affinity for oxygen
b. It reduces carbon dioxide transport by converting CO_2 to bicarbonate in red blood cells
c. It facilitates carbon dioxide removal by decreasing hemoglobin's affinity for CO_2 in the presence of high oxygen levels
d. It increases oxygen uptake by alveoli through direct chemical reactions with carbon dioxide

Answer: c. It facilitates carbon dioxide removal by decreasing hemoglobin's affinity for CO_2 in the presence of high oxygen levels. Explanation: The Haldane effect describes how oxygenation of blood in the lungs decreases hemoglobin's affinity for carbon dioxide, facilitating CO_2 release from hemoglobin and its subsequent exhalation. This effect enhances CO_2 removal during gas exchange.

433. In patients with right-to-left cardiac shunts, how is gas exchange affected?
a. Oxygenation improves due to increased transit time through the lungs

b. Carbon dioxide removal is enhanced, leading to respiratory alkalosis
c. Oxygenated and deoxygenated blood mix, leading to systemic arterial desaturation
d. Pulmonary capillary pressure decreases, improving alveolar gas exchange

Answer: c. Oxygenated and deoxygenated blood mix, leading to systemic arterial desaturation. Explanation: Right-to-left cardiac shunts allow deoxygenated blood from the right side of the heart to bypass the lungs and mix with oxygenated blood in the left side of the heart, leading to systemic arterial desaturation and reduced oxygen delivery to tissues.

434. How does positive pressure ventilation affect intrapulmonary shunting?
a. It increases shunting by compressing pulmonary capillaries
b. It decreases shunting by improving alveolar inflation and reducing atelectasis
c. It has no effect on shunting as it primarily affects dead space ventilation
d. It exacerbates shunting by diverting blood flow to non-ventilated regions of the lung

Answer: b. It decreases shunting by improving alveolar inflation and reducing atelectasis. Explanation: Positive pressure ventilation can help decrease intrapulmonary shunting by opening collapsed alveoli (reducing atelectasis) and improving the distribution of ventilation, thereby enhancing the matching of ventilation and perfusion in the lungs.

435. What is the primary cause of hypoxemia in patients with ventilation-perfusion (V/Q) mismatch?
a. Decreased total lung capacity
b. Impaired diffusion across the alveolar-capillary membrane
c. Inequalities in the distribution of air and blood flow in the lungs
d. Reduced hemoglobin concentration in the blood

Answer: c. Inequalities in the distribution of air and blood flow in the lungs. Explanation: Hypoxemia in the context of V/Q mismatch is primarily due to inequalities in the distribution of ventilation and perfusion within the lungs. Areas with low ventilation relative to perfusion (low V/Q ratios) contribute to poor oxygenation of blood, leading to hypoxemia.

436. An ABG of a patient presents with pH 7.32, PaCO2 50 mmHg, and HCO3- 24 mEq/L. What is the primary disturbance?
a. Metabolic acidosis
b. Metabolic alkalosis
c. Respiratory acidosis
d. Respiratory alkalosis

Answer: c. Respiratory acidosis. Explanation: The primary disturbance is respiratory acidosis, indicated by a decreased pH (acidemia) and elevated PaCO2, suggesting hypoventilation or impaired gas exchange. The HCO3- level is within the normal range, indicating that this is a primary respiratory issue without full metabolic compensation.

437. A patient's ABG shows pH 7.48, PaCO2 32 mmHg, and HCO3- 22 mEq/L. How would you interpret these results?
a. Compensated respiratory acidosis
b. Compensated respiratory alkalosis
c. Uncompensated metabolic alkalosis
d. Partially compensated metabolic acidosis

Answer: b. Compensated respiratory alkalosis. Explanation: The ABG indicates respiratory alkalosis, shown by the elevated pH (alkalemia) and decreased PaCO2, which suggests hyperventilation. The slightly decreased HCO3- level suggests renal compensation attempting to restore acid-base balance.

438. In a patient with chronic obstructive pulmonary disease (COPD), an ABG reveals pH 7.36, PaCO2 60 mmHg, and HCO3- 32 mEq/L. What does this suggest?
a. Uncompensated respiratory acidosis
b. Partially compensated respiratory acidosis
c. Fully compensated respiratory alkalosis
d. Metabolic alkalosis with respiratory compensation

Answer: b. Partially compensated respiratory acidosis. Explanation: The ABG suggests partially compensated respiratory acidosis, common in COPD due to retention of CO2. The near-normal pH indicates partial compensation, likely renal, as evidenced by the elevated HCO3- in response to chronic hypercapnia.

439. A patient presents with vomiting for 3 days. ABG shows pH 7.55, PaCO2 45 mmHg, and HCO3- 34 mEq/L. What is the most likely diagnosis?
a. Respiratory acidosis
b. Respiratory alkalosis
c. Metabolic alkalosis
d. Metabolic acidosis

Answer: c. Metabolic alkalosis. Explanation: Prolonged vomiting can lead to loss of gastric acid, resulting in metabolic alkalosis, as indicated by the elevated pH and HCO3-. The PaCO2 is normal, suggesting that this is a primary metabolic disturbance without respiratory compensation.

440. An ABG analysis of a patient with diarrhea shows pH 7.30, PaCO2 38 mmHg, and HCO3- 18 mEq/L. How would you interpret this?
a. Metabolic acidosis with respiratory compensation
b. Metabolic alkalosis with respiratory compensation
c. Respiratory acidosis with metabolic compensation
d. Respiratory alkalosis without compensation

Answer: a. Metabolic acidosis with respiratory compensation. Explanation: Diarrhea often leads to loss of bicarbonate, resulting in metabolic acidosis, as evidenced by the decreased pH and HCO3-. The slightly lowered PaCO2 suggests a respiratory compensatory attempt to increase acid elimination through hyperventilation.

441. A patient in the ICU has an ABG reading of pH 7.50, PaCO2 30 mmHg, and HCO3- 24 mEq/L. What is the primary acid-base disturbance?
a. Acute respiratory alkalosis
b. Chronic respiratory alkalosis
c. Acute metabolic alkalosis
d. Chronic metabolic alkalosis

Answer: a. Acute respiratory alkalosis. Explanation: The primary disturbance is acute respiratory alkalosis, indicated by the elevated pH and decreased PaCO2, likely due to hyperventilation. The normal HCO3- suggests that this is an acute process without significant renal compensation.

442. In a patient with renal failure, the ABG shows pH 7.25, PaCO2 35 mmHg, and HCO3- 15 mEq/L. What does this indicate?
a. Respiratory alkalosis with renal compensation
b. Metabolic alkalosis with respiratory compensation
c. Metabolic acidosis with partial respiratory compensation
d. Uncompensated metabolic acidosis

Answer: d. Uncompensated metabolic acidosis. Explanation: In renal failure, the inability to excrete acid leads to metabolic acidosis, as shown by the decreased pH and HCO3-. The normal PaCO2 indicates a lack of respiratory compensation, suggesting an uncompensated metabolic acidosis.

443. A patient with anxiety is hyperventilating. ABG results are pH 7.48, PaCO2 28 mmHg, and HCO3- 22 mEq/L. This is indicative of:
a. Compensated metabolic acidosis
b. Uncompensated respiratory alkalosis
c. Compensated respiratory acidosis
d. Compensated metabolic alkalosis

Answer: b. Uncompensated respiratory alkalosis. Explanation: Hyperventilation can lead to respiratory alkalosis, characterized by elevated pH and decreased PaCO2. The normal HCO3- suggests that this is an acute, uncompensated state, as the kidneys have not yet had time to respond.

444. In a patient with aspirin overdose, the ABG reveals pH 7.50, PaCO2 32 mmHg, and HCO3- 28 mEq/L. What acid-base disorder is present?
a. Primary respiratory alkalosis with metabolic compensation
b. Primary metabolic alkalosis with respiratory compensation
c. Mixed respiratory and metabolic alkalosis

d. Mixed respiratory alkalosis and metabolic acidosis

Answer: c. Mixed respiratory and metabolic alkalosis. Explanation: Aspirin overdose can lead to mixed acid-base disorders. Initially, it causes respiratory alkalosis due to stimulation of the respiratory center, and later, metabolic alkalosis due to increased renal bicarbonate retention. The ABG shows features of both disorders.

445. A patient presents with a primary complaint of persistent vomiting for 2 days. Blood gas analysis shows a high bicarbonate level. This scenario is indicative of:
a. Respiratory acidosis
b. Metabolic acidosis
c. Respiratory alkalosis
d. Metabolic alkalosis

Answer: d. Metabolic alkalosis. Explanation: Persistent vomiting can lead to loss of gastric acid, which contains hydrochloric acid, leading to an increase in blood bicarbonate levels and consequently metabolic alkalosis characterized by elevated pH.

446. In a patient with chronic obstructive pulmonary disease (COPD), blood gas analysis reveals elevated pCO2 levels. This condition is most likely:
a. Respiratory acidosis
b. Metabolic acidosis
c. Respiratory alkalosis
d. Metabolic alkalosis

Answer: a. Respiratory acidosis. Explanation: In patients with COPD, impaired gas exchange can lead to retention of CO2, resulting in respiratory acidosis, characterized by elevated pCO2 levels and decreased pH.

447. A patient with severe diarrhea is likely to develop which acid-base disturbance?
a. Respiratory acidosis
b. Metabolic acidosis
c. Respiratory alkalosis
d. Metabolic alkalosis

Answer: b. Metabolic acidosis. Explanation: Severe diarrhea can lead to loss of bicarbonate-rich intestinal fluids, resulting in metabolic acidosis characterized by decreased bicarbonate levels and reduced blood pH.

448. A patient on mechanical ventilation is set on a high respiratory rate. Blood gas analysis shows decreased pCO2 levels. This finding suggests:
a. Respiratory acidosis
b. Metabolic acidosis

c. Respiratory alkalosis
d. Metabolic alkalosis

Answer: c. Respiratory alkalosis. Explanation: A high respiratory rate can lead to excessive CO2 elimination, resulting in respiratory alkalosis, characterized by decreased pCO2 levels and increased pH.

449. A patient with renal failure is most likely to develop which acid-base disturbance?
a. Respiratory acidosis
b. Metabolic acidosis
c. Respiratory alkalosis
d. Metabolic alkalosis

Answer: b. Metabolic acidosis. Explanation: Renal failure can lead to impaired acid excretion and bicarbonate reabsorption, resulting in metabolic acidosis characterized by decreased bicarbonate levels and reduced blood pH.

450. In a patient with anxiety-induced hyperventilation, you would expect to find:
a. Respiratory acidosis
b. Metabolic acidosis
c. Respiratory alkalosis
d. Metabolic alkalosis

Answer: c. Respiratory alkalosis. Explanation: Anxiety-induced hyperventilation leads to excessive exhalation of CO2, causing respiratory alkalosis, characterized by decreased pCO2 levels and increased pH.

451. A patient with primary hyperaldosteronism would most likely present with:
a. Respiratory acidosis
b. Metabolic acidosis
c. Respiratory alkalosis
d. Metabolic alkalosis

Answer: d. Metabolic alkalosis. Explanation: Primary hyperaldosteronism can lead to increased renal bicarbonate reabsorption and hydrogen ion excretion, resulting in metabolic alkalosis characterized by elevated bicarbonate levels and increased blood pH.

452. In a patient with salicylate overdose, you would expect to find:
a. Respiratory acidosis and metabolic alkalosis
b. Metabolic acidosis and respiratory alkalosis
c. Respiratory acidosis and metabolic acidosis
d. Metabolic alkalosis and respiratory alkalosis

Answer: b. Metabolic acidosis and respiratory alkalosis. Explanation: Salicylate overdose initially causes respiratory alkalosis due to direct stimulation of the respiratory center, followed by metabolic acidosis due to accumulation of organic acids.

453. A patient with a high-altitude illness would most likely develop:
a. Respiratory acidosis
b. Metabolic acidosis
c. Respiratory alkalosis
d. Metabolic alkalosis

Answer: c. Respiratory alkalosis. Explanation: High-altitude exposure leads to hyperventilation in response to lower oxygen levels, causing respiratory alkalosis characterized by decreased pCO2 levels and increased pH.

454. A patient recovering from diabetic ketoacidosis (DKA) is administered bicarbonate therapy. This intervention risks causing:
a. Respiratory acidosis
b. Metabolic acidosis
c. Respiratory alkalosis
d. Metabolic alkalosis

Answer: d. Metabolic alkalosis. Explanation: Administration of bicarbonate in recovering DKA patients can overshoot the correction of acidosis, leading to metabolic alkalosis characterized by increased bicarbonate levels and elevated blood pH.

455. In a patient with metabolic acidosis, which compensatory mechanism is most likely to occur?
a. Hyperventilation to increase pCO2
b. Hypoventilation to decrease pCO2
c. Hyperventilation to decrease pCO2
d. Renal retention of bicarbonate

Answer: c. Hyperventilation to decrease pCO2. Explanation: In metabolic acidosis, the primary compensatory mechanism is respiratory compensation through hyperventilation, which decreases pCO2 (carbon dioxide) levels to help offset the acidosis by increasing the pH.

456. A patient with chronic obstructive pulmonary disease (COPD) develops respiratory acidosis. Which compensatory response is expected?
a. Increased renal excretion of bicarbonate
b. Decreased renal excretion of bicarbonate
c. Increased renal excretion of hydrogen ions
d. Decreased renal reabsorption of bicarbonate

Answer: b. Decreased renal excretion of bicarbonate. Explanation: In response to respiratory acidosis, as seen in COPD, the kidneys compensate by decreasing the excretion of bicarbonate and increasing the reabsorption and generation of bicarbonate, as well as excreting more hydrogen ions, to help normalize blood pH.

457. In a patient with metabolic alkalosis, what compensatory change is expected in respiratory function?
a. Increased respiratory rate to decrease pCO2
b. Decreased respiratory rate to increase pCO2
c. Increased tidal volume to decrease pCO2
d. Decreased tidal volume to increase pCO2

Answer: b. Decreased respiratory rate to increase pCO2. Explanation: The compensatory mechanism for metabolic alkalosis involves a decrease in respiratory rate or hypoventilation to retain CO2, which increases pCO2, helping to lower the pH towards normal.

458. A patient presents with acute renal failure and metabolic acidosis. What compensatory mechanism is observed in the respiratory system?
a. Decreased respiratory rate and depth
b. Increased respiratory rate and depth
c. No change in respiratory rate or depth
d. Periodic breathing patterns

Answer: b. Increased respiratory rate and depth. Explanation: In response to metabolic acidosis from acute renal failure, the respiratory system compensates by increasing the rate and depth of breathing (Kussmaul respirations), leading to decreased pCO2 and an increase in pH towards normal levels.

459. For a patient with severe diarrhea leading to metabolic acidosis, which compensatory mechanism would you expect to observe?
a. Renal excretion of HCO3-
b. Renal conservation of HCO3-
c. Respiratory conservation of CO2
d. Respiratory excretion of CO2

Answer: d. Respiratory excretion of CO2. Explanation: The primary compensatory mechanism for metabolic acidosis, such as that caused by severe diarrhea, is an increase in respiratory rate and depth to excrete more CO2, thereby decreasing pCO2 and helping to increase the pH towards normal levels.

460. In a patient experiencing anxiety-induced hyperventilation leading to respiratory alkalosis, how does the body attempt to compensate?
a. Kidneys excrete more bicarbonate

b. Kidneys retain more bicarbonate
c. Lungs decrease respiratory rate
d. Lungs increase respiratory rate

Answer: a. Kidneys excrete more bicarbonate. Explanation: To compensate for respiratory alkalosis, the kidneys increase the excretion of bicarbonate (HCO3-) to decrease the blood's base concentration, helping to bring the pH down towards normal.

461. A patient with a high altitude illness develops respiratory alkalosis. Which renal compensatory change helps to restore acid-base balance?
a. Increased bicarbonate reabsorption
b. Increased bicarbonate excretion
c. Increased hydrogen ion excretion
d. Decreased ammonia production

Answer: b. Increased bicarbonate excretion. Explanation: In response to respiratory alkalosis, such as that seen with high altitude illness, the kidneys compensate by increasing bicarbonate excretion to lower the blood bicarbonate levels and help normalize the pH.

462. In a patient with vomiting-induced metabolic alkalosis, what compensatory respiratory change is expected?
a. Increased respiratory rate to decrease pCO2
b. Decreased respiratory rate to increase pCO2
c. Increased tidal volume to decrease pCO2
d. Decreased tidal volume to increase pCO2

Answer: b. Decreased respiratory rate to increase pCO2. Explanation: The compensatory mechanism for metabolic alkalosis involves a decrease in respiratory rate or hypoventilation to increase pCO2, which adds acid to the blood, helping to lower the pH towards normal.

463. A patient with salicylate toxicity develops metabolic acidosis. Which compensatory mechanism is expected to coexist?
a. Respiratory acidosis
b. Respiratory alkalosis
c. Metabolic alkalosis
d. No compensatory mechanism

Answer: b. Respiratory alkalosis. Explanation: In salicylate toxicity, metabolic acidosis often coexists with respiratory alkalosis due to direct stimulation of the respiratory center by salicylates, leading to hyperventilation and decreased pCO2 as a compensatory mechanism.

464. In the setting of chronic respiratory acidosis, such as with advanced COPD, what is the primary renal compensatory mechanism?
a. Increased excretion of bicarbonate
b. Decreased excretion of bicarbonate
c. Increased production of ammonia
d. Decreased excretion of hydrogen ions

Answer: b. Decreased excretion of bicarbonate. Explanation: The kidneys compensate for chronic respiratory acidosis by decreasing the excretion of bicarbonate and increasing the reabsorption and generation of bicarbonate, along with increased excretion of hydrogen ions, to help normalize the blood pH.

465. Which of the following is a hallmark finding on the chest X-ray of a patient with Acute Respiratory Distress Syndrome (ARDS)?
a. Unilateral pleural effusion
b. Bilateral infiltrates resembling a "white-out"
c. Focal consolidation in the right lower lobe
d. Cavitary lesions in the upper lobes

Answer: b. Bilateral infiltrates resembling a "white-out". Explanation: A classic finding in ARDS on chest X-ray is the presence of diffuse bilateral pulmonary infiltrates, often described as a "white-out", which reflects the extensive alveolar damage and fluid-filled alveoli that characterize this condition.

466. What is the primary pathophysiological process in ARDS?
a. Cardiogenic pulmonary edema
b. Alveolar hypoventilation
c. Increased capillary permeability leading to non-cardiogenic pulmonary edema
d. Obstructive airway disease

Answer: c. Increased capillary permeability leading to non-cardiogenic pulmonary edema. Explanation: ARDS involves an acute inflammatory response leading to increased permeability of the alveolar-capillary barrier, resulting in the leakage of protein-rich fluid into the alveoli, causing non-cardiogenic pulmonary edema and impaired gas exchange.

467. In ARDS management, what is the primary goal of using low tidal volume ventilation?
a. To increase oxygenation by maximizing alveolar recruitment
b. To reduce the risk of ventilator-associated pneumonia
c. To minimize alveolar overdistension and ventilator-induced lung injury
d. To eliminate the need for supplemental oxygen

Answer: c. To minimize alveolar overdistension and ventilator-induced lung injury. Explanation: The use of low tidal volume ventilation in ARDS aims to minimize ventilator-induced lung injury (VILI) by preventing alveolar overdistension, also known as volutrauma, which can exacerbate lung injury and inflammation.

468. What role does positive end-expiratory pressure (PEEP) play in the management of ARDS?
a. To reduce the work of breathing by the patient
b. To decrease the oxygen-carrying capacity of hemoglobin
c. To prevent alveolar collapse and maintain functional residual capacity
d. To increase airway resistance and improve ventilation

Answer: c. To prevent alveolar collapse and maintain functional residual capacity. Explanation: In ARDS, PEEP is used to prevent end-expiratory alveolar collapse (atelectasis) by maintaining positive pressure in the lungs at the end of expiration, thereby improving oxygenation and functional residual capacity.

469. Which clinical criteria must be met to diagnose ARDS according to the Berlin Definition?
a. Acute onset, bilateral opacities on chest imaging, and a PaO2/FiO2 ratio < 300 mmHg
b. Chronic respiratory symptoms, unilateral infiltrates on chest X-ray, and PaCO2 > 45 mmHg
c. Acute onset, pleural effusions on chest imaging, and a PaO2/FiO2 ratio < 200 mmHg with PEEP ≥ 5 cm H2O
d. Acute onset, diffuse alveolar damage on biopsy, and a history of significant trauma

Answer: a. Acute onset, bilateral opacities on chest imaging, and a PaO2/FiO2 ratio < 300 mmHg. Explanation: The Berlin Definition of ARDS includes acute onset within one week of a known clinical insult, bilateral opacities on chest imaging not fully explained by effusions, lobar/lung collapse, or nodules, and a PaO2/FiO2 ratio ≤ 300 mmHg with PEEP or CPAP ≥ 5 cm H2O in the absence of left atrial hypertension.

470. What is the significance of the PaO2/FiO2 ratio in the context of ARDS?
a. It is used to determine the need for mechanical ventilation
b. It serves as a marker for the severity of hypoxemia and classification of ARDS severity
c. It indicates the level of carbon dioxide retention
d. It reflects the adequacy of hemoglobin in oxygen transport

Answer: b. It serves as a marker for the severity of hypoxemia and classification of ARDS severity. Explanation: The PaO2/FiO2 ratio is a key indicator of oxygenation efficiency and is used to classify the severity of ARDS. Lower ratios indicate more severe gas exchange abnormalities and hypoxemia.

471. In ARDS, what is the primary mechanism leading to hypoxemia?
a. Decreased cardiac output and tissue hypoperfusion
b. Ventilation-perfusion (V/Q) mismatch and shunting
c. Hypercapnia and respiratory acidosis
d. Reduced diffusion capacity of the alveolar membrane

Answer: b. Ventilation-perfusion (V/Q) mismatch and shunting. Explanation: The primary mechanism leading to hypoxemia in ARDS is a ventilation-perfusion mismatch, where areas of the lung are ventilated but not adequately perfused, along with intrapulmonary shunting of blood from the right to the left side of the heart without oxygenation.

472. What is the role of prone positioning in the management of severe ARDS?
a. To improve comfort and reduce the need for sedation
b. To enhance secretion clearance and prevent ventilator-associated pneumonia
c. To improve ventilation-perfusion matching and oxygenation
d. To increase lung compliance and reduce airway resistance

Answer: c. To improve ventilation-perfusion matching and oxygenation. Explanation: Prone positioning in severe ARDS can improve oxygenation by enhancing ventilation-perfusion matching. This position redistributes lung perfusion towards better-ventilated lung regions, reducing shunt and improving gas exchange.

473. Which extracorporeal support strategy may be considered in patients with severe ARDS unresponsive to conventional treatments?
a. Continuous renal replacement therapy (CRRT)
b. Intra-aortic balloon pump (IABP)
c. Extracorporeal membrane oxygenation (ECMO)
d. Ventricular assist device (VAD) implantation

Answer: c. Extracorporeal membrane oxygenation (ECMO). Explanation: In patients with severe ARDS who do not respond to conventional mechanical ventilation and adjunctive therapies, ECMO can be considered as a life-saving intervention. ECMO provides extracorporeal support by oxygenating the blood and removing carbon dioxide, allowing the lungs to rest and heal.

474. Sepsis is commonly defined as:
a. A localized infection that has not yet spread to the bloodstream
b. A systemic response to infection involving widespread inflammation
c. An infection solely confined to the urinary tract
d. A viral infection that causes elevated white blood cell count

Answer: b. A systemic response to infection involving widespread inflammation. Explanation: Sepsis is defined as a life-threatening organ dysfunction caused by a dysregulated host response to infection, characterized by widespread inflammation, leading to tissue damage and organ failure.

475. The pathophysiology of acute myocardial infarction primarily involves:
a. Bacterial infection of the myocardial tissue
b. Interruption of myocardial oxygen supply due to coronary artery occlusion
c. Overstimulation of the parasympathetic nervous system
d. Excessive potassium loss from cardiac cells

Answer: b. Interruption of myocardial oxygen supply due to coronary artery occlusion. Explanation: Acute myocardial infarction typically results from an interruption in blood flow, often due to thrombosis formed on a ruptured atherosclerotic plaque in a coronary artery, leading to ischemia and necrosis of heart tissue.

476. Asthma is characterized by:
a. Fixed airway obstruction that is not reversible with bronchodilators
b. Chronic systemic inflammation affecting multiple organs
c. Reversible airway obstruction, bronchial hyperresponsiveness, and inflammation
d. Destruction of alveoli and permanent enlargement of air spaces

Answer: c. Reversible airway obstruction, bronchial hyperresponsiveness, and inflammation. Explanation: Asthma is characterized by chronic airway inflammation, reversible airflow obstruction, and bronchial hyperresponsiveness to various stimuli, leading to episodes of wheezing, breathlessness, chest tightness, and coughing.

477. The primary mechanism of injury in acute pancreatitis is:
a. Auto-digestion of pancreatic tissue by its own enzymes
b. Direct infection of the pancreas by hepatotropic viruses
c. Obstruction of the pancreatic duct by a gallstone
d. Ischemic injury due to reduced arterial blood supply

Answer: a. Auto-digestion of pancreatic tissue by its own enzymes. Explanation: Acute pancreatitis primarily results from the premature activation of pancreatic enzymes within the pancreas itself, leading to auto-digestion of pancreatic tissue, causing inflammation, edema, and potentially necrosis.

478. Chronic kidney disease (CKD) involves:
a. Rapid loss of kidney function over days to weeks
b. Reversible kidney damage with appropriate treatment
c. Progressive loss of renal function over months to years
d. Isolated proteinuria without a decrease in glomerular filtration rate (GFR)

Answer: c. Progressive loss of renal function over months to years. Explanation: CKD is characterized by a gradual loss of kidney function over time, typically months to years, leading to the accumulation of waste products and fluid imbalances as the kidneys lose their filtering abilities.

479. The pathophysiological process of atherosclerosis begins with:
a. Smooth muscle cell proliferation in the absence of endothelial injury
b. The formation of fibrous plaques within the venous system
c. Endothelial injury and the subsequent accumulation of lipid-laden macrophages
d. Calcification of the arterial walls without lipid accumulation

Answer: c. Endothelial injury and the subsequent accumulation of lipid-laden macrophages. Explanation: Atherosclerosis starts with endothelial injury, followed by the accumulation of lipids, particularly low-density lipoproteins (LDL), which become oxidized and engulfed by macrophages, forming foam cells and fatty streaks, eventually leading to plaque formation.

480. In congestive heart failure (CHF), the heart is unable to:
a. Maintain adequate blood flow to meet the body's metabolic demands
b. Generate sufficient electrical impulses to maintain a regular heart rhythm
c. Prevent backflow of blood through the atrioventricular valves
d. Isolate pulmonary circulation from systemic circulation

Answer: a. Maintain adequate blood flow to meet the body's metabolic demands. Explanation: CHF is a condition where the heart's pumping efficiency is compromised, leading to inadequate blood flow to meet the metabolic demands of the body, resulting in symptoms such as shortness of breath, fatigue, and fluid accumulation.

481. Type 1 diabetes mellitus is primarily caused by:
a. Resistance of body cells to insulin
b. Obesity and lack of physical activity
c. Autoimmune destruction of pancreatic beta cells
d. Overproduction of glucagon by pancreatic alpha cells

Answer: c. Autoimmune destruction of pancreatic beta cells. Explanation: Type 1 diabetes is an autoimmune condition where the body's immune system attacks and destroys the insulin-producing beta cells in the pancreas, leading to insulin deficiency.

482. The fundamental defect in cystic fibrosis is related to:
a. A deficiency in surfactant production in the alveoli
b. Abnormalities in the CFTR gene leading to dysfunctional chloride channels
c. Chronic inflammation of the bronchi without an underlying genetic cause
d. Excessive production of normal mucus by the goblet cells

Answer: b. Abnormalities in the CFTR gene leading to dysfunctional chloride channels. Explanation: Cystic fibrosis is caused by mutations in the CFTR gene, which result in dysfunctional chloride channels, leading to thick, sticky mucus production, affecting various organs, especially the lungs and pancreas.

483. Pulmonary embolism (PE) pathophysiology primarily involves:
a. Chronic inflammation of the pulmonary arteries
b. Obstruction of pulmonary arterial blood flow by a thrombus
c. Spasm of the bronchial smooth muscle in the lungs
d. Accumulation of fluid in the alveolar spaces

Answer: b. Obstruction of pulmonary arterial blood flow by a thrombus. Explanation: PE is caused by the obstruction of pulmonary arteries by a thrombus, typically originating from the deep veins in the legs (deep vein thrombosis), leading to impaired gas exchange and potentially life-threatening respiratory and hemodynamic consequences.

484. According to the Berlin criteria, which of the following is NOT a requirement for the diagnosis of ARDS?
a. Acute onset within one week of a known clinical insult
b. Presence of bilateral opacities on chest imaging not fully explained by effusions, lobar/lung collapse, or nodules
c. Pulmonary artery wedge pressure (PAWP) ≤ 18 mmHg or no clinical evidence of left atrial hypertension
d. PaO2/FiO2 ratio > 300 mmHg with PEEP or CPAP ≥ 5 cm H2O

Answer: d. PaO2/FiO2 ratio > 300 mmHg with PEEP or CPAP ≥ 5 cm H2O. Explanation: The Berlin criteria for ARDS include a PaO2/FiO2 ratio ≤ 300 mmHg with PEEP or CPAP ≥ 5 cm H2O. A PaO2/FiO2 ratio > 300 mmHg would not meet the criteria for ARDS and instead might indicate a less severe form of acute lung injury or respiratory distress.

485. What is the significance of the timing of symptom onset in the Berlin criteria for ARDS?
a. It helps differentiate between ARDS and chronic respiratory conditions.
b. It is used to determine the appropriate ventilator settings.
c. It guides the choice of pharmacological treatments.
d. It is not considered important in the diagnosis of ARDS.

Answer: a. It helps differentiate between ARDS and chronic respiratory conditions. Explanation: The acute onset within one week of a known clinical insult, as specified in the Berlin criteria, is essential for differentiating ARDS from chronic respiratory conditions. This timing helps to link the respiratory distress directly to a recent insult or injury, which is characteristic of ARDS.

486. In the Berlin criteria for ARDS, what does the requirement of "bilateral opacities on chest imaging" imply?
a. It confirms the diagnosis of pneumonia.
b. It indicates the presence of diffuse alveolar damage.
c. It excludes cardiac causes of pulmonary edema.
d. It suggests a widespread involvement of both lungs, not explained by other local lung diseases.

Answer: d. It suggests a widespread involvement of both lungs, not explained by other local lung diseases. Explanation: The requirement of bilateral opacities on chest imaging in the Berlin criteria suggests that the lung involvement is widespread and diffuse, characteristic of ARDS, and not attributable to localized lung diseases or conditions such as lobar pneumonia or lung collapse.

487. How does the Berlin criteria categorize the severity of ARDS based on the PaO2/FiO2 ratio?
a. Mild ARDS: PaO2/FiO2 > 300 mmHg
b. Moderate ARDS: PaO2/FiO2 201-300 mmHg
c. Severe ARDS: PaO2/FiO2 ≤ 100 mmHg

d. The Berlin criteria do not categorize ARDS severity based on the PaO2/FiO2 ratio.

Answer: b. Moderate ARDS: PaO2/FiO2 201-300 mmHg. Explanation: The Berlin criteria categorize ARDS severity based on the PaO2/FiO2 ratio as follows: Mild ARDS (PaO2/FiO2 ≤ 300 but > 200 mmHg), Moderate ARDS (PaO2/FiO2 ≤ 200 but > 100 mmHg), and Severe ARDS (PaO2/FiO2 ≤ 100 mmHg), all with PEEP or CPAP ≥ 5 cm H2O. This classification helps in assessing the severity of gas exchange impairment and guiding treatment decisions.

488. Under the Berlin criteria, what is the relevance of excluding cardiac failure as the cause of pulmonary edema in diagnosing ARDS?
a. To ensure the use of inotropic agents in management
b. To confirm that the pulmonary edema is non-cardiogenic and due to increased permeability
c. To guide the administration of diuretics
d. To facilitate the decision for heart transplantation

Answer: b. To confirm that the pulmonary edema is non-cardiogenic and due to increased permeability. Explanation: Excluding cardiac failure as the cause of pulmonary edema is crucial in diagnosing ARDS to confirm that the edema is non-cardiogenic, resulting from increased alveolar-capillary membrane permeability, a hallmark of ARDS, rather than from elevated hydrostatic pressure typical of cardiogenic pulmonary edema.

489. What role does PEEP play in the Berlin criteria for diagnosing ARDS?
a. It is used as a therapeutic intervention to immediately reverse hypoxemia.
b. It serves as a parameter to differentiate ARDS from asthma.
c. It is a criterion to ensure that hypoxemia is assessed under standardized ventilatory conditions.
d. It is used to calculate the severity of lung injury.

Answer: c. It is a criterion to ensure that hypoxemia is assessed under standardized ventilatory conditions. Explanation: The inclusion of PEEP or CPAP ≥ 5 cm H2O in the Berlin criteria for diagnosing ARDS ensures that the assessment of hypoxemia (PaO2/FiO2 ratio) is made under standardized ventilatory conditions, providing a more accurate evaluation of the lung's gas exchange capabilities and the severity of lung injury.

490. In the context of the Berlin criteria, why is it important to establish the onset of ARDS symptoms within one week of a known clinical insult?
a. To differentiate ARDS from acute bronchitis
b. To establish a direct link between the insult and the acute lung injury
c. To determine the appropriate antibiotic regimen
d. To assess the need for long-term oxygen therapy

Answer: b. To establish a direct link between the insult and the acute lung injury. Explanation: Establishing the onset of ARDS symptoms within one week of a known clinical insult is crucial to link the acute lung injury directly to the insult, whether it's an infectious, traumatic, or inflammatory cause. This temporal relationship helps to differentiate ARDS from other forms of chronic or acute lung injury unrelated to a specific recent event.

491. How do the Berlin criteria address the issue of left atrial hypertension in diagnosing ARDS?
a. By requiring echocardiographic evidence of left ventricular dysfunction
b. By specifying a pulmonary artery wedge pressure (PAWP) ≤ 18 mmHg or no clinical evidence of left atrial hypertension
c. By mandating the use of left ventricular assist devices in all ARDS patients
d. By excluding patients with any history of left atrial hypertension from the ARDS diagnosis

Answer: b. By specifying a pulmonary artery wedge pressure (PAWP) ≤ 18 mmHg or no clinical evidence of left atrial hypertension. Explanation: The Berlin criteria specify that for a diagnosis of ARDS, there should be a PAWP ≤ 18 mmHg or no clinical evidence of left atrial hypertension, to exclude hydrostatic edema due to heart failure as the cause of pulmonary infiltrates, ensuring that diagnosed cases of ARDS are due to increased permeability pulmonary edema.

492. What is the clinical significance of categorizing ARDS severity using the Berlin criteria?
a. It determines the specific antiviral medication to be used.
b. It predicts the need for tracheostomy in all ARDS patients.
c. It helps in prognostication and guiding therapeutic interventions.
d. It identifies candidates for immediate lung transplantation.

Answer: c. It helps in prognostication and guiding therapeutic interventions. Explanation: Categorizing ARDS severity using the Berlin criteria (based on the PaO2/FiO2 ratio) aids in assessing the prognosis and guiding the intensity of therapeutic interventions needed. More severe categories indicate worse gas exchange and are associated with higher mortality, influencing decisions regarding ventilation strategies, the use of adjunctive therapies, and the level of monitoring required.

493. In lung-protective ventilation for ARDS, what is the recommended tidal volume?
a. 4-6 mL/kg of predicted body weight
b. 6-8 mL/kg of predicted body weight
c. 8-10 mL/kg of predicted body weight
d. 10-12 mL/kg of predicted body weight

Answer: a. 4-6 mL/kg of predicted body weight. Explanation: Lung-protective ventilation strategies for ARDS include using lower tidal volumes of 4-6 mL/kg of predicted body weight to minimize barotrauma and volutrauma, preventing ventilator-induced lung injury.

494. When applying lung-protective ventilation, what is the target plateau pressure to minimize the risk of barotrauma?
a. Less than 20 cm H2O
b. Less than 30 cm H2O
c. Less than 40 cm H2O
d. Less than 50 cm H2O

Answer: b. Less than 30 cm H2O. Explanation: In lung-protective ventilation strategies, keeping the plateau pressure below 30 cm H2O is crucial to minimize the risk of barotrauma and ventilator-induced lung injury by avoiding excessive alveolar distension.

495. For a patient with severe ARDS, which ventilation mode is often considered part of lung-protective strategies?
a. Volume-controlled ventilation
b. Pressure-controlled ventilation
c. High-frequency oscillatory ventilation
d. Inverse ratio ventilation

Answer: b. Pressure-controlled ventilation. Explanation: Pressure-controlled ventilation is often used in lung-protective strategies for patients with ARDS because it allows control of the peak inspiratory pressure, potentially reducing the risk of barotrauma while ensuring adequate gas exchange.

496. In the context of lung-protective ventilation, what role does positive end-expiratory pressure (PEEP) play?
a. It decreases functional residual capacity to reduce oxygenation.
b. It increases airway resistance to improve CO2 elimination.
c. It prevents alveolar collapse at end-expiration to improve oxygenation.
d. It increases tidal volume to reduce the respiratory rate.

Answer: c. It prevents alveolar collapse at end-expiration to improve oxygenation. Explanation: In lung-protective ventilation, PEEP is used to prevent alveolar collapse at end-expiration, thereby improving oxygenation and reducing the intrapulmonary shunt effect commonly seen in ARDS.

497. What is the primary goal of implementing a lung-protective ventilation strategy in patients with ARDS?
a. To maximize oxygen delivery by increasing tidal volume
b. To minimize ventilator-induced lung injury by using lower tidal volumes and appropriate PEEP
c. To eliminate CO2 as rapidly as possible by increasing the respiratory rate
d. To reduce the need for sedation and paralysis in mechanically ventilated patients

Answer: b. To minimize ventilator-induced lung injury by using lower tidal volumes and appropriate PEEP. Explanation: The primary goal of lung-protective ventilation in ARDS is to minimize ventilator-induced lung injury. This is achieved by using lower tidal volumes (4-6 mL/kg of predicted body weight) and applying appropriate levels of PEEP to maintain alveolar stability and improve oxygenation while avoiding overdistension of the lungs.

498. When considering lung-protective ventilation, why is it important to monitor for auto-PEEP?
a. Auto-PEEP can indicate excessive sedation levels.
b. Auto-PEEP can reduce the need for supplemental oxygen.
c. Auto-PEEP can lead to hemodynamic instability due to increased intrathoracic pressure.

d. Auto-PEEP signifies improved lung compliance and reduced ARDS severity.

Answer: c. Auto-PEEP can lead to hemodynamic instability due to increased intrathoracic pressure. Explanation: Auto-PEEP, or intrinsic PEEP, occurs when there is incomplete exhalation before the next breath starts, leading to the buildup of pressure in the alveoli. It can cause hemodynamic instability by increasing intrathoracic pressure, reducing venous return to the heart, and potentially leading to decreased cardiac output.

499. In lung-protective ventilation, how does the initial setting of PEEP affect oxygenation?
a. Higher initial PEEP settings decrease oxygenation by reducing alveolar recruitment.
b. Lower initial PEEP settings improve oxygenation by increasing alveolar ventilation.
c. Higher initial PEEP settings improve oxygenation by preventing alveolar collapse and maintaining recruitment.
d. Lower initial PEEP settings decrease oxygenation by increasing dead space ventilation.

Answer: c. Higher initial PEEP settings improve oxygenation by preventing alveolar collapse and maintaining recruitment. Explanation: In lung-protective ventilation, especially for ARDS patients, higher initial PEEP settings help improve oxygenation by preventing derecruitment and collapse of alveoli at end-expiration, thus maintaining a greater amount of aerated lung tissue to participate in gas exchange.

500. What is the impact of lung-protective ventilation on the duration of mechanical ventilation in ARDS patients?
a. It significantly increases the duration due to lower tidal volumes.
b. It has no impact on the duration of mechanical ventilation.
c. It may decrease the duration by reducing ventilator-induced lung injury.
d. It unpredictably varies without a clear pattern.

Answer: c. It may decrease the duration by reducing ventilator-induced lung injury. Explanation: Lung-protective ventilation strategies in ARDS can potentially decrease the duration of mechanical ventilation by minimizing further lung injury and promoting lung healing, thereby facilitating weaning from the ventilator.

501. In adjusting ventilation settings for lung-protective ventilation, what is the recommended approach if oxygenation remains inadequate?
a. Increase the tidal volume beyond 8 mL/kg of predicted body weight.
b. Increase the respiratory rate to more than 35 breaths per minute.
c. Increase PEEP while monitoring hemodynamics and oxygenation.
d. Decrease the inspiratory to expiratory (I:E) ratio to 1:1.

Answer: c. Increase PEEP while monitoring hemodynamics and oxygenation. Explanation: If oxygenation remains inadequate in lung-protective ventilation, increasing PEEP can be beneficial for improving oxygenation by enhancing alveolar recruitment. Careful monitoring is necessary to avoid potential adverse effects on hemodynamics.

502. How does the application of lung-protective ventilation affect the risk of developing ventilator-associated pneumonia (VAP)?
a. It increases the risk due to higher PEEP levels.
b. It decreases the risk by reducing ventilator-induced lung injury and duration of ventilation.
c. It has no effect on the risk of VAP.
d. It increases the risk by prolonging the need for mechanical ventilation.

Answer: b. It decreases the risk by reducing ventilator-induced lung injury and duration of ventilation. Explanation: Lung-protective ventilation can potentially decrease the risk of VAP by minimizing lung injury and possibly reducing the overall duration of mechanical ventilation, thereby decreasing the exposure time to ventilator-associated complications.

503. What is the primary purpose of applying Positive End-Expiratory Pressure (PEEP) in mechanical ventilation?
a. To increase oxygen delivery by raising the inspired oxygen concentration
b. To reduce the work of breathing by the patient
c. To prevent alveolar collapse and improve oxygenation
d. To decrease carbon dioxide levels by increasing the respiratory rate

Answer: c. To prevent alveolar collapse and improve oxygenation. Explanation: PEEP is applied in mechanical ventilation to maintain positive pressure in the lungs at the end of expiration, preventing alveolar collapse (atelectasis), thus improving gas exchange and oxygenation.

504. In volume-controlled ventilation, what parameter is set by the clinician and remains constant during delivery?
a. Inspiratory pressure
b. Tidal volume
c. Respiratory rate
d. Inspiratory flow rate

Answer: b. Tidal volume. Explanation: In volume-controlled ventilation, the clinician sets a specific tidal volume that the ventilator delivers with each breath. This ensures a consistent volume delivery despite variations in airway pressure or patient effort.

505. What is the primary mechanism by which mechanical ventilation can lead to ventilator-induced lung injury (VILI)?
a. Hypoventilation and resultant hypercapnia
b. Excessive use of PEEP leading to hyperoxygenation
c. Alveolar overdistension and repetitive opening and closing of alveoli
d. Decreased mucociliary clearance due to dry ventilator circuits

Answer: c. Alveolar overdistension and repetitive opening and closing of alveoli. Explanation: VILI is primarily caused by alveolar overdistension (volutrauma) from excessive tidal volumes and the repetitive opening and closing of alveoli (atelectrauma), leading to lung tissue damage and inflammation.

506. When adjusting mechanical ventilation settings for a patient with ARDS, which strategy is recommended to minimize lung injury?
a. High tidal volumes to ensure adequate oxygenation
b. Low tidal volumes (4-8 ml/kg of ideal body weight) to reduce volutrauma
c. High respiratory rates to compensate for low tidal volumes
d. Zero PEEP to minimize pressure on the alveoli

Answer: b. Low tidal volumes (4-8 ml/kg of ideal body weight) to reduce volutrauma. Explanation: In ARDS, a lung-protective ventilation strategy with low tidal volumes (4-8 ml/kg of ideal body weight) is recommended to minimize the risk of volutrauma and subsequent ventilator-induced lung injury.

507. What does the term "auto-PEEP" or "intrinsic PEEP" refer to in mechanical ventilation?
a. Additional PEEP set by the clinician to improve oxygenation
b. Unintended positive pressure that builds up due to incomplete exhalation
c. The pressure difference between the alveoli and the atmosphere at end-expiration
d. The pressure applied during the inspiratory phase to enhance tidal volume

Answer: b. Unintended positive pressure that builds up due to incomplete exhalation. Explanation: Auto-PEEP or intrinsic PEEP occurs when there is incomplete exhalation before the start of the next breath, leading to the accumulation of positive pressure in the alveoli. This can impair venous return, decrease cardiac output, and increase the work of breathing.

508. In the management of a patient with obstructive lung disease on mechanical ventilation, why might longer expiratory times be beneficial?
a. To increase the rate of oxygen delivery
b. To ensure complete alveolar filling during inspiration
c. To prevent air trapping and reduce the risk of auto-PEEP
d. To decrease the overall respiratory rate and reduce oxygen consumption

Answer: c. To prevent air trapping and reduce the risk of auto-PEEP. Explanation: In obstructive lung diseases, longer expiratory times can help prevent air trapping and the development of auto-PEEP by allowing more time for complete exhalation, especially important in conditions like COPD or asthma where expiratory flow rates are reduced.

509. How does the use of a high inspiratory flow rate affect patient comfort during mechanical ventilation?
a. It increases comfort by reducing the duration of inspiration and allowing for longer exhalation
b. It decreases comfort by causing rapid lung inflation and potential discomfort
c. It has no effect on comfort as it only influences oxygenation levels
d. It enhances comfort by synchronizing better with the patient's spontaneous breathing efforts

Answer: a. It increases comfort by reducing the duration of inspiration and allowing for longer exhalation. Explanation: A high inspiratory flow rate can shorten the duration of the inspiratory phase, potentially increasing patient comfort by allowing for a longer exhalation time, which can be more in sync with the patient's natural breathing pattern.

510. What is the significance of monitoring plateau pressure in patients receiving mechanical ventilation?
a. It is directly correlated with the risk of pneumothorax
b. It reflects the pressure in the airways during inspiration
c. It is an indicator of alveolar pressure and helps assess the risk of volutrauma
d. It determines the effectiveness of oxygen transfer in the alveoli

Answer: c. It is an indicator of alveolar pressure and helps assess the risk of volutrauma. Explanation: Plateau pressure, measured during an inspiratory hold when airflow is zero, reflects the pressure within the alveoli and is used to assess the risk of volutrauma. Keeping plateau pressure below 30 cm H2O is recommended to minimize the risk of lung injury.

511. In mechanically ventilated patients, what is the primary goal of implementing a spontaneous breathing trial (SBT)?
a. To evaluate the patient's ability to breathe independently without ventilatory support
b. To assess the need for increased sedation and muscle relaxation
c. To determine the optimal level of PEEP for lung recruitment
d. To measure the patient's maximal inspiratory and expiratory pressures

Answer: a. To evaluate the patient's ability to breathe independently without ventilatory support. Explanation: A spontaneous breathing trial (SBT) is conducted to assess a patient's readiness for extubation and ability to maintain adequate ventilation and oxygenation without the assistance of the mechanical ventilator, indicating potential readiness for weaning from mechanical ventilation.

512. In Assist Control (AC) ventilation, what happens when the patient initiates a breath above the set rate?
a. The ventilator delivers a breath at the preset tidal volume.
b. The ventilator switches to a spontaneous mode for that breath.
c. The ventilator does not deliver any additional support for that breath.
d. The ventilator delivers a breath at a lower tidal volume.

Answer: a. The ventilator delivers a breath at the preset tidal volume. Explanation: In AC ventilation, every breath initiated by the patient or delivered by the machine is provided at the preset tidal volume. If the patient initiates a breath above the set rate, the ventilator will support that breath with the full preset tidal volume.

513. What is the primary difference between Synchronized Intermittent Mandatory Ventilation (SIMV) and Assist Control (AC) ventilation?
a. SIMV provides a set number of mandatory breaths with the patient able to breathe spontaneously in between.
b. SIMV does not allow spontaneous breathing.

c. AC provides support for all spontaneous breaths.
d. AC allows the patient to control the respiratory rate.

Answer: a. SIMV provides a set number of mandatory breaths with the patient able to breathe spontaneously in between. Explanation: SIMV mode delivers a preset number of mandatory breaths while allowing the patient to breathe spontaneously between these breaths. In contrast, AC mode supports every breath with a preset tidal volume, whether the breath is patient-initiated or machine-delivered.

514. In Pressure Support Ventilation (PSV), what determines the tidal volume of each breath?
a. The preset tidal volume
b. The preset pressure support level
c. The patient's respiratory rate
d. The machine's respiratory rate

Answer: b. The preset pressure support level. Explanation: In PSV, the tidal volume of each breath is determined by the preset pressure support level and the patient's lung compliance and airway resistance. There is no preset tidal volume in PSV; the pressure support helps the patient's spontaneous breaths reach an adequate tidal volume based on the pressure provided.

515. How does the Bi-Level Positive Airway Pressure (BiPAP) mode differ from Continuous Positive Airway Pressure (CPAP)?
a. BiPAP provides two levels of pressure, while CPAP provides a single continuous pressure.
b. BiPAP is used only in mechanically ventilated patients, while CPAP is used for spontaneously breathing patients.
c. CPAP provides inspiratory and expiratory pressure support, while BiPAP provides only inspiratory support.
d. CPAP is used during the day, while BiPAP is used at night.

Answer: a. BiPAP provides two levels of pressure, while CPAP provides a single continuous pressure. Explanation: BiPAP delivers two levels of pressure: a higher pressure during inspiration (IPAP) and a lower pressure during expiration (EPAP), whereas CPAP maintains a single, continuous positive airway pressure throughout the respiratory cycle.

516. For a patient with acute respiratory distress syndrome (ARDS) on mechanical ventilation, which mode is often preferred due to its lung-protective strategy?
a. Volume Control Ventilation (VCV)
b. High-Frequency Oscillatory Ventilation (HFOV)
c. Pressure Regulated Volume Control (PRVC)
d. Pressure Control Ventilation (PCV)

Answer: d. Pressure Control Ventilation (PCV). Explanation: PCV is often preferred for patients with ARDS as part of a lung-protective strategy because it allows control over peak inspiratory pressures, potentially reducing the risk of barotrauma and volutrauma by limiting the maximum pressure applied to the lungs during ventilation.

517. When using Volume Control Ventilation (VCV), what parameter does the clinician set directly?
a. Inspiratory pressure
b. Tidal volume
c. Expiratory pressure
d. Inspiratory time

Answer: b. Tidal volume. Explanation: In VCV, the clinician sets the tidal volume directly, and the ventilator adjusts the inspiratory pressure needed to deliver that volume based on the patient's lung compliance and airway resistance.

518. What is the primary advantage of using Adaptive Support Ventilation (ASV)?
a. It completely removes the need for clinician intervention in ventilator settings.
b. It automatically adjusts ventilation parameters to meet the patient's needs while minimizing work of breathing.
c. It allows for higher tidal volumes to improve oxygenation rapidly.
d. It uses lower levels of positive end-expiratory pressure (PEEP) to maintain lung compliance.

Answer: b. It automatically adjusts ventilation parameters to meet the patient's needs while minimizing work of breathing. Explanation: ASV is a closed-loop ventilation mode that continuously monitors the patient's respiratory status and automatically adjusts the ventilatory support to meet the patient's needs, aiming to provide optimal ventilation with minimal work of breathing.

519. In Pressure Regulated Volume Control (PRVC) ventilation, what happens if the patient's lung compliance decreases?
a. The ventilator increases the inspiratory pressure to maintain the set tidal volume.
b. The ventilator decreases the inspiratory pressure to prevent barotrauma.
c. The tidal volume delivered decreases to protect the lungs.
d. The respiratory rate automatically increases to compensate for the lower tidal volume.

Answer: a. The ventilator increases the inspiratory pressure to maintain the set tidal volume. Explanation: In PRVC, the ventilator aims to deliver a preset tidal volume by automatically adjusting the inspiratory pressure. If the patient's lung compliance decreases, the ventilator increases the inspiratory pressure within set limits to maintain the preset tidal volume.

520. How does the use of Neurally Adjusted Ventilatory Assist (NAVA) differ from traditional ventilation modes?
a. NAVA delivers a fixed tidal volume and respiratory rate.
b. NAVA uses the electrical activity of the diaphragm to trigger and cycle breaths.
c. NAVA applies continuous positive pressure without patient-ventilator synchrony.
d. NAVA provides pressure support without monitoring the patient's respiratory effort.

Answer: b. NAVA uses the electrical activity of the diaphragm to trigger and cycle breaths. Explanation: NAVA mode utilizes the electrical activity of the diaphragm (Edi) as a signal to trigger and cycle the ventilator in synchrony with the patient's respiratory effort, improving patient-ventilator synchrony and potentially reducing the risk of ventilator-induced lung injury.

521. What is a key consideration when transitioning a patient from Assist Control (AC) to Synchronized Intermittent Mandatory Ventilation (SIMV)?
a. Ensuring the patient can maintain adequate minute ventilation spontaneously
b. Increasing the tidal volume to compensate for the reduced respiratory rate
c. Decreasing the positive end-expiratory pressure (PEEP) to reduce the work of breathing
d. Increasing the inspiratory pressure to maintain oxygenation

Answer: a. Ensuring the patient can maintain adequate minute ventilation spontaneously. Explanation: When transitioning from AC to SIMV, it's crucial to ensure the patient has the ability to maintain adequate minute ventilation spontaneously, as SIMV allows for spontaneous breathing between mandatory breaths, requiring the patient to contribute more to their ventilation.

522. What is the primary goal of adjusting the Fraction of Inspired Oxygen (FiO2) in mechanically ventilated patients?
a. To decrease the respiratory rate
b. To increase lung compliance
c. To ensure adequate oxygenation
d. To reduce carbon dioxide levels

Answer: c. To ensure adequate oxygenation. Explanation: The primary goal of adjusting FiO2 in mechanically ventilated patients is to ensure adequate oxygenation by providing the necessary amount of oxygen to meet the patient's metabolic demands and maintain arterial oxygen saturation (SaO2) within target ranges, typically above 90%.

523. When setting Positive End-Expiratory Pressure (PEEP) in a patient with Acute Respiratory Distress Syndrome (ARDS), what is the primary consideration?
a. Minimizing oxygen toxicity
b. Preventing alveolar collapse at end-expiration
c. Maximizing carbon dioxide elimination
d. Increasing tidal volume delivery

Answer: b. Preventing alveolar collapse at end-expiration. Explanation: In ARDS, the primary consideration when setting PEEP is to prevent alveolar collapse at end-expiration, thus improving gas exchange and oxygenation by maintaining alveolar recruitment and increasing functional residual capacity.

524. What is the significance of setting the appropriate tidal volume (Vt) in patients on mechanical ventilation?
a. To ensure rapid sedation of the patient
b. To prevent ventilator-induced lung injury (VILI)

c. To increase the patient's heart rate
d. To reduce the need for renal replacement therapy

Answer: b. To prevent ventilator-induced lung injury (VILI). Explanation: Setting an appropriate tidal volume, typically 6-8 ml/kg of ideal body weight in patients with ARDS, is crucial to prevent ventilator-induced lung injury, including volutrauma (damage due to overdistension) and barotrauma (damage due to high pressures).

525. How does increasing FiO2 affect the risk of oxygen toxicity in mechanically ventilated patients?
a. There is no risk of oxygen toxicity with mechanical ventilation.
b. Increasing FiO2 decreases the risk of oxygen toxicity.
c. Increasing FiO2 increases the risk of oxygen toxicity.
d. FiO2 adjustments have no impact on oxygen levels.

Answer: c. Increasing FiO2 increases the risk of oxygen toxicity. Explanation: Prolonged administration of high concentrations of oxygen can lead to oxygen toxicity, characterized by damage to lung tissues. It is important to use the lowest FiO2 necessary to achieve adequate oxygenation to minimize this risk.

526. In the context of lung-protective ventilation strategies, what is the rationale behind using lower tidal volumes?
a. To increase the rate of spontaneous breathing
b. To decrease the risk of atelectasis
c. To reduce the incidence of pneumothorax
d. To minimize alveolar overdistension and barotrauma

Answer: d. To minimize alveolar overdistension and barotrauma. Explanation: Lung-protective ventilation strategies, including the use of lower tidal volumes, aim to minimize the risk of alveolar overdistension and barotrauma, thus reducing the likelihood of ventilator-induced lung injury and improving outcomes in patients with acute lung injury or ARDS.

527. What effect does the application of PEEP have on intrathoracic pressure and cardiac output?
a. PEEP decreases intrathoracic pressure and increases cardiac output.
b. PEEP increases intrathoracic pressure and has no effect on cardiac output.
c. PEEP increases intrathoracic pressure and can decrease cardiac output.
d. PEEP decreases intrathoracic pressure and has no effect on cardiac output.

Answer: c. PEEP increases intrathoracic pressure and can decrease cardiac output. Explanation: PEEP increases intrathoracic pressure, which can lead to decreased venous return to the heart and potentially reduce cardiac output, particularly in patients with hypovolemia or compromised cardiac function.

528. When titrating FiO2 and PEEP in a patient with hypoxemic respiratory failure, what is the primary objective?
a. To maximize FiO2 before adjusting PEEP

b. To achieve the highest possible PEEP level
c. To balance oxygenation with the risk of lung injury
d. To minimize FiO2 regardless of oxygenation status

Answer: c. To balance oxygenation with the risk of lung injury. Explanation: The primary objective when titrating FiO2 and PEEP in patients with hypoxemic respiratory failure is to optimize oxygenation while minimizing the risk of lung injury. This often involves increasing PEEP to improve alveolar recruitment and using the lowest FiO2 necessary to maintain adequate oxygen saturation.

529. How does the choice of tidal volume affect the PaCO2 levels in mechanically ventilated patients?
a. Larger tidal volumes always decrease PaCO2 levels.
b. Smaller tidal volumes have no effect on PaCO2 levels.
c. Larger tidal volumes can lead to increased PaCO2 levels.
d. Smaller tidal volumes can lead to increased PaCO2 levels due to hypoventilation.

Answer: d. Smaller tidal volumes can lead to increased PaCO2 levels due to hypoventilation. Explanation: Using smaller tidal volumes can lead to hypoventilation if the total minute ventilation is insufficient, potentially resulting in increased PaCO2 levels (hypercapnia). Adjustments may need to be made to the respiratory rate to ensure adequate ventilation and CO2 elimination.

530. In mechanically ventilated patients, what is the primary goal of adjusting ventilator settings to achieve a low tidal volume strategy?
a. To increase the patient's comfort and reduce sedation needs
b. To enhance diuresis and fluid removal
c. To prevent or minimize ventilator-induced lung injury
d. To accelerate the process of weaning from the ventilator

Answer: c. To prevent or minimize ventilator-induced lung injury. Explanation: The primary goal of a low tidal volume strategy in mechanically ventilated patients, particularly those with ARDS, is to prevent or minimize ventilator-induced lung injury by avoiding alveolar overdistension and reducing the risk of volutrauma and barotrauma.

531. Which parameter is most commonly used to assess readiness for ventilator weaning?
a. Tidal volume (VT) of 4-6 mL/kg of ideal body weight
b. Rapid shallow breathing index (RSBI) less than 105 breaths/min/L
c. Positive end-expiratory pressure (PEEP) below 5 cm H2O
d. Arterial oxygen saturation (SaO2) above 95%

Answer: b. Rapid shallow breathing index (RSBI) less than 105 breaths/min/L. Explanation: RSBI, calculated as respiratory rate divided by tidal volume (in liters), is a commonly used parameter to assess a patient's readiness for ventilator weaning. An RSBI less than 105 breaths/min/L indicates a lower risk of weaning failure.

532. During a spontaneous breathing trial (SBT), which finding suggests that a patient may not be ready for extubation?
a. Heart rate increase by 10 beats per minute
b. Slight increase in blood pressure
c. Respiratory rate above 35 breaths per minute
d. Occasional sigh breaths

Answer: c. Respiratory rate above 35 breaths per minute. Explanation: A respiratory rate above 35 breaths per minute during an SBT can indicate inadequate respiratory muscle strength or endurance, suggesting the patient may not be ready for extubation due to the risk of respiratory fatigue.

533. What is the primary goal of implementing a T-piece trial in ventilator weaning?
a. To assess the patient's ability to maintain oxygenation without ventilator support
b. To determine the optimal level of PEEP for lung recruitment
c. To evaluate the effectiveness of nebulized medications
d. To measure the patient's inspiratory force

Answer: a. To assess the patient's ability to maintain oxygenation without ventilator support. Explanation: A T-piece trial involves disconnecting the patient from the ventilator and supplying oxygen through a T-piece, allowing assessment of the patient's ability to breathe spontaneously and maintain adequate oxygenation without the assistance of the ventilator.

534. Which clinical sign indicates poor tolerance to ventilator weaning?
a. Diaphoresis
b. Decreased urine output
c. Mild anxiety
d. Slight increase in diastolic blood pressure

Answer: a. Diaphoresis. Explanation: Diaphoresis during a weaning trial can be a sign of increased work of breathing and distress, indicating poor tolerance to the weaning process. It may suggest that the patient is not yet ready to be weaned off the ventilator.

535. In the context of ventilator weaning, what does a negative inspiratory force (NIF) of less than -20 cm H2O typically indicate?
a. Adequate respiratory muscle strength for weaning
b. Need for increased ventilatory support
c. Lung overdistension
d. Optimal PEEP level

Answer: a. Adequate respiratory muscle strength for weaning. Explanation: A negative inspiratory force (NIF) or maximal inspiratory pressure (MIP) of less than -20 cm H2O (more negative) is generally considered indicative of sufficient respiratory muscle strength, suggesting that the patient may be ready for ventilator weaning.

536. What role does the spontaneous breathing trial (SBT) play in the ventilator weaning process?
a. It is used to determine the patient's response to increased PEEP.
b. It assesses the patient's ability to breathe independently without mechanical assistance.
c. It evaluates the need for sedation adjustment.
d. It measures the lung compliance and airway resistance.

Answer: b. It assesses the patient's ability to breathe independently without mechanical assistance. Explanation: An SBT is a key component of the weaning process, where the patient is allowed to breathe spontaneously with minimal or no support from the ventilator, assessing their ability to maintain effective gas exchange and respiratory muscle endurance without mechanical assistance.

537. Which factor is NOT typically considered a contraindication to initiating a weaning trial?
a. Severe acidosis
b. Hemodynamic instability
c. Controlled infection
d. Myocardial ischemia

Answer: c. Controlled infection. Explanation: A controlled infection is not typically a contraindication to initiating a weaning trial. In contrast, severe acidosis, hemodynamic instability, and myocardial ischemia are conditions that may need to be stabilized before attempting to wean a patient from mechanical ventilation.

538. How does the use of Pressure Support Ventilation (PSV) aid in the weaning process?
a. By delivering a preset tidal volume for each spontaneous breath
b. By providing a constant pressure to augment the patient's spontaneous breaths
c. By fully controlling the patient's ventilation with a set respiratory rate and tidal volume
d. By applying high-frequency oscillations to reduce airway resistance

Answer: b. By providing a constant pressure to augment the patient's spontaneous breaths. Explanation: PSV aids in the weaning process by providing an adjustable level of pressure support to augment the patient's spontaneous breaths, reducing the work of breathing and allowing the patient to gradually assume more of the respiratory effort as their condition improves.

539. When considering extubation, which parameter is least important in the decision-making process?
a. Arterial blood gas analysis
b. Level of consciousness
c. Cuff leak test result
d. Duration of mechanical ventilation

Answer: d. Duration of mechanical ventilation. Explanation: While the duration of mechanical ventilation is a consideration, it is not as critical as the patient's current physiological status, including arterial blood gas analysis, level of consciousness, and cuff leak test results, in making extubation decisions.

540. Which pathogen is most commonly associated with community-acquired pneumonia in adults?
a. Mycoplasma pneumoniae
b. Haemophilus influenzae
c. Streptococcus pneumoniae
d. Legionella pneumophila

Answer: c. Streptococcus pneumoniae. Explanation: Streptococcus pneumoniae is the most common cause of community-acquired pneumonia in adults, responsible for a significant proportion of cases. It is known for causing typical pneumonia, which presents with sudden onset of symptoms like high fever, chills, and productive cough.

541. In the treatment of pneumonia caused by atypical pathogens, which class of antibiotics is generally considered most effective?
a. Beta-lactams
b. Aminoglycosides
c. Macrolides
d. Cephalosporins

Answer: c. Macrolides. Explanation: Macrolides, such as azithromycin and clarithromycin, are generally considered effective against atypical pathogens like Mycoplasma pneumoniae, Chlamydophila pneumoniae, and Legionella pneumophila, commonly implicated in atypical pneumonia.

542. For a patient diagnosed with hospital-acquired pneumonia (HAP), what is a critical factor in choosing empirical antibiotic therapy?
a. The patient's age
b. The presence of multidrug-resistant organisms in the hospital setting
c. The duration of hospital stay prior to pneumonia onset
d. The patient's blood type

Answer: b. The presence of multidrug-resistant organisms in the hospital setting. Explanation: When choosing empirical antibiotic therapy for HAP, it is crucial to consider the prevalence of multidrug-resistant organisms in the hospital setting, as these infections are often caused by bacteria that are more resistant to standard antibiotics.

543. What is the significance of the CURB-65 score in the management of pneumonia?
a. It predicts the 30-day mortality rate for patients with tuberculosis.
b. It assesses the severity of pneumonia to guide decisions regarding hospital admission.
c. It determines the need for antiviral therapy in viral pneumonia.

d. It measures the patient's response to bronchodilator therapy in obstructive lung disease.

Answer: b. It assesses the severity of pneumonia to guide decisions regarding hospital admission. Explanation: The CURB-65 score is a clinical prediction tool that assesses the severity of pneumonia based on five factors: Confusion, Urea, Respiratory rate, Blood pressure, and age ≥65 years. It helps clinicians decide whether outpatient treatment is safe or if hospitalization is needed.

544. In patients with pneumonia, what is a common radiographic finding on a chest X-ray?
a. Bilateral hilar lymphadenopathy
b. A hyperlucent lung field indicating pneumothorax
c. Consolidation in the affected lung segment or lobe
d. Diffuse interstitial patterns typical of pulmonary fibrosis

Answer: c. Consolidation in the affected lung segment or lobe. Explanation: A common radiographic finding in pneumonia is consolidation, which appears as an area of increased opacity in the affected lung segment or lobe. This is due to the filling of alveoli with inflammatory cells, bacteria, and exudate.

545. What role does vaccination play in the prevention of pneumonia?
a. Vaccines are primarily used to treat acute pneumonia episodes.
b. Vaccines are effective in preventing viral pneumonia only.
c. Vaccines, like pneumococcal and influenza, help prevent pneumonia by protecting against specific pathogens.
d. Vaccination has no significant role in pneumonia prevention and is not recommended.

Answer: c. Vaccines, like pneumococcal and influenza, help prevent pneumonia by protecting against specific pathogens. Explanation: Vaccination is a key strategy in the prevention of pneumonia. Pneumococcal vaccines protect against Streptococcus pneumoniae, and influenza vaccines reduce the risk of secondary bacterial pneumonia following influenza infection.

546. In the context of aspiration pneumonia, which intervention is crucial for prevention in at-risk patients?
a. Routine administration of antitussive medications
b. Elevating the head of the bed for patients with a high risk of aspiration
c. Daily chest physiotherapy to enhance mucociliary clearance
d. Prophylactic antibiotics for all patients with dysphagia

Answer: b. Elevating the head of the bed for patients with a high risk of aspiration. Explanation: For patients at high risk of aspiration, such as those with dysphagia or who are receiving enteral feeding, elevating the head of the bed (ideally to 30-45 degrees) is a crucial intervention to reduce the risk of aspiration pneumonia.

547. What is the typical clinical presentation of "walking pneumonia" caused by Mycoplasma pneumoniae?
a. Rapid onset of high fever and productive cough with green sputum

b. Severe chest pain with respiratory distress and cyanosis
c. Mild, flu-like symptoms with a dry cough and minimal systemic manifestations
d. Profound hypoxemia requiring immediate mechanical ventilation

Answer: c. Mild, flu-like symptoms with a dry cough and minimal systemic manifestations. Explanation: "Walking pneumonia" caused by Mycoplasma pneumoniae typically presents with mild, flu-like symptoms, including a persistent dry cough, low-grade fever, and malaise, with patients often remaining ambulatory and not appearing severely ill.

548. For a patient with severe community-acquired pneumonia and a penicillin allergy, which antibiotic regimen is a suitable alternative?
a. Penicillin G with an aminoglycoside
b. A combination of a fluoroquinolone and a macrolide
c. Vancomycin monotherapy
d. High-dose amoxicillin-clavulanate

Answer: b. A combination of a fluoroquinolone and a macrolide. Explanation: For patients with severe community-acquired pneumonia who have a penicillin allergy, a combination of a fluoroquinolone (like levofloxacin or moxifloxacin) and a macrolide (like azithromycin) is a suitable alternative, providing broad coverage against common pathogens including atypical bacteria.

549. Which of the following is considered a major risk factor for the development of acute respiratory distress syndrome (ARDS)?
a. Chronic obstructive pulmonary disease (COPD)
b. High altitude exposure
c. Severe sepsis
d. Vitamin D deficiency

Answer: c. Severe sepsis. Explanation: Severe sepsis is a well-known major risk factor for the development of ARDS due to the systemic inflammatory response that can lead to widespread lung injury and increased capillary permeability, resulting in non-cardiogenic pulmonary edema characteristic of ARDS.

550. In diagnosing heart failure, which test is considered the gold standard for assessing left ventricular ejection fraction?
a. Electrocardiogram (ECG)
b. Chest X-ray
c. Echocardiography
d. Cardiac catheterization

Answer: c. Echocardiography. Explanation: Echocardiography is considered the gold standard for assessing left ventricular ejection fraction, as it provides direct visualization and measurement of cardiac structures and function, allowing for accurate assessment of heart failure.

551. Which condition is a significant risk factor for the development of venous thromboembolism (VTE)?
a. Hypertension
b. Prolonged immobilization
c. Hyperthyroidism
d. Peptic ulcer disease

Answer: b. Prolonged immobilization. Explanation: Prolonged immobilization is a significant risk factor for the development of VTE, as it leads to stasis of blood in the veins, particularly in the lower extremities, increasing the risk of clot formation.

552. For diagnosing diabetes mellitus, which diagnostic criterion is accurate according to the American Diabetes Association (ADA)?
a. Fasting plasma glucose ≥ 126 mg/dL
b. Random plasma glucose ≥ 160 mg/dL
c. 2-hour plasma glucose during OGTT ≥ 180 mg/dL
d. HbA1c ≥ 5.5%

Answer: a. Fasting plasma glucose ≥ 126 mg/dL. Explanation: According to the ADA, a fasting plasma glucose level of ≥ 126 mg/dL is one of the criteria for diagnosing diabetes mellitus, indicating impaired fasting glucose.

553. Which is a well-established risk factor for the development of chronic kidney disease (CKD)?
a. Osteoporosis
b. Diabetes mellitus
c. Hypothyroidism
d. Gastroesophageal reflux disease (GERD)

Answer: b. Diabetes mellitus. Explanation: Diabetes mellitus is a well-established risk factor for CKD due to the long-term damage high blood sugar levels can inflict on the kidneys, leading to diabetic nephropathy.

554. In the diagnosis of pulmonary embolism (PE), which imaging study is considered the most definitive?
a. Chest X-ray
b. Ventilation-perfusion (V/Q) scan
c. Computed Tomography Pulmonary Angiography (CTPA)
d. Transthoracic echocardiogram

Answer: c. Computed Tomography Pulmonary Angiography (CTPA). Explanation: CTPA is considered the most definitive imaging study for diagnosing PE, as it allows direct visualization of the pulmonary arteries and can reliably detect clots that may be causing the embolism.

555. What is a primary risk factor for the development of osteoporosis?
a. Excessive physical activity
b. High calcium intake
c. Post-menopausal status in women
d. Use of proton pump inhibitors for less than one year

Answer: c. Post-menopausal status in women. Explanation: Post-menopausal status in women is a primary risk factor for osteoporosis due to the decrease in estrogen levels, which plays a crucial role in maintaining bone density.

556. For the diagnosis of an acute myocardial infarction (AMI), which biomarker is considered highly specific?
a. C-reactive protein (CRP)
b. Creatinine kinase-MB (CK-MB)
c. Cardiac troponins
d. Aspartate aminotransferase (AST)

Answer: c. Cardiac troponins. Explanation: Cardiac troponins are highly specific biomarkers for diagnosing AMI, as they are released into the bloodstream when heart muscle cells are injured, providing high specificity and sensitivity for myocardial injury.

557. Which lifestyle factor is a significant risk for the development of hypertension?
a. High sodium intake
b. Low-fat diet
c. Aerobic exercise
d. Moderate alcohol consumption

Answer: a. High sodium intake. Explanation: A high sodium intake is a significant lifestyle risk factor for the development of hypertension, as it can lead to fluid retention, increased blood volume, and subsequently increased blood pressure.

558. In diagnosing acute pancreatitis, which laboratory test is most indicative of the condition?
a. Elevated alanine aminotransferase (ALT)
b. Elevated blood urea nitrogen (BUN)
c. Elevated lipase
d. Elevated direct bilirubin

Answer: c. Elevated lipase. Explanation: Elevated serum lipase levels are most indicative of acute pancreatitis, as lipase is an enzyme produced by the pancreas, and its levels increase significantly in the blood during acute inflammation or injury to the pancreas.

559. What is a key consideration when initiating antibiotic therapy for community-acquired pneumonia (CAP)?
a. The need for broad-spectrum antibiotics to cover all potential hospital-acquired pathogens
b. Prioritization of antiviral agents due to the high likelihood of viral etiology
c. Selection of antibiotics based on local antimicrobial susceptibility patterns
d. Immediate initiation of tuberculosis-specific treatment until TB is ruled out

Answer: c. Selection of antibiotics based on local antimicrobial susceptibility patterns. Explanation: When initiating antibiotic therapy for CAP, it's crucial to select antibiotics based on local antimicrobial susceptibility patterns to ensure effectiveness against the most likely pathogens, such as Streptococcus pneumoniae, while considering patient-specific factors like allergies and comorbidities.

560. For hospital-acquired pneumonia (HAP), why is empirical therapy often broad-spectrum initially?
a. Patients with HAP are usually less responsive to narrow-spectrum antibiotics.
b. Broad-spectrum antibiotics are less likely to cause allergic reactions.
c. HAP pathogens often include more resistant bacteria, necessitating broader coverage until cultures identify specific organisms.
d. Broad-spectrum antibiotics speed up the recovery process, reducing hospital stay.

Answer: c. HAP pathogens often include more resistant bacteria, necessitating broader coverage until cultures identify specific organisms. Explanation: HAP is often caused by multidrug-resistant organisms, requiring initial broad-spectrum antibiotic therapy to cover a wide range of potential pathogens, including MRSA and Pseudomonas aeruginosa, until culture results allow for de-escalation to more targeted treatment.

561. In treating CAP, why is macrolide therapy (e.g., azithromycin) often recommended?
a. Macrolides effectively target the anaerobes commonly found in hospital environments.
b. They have a narrow spectrum of activity that specifically targets typical CAP pathogens.
c. Macrolides cover typical and atypical pathogens, making them suitable for empirical CAP therapy.
d. They are the most effective class against MRSA, a common cause of CAP.

Answer: c. Macrolides cover typical and atypical pathogens, making them suitable for empirical CAP therapy. Explanation: Macrolides like azithromycin are recommended for CAP due to their effectiveness against a broad range of pathogens involved in CAP, including atypical bacteria like Mycoplasma pneumoniae and Chlamydophila pneumoniae, offering a good empirical coverage.

562. What is the rationale behind the use of vancomycin or linezolid in the treatment of HAP?
a. To cover atypical pathogens that are common in the community setting
b. As first-line agents for viral pneumonias acquired in the hospital
c. To target MRSA, which is a potential pathogen in the hospital setting

d. For their effectiveness against typical bacteria causing CAP

Answer: c. To target MRSA, which is a potential pathogen in the hospital setting. Explanation: Vancomycin or linezolid are used in HAP treatment primarily to cover MRSA, a significant concern in the hospital setting due to its resistance to many antibiotics. Their use is based on risk factors for MRSA and local prevalence rates.

563. How does the approach to empirical antibiotic therapy differ between CAP and HAP in terms of pathogen coverage?
a. CAP treatment focuses exclusively on fungal pathogens, while HAP treatment does not.
b. HAP empirical therapy often includes coverage for a wider range of resistant bacteria compared to CAP.
c. Antibiotics for CAP are selected based on the duration of hospital stay, whereas HAP antibiotics are not.
d. CAP requires immediate antiviral treatment, while HAP focuses on antibacterial agents only.

Answer: b. HAP empirical therapy often includes coverage for a wider range of resistant bacteria compared to CAP. Explanation: Empirical therapy for HAP typically covers a broader spectrum of bacteria, including multidrug-resistant organisms, due to the different pathogen profile and resistance patterns seen in hospital settings, unlike CAP, where the focus is on community-prevalent pathogens.

564. When might a combination therapy with a beta-lactam and a macrolide be considered for CAP?
a. When the patient has a documented allergy to penicillin
b. In cases of mild CAP without any comorbidities
c. For severe CAP requiring hospitalization, to cover both typical and atypical pathogens
d. As a standard approach for all CAP cases regardless of severity

Answer: c. For severe CAP requiring hospitalization, to cover both typical and atypical pathogens. Explanation: Combination therapy with a beta-lactam antibiotic (to cover typical bacteria like Streptococcus pneumoniae) and a macrolide (to cover atypical pathogens) is often used for severe CAP requiring hospitalization, enhancing empirical coverage and potentially improving outcomes.

565. In the context of pneumonia treatment, how does the presence of comorbidities influence antibiotic selection for CAP?
a. Comorbidities necessitate the exclusive use of antiviral agents.
b. Patients with comorbidities are always treated with the same antibiotics as HAP to cover resistant strains.
c. Comorbidities such as chronic heart, lung, liver, or renal diseases may warrant broader-spectrum or combination antibiotic therapy.
d. Comorbidities require the use of antibiotics that target anaerobic bacteria only.

Answer: c. Comorbidities such as chronic heart, lung, liver, or renal diseases may warrant broader-spectrum or combination antibiotic therapy. Explanation: In CAP patients with significant comorbidities, broader-spectrum or combination therapy is often used to ensure adequate coverage against potential pathogens, given the increased risk of complications and more severe disease.

566. What is the impact of prior antibiotic use within the past 3 months on the selection of empirical therapy for CAP?
a. Prior antibiotic use has no impact on the selection of empirical therapy.
b. It may necessitate the use of more potent antifungal medications.
c. Empirical therapy may need adjustment to cover potential resistant pathogens due to recent antibiotic exposure.
d. Treatment must shift focus exclusively to viral etiologies.

Answer: c. Empirical therapy may need adjustment to cover potential resistant pathogens due to recent antibiotic exposure. Explanation: Recent antibiotic use can select for resistant strains, requiring an adjustment in empirical therapy for CAP to ensure coverage of potential drug-resistant pathogens, thereby tailoring the treatment to the individual risk profile.

567. For a patient with CAP showing signs of treatment failure, what step should be considered in the management plan?
a. Immediate discontinuation of all antibiotics
b. Reevaluation of the diagnosis and consideration of alternative or additional pathogens, including drug-resistant organisms
c. Switch to a less potent antibiotic to minimize side effects
d. Continuation of the initial therapy without changes for an extended duration

Answer: b. Reevaluation of the diagnosis and consideration of alternative or additional pathogens, including drug-resistant organisms. Explanation: Treatment failure in CAP necessitates a thorough reevaluation of the diagnosis and treatment plan, considering factors like incorrect initial diagnosis, presence of drug-resistant pathogens, or complications such as abscess formation, indicating the need for alternative or additional therapeutic strategies.

568. What is the most common source of pulmonary embolism (PE)?
a. Right atrial thrombus
b. Deep vein thrombosis in the lower extremities
c. Atherosclerotic plaques in the pulmonary artery
d. Renal vein thrombosis

Answer: b. Deep vein thrombosis in the lower extremities. Explanation: The most common source of pulmonary embolism is a thrombus originating from deep vein thrombosis (DVT) in the lower extremities. These clots can dislodge and travel through the venous system to the lungs, causing a PE.

569. Which clinical feature is most characteristic of a massive pulmonary embolism?
a. Wheezing
b. Hemoptysis
c. Sudden onset of dyspnea
d. Chronic cough

Answer: c. Sudden onset of dyspnea. Explanation: A sudden onset of dyspnea is one of the most characteristic and common features of a massive pulmonary embolism, often accompanied by pleuritic chest pain, hypoxia, and hemodynamic instability.

570. In the diagnostic workup for suspected PE, what role does the D-dimer test serve?
a. It confirms the diagnosis of PE.
b. It is used to stratify the risk of mortality in PE.
c. It helps to exclude PE in patients with a low pre-test probability.
d. It identifies the specific location of the thrombus.

Answer: c. It helps to exclude PE in patients with a low pre-test probability. Explanation: The D-dimer test is used to exclude pulmonary embolism in patients with a low pre-test probability, as it is a sensitive marker of clot formation and degradation. A negative D-dimer test in such patients makes PE unlikely.

571. Which imaging study is considered the gold standard for the diagnosis of pulmonary embolism?
a. Chest X-ray
b. Ventilation-perfusion (V/Q) scan
c. Computed Tomography Pulmonary Angiography (CTPA)
d. Transthoracic echocardiogram

Answer: c. Computed Tomography Pulmonary Angiography (CTPA). Explanation: CTPA is considered the gold standard for diagnosing pulmonary embolism as it allows direct visualization of the pulmonary arteries and can accurately detect the presence of emboli.

572. What is the initial anticoagulation treatment of choice for most patients with acute PE?
a. Unfractionated heparin
b. Direct oral anticoagulants (DOACs)
c. Aspirin
d. Warfarin, started without bridging anticoagulation

Answer: b. Direct oral anticoagulants (DOACs). Explanation: Direct oral anticoagulants (DOACs) are often the treatment of choice for most patients with acute pulmonary embolism due to their rapid onset of action, predictable pharmacokinetics, and fewer dietary and drug interactions compared to warfarin.

573. In the context of PE, what is the significance of the presence of right ventricular strain on echocardiography?
a. It indicates a low-risk PE.
b. It is a marker of chronic pulmonary hypertension.
c. It suggests a high-risk PE with potential hemodynamic compromise.
d. It is an incidental finding with no clinical significance.

Answer: c. It suggests a high-risk PE with potential hemodynamic compromise. Explanation: Right ventricular strain on echocardiography in the context of PE indicates pressure overload due to acute obstruction of pulmonary circulation, suggesting a high-risk PE that may lead to hemodynamic instability.

574. For patients with a confirmed PE, what is the recommended duration of anticoagulant therapy for a first unprovoked event?
a. 3 months
b. 6 months
c. At least 12 months
d. Indefinite duration

Answer: b. 6 months. Explanation: For a first unprovoked PE, the recommended duration of anticoagulant therapy is at least 6 months. Extended or indefinite therapy may be considered in patients with recurrent, unprovoked events or persistent risk factors, balancing the risk of bleeding.

575. What is the primary mechanism of action of thrombolytic therapy in the treatment of PE?
a. It stabilizes the thrombus to prevent further embolization.
b. It dilates the pulmonary arteries to reduce right ventricular strain.
c. It mechanically removes the thrombus.
d. It dissolves the thrombus to restore pulmonary artery patency.

Answer: d. It dissolves the thrombus to restore pulmonary artery patency. Explanation: Thrombolytic therapy works by dissolving the existing thrombus in the pulmonary artery, thereby restoring patency and improving blood flow, and is primarily considered in massive PE with hemodynamic instability.

576. In PE management, what is the primary purpose of using an inferior vena cava (IVC) filter?
a. To dissolve clots in the lower extremities
b. To prevent recurrent PE in patients with contraindications to anticoagulation
c. To reduce the size of existing pulmonary emboli
d. As first-line treatment in all patients diagnosed with PE

Answer: b. To prevent recurrent PE in patients with contraindications to anticoagulation. Explanation: An IVC filter is used to prevent recurrent PE in patients who have contraindications to anticoagulation (e.g., significant bleeding risk), by catching thrombi from the lower extremities before they can embolize to the lungs.

577. Which clinical scoring system is used to assess the severity and prognosis of PE?
a. CHA2DS2-VASc score
b. Wells' score
c. Pulmonary Embolism Severity Index (PESI)
d. CURB-65 score

Answer: c. Pulmonary Embolism Severity Index (PESI). Explanation: The Pulmonary Embolism Severity Index (PESI) is a clinical scoring system used to assess the severity and prognosis of PE, helping to stratify patients based on the risk of mortality and guiding decisions regarding the level of care (e.g., outpatient vs. inpatient treatment).

578. Which component of Virchow's triad refers to changes in the blood's composition that promote clotting?
a. Endothelial injury
b. Hemodynamic changes
c. Hypercoagulability
d. Vascular stasis

Answer: c. Hypercoagulability. Explanation: Hypercoagulability, one of the components of Virchow's triad, refers to alterations in the blood that predispose it to clot more easily. This can be due to genetic factors, such as factor V Leiden mutation, or acquired conditions, like malignancy or prolonged immobilization.

579. A patient with a recent orthopedic surgery is at risk for deep vein thrombosis (DVT) primarily due to which aspect of Virchow's triad?
a. Increased blood vessel diameter
b. Endothelial damage caused by surgical manipulation
c. Enhanced erythropoiesis post-surgery
d. Reduced cardiac output postoperatively

Answer: b. Endothelial damage caused by surgical manipulation. Explanation: Surgical procedures, especially orthopedic surgeries, can cause direct endothelial damage due to mechanical manipulation, which is a key factor in Virchow's triad for the development of thrombosis, including DVT.

580. In the context of Virchow's triad, how does prolonged bed rest contribute to thromboembolism?
a. By promoting hypercoagulability due to increased synthesis of clotting factors
b. By causing endothelial injury due to pressure points
c. By leading to vascular stasis as a result of reduced muscle contraction and blood flow
d. By inducing hemodynamic changes that increase blood pressure

Answer: c. By leading to vascular stasis as a result of reduced muscle contraction and blood flow. Explanation: Prolonged bed rest or immobility leads to vascular stasis, a key component of Virchow's triad, by reducing venous return and blood flow, particularly in the lower limbs, which increases the risk of clot formation.

581. Which factor is considered a primary contributor to hypercoagulability in cancer patients, according to Virchow's triad?
a. Direct endothelial damage by tumor cells
b. Tumor secretion of procoagulant substances and cytokines
c. Increased blood viscosity due to chemotherapy

d. Immune-mediated destruction of clotting inhibitors

Answer: b. Tumor secretion of procoagulant substances and cytokines. Explanation: Cancer patients often exhibit hypercoagulability, part of Virchow's triad, due to the tumor's secretion of procoagulant substances and cytokines that alter the normal coagulation pathway, increasing the risk of thromboembolic events.

582. In patients with atrial fibrillation, which aspect of Virchow's triad is primarily implicated in stroke risk?
a. Hypercoagulability due to irregular heart rhythm
b. Hemodynamic changes leading to increased shear stress
c. Vascular stasis within the atria due to ineffective contractions
d. Endothelial injury from high atrial pressures

Answer: c. Vascular stasis within the atria due to ineffective contractions. Explanation: In atrial fibrillation, the risk of stroke is primarily due to vascular stasis within the atria. The loss of effective atrial contractions leads to blood pooling and stasis, a key component of Virchow's triad, increasing the risk of clot formation that can embolize to the brain.

583. What role does smoking play in the development of thrombosis via Virchow's triad?
a. It reduces plasma antithrombin levels, leading to hypercoagulability.
b. It causes direct endothelial injury through toxic exposure to chemicals in smoke.
c. It increases blood flow velocity, reducing the risk of vascular stasis.
d. It enhances fibrinolysis, counteracting the effects of hypercoagulability.

Answer: b. It causes direct endothelial injury through toxic exposure to chemicals in smoke. Explanation: Smoking contributes to thrombosis risk by causing direct endothelial injury, one of the elements of Virchow's triad, through the toxic effects of chemicals in tobacco smoke on the vascular endothelium, promoting a prothrombotic state.

584. How does dehydration influence thrombosis risk in relation to Virchow's triad?
a. By causing endothelial swelling and narrowing of vessels
b. By increasing blood viscosity, contributing to vascular stasis
c. By enhancing the synthesis of natural anticoagulants
d. By promoting vasodilation and increased blood flow

Answer: b. By increasing blood viscosity, contributing to vascular stasis. Explanation: Dehydration can lead to increased blood viscosity, which is a factor contributing to vascular stasis, part of Virchow's triad. This increased viscosity can impede normal blood flow and increase the risk of clot formation.

585. In the management of a patient with a history of recurrent DVTs, what is a key target for reducing future risk based on Virchow's triad?
a. Administration of vasodilators to increase vessel diameter

b. Use of anticoagulants to address hypercoagulability
c. Surgical intervention to repair endothelial damage
d. Physical therapy to increase blood pressure and flow

Answer: b. Use of anticoagulants to address hypercoagulability. Explanation: For patients with a history of recurrent DVTs, targeting hypercoagulability through the use of anticoagulants is a key strategy to reduce future risk. Anticoagulants prevent further clot formation by interfering with the blood's clotting process, addressing one of the critical elements of Virchow's triad.

586. Which intervention effectively addresses all three components of Virchow's triad in the prevention of post-operative DVT?
a. Prophylactic use of low-molecular-weight heparin
b. Routine post-operative insertion of inferior vena cava filters
c. High-dose aspirin therapy initiated pre-operatively
d. Application of compression stockings and early ambulation

Answer: d. Application of compression stockings and early ambulation. Explanation: Compression stockings and early ambulation post-surgery are effective interventions that address all three components of Virchow's triad. They help reduce vascular stasis by promoting venous return, minimize endothelial injury by reducing venous distension, and may indirectly influence hypercoagulability by enhancing blood flow and reducing the opportunity for clot formation.

587. What is the primary purpose of a B-type natriuretic peptide (BNP) test in a patient presenting with dyspnea?
a. To confirm a diagnosis of acute asthma exacerbation
b. To identify the presence of electrolyte imbalances
c. To assess for cardiac ischemia
d. To differentiate between cardiac and non-cardiac causes of dyspnea

Answer: d. To differentiate between cardiac and non-cardiac causes of dyspnea. Explanation: BNP is released by the ventricles in response to excessive stretching of heart muscle cells. Elevated levels are indicative of heart failure, making the BNP test valuable for distinguishing cardiac causes of dyspnea from non-cardiac causes, such as pulmonary conditions.

588. In diagnosing myocardial infarction, which biomarker is considered the most sensitive and specific?
a. Creatine kinase-MB (CK-MB)
b. Aspartate aminotransferase (AST)
c. Lactate dehydrogenase (LDH)
d. Troponin

Answer: d. Troponin. Explanation: Cardiac troponins (I and T) are highly sensitive and specific biomarkers for myocardial injury. Their levels rise within hours of cardiac injury and remain elevated for an extended period, making them critical for diagnosing myocardial infarction.

589. Which diagnostic test provides the most definitive evidence of a pulmonary embolism (PE)?
a. Ventilation-perfusion (V/Q) scan
b. D-dimer assay
c. Computed tomography pulmonary angiography (CTPA)
d. Pulmonary function tests (PFTs)

Answer: c. Computed tomography pulmonary angiography (CTPA). Explanation: CTPA is the most definitive diagnostic test for PE as it allows direct visualization of the pulmonary arteries and can detect the presence of thrombi obstructing blood flow, making it the gold standard for PE diagnosis.

590. For a patient suspected of having a deep vein thrombosis (DVT), which test is typically the first-line diagnostic tool?
a. Venography
b. Doppler ultrasound
c. D-dimer assay
d. Magnetic resonance imaging (MRI)

Answer: b. Doppler ultrasound. Explanation: Doppler ultrasound is the first-line diagnostic tool for suspected DVT. It is non-invasive, widely available, and capable of visualizing blood flow and thrombi within the veins, particularly in the lower extremities.

591. In evaluating a patient for chronic obstructive pulmonary disease (COPD), which test is most useful for assessing the severity of airflow obstruction?
a. Arterial blood gas (ABG) analysis
b. Chest X-ray
c. Spirometry
d. Complete blood count (CBC)

Answer: c. Spirometry. Explanation: Spirometry is the most useful test for diagnosing and assessing the severity of COPD. It measures the volume and flow of air during inhalation and exhalation, providing objective data on the presence and extent of airflow obstruction.

592. What is the significance of a positive antinuclear antibody (ANA) test in a patient with joint pain and fatigue?
a. It confirms a diagnosis of rheumatoid arthritis.
b. It is indicative of acute bacterial infection.
c. It suggests the presence of an autoimmune disorder.
d. It is specific to systemic lupus erythematosus (SLE).

Answer: c. It suggests the presence of an autoimmune disorder. Explanation: A positive ANA test is indicative of the presence of autoantibodies and suggests an autoimmune disorder. While not specific, it is commonly seen in various autoimmune diseases, including SLE, rheumatoid arthritis, and scleroderma, and warrants further evaluation.

593. In diagnosing acute pancreatitis, which laboratory test is most indicative of the condition?
a. Elevated alanine aminotransferase (ALT)
b. Elevated blood urea nitrogen (BUN)
c. Elevated lipase
d. Elevated direct bilirubin

Answer: c. Elevated lipase. Explanation: Elevated serum lipase levels are most indicative of acute pancreatitis, as lipase is an enzyme produced by the pancreas, and its levels increase significantly in the blood during acute inflammation or injury to the pancreas.

594. For a patient with suspected liver disease, which test is most useful for assessing liver fibrosis and cirrhosis?
a. Liver function tests (LFTs)
b. Alpha-fetoprotein (AFP)
c. Hepatitis serologies
d. Transient elastography (FibroScan)

Answer: d. Transient elastography (FibroScan). Explanation: Transient elastography, such as FibroScan, is a non-invasive imaging test that measures liver stiffness, which correlates with the degree of fibrosis and cirrhosis, providing valuable information about the extent of liver disease without the need for a biopsy.

595. In evaluating a patient with suspected inflammatory bowel disease (IBD), which diagnostic test is considered most definitive?
a. Colonoscopy with biopsy
b. Stool culture
c. Abdominal ultrasound
d. Complete blood count (CBC)

Answer: a. Colonoscopy with biopsy. Explanation: Colonoscopy with biopsy is considered the most definitive diagnostic test for IBD. It allows direct visualization of the intestinal mucosa and the ability to obtain tissue samples for histopathological examination, aiding in the diagnosis and differentiation between Crohn's disease and ulcerative colitis.

596. In the context of deep vein thrombosis (DVT) treatment, which anticoagulant is commonly initiated for immediate therapeutic effect?
a. Warfarin
b. Aspirin
c. Low-molecular-weight heparin (LMWH)
d. Vitamin C

Answer: c. Low-molecular-weight heparin (LMWH). Explanation: LMWH is commonly used for the immediate treatment of DVT due to its rapid onset of action, predictable pharmacokinetics, and lower risk of thrombocytopenia compared to unfractionated heparin, making it a preferred choice for initial anticoagulation.

597. Which therapeutic approach is preferred for a patient with a massive pulmonary embolism (PE) presenting with hemodynamic instability?
a. Oral anticoagulation therapy alone
b. Thrombolytic therapy
c. Inferior vena cava (IVC) filter placement without anticoagulation
d. Compression stockings

Answer: b. Thrombolytic therapy. Explanation: Thrombolytic therapy is indicated for patients with massive PE accompanied by hemodynamic instability, as it can rapidly dissolve the clot, restore pulmonary circulation, and improve hemodynamics. This approach is reserved for patients without contraindications to thrombolysis due to the risk of bleeding.

598. When transitioning a patient from LMWH to warfarin for long-term anticoagulation, what is an important consideration?
a. Warfarin should be started only after LMWH is discontinued.
b. Overlap LMWH and warfarin until the INR is therapeutic for at least 24 hours.
c. Vitamin K should be administered concurrently to prevent warfarin-induced skin necrosis.
d. LMWH doses should be doubled during the overlap period to ensure therapeutic anticoagulation.

Answer: b. Overlap LMWH and warfarin until the INR is therapeutic for at least 24 hours. Explanation: When transitioning to warfarin, it is essential to overlap with LMWH until the INR is within the therapeutic range (typically 2.0-3.0) for at least 24 hours to ensure continuous anticoagulation, as warfarin has a delayed onset of action.

599. In the management of DVT, what is the primary role of compression stockings?
a. To dissolve clots within the deep veins
b. To provide symptomatic relief and reduce the risk of post-thrombotic syndrome
c. To replace anticoagulation therapy in patients with contraindications
d. To increase the INR to a therapeutic level

Answer: b. To provide symptomatic relief and reduce the risk of post-thrombotic syndrome. Explanation: Compression stockings are used in the management of DVT to reduce swelling, pain, and the risk of post-thrombotic syndrome by improving venous return and reducing venous stasis, not as a replacement for anticoagulation therapy.

600. What is the main advantage of direct oral anticoagulants (DOACs) over warfarin in the treatment of venous thromboembolism (VTE)?

a. DOACs require regular INR monitoring.
b. DOACs have a higher risk of major bleeding.
c. DOACs offer the convenience of fixed dosing without the need for routine coagulation monitoring.
d. Warfarin is more effective in preventing recurrent VTE.

Answer: c. DOACs offer the convenience of fixed dosing without the need for routine coagulation monitoring. Explanation: DOACs, such as rivaroxaban, apixaban, and dabigatran, provide the advantage of fixed dosing and do not require routine INR monitoring like warfarin, making them more convenient for patients and potentially improving adherence.

601. For a patient with VTE and a history of heparin-induced thrombocytopenia (HIT), which anticoagulant is appropriate?
a. Unfractionated heparin
b. Fondaparinux
c. Warfarin, initiated immediately
d. Low-molecular-weight heparin

Answer: b. Fondaparinux. Explanation: Fondaparinux, a synthetic pentasaccharide factor Xa inhibitor, is an appropriate choice for patients with a history of HIT, as it does not carry the risk of HIT. It can be used safely in such patients for the treatment and prevention of VTE.

602. What is a critical safety consideration when using thrombolytic therapy for the treatment of VTE?
a. Ensuring the patient has a low INR before administration
b. Screening for risk factors for bleeding, such as recent surgery or active peptic ulcer disease
c. Avoiding the use of compression stockings concurrently
d. Administering a loading dose of warfarin concurrently with thrombolytics

Answer: b. Screening for risk factors for bleeding, such as recent surgery or active peptic ulcer disease. Explanation: Before initiating thrombolytic therapy, it is crucial to screen patients for contraindications and risk factors for bleeding, including recent major surgery, active bleeding, or a history of hemorrhagic stroke, to minimize the risk of serious bleeding complications.

603. In patients with recurrent VTE on therapeutic anticoagulation, what is a potential treatment adjustment?
a. Discontinuation of anticoagulation due to treatment failure
b. Switching to a different class of anticoagulant, such as from a vitamin K antagonist to a DOAC
c. Addition of antiplatelet therapy to existing anticoagulant regimen
d. Increasing the target INR range for patients on warfarin

Answer: b. Switching to a different class of anticoagulant, such as from a vitamin K antagonist to a DOAC. Explanation: For patients with recurrent VTE despite therapeutic anticoagulation, switching to a different class of anticoagulant, for example from warfarin (a vitamin K antagonist) to a DOAC, may be considered to improve efficacy and reduce the risk of further recurrence.

604. What is the recommended duration of anticoagulation therapy for a first unprovoked DVT or PE?
a. At least 3 months
b. A minimum of 6 weeks
c. Indefinite anticoagulation with annual reassessment
d. Lifelong anticoagulation without reassessment

Answer: a. At least 3 months. Explanation: For a first unprovoked DVT or PE, the minimum recommended duration of anticoagulation therapy is at least 3 months. Beyond this, the decision to extend therapy is individualized based on the patient's risk of recurrence versus the risk of bleeding, with indefinite anticoagulation considered for those with high risk of recurrence and low bleeding risk.

605. Which of the following is a common cause of pre-renal acute kidney injury (AKI)?
a. Acute tubular necrosis
b. Renal artery stenosis
c. Uncontrolled hypertension
d. Volume depletion

Answer: d. Volume depletion. Explanation: Volume depletion, such as from dehydration or bleeding, can lead to decreased renal perfusion and pre-renal AKI, as the kidneys receive insufficient blood flow to maintain normal function.

606. In the context of AKI, what does the presence of muddy brown casts in the urine sediment suggest?
a. Glomerulonephritis
b. Acute tubular necrosis (ATN)
c. Urinary tract infection
d. Nephrotic syndrome

Answer: b. Acute tubular necrosis (ATN). Explanation: Muddy brown casts are typically seen in acute tubular necrosis, a type of intrinsic AKI, indicating damage to the tubular cells of the kidneys.

607. What is the most reliable laboratory marker for evaluating the progression of AKI?
a. Serum creatinine
b. Blood urea nitrogen (BUN)
c. Ur

608. ine specific gravity
d. Serum potassium

Answer: a. Serum creatinine. Explanation: Serum creatinine is the most reliable laboratory marker for evaluating the progression of AKI because it directly reflects the kidneys' filtration function. Rapid increases in serum creatinine indicate a decline in kidney function.

609. Which diagnostic test is most useful for distinguishing between pre-renal AKI and intrinsic renal AKI?
a. Renal ultrasound
b. Urinalysis
c. Fractional excretion of sodium (FeNa)
d. Serum electrolytes

Answer: c. Fractional excretion of sodium (FeNa). Explanation: The fractional excretion of sodium (FeNa) is a valuable diagnostic test for differentiating between pre-renal AKI, where FeNa is typically low (<1%) due to increased sodium reabsorption, and intrinsic renal AKI, where FeNa is often higher (>2%) due to tubular damage and reduced sodium reabsorption.

610. In AKI, what role does oliguria play in the diagnosis?
a. It is a definitive indicator of intrinsic renal damage.
b. It is a common finding in post-renal AKI only.
c. It signifies severe dehydration as the sole cause.
d. It is an early sign that may be present in all types of AKI.

Answer: d. It is an early sign that may be present in all types of AKI. Explanation: Oliguria, defined as urine output less than 400 mL per day, can be an early sign of AKI regardless of the underlying cause. It indicates a significant reduction in kidney function.

611. What is the significance of hyperkalemia in a patient with AKI?
a. It is a specific sign of post-renal AKI.
b. It indicates an immediate need for dialysis.
c. It is a potentially life-threatening complication.
d. It suggests overhydration as the primary cause.

Answer: c. It is a potentially life-threatening complication. Explanation: Hyperkalemia in AKI is a potentially life-threatening complication due to the risk of cardiac arrhythmias. It reflects the kidneys' reduced ability to excrete potassium.

612. Which therapeutic intervention is most appropriate for managing volume overload in AKI?
a. Administration of high-dose loop diuretics
b. Immediate initiation of high-flux hemodialysis
c. Restriction of fluid and sodium intake
d. Aggressive hydration with isotonic saline

Answer: a. Administration of high-dose loop diuretics. Explanation: High-dose loop diuretics are often used to manage volume overload in AKI to promote diuresis, although their effectiveness may be limited in advanced AKI stages.

613. In AKI management, what is the primary goal of renal replacement therapy (RRT)?
a. To permanently replace kidney function
b. To correct electrolyte imbalances and remove waste products
c. To stimulate the kidneys to produce more urine
d. To reduce proteinuria and slow the progression of CKD

Answer: b. To correct electrolyte imbalances and remove waste products. Explanation: The primary goal of renal replacement therapy (RRT) in AKI is to correct life-threatening electrolyte imbalances and remove uremic toxins and excess fluid, serving as a temporary support until kidney function potentially recovers.

614. What is the role of kidney biopsy in the management of AKI?
a. It is routinely performed in all cases of AKI to confirm the diagnosis.
b. It is primarily used to diagnose post-renal causes of AKI.
c. It may be indicated when the cause of AKI is unclear or to diagnose specific renal pathologies.
d. It is contraindicated in AKI due to the risk of worsening renal function.

Answer: c. It may be indicated when the cause of AKI is unclear or to diagnose specific renal pathologies. Explanation: A kidney biopsy is not routinely performed in AKI but may be indicated in select cases where the cause of AKI is unclear, or there is suspicion of specific intrinsic renal diseases that require histological diagnosis to guide treatment.

615. How does the use of continuous renal replacement therapy (CRRT) compare to intermittent hemodialysis in critically ill patients with AKI?
a. CRRT is associated with higher mortality rates.
b. CRRT is only used in patients with chronic kidney disease.
c. CRRT offers the advantage of slower, more continuous fluid removal and solute clearance.
d. Intermittent hemodialysis is always preferred due to lower complication rates.

Answer: c. CRRT offers the advantage of slower, more continuous fluid removal and solute clearance. Explanation: CRRT is often preferred in hemodynamically unstable critically ill patients with AKI because it allows for slower, more continuous fluid and solute clearance, minimizing the risk of hemodynamic instability associated with intermittent hemodialysis.

616. What is the most common cause of pre-renal acute kidney injury (AKI)?
a. Acute tubular necrosis
b. Renal artery stenosis
c. Severe dehydration
d. Urinary tract obstruction

Answer: c. Severe dehydration. Explanation: Severe dehydration leads to reduced blood flow to the kidneys, which is the most common cause of pre-renal AKI. This condition results from inadequate circulating blood volume, affecting the kidney's ability to perform its normal filtration function.

617. Intrinsic AKI due to acute tubular necrosis (ATN) can be caused by which of the following?
a. Prolonged hypotension
b. Nephrolithiasis
c. Bladder cancer
d. Benign prostatic hyperplasia

Answer: a. Prolonged hypotension. Explanation: Prolonged hypotension can lead to ischemia of the renal tubules, resulting in acute tubular necrosis (ATN), a common cause of intrinsic AKI. ATN can also be caused by nephrotoxic drugs or substances.

618. Which condition is a typical post-renal cause of AKI?
a. Glomerulonephritis
b. Bilateral ureteral obstruction
c. Hemolytic uremic syndrome
d. Diabetic nephropathy

Answer: b. Bilateral ureteral obstruction. Explanation: Bilateral ureteral obstruction, which can be caused by conditions such as nephrolithiasis, tumors, or strictures, is a typical post-renal cause of AKI. It impedes the flow of urine from the kidneys, leading to increased pressure and potential kidney damage.

619. What is a primary risk factor for the development of intrinsic AKI due to interstitial nephritis?
a. Overuse of NSAIDs
b. Excessive alcohol consumption
c. High protein diet
d. Sedentary lifestyle

Answer: a. Overuse of NSAIDs. Explanation: Overuse of nonsteroidal anti-inflammatory drugs (NSAIDs) can lead to acute interstitial nephritis, an inflammatory condition of the kidney's interstitium, which is a common cause of intrinsic AKI.

620. In the context of pre-renal AKI, what role does heart failure play?
a. It directly damages renal tubules through toxic metabolites.
b. It leads to decreased renal perfusion due to reduced cardiac output.
c. It causes obstruction of the urinary tract, leading to increased pressures.
d. It induces renal artery stenosis, reducing blood flow to the kidneys.

Answer: b. It leads to decreased renal perfusion due to reduced cardiac output. Explanation: Heart failure can lead to pre-renal AKI by reducing cardiac output, which in turn decreases renal perfusion and impairs kidney function, as the kidneys receive less blood flow.

621. How does rhabdomyolysis contribute to intrinsic AKI?
a. By causing direct obstruction of the urinary tract
b. Through ischemic injury to the renal parenchyma
c. By the nephrotoxic effects of myoglobin released from damaged muscle cells
d. By inducing severe dehydration leading to reduced renal perfusion

Answer: c. By the nephrotoxic effects of myoglobin released from damaged muscle cells. Explanation: Rhabdomyolysis leads to the release of myoglobin into the bloodstream, which has nephrotoxic effects on the renal tubules, causing intrinsic AKI.

622. Which mechanism explains the development of post-renal AKI due to benign prostatic hyperplasia (BPH)?
a. The inflammatory response in the prostate gland damages nearby renal tissue.
b. BPH leads to decreased blood flow to the renal cortex.
c. BPH causes bladder outlet obstruction, leading to increased pressures transmitted backward to the kidneys.
d. The hormonal changes associated with BPH directly affect glomerular filtration.

Answer: c. BPH causes bladder outlet obstruction, leading to increased pressures transmitted backward to the kidneys. Explanation: Benign prostatic hyperplasia can cause bladder outlet obstruction, which if severe, can lead to increased back pressure on the kidneys, resulting in post-renal AKI.

623. What distinguishes pre-renal AKI from intrinsic AKI in terms of laboratory findings?
a. Elevated serum creatinine in pre-renal AKI only
b. Presence of urinary casts in intrinsic AKI
c. Lower fractional excretion of sodium (FeNa) in pre-renal AKI
d. Higher urine osmolality in intrinsic AKI

Answer: c. Lower fractional excretion of sodium (FeNa) in pre-renal AKI. Explanation: Pre-renal AKI is characterized by a lower fractional excretion of sodium (FeNa <1%) due to the kidney's attempt to conserve sodium in the setting of reduced renal perfusion, whereas intrinsic AKI often has a higher FeNa due to tubular damage.

624. In a patient with AKI, what finding would most strongly suggest a post-renal cause?
a. Proteinuria and hematuria
b. High urine specific gravity
c. Hydronephrosis on renal ultrasound
d. Elevated blood urea nitrogen (BUN) to creatinine ratio

Answer: c. Hydronephrosis on renal ultrasound. Explanation: Hydronephrosis, or swelling of the kidneys due to urine buildup, seen on renal ultrasound, strongly suggests a post-renal cause of AKI, indicating an obstruction in the urinary tract that prevents urine from draining properly.

625. In the RIFLE classification for acute kidney injury (AKI), what does the "I" stand for, and how is it defined?
a. Increase: An increase in serum creatinine by 2 times baseline
b. Injury: An increase in serum creatinine by 2 times baseline or urine output <0.5 mL/kg/h for 12 hours
c. Inflammation: Presence of markers of renal inflammation without significant change in creatinine
d. Insufficiency: A 50% decrease in glomerular filtration rate (GFR) from baseline

Answer: b. Injury: An increase in serum creatinine by 2 times baseline or urine output <0.5 mL/kg/h for 12 hours. Explanation: In the RIFLE criteria, "I" stands for Injury, which indicates a more severe stage of AKI than "Risk" and is defined by a doubling of the baseline serum creatinine or a significant reduction in urine output.

626. What is the key difference between the RIFLE and AKIN criteria for diagnosing AKI?
a. RIFLE requires a change in GFR, whereas AKIN does not.
b. AKIN includes a criterion for an absolute increase in serum creatinine of ≥0.3 mg/dL within 48 hours.
c. RIFLE incorporates urine output criteria only, whereas AKIN includes both creatinine and urine output.
d. AKIN classification is based solely on biomarkers other than creatinine and urine output.

Answer: b. AKIN includes a criterion for an absolute increase in serum creatinine of ≥0.3 mg/dL within 48 hours. Explanation: The Acute Kidney Injury Network (AKIN) criteria modified the RIFLE criteria by including a criterion for an absolute increase in serum creatinine of ≥0.3 mg/dL within 48 hours, allowing for earlier detection of AKI.

627. Under the KDIGO criteria for AKI, what serum creatinine change qualifies for Stage 1 AKI?
a. An increase in serum creatinine by ≥0.3 mg/dL within 48 hours
b. A 1.5-1.9 times increase from baseline within 7 days
c. A doubling of serum creatinine from baseline
d. Both a and b

Answer: d. Both a and b. Explanation: The KDIGO (Kidney Disease: Improving Global Outcomes) criteria for Stage 1 AKI include either an increase in serum creatinine by ≥0.3 mg/dL within 48 hours or a 1.5-1.9 times increase from baseline within the previous 7 days.

628. Which criteria use urine output as a parameter for defining AKI?
a. RIFLE only
b. AKIN only
c. Both RIFLE and AKIN
d. KDIGO only

Answer: c. Both RIFLE and AKIN. Explanation: Both the RIFLE and AKIN criteria use urine output as a parameter for defining and staging AKI, recognizing oliguria as an important indicator of renal dysfunction.

629. In the context of AKI staging, what does a urine output of <0.3 mL/kg/h for 24 hours indicate according to the KDIGO criteria?
a. Stage 1 AKI
b. Stage 2 AKI
c. Stage 3 AKI
d. Not used for staging in KDIGO

Answer: c. Stage 3 AKI. Explanation: According to the KDIGO criteria, a urine output of <0.3 mL/kg/h for 24 hours or anuria for 12 hours is indicative of Stage 3 AKI, representing the most severe form of AKI in these criteria.

630. How do the KDIGO criteria for AKI integrate the RIFLE and AKIN classifications?
a. By adopting the GFR criteria from RIFLE and the creatinine criteria from AKIN
b. By using the stricter of the two classifications for each stage of AKI
c. By combining the criteria and making modifications to create a unified staging system
d. KDIGO does not integrate RIFLE and AKIN but rather replaces them entirely

Answer: c. By combining the criteria and making modifications to create a unified staging system. Explanation: The KDIGO criteria for AKI integrate elements from both the RIFLE and AKIN classifications, combining and modifying them to create a unified, consensus-based staging system for AKI.

631. What is the primary purpose of establishing standardized criteria like RIFLE, AKIN, and KDIGO for AKI?
a. To provide specific treatment protocols for each stage of AKI
b. To standardize the definition and staging of AKI across clinical studies and practices
c. To identify the underlying cause of AKI in individual patients
d. To predict the long-term outcomes of AKI, such as chronic kidney disease (CKD)

Answer: b. To standardize the definition and staging of AKI across clinical studies and practices. Explanation: The primary purpose of establishing criteria like RIFLE, AKIN, and KDIGO is to standardize the definition and staging of AKI, facilitating more consistent diagnosis, management, and research across various clinical settings.

632. In the AKIN classification, what is the significance of Stage 3 AKI?
a. It indicates a need for immediate renal replacement therapy.
b. It is defined by a tripling of serum creatinine or initiation of renal replacement therapy.
c. It suggests reversible kidney injury with prompt treatment.
d. It is associated with the lowest risk of mortality among the AKIN stages.

Answer: b. It is defined by a tripling of serum creatinine or initiation of renal replacement therapy. Explanation: In the AKIN classification, Stage 3 AKI is defined by a tripling of serum creatinine from baseline, an increase in serum creatinine to ≥4.0 mg/dL, a reduction in GFR by ≥75%, or the initiation of renal replacement therapy, indicating severe renal dysfunction.

633. Under which criteria is the duration of AKI considered in the staging process?
a. RIFLE
b. AKIN
c. KDIGO
d. Duration is not considered in any of these criteria

Answer: d. Duration is not considered in any of these criteria. Explanation: The RIFLE, AKIN, and KDIGO criteria focus on changes in serum creatinine, GFR, and urine output to define and stage AKI, without specifically considering the duration of these changes in their staging processes.

634. In managing fluid balance for a patient with acute decompensated heart failure, which intervention is most appropriate?
a. Administration of high-volume intravenous fluids to improve cardiac output
b. Use of loop diuretics to reduce preload and relieve pulmonary congestion
c. Restriction of all oral and intravenous fluids to minimize fluid overload
d. Aggressive hydration with isotonic saline to correct hypotension

Answer: b. Use of loop diuretics to reduce preload and relieve pulmonary congestion. Explanation: In acute decompensated heart failure, loop diuretics are often used to reduce fluid volume, decreasing preload and relieving symptoms of pulmonary congestion and peripheral edema, thereby improving the patient's clinical status.

635. For a patient with chronic kidney disease (CKD) and hyperkalemia, which medication is preferred to help manage potassium levels?
a. Calcium gluconate
b. Sodium polystyrene sulfonate (Kayexalate)
c. Intravenous insulin with glucose
d. High-dose furosemide

Answer: b. Sodium polystyrene sulfonate (Kayexalate). Explanation: Sodium polystyrene sulfonate is used in patients with CKD to treat hyperkalemia by exchanging sodium ions for potassium ions in the intestine, which helps to lower serum potassium levels.

636. What is the primary goal of using beta-blockers in the management of chronic heart failure?
a. To increase heart rate and improve cardiac output
b. To reduce myocardial oxygen demand by decreasing heart rate and contractility

c. To promote diuresis and reduce fluid overload
d. To directly dilate coronary arteries and improve myocardial perfusion

Answer: b. To reduce myocardial oxygen demand by decreasing heart rate and contractility. Explanation: In chronic heart failure, beta-blockers are used to reduce the heart's workload and oxygen demand by slowing the heart rate and reducing myocardial contractility, which can improve symptoms and potentially enhance survival.

637. When managing a patient with septic shock, why is norepinephrine the first-line vasopressor?
a. It primarily increases cardiac output with minimal effects on blood pressure.
b. It has a strong vasodilatory effect that improves microcirculation.
c. It increases blood pressure by vasoconstriction without significantly increasing heart rate.
d. It selectively dilates renal and mesenteric blood vessels, improving perfusion.

Answer: c. It increases blood pressure by vasoconstriction without significantly increasing heart rate. Explanation: Norepinephrine is preferred in septic shock for its potent vasoconstrictive effects, which increase systemic vascular resistance and blood pressure, essential for counteracting the profound vasodilation seen in sepsis without causing excessive tachycardia.

638. In a patient with acute pulmonary edema, why is morphine used cautiously?
a. It can lead to a rapid increase in heart rate, worsening cardiac output.
b. It may cause respiratory depression and worsen gas exchange.
c. It has a diuretic effect that can lead to electrolyte imbalances.
d. It increases preload, further stressing the heart.

Answer: b. It may cause respiratory depression and worsen gas exchange. Explanation: Morphine is used cautiously in acute pulmonary edema primarily due to the risk of respiratory depression, which can further compromise gas exchange in a patient already experiencing respiratory distress from pulmonary edema.

639. For the management of atrial fibrillation with rapid ventricular response, which medication is preferred to control heart rate?
a. Intravenous amiodarone
b. Oral digoxin
c. Intravenous diltiazem
d. Subcutaneous heparin

Answer: c. Intravenous diltiazem. Explanation: Intravenous diltiazem, a calcium channel blocker, is often preferred for acute rate control in atrial fibrillation with rapid ventricular response due to its effectiveness in slowing the ventricular rate without causing significant hypotension.

640. In treating a patient with acute kidney injury (AKI) due to nephrotoxins, what is the first step in management?

a. Immediate initiation of renal replacement therapy
b. Administration of high-dose corticosteroids to reduce inflammation
c. Discontinuation or adjustment of the offending nephrotoxic agents
d. Aggressive fluid resuscitation with albumin

Answer: c. Discontinuation or adjustment of the offending nephrotoxic agents. Explanation: The first step in managing AKI due to nephrotoxins is to discontinue or adjust the dosage of the nephrotoxic medications or substances, thereby removing the primary cause of the injury and allowing for renal recovery.

641. When considering fluid management in a patient with acute pancreatitis, which strategy is most appropriate?
a. Restriction of fluids to prevent fluid sequestration in the third space
b. Aggressive hydration with crystalloids to prevent hypovolemia and support organ perfusion
c. Administration of hypertonic saline to reduce inflammation
d. Use of colloids as the first-line fluid choice to improve oncotic pressure

Answer: b. Aggressive hydration with crystalloids to prevent hypovolemia and support organ perfusion. Explanation: In acute pancreatitis, aggressive hydration with crystalloids, especially in the initial 24-48 hours, is crucial to prevent hypovolemia, support organ perfusion, and reduce the risk of complications such as necrotizing pancreatitis.

642. For a patient undergoing major surgery, what is the rationale behind using low-molecular-weight heparin (LMWH) for venous thromboembolism (VTE) prophylaxis?
a. LMWH has a long half-life, allowing for once-daily dosing.
b. It preferentially increases fibrinolysis, quickly dissolving any formed clots.
c. LMWH significantly increases platelet count, enhancing clot stability.
d. It has a predictable dose-response and lower risk of heparin-induced thrombocytopenia (HIT) compared to unfractionated heparin.

Answer: d. It has a predictable dose-response and lower risk of heparin-induced thrombocytopenia (HIT) compared to unfractionated heparin. Explanation: LMWH is used for VTE prophylaxis in surgical patients due to its predictable pharmacokinetics, allowing for fixed dosing without the need for routine monitoring, and a lower risk of HIT compared to unfractionated heparin, making it safer and more convenient for preventing postoperative thrombosis.

643. Which of the following ECG changes is most commonly associated with hyperkalemia?
a. Prolonged QT interval
b. ST segment depression
c. Peaked T waves
d. Presence of U waves

Answer: c. Peaked T waves. Explanation: Hyperkalemia often manifests on the ECG with peaked T waves due to the effect of elevated potassium levels on cardiac myocyte repolarization. This is one of the earliest ECG changes seen with rising serum potassium levels.

644. A patient with severe diarrhea is likely to develop which electrolyte imbalance?
a. Hyperkalemia
b. Hypercalcemia
c. Hyponatremia
d. Hypernatremia

Answer: c. Hyponatremia. Explanation: Severe diarrhea can lead to significant loss of fluids that contain not only water but also electrolytes, including sodium. The loss of sodium-rich fluids can lead to hyponatremia, especially in the setting of continued water intake or administration of hypotonic fluids.

645. What is the primary treatment for symptomatic hypocalcemia?
a. Oral calcium supplementation
b. Intravenous magnesium sulfate
c. Intravenous calcium gluconate
d. Oral vitamin D supplementation

Answer: c. Intravenous calcium gluconate. Explanation: For symptomatic hypocalcemia, especially when symptoms are acute or severe, intravenous calcium gluconate is the treatment of choice to rapidly increase serum calcium levels and alleviate symptoms.

646. In the setting of acute renal failure, which electrolyte imbalance is most commonly encountered?
a. Hypokalemia
b. Hyperkalemia
c. Hypophosphatemia
d. Hypercalcemia

Answer: b. Hyperkalemia. Explanation: Acute renal failure can lead to impaired potassium excretion, resulting in hyperkalemia. This is a common and potentially life-threatening complication of renal insufficiency.

647. A patient presenting with muscle weakness, arrhythmias, and constipation could be suffering from which of the following?
a. Hypokalemia
b. Hyperkalemia
c. Hypercalcemia
d. Hypocalcemia

Answer: c. Hypercalcemia. Explanation: Hypercalcemia can cause muscle weakness, cardiac arrhythmias due to its effects on cardiac conduction, and constipation due to decreased smooth muscle activity in the gastrointestinal tract.

648. Which of the following is a common cause of hypomagnesemia?
a. Renal insufficiency
b. Excessive intake of antacids
c. Prolonged intravenous fluid administration without magnesium supplementation
d. Hyperparathyroidism

Answer: c. Prolonged intravenous fluid administration without magnesium supplementation. Explanation: Prolonged administration of intravenous fluids that lack magnesium can lead to hypomagnesemia, especially in settings where there is increased urinary loss or inadequate dietary intake.

649. What ECG changes are associated with hypokalemia?
a. Peaked T waves and widened QRS complexes
b. ST elevation and tall QRS complexes
c. Flattened T waves, prominent U waves, and ST depression
d. Prolonged PR interval and shortened QT interval

Answer: c. Flattened T waves, prominent U waves, and ST depression. Explanation: Hypokalemia can lead to flattened T waves, the appearance of prominent U waves (best seen in the precordial leads), and ST-segment depression due to its effects on cardiac repolarization.

650. In treating hyperphosphatemia in a patient with chronic kidney disease, which approach is most effective?
a. Increasing dietary phosphate intake
b. Phosphate binder administration
c. High doses of oral calcium supplements
d. Aggressive hydration with intravenous fluids

Answer: b. Phosphate binder administration. Explanation: Phosphate binders are effective in treating hyperphosphatemia in patients with chronic kidney disease by binding dietary phosphate in the gastrointestinal tract, thereby reducing its absorption and serum levels.

651. What is the typical presentation of a patient with hypermagnesemia?
a. Tetany and muscular spasms
b. Nausea, vomiting, and diarrhea
c. Hypertension and tachycardia
d. Decreased deep tendon reflexes and respiratory depression

Answer: d. Decreased deep tendon reflexes and respiratory depression. Explanation: Hypermagnesemia can lead to neuromuscular and cardiovascular symptoms, including decreased deep tendon reflexes, muscle weakness, and in severe cases, respiratory depression due to the depressant effects of magnesium on the neuromuscular junction.

652. Which electrolyte imbalance is most commonly associated with the use of diuretics?
a. Hyperkalemia
b. Hypokalemia
c. Hypercalcemia
d. Hypermagnesemia

Answer: b. Hypokalemia. Explanation: The use of diuretics, particularly loop and thiazide diuretics, is a common cause of hypokalemia due to increased renal potassium excretion.

653. What ECG changes are commonly seen in hyperkalemia?
a. Prolonged QT interval
b. Peaked T waves
c. Absence of P waves
d. Both b and c

Answer: d. Both b and c. Explanation: Hyperkalemia often presents with peaked T waves and the absence of P waves on an ECG. These changes reflect the effects of elevated potassium levels on cardiac cell membrane potentials, leading to altered electrical activity.

654. Which of the following is a common cause of hypokalemia?
a. Renal failure
b. Excessive intake of potassium supplements
c. Use of loop diuretics
d. Hemolysis

Answer: c. Use of loop diuretics. Explanation: Loop diuretics are a common cause of hypokalemia because they increase the renal excretion of potassium. This can lead to a significant depletion of potassium levels in the body.

655. In treating severe hyperkalemia, which medication can rapidly stabilize the myocardial cell membrane?
a. Oral potassium chloride
b. Intravenous calcium gluconate
c. Subcutaneous insulin
d. Nebulized albuterol

Answer: b. Intravenous calcium gluconate. Explanation: Intravenous calcium gluconate is used in the treatment of severe hyperkalemia to rapidly stabilize the myocardial cell membrane, thereby reducing the risk of fatal cardiac arrhythmias.

656. What dietary modification is recommended for a patient with chronic hypokalemia?

a. Increased sodium intake
b. Increased potassium intake through foods like bananas and potatoes
c. Decreased carbohydrate intake
d. Increased calcium intake

Answer: b. Increased potassium intake through foods like bananas and potatoes. Explanation: For a patient with chronic hypokalemia, dietary modifications to increase potassium intake through potassium-rich foods, such as bananas, oranges, potatoes, and spinach, are recommended to help restore normal potassium levels.

657. Which condition is most likely to result in transcellular potassium shifts leading to hypokalemia?
a. Metabolic acidosis
b. Metabolic alkalosis
c. Hypernatremia
d. Hyponatremia

Answer: b. Metabolic alkalosis. Explanation: Metabolic alkalosis can cause a transcellular shift of potassium from the extracellular to the intracellular space, leading to hypokalemia. This shift is often a compensatory mechanism to balance the pH levels in the body.

658. How does the administration of insulin and glucose affect serum potassium levels in hyperkalemia?
a. Increases potassium excretion through the kidneys
b. Shifts potassium from extracellular to intracellular space
c. Reduces potassium absorption in the gut
d. Increases potassium uptake by skeletal muscles

Answer: b. Shifts potassium from extracellular to intracellular space. Explanation: Insulin, often given with glucose to prevent hypoglycemia, promotes the cellular uptake of potassium, thereby lowering serum potassium levels by shifting it from the extracellular to the intracellular space.

659. What is the role of sodium polystyrene sulfonate (Kayexalate) in hyperkalemia management?
a. It increases renal potassium excretion.
b. It shifts potassium into cells.
c. It binds potassium in the gastrointestinal tract, leading to its excretion.
d. It stabilizes the cardiac membrane.

Answer: c. It binds potassium in the gastrointestinal tract, leading to its excretion. Explanation: Sodium polystyrene sulfonate (Kayexalate) works by binding potassium in the gastrointestinal tract, which is then excreted in the feces, effectively reducing serum potassium levels.

660. In a patient with renal tubular acidosis, why might hypokalemia occur?

a. Due to excessive urinary excretion of potassium
b. Because of decreased dietary potassium intake
c. Due to transcellular shift of potassium into cells
d. Because of binding of potassium in the GI tract

Answer: a. Due to excessive urinary excretion of potassium. Explanation: In renal tubular acidosis, the renal tubules fail to adequately reabsorb bicarbonate or excrete hydrogen ions, leading to acidosis and often resulting in excessive urinary potassium excretion and subsequent hypokalemia.

661. Which intravenous solution is preferred for rapid correction of hypokalemia?
a. 0.9% Saline
b. 5% Dextrose
c. Potassium chloride in 0.9% saline
d. Calcium gluconate

Answer: c. Potassium chloride in 0.9% saline. Explanation: For rapid correction of hypokalemia, potassium chloride in 0.9% saline is often used intravenously, as it provides a direct source of potassium to quickly restore serum levels while maintaining osmolarity.

662. What is the potential complication of rapid potassium administration?
a. Metabolic alkalosis
b. Hypoglycemia
c. Cardiac arrhythmias
d. Respiratory alkalosis

Answer: c. Cardiac arrhythmias. Explanation: Rapid administration of potassium can lead to hyperkalemia, which may induce cardiac arrhythmias, including potentially fatal conditions like ventricular fibrillation or asystole, necessitating careful monitoring during treatment.

663. A patient with severe hyponatremia is at risk for developing which neurological condition due to rapid correction of sodium levels?
a. Central pontine myelinolysis
b. Cerebral aneurysm
c. Guillain-Barré syndrome
d. Multiple sclerosis

Answer: a. Central pontine myelinolysis. Explanation: Rapid correction of severe hyponatremia can lead to central pontine myelinolysis, a neurological condition characterized by demyelination in the central part of the brainstem, which can result in serious neurological symptoms.

664. In a patient with hypercalcemia, which symptom is most commonly observed?
a. Tetany
b. Constipation
c. Diarrhea
d. Hyporeflexia

Answer: b. Constipation. Explanation: Hypercalcemia can lead to constipation due to decreased smooth muscle activity in the gastrointestinal tract, along with other symptoms such as renal dysfunction, bone pain, and neurological manifestations like confusion.

665. Which of the following is a common cause of hypomagnesemia?
a. Renal failure
b. Excessive use of antacids
c. Prolonged proton pump inhibitor therapy
d. High dietary magnesium intake

Answer: c. Prolonged proton pump inhibitor therapy. Explanation: Prolonged use of proton pump inhibitors has been associated with hypomagnesemia, possibly due to decreased intestinal absorption of magnesium.

666. What ECG changes are typically seen in a patient with hyperphosphatemia?
a. Prolonged PR interval
b. ST-segment elevation
c. Peaked T waves
d. Shortened QT interval

Answer: d. Shortened QT interval. Explanation: Hyperphosphatemia can lead to a shortened QT interval due to its association with hypocalcemia, as elevated phosphate levels can cause calcium to precipitate, reducing its serum levels and affecting cardiac repolarization.

667. In managing a patient with hypocalcemia, which intervention is crucial to prevent seizures?
a. Administration of oral calcium supplements
b. Intravenous infusion of calcium gluconate
c. High phosphate diet
d. Fluid restriction

Answer: b. Intravenous infusion of calcium gluconate. Explanation: Intravenous infusion of calcium gluconate is crucial in the acute management of hypocalcemia to prevent seizures and other neuromuscular irritability symptoms by rapidly increasing serum calcium levels.

668. Which symptom is indicative of severe hypernatremia?

a. Bradycardia
b. Muscle weakness
c. Profound thirst
d. Hypotension

Answer: c. Profound thirst. Explanation: Profound thirst is a hallmark symptom of hypernatremia, reflecting the body's attempt to correct the high sodium concentration by increasing fluid intake.

669. For a patient with renal insufficiency, which electrolyte imbalance is most concerning due to its cardiovascular effects?
a. Hypokalemia
b. Hyperkalemia
c. Hyponatremia
d. Hypernatremia

Answer: b. Hyperkalemia. Explanation: Hyperkalemia is particularly concerning in patients with renal insufficiency due to its potential to cause life-threatening cardiac arrhythmias, as the kidneys' ability to excrete potassium is compromised.

670. What is the first-line treatment for symptomatic hypophosphatemia?
a. Oral phosphate supplements
b. Intravenous phosphate administration
c. High-calcium diet
d. Sunlight exposure

Answer: b. Intravenous phosphate administration. Explanation: Intravenous phosphate administration is the first-line treatment for symptomatic hypophosphatemia, especially in severe cases, to rapidly replenish phosphate levels and prevent complications related to phosphate depletion.

671. In a patient with chronic alcoholism, which electrolyte imbalance is commonly seen due to nutritional deficiencies?
a. Hypercalcemia
b. Hyponatremia
c. Hypomagnesemia
d. Hyperkalemia

Answer: c. Hypomagnesemia. Explanation: Hypomagnesemia is commonly seen in patients with chronic alcoholism due to poor dietary intake, gastrointestinal losses, and renal dysfunction associated with alcohol use.

672. A patient presenting with muscle cramps, arrhythmias, and a positive Chvostek's sign likely has an imbalance in which electrolyte?
a. Sodium
b. Calcium
c. Magnesium
d. Phosphorus

Answer: b. Calcium. Explanation: Muscle cramps, arrhythmias, and a positive Chvostek's sign (facial muscle spasm upon tapping the facial nerve) are indicative of hypocalcemia, reflecting increased neuromuscular excitability due to low calcium levels.

673. What is the primary mechanism of solute removal in Continuous Venovenous Hemofiltration (CVVH)?
a. Diffusion
b. Convection
c. Adsorption
d. Ultrafiltration

Answer: b. Convection. Explanation: CVVH primarily uses convection for solute removal, where solutes are removed along with water through a semipermeable membrane by creating a hydrostatic pressure gradient. This process effectively clears larger molecules compared to diffusion-based methods.

674. In Continuous Venovenous Hemodialysis (CVVHD), what is the main process used to remove waste products from the blood?
a. Convection
b. Diffusion
c. Osmosis
d. Filtration

Answer: b. Diffusion. Explanation: CVVHD relies on the process of diffusion for solute removal, where waste products and excess ions move across a semipermeable membrane from an area of higher concentration (blood) to an area of lower concentration (dialysate), driven by their concentration gradients.

675. Continuous Venovenous Hemodiafiltration (CVVHDF) combines which two modalities for solute removal?
a. Diffusion and osmosis
b. Convection and ultrafiltration
c. Diffusion and convection
d. Ultrafiltration and osmosis

Answer: c. Diffusion and convection. Explanation: CVVHDF combines both diffusion and convection modalities for enhanced solute removal. Diffusion removes small solutes through concentration gradients, while convection provides added removal of larger molecules by solvent drag through a semipermeable membrane.

676. Which modality is most suitable for patients with hemodynamic instability requiring renal replacement therapy?
a. Intermittent Hemodialysis (IHD)
b. CVVHD
c. Peritoneal Dialysis (PD)
d. Sustained Low-Efficiency Dialysis (SLED)

Answer: b. CVVHD. Explanation: CVVHD is particularly suitable for patients with hemodynamic instability due to its continuous nature, allowing for slower fluid and solute removal over 24 hours. This minimizes the risk of hypotension and provides better hemodynamic tolerance compared to intermittent therapies.

677. What is a unique advantage of using CVVH in the management of fluid overload in critically ill patients?
a. Rapid correction of electrolyte imbalances
b. Efficient removal of high molecular weight toxins
c. Lower risk of clotting in the extracorporeal circuit
d. Ability to provide nutritional support

Answer: b. Efficient removal of high molecular weight toxins. Explanation: CVVH is particularly effective in removing larger molecules and mediators of inflammation due to its convective solute transport mechanism, making it advantageous in managing fluid overload and providing clearance of larger solutes in critically ill patients.

678. In CVVHD, how is the dialysate flow direction relative to the blood flow in the dialyzer?
a. In the same direction as blood flow (co-current)
b. In the opposite direction to blood flow (counter-current)
c. Perpendicular to the blood flow
d. Dialysate flow is not involved in CVVHD

Answer: b. In the opposite direction to blood flow (counter-current). Explanation: In CVVHD, the dialysate flows in the opposite direction to the blood flow within the dialyzer (counter-current flow), maximizing the concentration gradient for diffusion and enhancing the efficiency of solute removal.

679. For a patient on CVVHDF, what parameter is crucial to monitor to prevent electrolyte imbalances?
a. Dialysate sodium concentration
b. Replacement fluid conductivity
c. Anticoagulant dosage
d. Ultrafiltration rate

Answer: b. Replacement fluid conductivity. Explanation: In CVVHDF, monitoring the conductivity of the replacement fluid is crucial to ensure proper electrolyte balance. The conductivity reflects the ion concentration in the replacement fluid, which needs to be carefully managed to prevent electrolyte imbalances.

680. What role does anticoagulation play in Continuous Renal Replacement Therapy (CRRT) modalities like CVVH, CVVHD, and CVVHDF?
a. Prevents bacterial growth in the dialysis fluid
b. Enhances the diffusive transport of solutes
c. Prevents clotting in the extracorporeal circuit
d. Increases the permeability of the dialysis membrane

Answer: c. Prevents clotting in the extracorporeal circuit. Explanation: Anticoagulation is essential in CRRT to prevent the formation of clots in the extracorporeal circuit, ensuring the uninterrupted flow of blood through the dialyzer and maintaining the efficiency of the solute removal process.

681. How does the adjustment of ultrafiltration rate impact fluid management in patients undergoing CVVH?
a. It controls the rate of electrolyte removal.
b. It determines the rate of bicarbonate correction.
c. It regulates the removal of excess fluid from the patient.
d. It adjusts the clearance of low molecular weight solutes.

Answer: c. It regulates the removal of excess fluid from the patient. Explanation: In CVVH, the ultrafiltration rate is a key parameter that regulates the removal of excess fluid from the patient. Adjusting this rate allows for precise control of fluid balance, which is critical in managing fluid overload in critically ill patients.

682. What is the primary indication for initiating Continuous Renal Replacement Therapy (CRRT) in critically ill patients?
a. Hypertension refractory to medication
b. Acute kidney injury with hemodynamic instability
c. Chronic kidney disease stage 4 or 5
d. Electrolyte imbalances in a stable patient

Answer: b. Acute kidney injury with hemodynamic instability. Explanation: CRRT is primarily indicated for patients with acute kidney injury (AKI) who are hemodynamically unstable, making them poor candidates for intermittent hemodialysis due to the risk of further hemodynamic compromise.

683. Which CRRT modality is most effective for fluid removal while providing hemodynamic stability?
a. Continuous venovenous hemofiltration (CVVH)
b. Continuous venovenous hemodialysis (CVVHD)
c. Continuous venovenous hemodiafiltration (CVVHDF)
d. Slow continuous ultrafiltration (SCUF)

Answer: c. Continuous venovenous hemodiafiltration (CVVHDF). Explanation: CVVHDF combines both diffusive and convective solute removal methods, making it effective for fluid removal and solute clearance while maintaining hemodynamic stability through gradual fluid shifts.

684. In CRRT, what role does the anticoagulant citrate play?
a. It enhances solute clearance.
b. It prevents clotting in the extracorporeal circuit.
c. It increases ultrafiltration rate.
d. It stabilizes electrolyte levels in the blood.

Answer: b. It prevents clotting in the extracorporeal circuit. Explanation: Citrate is used as an anticoagulant in CRRT to chelate calcium, which is necessary for blood clotting, thereby preventing clot formation in the extracorporeal circuit without systemic anticoagulant effects.

685. What is a potential complication of using citrate anticoagulation in CRRT?
a. Hypernatremia
b. Citrate toxicity leading to metabolic alkalosis
c. Increased risk of bleeding
d. Hypercalcemia

Answer: b. Citrate toxicity leading to metabolic alkalosis. Explanation: Citrate toxicity can occur if citrate accumulates and is not adequately metabolized by the liver, leading to metabolic alkalosis due to excess bicarbonate generation during citrate metabolism.

686. When adjusting CRRT settings, what parameter is primarily increased to enhance clearance of small solutes like urea?
a. Blood flow rate (BFR)
b. Dialysate flow rate
c. Ultrafiltration rate (UFR)
d. Replacement fluid rate

Answer: b. Dialysate flow rate. Explanation: Increasing the dialysate flow rate in CRRT enhances the diffusive clearance of small solutes like urea by increasing the gradient for diffusion between the blood and dialysate.

687. How does CRRT differ from intermittent hemodialysis in terms of fluid removal?
a. CRRT removes fluid more rapidly.
b. CRRT allows for slower, more controlled fluid removal.
c. CRRT cannot remove fluid, only solutes.
d. There is no difference in fluid removal rates between the two modalities.

Answer: b. CRRT allows for slower, more controlled fluid removal. Explanation: CRRT allows for slower, continuous fluid removal over 24 hours, which is beneficial for hemodynamically unstable patients, as it minimizes the risk of intradialytic hypotension associated with the rapid fluid shifts in intermittent hemodialysis.

688. What is a key advantage of CRRT in managing electrolyte imbalances in AKI?
a. It rapidly corrects electrolyte imbalances within hours.
b. It provides a continuous, gradual correction of electrolyte imbalances.
c. It does not alter electrolyte levels, avoiding the risk of overcorrection.
d. It selectively removes only the electrolytes that are in excess.

Answer: b. It provides a continuous, gradual correction of electrolyte imbalances. Explanation: CRRT offers the advantage of continuous, gradual correction of electrolyte imbalances, allowing for more stable control compared to the potential rapid shifts seen with intermittent hemodialysis.

689. In the context of CRRT, what is the significance of achieving 'dialysis dose' targets?
a. It ensures adequate hydration status.
b. It correlates with improved survival rates in AKI patients.
c. It guarantees the removal of all nephrotoxins.
d. It primarily focuses on blood pressure control.

Answer: b. It correlates with improved survival rates in AKI patients. Explanation: Achieving prescribed 'dialysis dose' targets in CRRT, typically quantified in terms of effluent volume per unit of time relative to patient body weight, has been associated with improved survival rates in patients with AKI, as it ensures adequate clearance of uremic toxins and maintenance of fluid balance.

690. What monitoring parameter is essential in patients receiving CRRT to assess fluid balance and treatment efficacy?
a. Daily body weight measurements
b. Hourly urine output
c. Weekly creatinine clearance tests
d. Monthly blood urea nitrogen (BUN) levels

Answer: a. Daily body weight measurements. Explanation: Daily body weight measurements are essential in patients undergoing CRRT to accurately assess fluid balance and the efficacy of the treatment in removing excess fluid, as weight changes directly reflect changes in the patient's fluid status.

691. What is the most common cause of upper gastrointestinal (GI) bleeding in adults?
a. Esophageal varices
b. Peptic ulcer disease
c. Gastric cancer
d. Mallory-Weiss tear

Answer: b. Peptic ulcer disease. Explanation: Peptic ulcer disease, resulting from ulcers in the stomach or proximal duodenum, is the most common cause of upper GI bleeding in adults, often due to Helicobacter pylori infection or NSAID use.

692. Which of the following is a hallmark sign of lower GI bleeding?
a. Hematemesis
b. Melena
c. Hematochezia
d. Coffee-ground emesis

Answer: c. Hematochezia. Explanation: Hematochezia, the passage of fresh, red blood per rectum, is a hallmark sign of lower GI bleeding, indicating bleeding from sources distal to the ligament of Treitz, such as the colon or rectum.

693. In the management of GI bleeding, what is the role of a proton pump inhibitor (PPI)?
a. To stimulate clot formation at the bleeding site
b. To decrease gastric acid secretion and stabilize blood clots
c. To increase gastrointestinal motility and clear blood
d. To directly vasoconstrict arterioles at the bleeding site

Answer: b. To decrease gastric acid secretion and stabilize blood clots. Explanation: PPIs are used in the management of GI bleeding, particularly upper GI bleeding, to decrease gastric acid secretion, which helps stabilize clot formation on the ulcer base and promotes healing.

694. Which diagnostic tool is most commonly used to identify the source of upper GI bleeding?
a. Abdominal CT scan
b. Barium swallow study
c. Esophagogastroduodenoscopy (EGD)
d. Colonoscopy

Answer: c. Esophagogastroduodenoscopy (EGD). Explanation: EGD is the most commonly used diagnostic tool to identify the source of upper GI bleeding, allowing for direct visualization of the esophagus, stomach, and duodenum, and potential therapeutic interventions.

695. What is the significance of a "coffee-ground" appearance in vomitus?
a. It indicates active upper GI bleeding with rapid bleeding.
b. It suggests the presence of bile and pancreatic enzymes.
c. It signifies the oxidation of hemoglobin by gastric acid.
d. It is indicative of lower GI bleeding.

Answer: c. It signifies the oxidation of hemoglobin by gastric acid. Explanation: A "coffee-ground" appearance in vomitus is indicative of upper GI bleeding where blood has been in contact with gastric acid, leading to the oxidation of hemoglobin and the characteristic dark color.

696. In patients with cirrhosis, what is the most likely cause of upper GI bleeding?
a. Peptic ulcer disease
b. Gastric antral vascular ectasia
c. Esophageal varices
d. Dieulafoy's lesion

Answer: c. Esophageal varices. Explanation: In patients with cirrhosis, esophageal varices are a common cause of upper GI bleeding, resulting from portal hypertension that leads to the development of dilated submucosal veins in the esophagus.

697. How does Octreotide work in the management of GI bleeding due to esophageal varices?
a. By neutralizing gastric acid
b. By promoting mucosal healing
c. By reducing portal venous pressure
d. By directly cauterizing the varices

Answer: c. By reducing portal venous pressure. Explanation: Octreotide, a somatostatin analog, works in the management of GI bleeding due to esophageal varices by reducing portal venous pressure, which in turn decreases blood flow to the varices, reducing the risk of bleeding.

698. What is the first-line treatment for acute lower GI bleeding in hemodynamically stable patients?
a. Immediate surgery
b. Therapeutic colonoscopy
c. Intravenous vasopressin
d. Radiographic embolization

Answer: b. Therapeutic colonoscopy. Explanation: Therapeutic colonoscopy is often the first-line treatment for acute lower GI bleeding in hemodynamically stable patients, allowing for both diagnosis and treatment, including cauterization, clipping, or injection therapy at the bleeding site.

699. Which risk scoring system is used to stratify the risk of mortality in patients with upper GI bleeding?
a. Glasgow-Blatchford score
b. CHADS2 score
c. Child-Pugh score
d. MELD score

Answer: a. Glasgow-Blatchford score. Explanation: The Glasgow-Blatchford score is a clinical tool used to stratify the risk of mortality and the need for intervention in patients with upper GI bleeding, based on clinical and laboratory parameters.

700. In the context of GI bleeding, what is the role of transfusion of packed red blood cells?
a. To increase clotting factors in patients with coagulopathy
b. To restore and maintain hemodynamic stability in patients with significant blood loss
c. To neutralize gastric acid and prevent further bleeding
d. To provide immediate hemostasis at the bleeding site

Answer: b. To restore and maintain hemodynamic stability in patients with significant blood loss. Explanation: Transfusion of packed red blood cells in the context of GI bleeding is primarily aimed at restoring and maintaining hemodynamic stability in patients who have experienced significant blood loss, helping to ensure adequate oxygen delivery to vital organs.

701. What is a primary nursing consideration when caring for a patient on mechanical ventilation to prevent Ventilator-Associated Pneumonia (VAP)?
a. Administering sedatives regularly to ensure patient-ventilator synchrony
b. Maintaining the head of the bed elevated at 30-45 degrees
c. Increasing the rate of respiratory cycles to improve oxygenation
d. Decreasing humidification to reduce moisture buildup

Answer: b. Maintaining the head of the bed elevated at 30-45 degrees. Explanation: Elevating the head of the bed between 30 to 45 degrees is a key nursing intervention to prevent aspiration and subsequent Ventilator-Associated Pneumonia (VAP) in mechanically ventilated patients.

702. For a patient receiving Continuous Renal Replacement Therapy (CRRT), what is a crucial nursing consideration regarding vascular access?
a. Regularly changing the access site to prevent infection
b. Ensuring patency and monitoring for signs of infection at the access site
c. Using the largest possible catheter to increase blood flow
d. Administering anticoagulants directly into the access site to prevent clotting

Answer: b. Ensuring patency and monitoring for signs of infection at the access site. Explanation: For CRRT, maintaining vascular access patency and vigilantly monitoring for any signs of infection or thrombosis at the access site are critical nursing responsibilities to ensure the effectiveness and safety of the therapy.

703. In administering intravenous potassium for hypokalemia, what nursing consideration is most important?
a. Infusing potassium rapidly to quickly resolve hypokalemia
b. Diluting potassium adequately and administering it via a central line when possible
c. Providing potassium in bolus form to ascertain the immediate response

d. Mixing potassium with high-glucose solutions to enhance absorption

Answer: b. Diluting potassium adequately and administering it via a central line when possible. Explanation: When administering intravenous potassium, it's crucial to dilute it adequately and preferably use a central line for administration to prevent vein irritation and ensure patient safety, as rapid or undiluted potassium infusion can lead to life-threatening arrhythmias.

704. What is an essential nursing consideration when caring for a patient with an arterial line?
a. Frequent calibration to ensure accurate blood pressure readings
b. Applying a pressure dressing to prevent bleeding
c. Regular limb mobilization to prevent contractures
d. Ensuring the line is used exclusively for blood pressure monitoring and not for medication administration

Answer: a. Frequent calibration to ensure accurate blood pressure readings. Explanation: Ensuring frequent calibration of the arterial line system is crucial for obtaining accurate and reliable blood pressure readings, which is essential for the proper management of critically ill patients.

705. When providing care for a patient on Total Parenteral Nutrition (TPN), what is a key nursing consideration to prevent complications?
a. Rapidly increasing the rate of TPN infusion to meet nutritional needs
b. Using a dedicated central venous catheter for TPN infusion
c. Supplementing TPN with oral feedings to enhance gastrointestinal function
d. Administering TPN intermittently to mimic normal eating patterns

Answer: b. Using a dedicated central venous catheter for TPN infusion. Explanation: Using a dedicated central venous catheter for TPN infusion is essential to prevent infections and complications associated with TPN, as it helps to maintain sterility and reduces the risk of catheter-related bloodstream infections.

706. For a patient undergoing hemodialysis, what nursing action is crucial immediately post-procedure?
a. Encouraging ambulation to prevent blood clots
b. Monitoring for signs of disequilibrium syndrome
c. Applying heat to the access site to enhance blood flow
d. Providing high-phosphate foods to replace lost nutrients

Answer: b. Monitoring for signs of disequilibrium syndrome. Explanation: Post-hemodialysis, monitoring for signs of disequilibrium syndrome, such as nausea, headache, and disorientation, is crucial due to rapid changes in fluid and electrolytes that can affect the brain.

707. In the management of a patient with a chest tube, what is an essential nursing intervention to ensure proper function of the chest drainage system?

a. Clamping the tube daily to assess for air leaks
b. Regularly milking the tube to ensure patency
c. Keeping the drainage system below the level of the chest
d. Increasing suction if continuous bubbling is noted in the suction control chamber

Answer: c. Keeping the drainage system below the level of the chest. Explanation: Maintaining the chest drainage system below the level of the patient's chest is vital to ensure gravity drainage of air and fluids, preventing the risk of reflux into the pleural space.

708. What is a critical nursing consideration when managing a patient with an intra-aortic balloon pump (IABP)?
a. Encouraging leg exercises to promote circulation
b. Maintaining the patient in a flat position at all times
c. Monitoring for signs of limb ischemia distal to the insertion site
d. Adjusting the balloon inflation to synchronize with the patient's respiratory rate

Answer: c. Monitoring for signs of limb ischemia distal to the insertion site. Explanation: For patients with an IABP, vigilant monitoring for signs of limb ischemia, such as pain, pallor, or decreased pulses distal to the insertion site, is critical due to the risk of vascular compromise from the device.

709. In administering a blood transfusion, what is a priority nursing action to prevent a transfusion reaction?
a. Warming the blood to body temperature before infusion
b. Infusing the blood rapidly to prevent clotting in the line
c. Verifying the match of blood type and Rh factor with another nurse
d. Adding a standard IV solution to the blood to improve flow rates

Answer: c. Verifying the match of blood type and Rh factor with another nurse. Explanation: Double-checking the compatibility of the blood product, including blood type and Rh factor, with another nurse before administration is a critical safety measure to prevent transfusion reactions and ensure patient safety.

710. What hemoglobin level typically triggers consideration for red blood cell transfusion in a stable, non-bleeding adult patient?
a. Hemoglobin < 10 g/dL
b. Hemoglobin < 7 g/dL
c. Hemoglobin < 12 g/dL
d. Hemoglobin < 9 g/dL

Answer: b. Hemoglobin < 7 g/dL. Explanation: Current guidelines suggest considering red blood cell transfusion in stable, non-bleeding adult patients when hemoglobin levels fall below 7 g/dL. This threshold aims to balance the need for adequate oxygenation with the risks associated with transfusions.

711. In the context of massive transfusion protocols (MTP), what ratio of packed red blood cells (PRBCs) to fresh frozen plasma (FFP) is generally recommended?
a. 1:1
b. 2:1
c. 3:1
d. 4:1

Answer: a. 1:1. Explanation: Massive transfusion protocols often recommend a 1:1 ratio of packed red blood cells to fresh frozen plasma to approximate whole blood and minimize the risks of coagulopathy associated with large volume blood transfusions.

712. For a patient with chronic anemia and cardiovascular disease, at what hemoglobin level might transfusion be considered earlier than the standard threshold?
a. < 8 g/dL
b. < 7 g/dL
c. < 10 g/dL
d. < 6 g/dL

Answer: c. < 10 g/dL. Explanation: Patients with chronic anemia and coexisting cardiovascular disease may require transfusion at a higher hemoglobin threshold, such as < 10 g/dL, to prevent cardiac ischemia due to compromised oxygen-carrying capacity.

713. What clinical sign is a critical assessment parameter indicating potential need for transfusion in patients with acute bleeding?
a. Hypertension
b. Tachycardia
c. Peripheral edema
d. Polyuria

Answer: b. Tachycardia. Explanation: Tachycardia is an early compensatory mechanism in response to hypovolemia from acute bleeding, making it a critical assessment parameter that may indicate the need for transfusion to restore intravascular volume and maintain tissue perfusion.

714. In pediatric patients, what is a common trigger for considering transfusion, particularly in the context of acute blood loss?
a. Weight-based blood loss exceeding 10 mL/kg
b. Hemoglobin < 12 g/dL
c. Single episode of vomiting
d. Blood pressure within normal limits for age

Answer: a. Weight-based blood loss exceeding 10 mL/kg. Explanation: In pediatric patients, transfusion considerations often include weight-based assessment of blood loss, with >10 mL/kg being a common trigger, especially in the context of acute blood loss, due to their smaller circulating blood volume relative to body weight.

715. When managing a patient with septic shock, what transfusion trigger might be adjusted based on mixed venous oxygen saturation (SvO2) or central venous oxygen saturation (ScvO2) measurements?
a. Hemoglobin < 9 g/dL if SvO2 < 70%
b. Hemoglobin < 7 g/dL regardless of SvO2/ScvO2
c. Hemoglobin < 10 g/dL if ScvO2 > 75%
d. Hemoglobin < 8 g/dL if SvO2/ScvO2 measurements are not available

Answer: a. Hemoglobin < 9 g/dL if SvO2 < 70%. Explanation: In patients with septic shock, transfusion decisions might be influenced by oxygen delivery and consumption parameters. A hemoglobin trigger of < 9 g/dL might be considered if SvO2 is < 70%, suggesting inadequate oxygenation that could potentially be improved with transfusion.

716. For a patient with thalassemia undergoing regular transfusions, what is a key consideration to prevent transfusion-related complications?
a. Maximizing the interval between transfusions to >12 weeks
b. Using leukocyte-reduced PRBCs to prevent alloimmunization
c. Administering erythropoietin to stimulate endogenous erythropoiesis
d. Limiting transfusion volume to avoid iron overload

Answer: b. Using leukocyte-reduced PRBCs to prevent alloimmunization. Explanation: For patients with conditions like thalassemia requiring regular transfusions, using leukocyte-reduced PRBCs is important to minimize the risk of alloimmunization, which can complicate future transfusions.

717. What is an essential nursing action prior to initiating a blood transfusion to ensure patient safety?
a. Pre-medicate with antipyretics to prevent transfusion reactions
b. Confirm the patient's identity and blood product compatibility through a bedside check
c. Increase the infusion rate for the first 15 minutes to assess for adverse reactions
d. Administer diuretics to prevent fluid overload

Answer: b. Confirm the patient's identity and blood product compatibility through a bedside check. Explanation: An essential nursing action prior to transfusion is to confirm the patient's identity and the compatibility of the blood product through a bedside check, adhering to the "right patient, right blood" principle to prevent transfusion errors.

718. In a trauma setting, what is a key factor influencing the decision to initiate a massive transfusion protocol (MTP)?
a. Blood pressure > 100 mmHg systolic
b. Hemoglobin level on arrival
c. Estimated blood loss exceeding 1500 mL
d. Presence of limb fractures

Answer: c. Estimated blood loss exceeding 1500 mL. Explanation: In a trauma setting, the decision to initiate a massive transfusion protocol is often influenced by the estimated blood loss, with >1500 mL being a common threshold, indicating significant hemorrhage that may require aggressive and rapid transfusion support.

719. What is the primary goal of endoscopic retrograde cholangiopancreatography (ERCP) in the management of cholelithiasis?
a. Removal of gastric ulcers
b. Biopsy of pancreatic tissue
c. Relief of bile duct obstruction by stone extraction
d. Diagnosis of esophageal varices

Answer: c. Relief of bile duct obstruction by stone extraction. Explanation: ERCP is primarily used in the management of cholelithiasis to relieve bile duct obstruction by extracting stones from the bile duct, improving bile flow and alleviating symptoms associated with the obstruction.

720. In endoscopic variceal ligation (EVL), what is the mechanism used to prevent variceal bleeding?
a. Sclerotherapy to harden the varices
b. Application of a band to ligate the varices
c. Thermal coagulation to seal the varices
d. Injection of botulinum toxin to reduce pressure

Answer: b. Application of a band to ligate the varices. Explanation: EVL involves the application of a specialized band around the base of esophageal varices to ligate them, which can prevent bleeding by eliminating the varix through necrosis and eventual sloughing.

721. Which endoscopic intervention is typically used for the treatment of Barrett's esophagus with dysplasia?
a. Endoscopic mucosal resection (EMR)
b. Percutaneous endoscopic gastrostomy (PEG)
c. Transesophageal echocardiography (TEE)
d. Endoscopic submucosal dissection (ESD)

Answer: a. Endoscopic mucosal resection (EMR). Explanation: EMR is commonly used for the treatment of Barrett's esophagus with dysplasia, where abnormal cells are removed to reduce the risk of progression to esophageal cancer. This procedure involves resecting and removing the dysplastic mucosal layer.

722. What is the primary indication for performing a colonoscopy?
a. Assessment and treatment of nasal polyps
b. Screening and removal of colorectal polyps
c. Diagnosis of peptic ulcer disease
d. Evaluation of upper GI tract bleeding

Answer: b. Screening and removal of colorectal polyps. Explanation: The primary indication for a colonoscopy is the screening for colorectal cancer, including the identification and removal of colorectal polyps, which can be precancerous, thereby reducing the risk of colorectal cancer development.

723. During an upper endoscopy, what therapeutic action can be taken to control gastric ulcer bleeding?
a. Endoscopic balloon dilation
b. Endoscopic stent placement
c. Endoscopic injection of epinephrine
d. Transjugular intrahepatic portosystemic shunt (TIPS)

Answer: c. Endoscopic injection of epinephrine. Explanation: To control gastric ulcer bleeding during an upper endoscopy, an endoscopic injection of epinephrine can be performed. This causes vasoconstriction, reducing blood flow to the bleeding site and promoting hemostasis.

724. How does endoscopic ultrasound (EUS) enhance the staging of esophageal cancer?
a. By providing high-resolution images of the esophageal wall layers
b. Through measurement of gastric acid levels
c. By visualizing the surface of the esophagus only
d. Through direct biopsy of the liver

Answer: a. By providing high-resolution images of the esophageal wall layers. Explanation: EUS enhances the staging of esophageal cancer by providing detailed, high-resolution images of the esophageal wall layers, allowing for assessment of tumor depth and involvement of adjacent lymph nodes, which is crucial for accurate staging.

725. What role does percutaneous endoscopic gastrostomy (PEG) play in patient management?
a. Temporary reduction of stomach size for weight loss
b. Long-term enteral feeding in patients unable to take oral nutrition
c. Relief of gastric volvulus
d. Gastric decompression in cases of ileus

Answer: b. Long-term enteral feeding in patients unable to take oral nutrition. Explanation: PEG is primarily used for long-term enteral feeding in patients who are unable to maintain adequate nutrition orally, due to conditions such as neurological disorders or head and neck cancers, providing a direct feeding route into the stomach.

726. In the context of acute pancreatitis, what is the therapeutic goal of endoscopic transgastric necrosectomy?
a. Removal of gallstones from the common bile duct
b. Drainage and debridement of infected pancreatic necrosis
c. Bypass of the pancreatic duct
d. Injection of sclerosants into pancreatic cysts

Answer: b. Drainage and debridement of infected pancreatic necrosis. Explanation: Endoscopic transgastric necrosectomy is performed in the context of acute pancreatitis to drain and debride infected or sterile pancreatic necrosis, reducing the risk of further complications associated with necrotizing pancreatitis.

727. What is a common complication following endoscopic retrograde cholangiopancreatography (ERCP) that clinicians should monitor for?
a. Myocardial infarction
b. Post-ERCP pancreatitis
c. Appendicitis
d. Acute cholecystitis

Answer: b. Post-ERCP pancreatitis. Explanation: Post-ERCP pancreatitis is a common complication following ERCP, characterized by abdominal pain and elevated pancreatic enzymes. Clinicians should monitor patients for this complication and manage it appropriately to prevent severe outcomes.

728. What is the primary cause of tension pneumothorax in trauma patients?
a. Spontaneous bacterial infection
b. Rib fracture puncturing the lung
c. Chronic obstructive pulmonary disease (COPD)
d. Asthma

Answer: b. Rib fracture puncturing the lung. Explanation: In trauma patients, tension pneumothorax is most commonly caused by a rib fracture that punctures the lung, allowing air to enter the pleural space and become trapped, leading to increased intrathoracic pressure and potential life-threatening respiratory and hemodynamic compromise.

729. Which symptom is most indicative of acute decompensated heart failure?
a. Intermittent claudication
b. Paroxysmal nocturnal dyspnea
c. Epigastric pain
d. Dry cough

Answer: b. Paroxysmal nocturnal dyspnea. Explanation: Paroxysmal nocturnal dyspnea, characterized by sudden episodes of shortness of breath that awaken the patient from sleep, is a hallmark symptom of acute decompensated heart failure, reflecting fluid redistribution into the lungs when recumbent.

730. In diabetic ketoacidosis (DKA), what is a key distinguishing sign?
a. Bradycardia
b. Kussmaul respirations

c. Hypertension
d. Hyperactive bowel sounds

Answer: b. Kussmaul respirations. Explanation: Kussmaul respirations, a deep and labored breathing pattern, are a key sign of diabetic ketoacidosis, reflecting the body's attempt to eliminate excess carbon dioxide and compensate for metabolic acidosis.

731. What is a common cause of acute pancreatitis?
a. Viral infection
b. Gallstones
c. Hypothyroidism
d. Renal failure

Answer: b. Gallstones. Explanation: Gallstones are a common cause of acute pancreatitis, as they can obstruct the pancreatic duct, leading to pancreatic enzyme activation, inflammation, and autodigestion of the pancreas.

732. Which symptom is characteristic of aortic dissection?
a. Gradual onset of diffuse abdominal pain
b. Sudden, severe chest or upper back pain
c. Slow, progressive shortness of breath
d. Bilateral ankle swelling

Answer: b. Sudden, severe chest or upper back pain. Explanation: Aortic dissection typically presents with sudden, severe, and sharp chest or upper back pain, often described as "tearing" in nature, reflecting the acute development of a tear in the aortic intima, allowing blood to dissect into the media layer.

733. What is a cardinal sign of acute arterial occlusion in the lower extremities?
a. Unilateral leg swelling
b. Warmth and redness over the affected area
c. Pulsating mass in the groin
d. Pallor and coldness of the affected limb

Answer: d. Pallor and coldness of the affected limb. Explanation: Pallor and coldness of the affected limb are cardinal signs of acute arterial occlusion in the lower extremities, reflecting the sudden loss of arterial blood supply and resulting in ischemia.

734. In the setting of septic shock, what clinical sign is most commonly observed?
a. Hypothermia
b. Bradycardia
c. Warm, flushed skin

d. Hypotension unresponsive to fluid resuscitation

Answer: d. Hypotension unresponsive to fluid resuscitation. Explanation: In septic shock, a key clinical sign is hypotension that remains unresponsive to adequate fluid resuscitation, along with the presence of perfusion abnormalities, indicative of a systemic response to infection leading to circulatory collapse.

735. What is a leading cause of peptic ulcer disease leading to upper GI bleeding?
a. Prolonged use of acetaminophen
b. Helicobacter pylori infection
c. Excessive consumption of dairy products
d. Viral gastroenteritis

Answer: b. Helicobacter pylori infection. Explanation: Helicobacter pylori infection is a leading cause of peptic ulcer disease, which can lead to upper GI bleeding. The bacteria damage the gastric or duodenal mucosa, leading to ulcer formation and potential hemorrhage.

736. What neurological sign is commonly associated with subarachnoid hemorrhage?
a. Hemiparesis
b. Sudden, severe headache often described as "the worst headache of my life"
c. Gradual onset of confusion over several days
d. Unilateral facial droop

Answer: b. Sudden, severe headache often described as "the worst headache of my life". Explanation: A sudden, severe headache, often described by patients as "the worst headache of my life," is a hallmark sign of subarachnoid hemorrhage, reflecting the acute onset of bleeding into the subarachnoid space.

737. In the diagnosis of pulmonary embolism, what symptom is most frequently reported?
a. Hemoptysis
b. Pleuritic chest pain
c. Wheezing
d. Chronic cough

Answer: b. Pleuritic chest pain. Explanation: Pleuritic chest pain, which is sharp and worsens with deep breaths, is one of the most frequently reported symptoms in patients with pulmonary embolism, reflecting irritation of the pleura as the embolus obstructs pulmonary arterial flow.

738. What is the earliest clinical sign of increased intracranial pressure (ICP)?
a. Fixed and dilated pupils
b. Decerebrate posturing
c. Change in level of consciousness

d. Hypertension with a widened pulse pressure

Answer: c. Change in level of consciousness. Explanation: A change in the level of consciousness is often the earliest sign of increased ICP, as even slight elevations can affect cerebral perfusion and neuronal function, leading to alterations in alertness, cognition, and responsiveness.

739. Which imaging study is considered the gold standard for identifying the cause of increased ICP?
a. Skull X-ray
b. Computed Tomography (CT) scan of the head
c. Magnetic Resonance Imaging (MRI) of the brain
d. Cerebral angiography

Answer: b. Computed Tomography (CT) scan of the head. Explanation: A CT scan of the head is often considered the gold standard for initial assessment of increased ICP, as it quickly provides detailed images of the brain, can identify shifts in brain structures, masses, hemorrhage, or edema that may contribute to increased ICP.

740. In the management of increased ICP, what is the primary goal of using mannitol?
a. To increase cerebral blood flow
b. To reduce cerebral edema through osmotic diuresis
c. To induce systemic hypertension and improve perfusion
d. To sedate the patient and reduce metabolic demand

Answer: b. To reduce cerebral edema through osmotic diuresis. Explanation: Mannitol is an osmotic diuretic used in the management of increased ICP primarily to reduce cerebral edema. It works by creating an osmotic gradient that draws fluid from the brain parenchyma into the intravascular space, thereby reducing ICP.

741. What is the significance of Cushing's triad in the context of increased ICP?
a. It indicates an early compensatory stage of increased ICP.
b. It is a specific finding for brainstem herniation.
c. It represents a late and ominous sign of increased ICP comprising hypertension, bradycardia, and irregular respirations.
d. It signifies the resolution of increased ICP and improvement in patient status.

Answer: c. It represents a late and ominous sign of increased ICP comprising hypertension, bradycardia, and irregular respirations. Explanation: Cushing's triad is a classic but late sign of significantly increased ICP and impending brain herniation, characterized by the triad of systemic hypertension with a widened pulse pressure, bradycardia, and irregular respirations.

742. Which therapeutic intervention is NOT recommended in the routine management of increased ICP?
a. Elevation of the head of the bed to 30 degrees

b. Administration of prophylactic anticonvulsants
c. Hyperventilation to a PaCO2 of 25-30 mmHg
d. Therapeutic hypothermia

Answer: d. Therapeutic hypothermia. Explanation: While therapeutic hypothermia has been explored in the management of increased ICP, it is not routinely recommended due to mixed evidence on its efficacy and concerns about potential complications. The other options are commonly utilized strategies in managing increased ICP.

743. What nursing intervention is crucial in preventing secondary injury in a patient with increased ICP?
a. Maintaining strict bed rest with no repositioning
b. Frequent neurological assessments to detect changes in ICP
c. Limiting fluid intake to reduce cerebral edema
d. Administering high-dose corticosteroids routinely

Answer: b. Frequent neurological assessments to detect changes in ICP. Explanation: Frequent and detailed neurological assessments are crucial in patients with increased ICP to promptly detect changes that may indicate worsening of the condition or the effectiveness of interventions, thereby preventing secondary injury.

744. In patients with increased ICP, why is maintaining euvolemia important?
a. To ensure adequate cerebral perfusion pressure (CPP)
b. To facilitate the renal excretion of neurotoxic metabolites
c. To prepare the patient for potential surgical intervention
d. To increase the efficacy of osmotic diuretics like mannitol

Answer: a. To ensure adequate cerebral perfusion pressure (CPP). Explanation: Maintaining euvolemia is essential in managing increased ICP to ensure adequate CPP, which is the pressure gradient driving cerebral blood flow. Both hypovolemia and hypervolemia can adversely affect CPP and, consequently, brain tissue oxygenation.

745. What is a critical consideration when using barbiturates to manage increased ICP?
a. They should be the first-line treatment in all cases of increased ICP.
b. They may induce hypotension, requiring careful monitoring and management.
c. They improve cerebral perfusion by increasing systemic blood pressure.
d. They are most effective when administered orally rather than intravenously.

Answer: b. They may induce hypotension, requiring careful monitoring and management. Explanation: Barbiturates can be used to lower ICP by reducing metabolic demand and cerebral blood flow, but they may also induce hypotension, necessitating vigilant monitoring and potential vasopressor support to maintain adequate CPP.

746. What is the role of decompressive craniectomy in the management of increased ICP?
a. It is a diagnostic procedure to identify the cause of increased ICP.

b. It is a therapeutic measure to mechanically remove a portion of the skull to allow brain expansion and reduce ICP.
c. It is performed routinely in all patients with mild to moderate increased ICP.
d. It involves the infusion of hypertonic solutions directly into the cranial cavity to reduce edema.

Answer: b. It is a therapeutic measure to mechanically remove a portion of the skull to allow brain expansion and reduce ICP. Explanation: Decompressive craniectomy is a surgical intervention where part of the skull is removed to provide additional space for swollen brain tissue, thereby reducing ICP in cases where medical management is insufficient.

747. In the context of increased ICP, why is it important to avoid hyperglycemia?
a. Hyperglycemia can lead to increased cerebral edema through osmotic effects.
b. Hyperglycemia reduces the efficacy of osmotic diuretics like mannitol.
c. Hyperglycemia increases the risk of developing Cushing's triad.
d. Hyperglycemia directly increases ICP through vasodilation.

Answer: a. Hyperglycemia can lead to increased cerebral edema through osmotic effects. Explanation: Hyperglycemia can exacerbate cerebral edema and increase ICP through osmotic effects, drawing water into the brain tissue. Additionally, it may be associated with worse outcomes in brain-injured patients, making glycemic control an important aspect of managing increased ICP.

748. What is the primary mechanism of an ischemic stroke?
a. Bleeding within the brain tissue
b. Obstruction of a blood vessel supplying the brain
c. Inflammation of the brain's meninges
d. Excessive accumulation of cerebrospinal fluid

Answer: b. Obstruction of a blood vessel supplying the brain. Explanation: Ischemic stroke occurs when a blood vessel supplying blood to the brain is obstructed, leading to a reduction or cessation of blood flow and oxygen to brain tissue, causing cell death in the affected area.

749. Which clinical sign is indicative of a stroke affecting the brain's left hemisphere?
a. Right-sided weakness or paralysis
b. Loss of vision in the left eye
c. Difficulty in remembering past events
d. Loss of balance and coordination

Answer: a. Right-sided weakness or paralysis. Explanation: A stroke affecting the brain's left hemisphere typically presents with right-sided weakness or paralysis due to the brain's cross-representation, where the left hemisphere controls motor function on the body's right side.

750. In the management of acute ischemic stroke, what is the therapeutic window for the administration of intravenous tissue plasminogen activator (tPA)?
a. Within 12 hours of symptom onset
b. Within 24 hours of symptom onset
c. Within 4.5 hours of symptom onset
d. Within 72 hours of symptom onset

Answer: c. Within 4.5 hours of symptom onset. Explanation: The therapeutic window for the administration of intravenous tPA in acute ischemic stroke is within 4.5 hours of symptom onset. This time frame is critical for effective treatment to restore blood flow and minimize brain damage.

751. What is a key risk factor for hemorrhagic stroke?
a. Hypoglycemia
b. Hypotension
c. Uncontrolled hypertension
d. Low cholesterol levels

Answer: c. Uncontrolled hypertension. Explanation: Uncontrolled hypertension is a key risk factor for hemorrhagic stroke, as chronically elevated blood pressure can weaken blood vessel walls, leading to their rupture within the brain.

752. Which imaging modality is preferred for the initial assessment of a suspected stroke?
a. MRI with contrast
b. CT scan without contrast
c. Ultrasound of the carotid arteries
d. PET scan

Answer: b. CT scan without contrast. Explanation: A non-contrast CT scan is the preferred initial imaging modality for assessing a suspected stroke as it can quickly differentiate between ischemic and hemorrhagic stroke, guiding appropriate treatment decisions.

753. What is the significance of the NIH Stroke Scale in the management of stroke patients?
a. It determines the patient's eligibility for surgical intervention.
b. It provides a quantitative measure of stroke-related neurological deficit.
c. It predicts the long-term outcomes and rehabilitation potential.
d. It assesses the patient's cognitive function post-stroke.

Answer: b. It provides a quantitative measure of stroke-related neurological deficit. Explanation: The NIH Stroke Scale is a systematic assessment tool that provides a quantitative measure of stroke-related neurological deficit, helping to evaluate the stroke's severity and guide treatment decisions.

754. In stroke management, what is the goal of carotid endarterectomy?
a. To repair damaged brain tissue
b. To remove plaque from the carotid artery and restore blood flow
c. To drain accumulated cerebrospinal fluid
d. To relieve pressure within the skull

Answer: b. To remove plaque from the carotid artery and restore blood flow. Explanation: Carotid endarterectomy is a surgical procedure aimed at removing plaque from the carotid artery to restore blood flow and prevent stroke in patients with significant carotid artery stenosis.

755. What lifestyle modification is most effective in reducing the risk of recurrent strokes?
a. Increased intake of vitamin supplements
b. Regular aerobic exercise
c. Adoption of a nocturnal lifestyle
d. High protein diet

Answer: b. Regular aerobic exercise. Explanation: Regular aerobic exercise is a significant lifestyle modification that can help reduce the risk of recurrent strokes by improving cardiovascular health, lowering blood pressure, and maintaining a healthy weight.

756. Which symptom differentiates a transient ischemic attack (TIA) from a stroke?
a. Sudden onset of unilateral numbness
b. Complete resolution of symptoms within 24 hours
c. Severe headache with no known cause
d. Speech difficulties lasting more than 2 days

Answer: b. Complete resolution of symptoms within 24 hours. Explanation: A transient ischemic attack (TIA) is characterized by the sudden onset of stroke-like symptoms that completely resolve within 24 hours, differentiating it from a stroke where neurological deficits may persist.

757. What is the primary mechanism by which mannitol reduces increased intracranial pressure (ICP)?
a. Vasodilation of cerebral vessels
b. Induction of systemic hypotension
c. Osmotic diuresis leading to reduced brain edema
d. Direct absorption of cerebrospinal fluid (CSF)

Answer: c. Osmotic diuresis leading to reduced brain edema. Explanation: Mannitol works by creating an osmotic gradient across the blood-brain barrier, leading to osmotic diuresis. This process draws water out of the brain tissue, thereby reducing cerebral edema and intracranial pressure.

758. When administering hypertonic saline for increased ICP, what is a key nursing consideration to monitor for potential complications?
a. Hypoglycemia
b. Hyperkalemia
c. Central pontine myelinolysis
d. Metabolic acidosis

Answer: c. Central pontine myelinolysis. Explanation: Rapid changes in serum sodium levels due to hypertonic saline administration can lead to central pontine myelinolysis, a serious neurological condition. Careful monitoring of serum sodium levels and changes in neurological status is essential to avoid this complication.

759. In the context of traumatic brain injury (TBI), what is a potential advantage of using hypertonic saline over mannitol?
a. It can be used indefinitely without concern for renal effects.
b. It provides volume expansion in addition to reducing ICP.
c. It does not require monitoring of serum osmolality.
d. It is less likely to cause electrolyte imbalances.

Answer: b. It provides volume expansion in addition to reducing ICP. Explanation: Hypertonic saline not only reduces ICP through osmotic effects but also provides volume expansion, which can be beneficial in managing patients with TBI who may also be hypovolemic.

760. What is a significant risk associated with the rapid infusion of mannitol?
a. Pulmonary edema
b. Acute renal failure
c. Hypertensive crisis
d. Severe hypokalemia

Answer: a. Pulmonary edema. Explanation: Rapid infusion of mannitol can lead to acute expansion of intravascular volume, potentially leading to pulmonary edema, especially in patients with compromised cardiac function.

761. Why is continuous monitoring of serum sodium levels important when administering hypertonic saline for increased ICP?
a. To prevent the risk of hypernatremia and its associated complications
b. To ensure therapeutic levels of sodium for osmotic effect
c. To adjust the dosage of hypertonic saline accurately
d. All of the above

Answer: d. All of the above. Explanation: Continuous monitoring of serum sodium levels is crucial when administering hypertonic saline to prevent hypernatremia, ensure therapeutic levels of sodium for the desired osmotic effect, and accurately adjust the dosage as needed.

762. What is a contraindication for the use of mannitol in the management of increased ICP?
a. Anuria
b. Hyponatremia
c. Hypotension
d. Diabetes mellitus

Answer: a. Anuria. Explanation: Mannitol is contraindicated in patients with anuria due to the risk of acute kidney injury from the osmotic load and inability to excrete the mannitol, potentially leading to fluid overload and worsening of cerebral edema.

763. For a patient receiving mannitol, what is an essential component of nursing care related to monitoring its effectiveness and side effects?
a. Daily weight and input/output monitoring
b. Frequent neurological assessments
c. Monitoring for signs of dehydration
d. All of the above

Answer: d. All of the above. Explanation: Comprehensive nursing care for a patient receiving mannitol includes daily weight and input/output monitoring to assess for fluid balance, frequent neurological assessments to gauge effectiveness in reducing ICP, and monitoring for signs of dehydration, a common side effect of mannitol-induced diuresis.

764. When would hypertonic saline be preferred over mannitol for a patient with increased ICP and hemodynamic instability?
a. When there is a need for rapid ICP reduction
b. When there is coexisting hypovolemia
c. When renal function is impaired
d. Both b and c

Answer: d. Both b and c. Explanation: Hypertonic saline may be preferred over mannitol in patients with increased ICP who are also hemodynamically unstable, particularly when there is coexisting hypovolemia or impaired renal function, as hypertonic saline can provide both osmotic effect to reduce ICP and volume expansion to support blood pressure.

765. What is the recommended monitoring interval for serum osmolality when administering mannitol to ensure safety?
a. Every 6-8 hours during infusion
b. Every 12 hours

c. Every 24 hours
d. Only prior to the initiation of therapy

Answer: a. Every 6-8 hours during infusion. Explanation: Monitoring serum osmolality every 6-8 hours during mannitol infusion is recommended to prevent osmotic demyelination syndrome and kidney injury by ensuring osmolality remains within safe limits, generally not exceeding 320 mOsm/kg.

766. In managing a patient with increased ICP, what is a key consideration when choosing between mannitol and hypertonic saline?
a. The patient's neurological status only
b. The presence of coexisting medical conditions and overall fluid balance
c. The cost and availability of the medication
d. The preference of the healthcare provider

Answer: b. The presence of coexisting medical conditions and overall fluid balance. Explanation: The choice between mannitol and hypertonic saline for managing increased ICP should consider the patient's coexisting medical conditions, overall fluid and electrolyte balance, and specific therapeutic goals, rather than cost, availability, or provider preference alone.

767. What is the maximum time window from onset of ischemic stroke symptoms to administration of intravenous tissue plasminogen activator (tPA)?
a. 3 hours
b. 4.5 hours
c. 6 hours
d. 12 hours

Answer: b. 4.5 hours. Explanation: The maximum time window for the administration of intravenous tPA in eligible ischemic stroke patients is 4.5 hours from the onset of symptoms. Beyond this period, the risks of tPA, particularly hemorrhagic complications, may outweigh the potential benefits.

768. Which of the following is a contraindication for the use of tPA in ischemic stroke?
a. Blood pressure of 180/100 mmHg after treatment
b. A history of diabetes mellitus
c. Prior ischemic stroke more than 6 months ago
d. Evidence of intracranial hemorrhage on initial CT scan

Answer: d. Evidence of intracranial hemorrhage on initial CT scan. Explanation: The presence of intracranial hemorrhage on initial CT imaging is an absolute contraindication for tPA administration due to the high risk of exacerbating the hemorrhage.

769. In the context of tPA administration, what is the significance of a patient's blood pressure being above 185/110 mmHg?
a. It is an indication for immediate tPA administration.
b. It requires aggressive management to lower the blood pressure before tPA can be safely administered.
c. It is considered optimal and requires no intervention.
d. It indicates the need for immediate surgical intervention.

Answer: b. It requires aggressive management to lower the blood pressure before tPA can be safely administered. Explanation: A blood pressure above 185/110 mmHg is a relative contraindication for tPA administration due to the increased risk of hemorrhagic conversion. Blood pressure must be aggressively managed and stabilized below this threshold before tPA can be safely given.

770. What is the protocol for anticoagulant use in patients scheduled to receive tPA for acute ischemic stroke?
a. Anticoagulants are recommended to be administered concurrently with tPA.
b. Anticoagulants should be initiated 24 hours before tPA administration.
c. Anticoagulants are withheld for 24 hours after tPA administration.
d. Anticoagulants should be used only if atrial fibrillation is present.

Answer: c. Anticoagulants are withheld for 24 hours after tPA administration. Explanation: Following tPA administration, anticoagulants are typically withheld for 24 hours to minimize the risk of bleeding. This allows time to assess the patient's response to tPA and to perform follow-up imaging before introducing additional antithrombotic therapy.

771. For a patient with a rapidly improving stroke symptom (RIS), how does this affect eligibility for tPA administration?
a. RIS is considered a contraindication for tPA.
b. tPA is administered regardless of symptom improvement.
c. tPA administration is delayed to assess for sustained improvement.
d. RIS qualifies the patient for an increased dose of tPA.

Answer: a. RIS is considered a contraindication for tPA. Explanation: Rapidly improving stroke symptoms can indicate spontaneous recovery, and such patients may not be considered for tPA administration due to the potential risks of the treatment outweighing the benefits in a resolving stroke.

772. In patients with a history of recent major surgery, how does this impact tPA eligibility for acute ischemic stroke?
a. It has no impact on tPA administration.
b. It is considered a relative contraindication, requiring individual risk-benefit assessment.
c. It is an absolute contraindication for tPA.
d. tPA dose is halved in patients with recent major surgery.

Answer: b. It is considered a relative contraindication, requiring individual risk-benefit assessment. Explanation: A history of recent major surgery is a relative contraindication for tPA due to the increased risk of bleeding at the surgical site. A careful risk-benefit assessment is required to determine eligibility for tPA in such cases.

773. How does age affect the administration of tPA in acute ischemic stroke patients?
a. There is no upper age limit for tPA administration.
b. Patients over 80 years old are automatically excluded from tPA treatment.
c. tPA is only administered to patients between the ages of 18 and 50.
d. Patients under 18 years old receive a reduced dose of tPA.

Answer: a. There is no upper age limit for tPA administration. Explanation: Current guidelines do not impose an upper age limit for tPA administration in acute ischemic stroke patients. Eligibility is based on clinical and imaging criteria rather than age alone.

774. What is the role of platelet count in determining eligibility for tPA administration?
a. Platelet count is irrelevant to tPA administration.
b. A platelet count below 100,000/mm³ is a contraindication for tPA.
c. tPA can be administered regardless of low platelet count if transfusions are given concurrently.
d. A high platelet count requires dose adjustment of tPA.

Answer: b. A platelet count below 100,000/mm³ is a contraindication for tPA. Explanation: A platelet count below 100,000/mm³ is considered a contraindication for tPA administration due to the increased risk of bleeding. Adequate platelet function is necessary for safe tPA use.

775. Regarding glucose levels, what is a critical consideration before administering tPA in stroke patients?
a. Hyperglycemia is a contraindication for tPA.
b. Hypoglycemia must be corrected before tPA administration.
c. Glucose levels have no impact on tPA administration.
d. tPA requires concurrent insulin therapy in diabetic patients.

Answer: b. Hypoglycemia must be corrected before tPA administration. Explanation: Hypoglycemia can mimic stroke symptoms, and it is crucial to correct low glucose levels before administering tPA to ensure that symptoms are indeed due to ischemic stroke and not metabolic abnormalities.

776. What imaging study is considered the gold standard for the initial differentiation between ischemic and hemorrhagic stroke?
a. MRI with diffusion-weighted imaging
b. Non-contrast CT head scan
c. Cerebral angiography
d. Transcranial Doppler ultrasound

Answer: b. Non-contrast CT head scan. Explanation: A non-contrast CT head scan is considered the gold standard for the initial evaluation of stroke, as it can quickly differentiate between ischemic and hemorrhagic stroke by identifying the presence or absence of blood within the brain.

777. Which clinical symptom is more suggestive of a hemorrhagic stroke than an ischemic stroke?
a. Sudden onset of unilateral weakness
b. Severe headache of sudden onset
c. Aphasia
d. Visual field deficit

Answer: b. Severe headache of sudden onset. Explanation: While both ischemic and hemorrhagic strokes can present with neurological deficits, a sudden, severe headache, often described as "the worst headache of my life," is more characteristic of a hemorrhagic stroke due to the irritation of the meninges by blood.

778. In the management of ischemic stroke, what is the time window for the administration of intravenous thrombolytics from symptom onset?
a. Within 3 hours
b. Within 4.5 hours
c. Within 6 hours
d. Within 12 hours

Answer: b. Within 4.5 hours. Explanation: The current guideline for the administration of intravenous thrombolytics, such as alteplase, in acute ischemic stroke is within 4.5 hours from the onset of symptoms, as this has been shown to improve outcomes.

779. What is a key risk factor that predisposes an individual more to hemorrhagic stroke than to ischemic stroke?
a. Atrial fibrillation
b. Hypertension
c. Diabetes mellitus
d. Hyperlipidemia

Answer: b. Hypertension. Explanation: Uncontrolled hypertension is a significant risk factor for hemorrhagic stroke, as chronically elevated blood pressure can lead to weakening of the blood vessel walls, making them prone to rupture.

780. What is the primary goal of acute management in hemorrhagic stroke?
a. Reperfusion of the ischemic brain tissue
b. Prevention of rebleeding and management of intracranial pressure
c. Immediate anticoagulation to prevent clot propagation
d. Stabilization of plaque in cerebral arteries

Answer: b. Prevention of rebleeding and management of intracranial pressure. Explanation: In hemorrhagic stroke, the primary management goals are to prevent rebleeding and to manage intracranial pressure to protect brain tissue from further damage.

781. In differentiating ischemic vs. hemorrhagic stroke, what role does blood pressure management play in the acute setting?
a. Aggressive lowering of blood pressure is recommended in both types of stroke.
b. Blood pressure management is more critical in hemorrhagic stroke to prevent rebleeding.
c. Elevated blood pressure is beneficial in ischemic stroke to promote cerebral perfusion.
d. Blood pressure is not a significant concern in the acute management of stroke.

Answer: b. Blood pressure management is more critical in hemorrhagic stroke to prevent rebleeding. Explanation: While blood pressure management is important in both types of stroke, it is particularly crucial in hemorrhagic stroke to prevent rebleeding. Guidelines suggest careful blood pressure control to reduce the risk of further hemorrhage.

782. What is a contraindication for the use of thrombolytic therapy in stroke management?
a. Evidence of ischemic stroke on CT
b. Presentation within the therapeutic time window
c. History of prior ischemic stroke and diabetes mellitus
d. Signs of intracerebral hemorrhage on imaging

Answer: d. Signs of intracerebral hemorrhage on imaging. Explanation: The presence of intracerebral hemorrhage on imaging is a contraindication for the use of thrombolytic therapy, as this treatment could exacerbate bleeding and worsen the patient's condition.

783. How does the presence of a "hyperdense artery sign" on CT scan influence the management of stroke?
a. It indicates a need for immediate anticoagulation.
b. It suggests the presence of an ischemic stroke due to arterial occlusion.
c. It is indicative of a hemorrhagic stroke and the need for surgical intervention.
d. It has no significant impact on the immediate management of stroke.

Answer: b. It suggests the presence of an ischemic stroke due to arterial occlusion. Explanation: The "hyperdense artery sign" on a CT scan is indicative of a thrombus within a cerebral artery, suggesting an ischemic stroke due to arterial occlusion, which may influence the decision to use thrombolytic therapy if within the therapeutic window.

784. In evaluating a patient with suspected stroke, what finding on neurological examination is highly suggestive of a large vessel occlusion in ischemic stroke?
a. Isolated facial droop
b. Mild unilateral weakness
c. Aphasia or neglect
d. Bilateral sensory loss

Answer: c. Aphasia or neglect. Explanation: Aphasia (language disturbance) or neglect (inattention to one side of the body) is suggestive of a large vessel occlusion, particularly in the middle cerebral artery territory, and may indicate eligibility for mechanical thrombectomy in addition to thrombolytic therapy.

785. What is the first-line medication for the initial management of status epilepticus?
a. Phenytoin
b. Lorazepam
c. Levetiracetam
d. Valproate

Answer: b. Lorazepam. Explanation: Lorazepam is considered a first-line medication for the initial management of status epilepticus due to its rapid onset of action and effectiveness in terminating seizures. It is preferred for its longer duration of anticonvulsant effect compared to other benzodiazepines.

786. If the first dose of a benzodiazepine is ineffective in status epilepticus, what is the recommended next step?
a. Repeat the same benzodiazepine at double the dose.
b. Administer a second dose of a different benzodiazepine.
c. Initiate an intravenous antiepileptic drug (AED) such as fosphenytoin.
d. Proceed to general anesthesia with propofol.

Answer: c. Initiate an intravenous antiepileptic drug (AED) such as fosphenytoin. Explanation: If the initial benzodiazepine dose is ineffective, the recommended next step is to initiate an intravenous AED such as fosphenytoin, phenytoin, valproate, or levetiracetam, rather than repeating or increasing the dose of benzodiazepine, to avoid excessive sedation and respiratory depression.

787. In the treatment protocol for status epilepticus, when is intubation generally recommended?
a. Immediately upon diagnosis
b. After the first line of medication fails
c. During the administration of the second line AEDs
d. If respiratory depression or compromised airway occurs

Answer: d. If respiratory depression or compromised airway occurs. Explanation: Intubation is generally recommended in the treatment of status epilepticus if there is respiratory depression, compromised airway protection, or during the administration of anesthetic agents for refractory status epilepticus, to ensure patient safety.

788. Which medication is considered a second-line treatment for status epilepticus when initial benzodiazepines are ineffective?
a. Carbamazepine

b. Fosphenytoin or phenytoin
c. Gabapentin
d. Topiramate

Answer: b. Fosphenytoin or phenytoin. Explanation: Fosphenytoin or phenytoin is considered a second-line treatment for status epilepticus when initial benzodiazepines are ineffective. These medications are used for their antiepileptic properties and can be administered intravenously.

789. For refractory status epilepticus, which treatment is typically considered?
a. Oral anticonvulsants
b. Intravenous immunoglobulins
c. Continuous intravenous anesthetic agents (e.g., midazolam, propofol, or barbiturates)
d. Corticosteroids

Answer: c. Continuous intravenous anesthetic agents (e.g., midazolam, propofol, or barbiturates). Explanation: For refractory status epilepticus, continuous intravenous anesthetic agents such as midazolam, propofol, or barbiturates are typically considered to achieve seizure control, often requiring intensive care monitoring.

790. In the management of status epilepticus, what is the role of continuous EEG monitoring?
a. To confirm the diagnosis of epilepsy
b. To guide anesthesia depth during surgery
c. To detect non-convulsive seizures or non-convulsive status epilepticus
d. As a standard procedure for all seizure patients

Answer: c. To detect non-convulsive seizures or non-convulsive status epilepticus. Explanation: Continuous EEG monitoring is crucial in the management of status epilepticus, particularly to detect non-convulsive seizures or non-convulsive status epilepticus, which may occur without overt clinical signs, allowing for timely intervention and adjustment of therapy.

791. What is the significance of loading doses of antiepileptic drugs (AEDs) in status epilepticus?
a. To decrease the risk of allergic reactions
b. To rapidly achieve therapeutic drug levels
c. To assess the patient's tolerance to the medication
d. To prolong the duration of the drug's effect

Answer: b. To rapidly achieve therapeutic drug levels. Explanation: Loading doses of AEDs are used in the management of status epilepticus to rapidly achieve therapeutic drug levels in the bloodstream, providing immediate seizure control, which is critical in this acute and potentially life-threatening condition.

792. In status epilepticus management, when is neuroimaging (CT/MRI) typically indicated?

a. As the initial step before administering any medication
b. After the first seizure episode in a known epilepsy patient
c. When the underlying cause of status epilepticus is unclear or if there is no response to initial treatments
d. Routinely every 24 hours during hospitalization

Answer: c. When the underlying cause of status epilepticus is unclear or if there is no response to initial treatments. Explanation: Neuroimaging, such as CT or MRI, is indicated in the management of status epilepticus when the underlying cause is unclear or if there is no response to initial treatments, to identify potentially reversible causes like stroke, tumor, or infection.

793. How does the ketogenic diet play a role in the management of refractory status epilepticus?
a. As a first-line dietary intervention
b. To supplement pharmacological treatments in refractory cases
c. As an alternative to intravenous anesthetic agents
d. There is no role for the ketogenic diet in status epilepticus management

Answer: b. To supplement pharmacological treatments in refractory cases. Explanation: The ketogenic diet can play a supplementary role in the management of refractory status epilepticus, especially in cases where pharmacological treatments are not fully effective. The diet alters the body's energy metabolism, which can have an antiepileptic effect.

794. What is the recommended approach to fluid and electrolyte management in a patient with status epilepticus?
a. Aggressive fluid resuscitation regardless of electrolyte levels
b. Restrict fluids to minimize cerebral edema
c. Careful monitoring and correction of electrolyte imbalances, particularly sodium
d. High-dose diuretics to prevent fluid overload

Answer: c. Careful monitoring and correction of electrolyte imbalances, particularly sodium. Explanation: Careful monitoring and correction of electrolyte imbalances, particularly sodium, is recommended in patients with status epilepticus, as imbalances can exacerbate or precipitate seizures. Fluid management should be tailored to the individual's needs, avoiding both overhydration and dehydration.

795. Which anticonvulsant is considered first-line treatment for status epilepticus?
a. Carbamazepine
b. Phenobarbital
c. Lorazepam
d. Gabapentin

Answer: c. Lorazepam. Explanation: Lorazepam is considered a first-line treatment for status epilepticus due to its rapid onset of action and effectiveness in controlling seizures. Benzodiazepines like lorazepam are typically used initially to halt the progression of status epilepticus before longer-acting anticonvulsants are administered.

796. For a patient with newly diagnosed temporal lobe epilepsy, which medication is commonly initiated?
a. Valproate
b. Levetiracetam
c. Phenytoin
d. Ethosuximide

Answer: b. Levetiracetam. Explanation: Levetiracetam is commonly used for the treatment of temporal lobe epilepsy due to its broad spectrum of activity and favorable side effect profile. It can be effective in both partial and generalized seizures, making it a versatile choice in epilepsy management.

797. In the management of absence seizures, which anticonvulsant is most effective?
a. Topiramate
b. Ethosuximide
c. Oxcarbazepine
d. Pregabalin

Answer: b. Ethosuximide. Explanation: Ethosuximide is considered the drug of choice for absence seizures. It specifically targets the thalamic T-type calcium channels, which are thought to be involved in the generation of absence seizures, making it highly effective for this seizure type.

798. What is a major side effect of phenytoin that requires monitoring?
a. Hypertension
b. Gingival hyperplasia
c. Acute renal failure
d. Pulmonary fibrosis

Answer: b. Gingival hyperplasia. Explanation: Gingival hyperplasia is a well-documented side effect of phenytoin, one of the older anticonvulsants. Regular dental check-ups and oral hygiene are recommended for patients on long-term phenytoin therapy to monitor and manage this side effect.

799. Which anticonvulsant requires regular blood level monitoring to ensure therapeutic efficacy and avoid toxicity?
a. Lamotrigine
b. Valproate
c. Carbamazepine
d. Gabapentin

Answer: c. Carbamazepine. Explanation: Carbamazepine requires regular blood level monitoring due to its narrow therapeutic index. Maintaining blood levels within the therapeutic range is crucial to maximize efficacy while minimizing the risk of toxicity.

800. When transitioning a patient from intravenous to oral anticonvulsants, which factor is most important to ensure continuous seizure control?
a. The half-life of the medication
b. The bioavailability of the oral form
c. The patient's weight
d. The time of day the medication is administered

Answer: b. The bioavailability of the oral form. Explanation: When transitioning from intravenous to oral anticonvulsants, it is crucial to consider the bioavailability of the oral form to ensure that the patient receives an equivalent dose that maintains seizure control without leading to toxicity.

801. For a patient with a history of renal impairment, which anticonvulsant requires dose adjustment?
a. Levetiracetam
b. Phenobarbital
c. Clonazepam
d. Zonisamide

Answer: a. Levetiracetam. Explanation: Levetiracetam is primarily excreted by the kidneys, requiring dose adjustments in patients with renal impairment to prevent drug accumulation and potential toxicity.

802. In managing a pregnant patient with epilepsy, which anticonvulsant is generally considered safe with the least teratogenic risk?
a. Valproate
b. Lamotrigine
c. Felbamate
d. Phenobarbital

Answer: b. Lamotrigine. Explanation: Lamotrigine is generally considered one of the safer anticonvulsants for use during pregnancy, with a lower risk of teratogenic effects compared to others like valproate, which is associated with a higher risk of fetal malformations.

803. What is the mechanism of action of sodium valproate in seizure management?
a. Selective inhibition of sodium channels
b. Enhancement of GABAergic neurotransmission
c. Blockade of calcium channels
d. Inhibition of glutamate receptors

Answer: b. Enhancement of GABAergic neurotransmission. Explanation: Sodium valproate primarily works by enhancing GABAergic neurotransmission, which increases the inhibitory action of GABA in the brain, thereby stabilizing neuronal activity and preventing seizures.

804. For a patient experiencing focal seizures with secondary generalization, which anticonvulsant is commonly preferred?
a. Ethosuximide
b. Clonazepam
c. Oxcarbazepine
d. Vigabatrin

Answer: c. Oxcarbazepine. Explanation: Oxcarbazepine is commonly preferred for the treatment of focal (partial) seizures that may secondarily generalize, due to its effectiveness in controlling this seizure type and a side effect profile that is generally more favorable than older medications like carbamazepine.

805. In the Glasgow Coma Scale (GCS), what is the highest possible score a patient can achieve?
a. 8
b. 10
c. 15
d. 12

Answer: c. 15. Explanation: The Glasgow Coma Scale (GCS) is a neurological scale designed to assess a patient's level of consciousness after a brain injury. The scale comprises three tests: eye, verbal, and motor responses. The highest possible score, indicating optimal neurological function, is 15.

806. What does a unilateral dilated pupil suggest in a neurological assessment?
a. Normal physiological variation
b. Increased intracranial pressure affecting the oculomotor nerve
c. Early sign of meningitis
d. Dehydration

Answer: b. Increased intracranial pressure affecting the oculomotor nerve. Explanation: A unilateral dilated pupil, especially when non-reactive to light, can indicate increased intracranial pressure (ICP) compressing the oculomotor nerve (cranial nerve III). This is often considered a neurological emergency requiring immediate attention.

807. In the GCS, what does a motor response score of 6 indicate?
a. No motor response
b. Extension to painful stimuli
c. Flexion to painful stimuli
d. Obeys commands for movement

Answer: d. Obeys commands for movement. Explanation: In the Glasgow Coma Scale, a motor response score of 6 indicates that the patient obeys commands for movement, representing the highest level of motor response and suggesting intact motor pathways and higher cognitive function to comprehend and follow commands.

808. How is the pupillary light reflex used in a neurological assessment?
a. To assess the balance between sympathetic and parasympathetic nervous systems
b. To evaluate the visual acuity and field of vision
c. To determine the level of hydration
d. To check for the integrity of the cranial nerves II and III

Answer: d. To check for the integrity of the cranial nerves II and III. Explanation: The pupillary light reflex involves shining a light into the pupil and observing its constriction, which assesses the integrity of the optic nerve (cranial nerve II) and the oculomotor nerve (cranial nerve III), indicating the functioning of the afferent and efferent pathways involved in the reflex.

809. What does a GCS score of 8 or less generally indicate?
a. Mild traumatic brain injury
b. Moderate traumatic brain injury
c. Severe traumatic brain injury
d. Full consciousness with no impairment

Answer: c. Severe traumatic brain injury. Explanation: A Glasgow Coma Scale score of 8 or less is generally indicative of a severe traumatic brain injury (TBI). This score suggests significant impairment of consciousness and potentially life-threatening neurological damage, often necessitating immediate medical intervention and intensive care.

810. What neurological assessment finding is indicative of a positive Babinski sign?
a. Curling of toes when the sole is stimulated
b. Dorsiflexion of the big toe with fanning of other toes upon stimulation of the foot's sole
c. Constriction of pupils in response to light
d. Symmetrical movement of both arms when the torso is stimulated

Answer: b. Dorsiflexion of the big toe with fanning of other toes upon stimulation of the foot's sole. Explanation: A positive Babinski sign is indicated by dorsiflexion (upward movement) of the big toe and fanning of the other toes in response to a stimulus applied to the sole of the foot. This reflex is normal in infants but in adults can indicate central nervous system disorders involving the corticospinal tract.

811. In assessing a patient's verbal response on the GCS, what does a score of 4 represent?
a. Incomprehensible sounds
b. Disoriented conversation
c. Uses inappropriate words
d. No verbal response

Answer: b. Disoriented conversation. Explanation: In the Glasgow Coma Scale, a verbal response score of 4 signifies disoriented conversation. This means the patient can speak, but the content may be disorganized or confused, indicating altered cerebral function or impairment.

812. During a neurological assessment, what does bilateral small and reactive pupils suggest?
a. Opioid overdose
b. Exposure to bright lights
c. Severe brain damage
d. Hypothermia

Answer: a. Opioid overdose. Explanation: Bilateral small and reactive pupils, often referred to as "pinpoint pupils," can suggest opioid overdose. Opioids cause constriction of the pupils (miosis) due to their action on the parasympathetic nervous system.

813. What does decerebrate posturing indicate in a patient with a severe brain injury?
a. A sign of localized lesion in the cerebral hemisphere
b. An indication of damage to the upper brain stem
c. A benign reflex in patients with mild concussions
d. A voluntary response to pain

Answer: b. An indication of damage to the upper brain stem. Explanation: Decerebrate posturing, characterized by extension of the arms and legs, pronation of the arms, and extension of the neck, typically indicates damage to the upper brain stem. It is a sign of severe brain injury and a poor prognostic indicator.

814. In the context of neurological assessment, what is implied by anisocoria?
a. Normal pupil size and reactivity
b. Equal pupil size in both eyes
c. Unequal pupil sizes
d. Absence of pupillary light reflex

Answer: c. Unequal pupil sizes. Explanation: Anisocoria refers to a condition where the pupils are of unequal sizes. It can be a benign finding or indicate underlying neurological conditions, necessitating further evaluation to determine its significance in the context of the patient's clinical presentation.

815. What laboratory finding is most indicative of diabetic ketoacidosis (DKA)?
a. Blood glucose > 250 mg/dL with arterial pH < 7.3
b. Serum sodium level of 135 mEq/L
c. White blood cell count of 12,000/mm³
d. Serum creatinine of 1.2 mg/dL

Answer: a. Blood glucose > 250 mg/dL with arterial pH < 7.3. Explanation: The diagnosis of DKA typically includes hyperglycemia (blood glucose > 250 mg/dL) combined with acidosis (arterial pH < 7.3) and the presence of ketones in the blood or urine, which are key indicators of this metabolic derangement.

816. In the treatment of DKA, what is the initial fluid therapy of choice?
a. 0.45% saline
b. 0.9% saline
c. Dextrose 5% in water
d. Ringer's lactate

Answer: b. 0.9% saline. Explanation: Initial fluid therapy for DKA usually involves isotonic saline (0.9% saline) to restore volume status and correct dehydration, which is a common finding in DKA due to osmotic diuresis from hyperglycemia.

817. When should insulin therapy be initiated in a patient with DKA?
a. Immediately upon diagnosis
b. After initial fluid resuscitation
c. Once blood glucose levels fall below 250 mg/dL
d. After correction of electrolyte imbalances

Answer: b. After initial fluid resuscitation. Explanation: Insulin therapy in DKA should be initiated after initial fluid resuscitation to avoid rapid shifts in osmolality and to ensure that the patient is hemodynamically stable.

818. What is the primary reason for administering potassium in the treatment of DKA, even if the initial serum potassium level is normal?
a. To prevent hypokalemia as insulin therapy and fluid replacement progress
b. To enhance the action of insulin
c. To correct acidosis
d. To increase urinary output

Answer: a. To prevent hypokalemia as insulin therapy and fluid replacement progress. Explanation: Potassium is administered in DKA treatment to prevent hypokalemia, which can occur as insulin therapy drives potassium from the extracellular fluid into the cells, and fluid replacement dilutes serum potassium levels.

819. Which acid-base disturbance is typically seen in DKA?
a. Respiratory alkalosis
b. Metabolic alkalosis
c. Metabolic acidosis
d. Respiratory acidosis

Answer: c. Metabolic acidosis. Explanation: DKA is characterized by metabolic acidosis, which results from the accumulation of ketoacids in the blood due to the breakdown of fatty acids in the absence of adequate insulin.

820. What is the role of bicarbonate therapy in DKA management?
a. Routinely administered to all patients with DKA
b. Indicated for patients with severe acidosis (pH < 6.9)
c. Used to correct hyperkalemia
d. Recommended for patients with mild acidosis (pH > 7.2)

Answer: b. Indicated for patients with severe acidosis (pH < 6.9). Explanation: Bicarbonate therapy in DKA is generally reserved for patients with severe acidosis (pH < 6.9), as its routine use can lead to complications such as hypokalemia, cerebral edema, and paradoxical central nervous system acidosis.

821. During the resolution of DKA, when is it appropriate to transition from intravenous to subcutaneous insulin?
a. As soon as blood glucose levels are <200 mg/dL
b. Once anion gap metabolic acidosis has resolved
c. After the first 24 hours of treatment
d. Immediately after the initial bolus of intravenous insulin

Answer: b. Once anion gap metabolic acidosis has resolved. Explanation: The transition from intravenous to subcutaneous insulin in DKA management should occur once the anion gap has closed and metabolic acidosis has resolved, indicating that the underlying metabolic derangements of DKA have been corrected.

822. What is a potential complication of rapid correction of hyperglycemia in DKA?
a. Hypertensive crisis
b. Cerebral edema
c. Acute renal failure
d. Cardiac arrhythmias

Answer: b. Cerebral edema. Explanation: A potential complication of rapid correction of hyperglycemia in DKA is cerebral edema, which is a serious condition that can occur due to osmotic shifts associated with rapid changes in serum glucose levels.

823. In assessing a patient with DKA, what clinical sign would suggest the development of cerebral edema?
a. Bradycardia
b. Polyuria
c. Headache and altered mental status
d. Flushed skin

Answer: c. Headache and altered mental status. Explanation: Headache and altered mental status in a patient with DKA can suggest the development of cerebral edema, a serious complication that requires immediate attention and management.

824. When managing a patient with DKA, what monitoring parameter is essential for guiding fluid and electrolyte replacement therapy?
a. Serum creatinine levels
b. Urine output
c. Serum osmolality
d. Anion gap

Answer: d. Anion gap. Explanation: Monitoring the anion gap in a patient with DKA is essential for guiding treatment, as closure of the anion gap indicates resolution of ketoacidosis, which is a key goal in the management of DKA.

825. Which laboratory finding is commonly associated with sepsis?
a. Decreased C-reactive protein
b. Increased white blood cell count
c. Elevated red blood cell count
d. Lowered platelet count

Answer: b. Increased white blood cell count. Explanation: An increased white blood cell (WBC) count is commonly associated with sepsis, indicating the body's immune response to infection. It's a key marker used alongside clinical signs to diagnose sepsis.

826. In the management of sepsis, what is the significance of lactate levels?
a. Elevated lactate levels indicate decreased oxygen delivery to tissues.
b. Low lactate levels confirm the absence of sepsis.
c. Elevated lactate levels suggest overhydration.
d. Low lactate levels indicate effective antibiotic therapy.

Answer: a. Elevated lactate levels indicate decreased oxygen delivery to tissues. Explanation: In sepsis, elevated lactate levels can indicate hypoperfusion and inadequate oxygen delivery to tissues, often signaling a more severe condition known as septic shock.

827. What is the first-line pharmacological treatment for sepsis?
a. Corticosteroids
b. Broad-spectrum antibiotics
c. Antipyretics
d. Vasopressors

Answer: b. Broad-spectrum antibiotics. Explanation: Broad-spectrum antibiotics are the first-line pharmacological treatment for sepsis, aimed at targeting the potential range of bacteria causing the infection, pending culture and sensitivity results.

828. How does the source control strategy play a role in the treatment of sepsis?
a. It involves fluid resuscitation to manage hypotension.
b. It includes the removal or drainage of the infectious source.
c. It is based on administering antiviral medications.
d. It focuses on the prophylactic use of antibiotics.

Answer: b. It includes the removal or drainage of the infectious source. Explanation: Source control is a critical component in the treatment of sepsis, involving the removal or drainage of the infectious focus, such as an abscess or infected device, to eliminate the source of the infection.

829. What is the goal of fluid resuscitation in the early management of septic shock?
a. To increase heart rate and reduce oxygen demand
b. To maintain adequate urine output and blood pressure
c. To decrease C-reactive protein levels
d. To promote diuresis and reduce edema

Answer: b. To maintain adequate urine output and blood pressure. Explanation: In the early management of septic shock, fluid resuscitation aims to maintain adequate urine output (>0.5 mL/kg/hr) and blood pressure, addressing hypovolemia and improving tissue perfusion.

830. Which clinical sign is an early indicator of sepsis in patients?
a. Bradycardia
b. Hypothermia
c. Tachypnea
d. Constricted pupils

Answer: c. Tachypnea. Explanation: Tachypnea, or rapid breathing, is often an early clinical sign of sepsis, resulting from the body's response to infection and systemic inflammation, leading to increased respiratory demand.

831. In sepsis, what role do vasopressors play when fluid resuscitation is not sufficient?
a. They decrease heart rate to improve perfusion.
b. They are used to reduce body temperature.
c. They increase blood pressure to ensure organ perfusion.
d. They act as diuretics to remove excess fluid.

Answer: c. They increase blood pressure to ensure organ perfusion. Explanation: When fluid resuscitation is not sufficient in septic shock, vasopressors are used to constrict blood vessels and increase blood pressure, ensuring adequate blood flow and organ perfusion.

832. What is the significance of the "hour-1 bundle" in the management of sepsis?
a. It outlines a set of interventions to be initiated within the first hour of recognizing sepsis.
b. It is a nutritional protocol to be administered in the first hour.
c. It involves administering all antibiotics within the first hour.
d. It specifies a series of diagnostic tests to be completed within an hour.

Answer: a. It outlines a set of interventions to be initiated within the first hour of recognizing sepsis. Explanation: The "hour-1 bundle" refers to a set of evidence-based interventions recommended to be initiated within the first hour of recognizing sepsis, including blood cultures, broad-spectrum antibiotics, lactate measurement, and fluid resuscitation, to improve outcomes.

833. How does the Sequential Organ Failure Assessment (SOFA) score relate to sepsis?
a. It is used to assess the initial response to antibiotics.
b. It predicts the likelihood of sepsis based on organ dysfunction.
c. It is a measure of the patient's nutritional status during sepsis.
d. It determines the type of vasopressors required.

Answer: b. It predicts the likelihood of sepsis based on organ dysfunction. Explanation: The SOFA score assesses the extent of a patient's organ function or rate of failure to determine the impact of sepsis. An increased SOFA score is associated with a higher probability of mortality and is used to identify patients with sepsis-induced organ dysfunction.

834. What is the primary goal of administering stress-dose steroids in septic shock?
a. To enhance the patient's immune response to infection
b. To reduce inflammation and support cardiovascular stability
c. To promote diuresis and manage fluid overload
d. To increase blood glucose levels for energy

Answer: b. To reduce inflammation and support cardiovascular stability. Explanation: In septic shock, administering stress-dose steroids aims to reduce systemic inflammation and support cardiovascular stability, especially in patients who show poor response to fluid resuscitation and vasopressors, indicating possible relative adrenal insufficiency.

835. What distinguishes the blood glucose levels typically seen in Hyperosmolar Hyperglycemic State (HHS) from those in Diabetic Ketoacidosis (DKA)?
a. HHS blood glucose levels are usually lower than in DKA.
b. HHS and DKA have similar ranges of blood glucose levels.
c. HHS blood glucose levels are usually higher than in DKA, often exceeding 600 mg/dL.

d. Blood glucose levels in DKA are too variable for comparison.

Answer: c. HHS blood glucose levels are usually higher than in DKA, often exceeding 600 mg/dL. Explanation: HHS is characterized by significantly higher blood glucose levels, often exceeding 600 mg/dL, compared to DKA, where blood glucose levels are elevated but not typically to the same extent.

836. In the context of HHS, what is a key clinical feature that differentiates it from DKA?
a. Profound neurological symptoms due to severe dehydration and hyperosmolarity
b. Rapid onset of symptoms
c. Kussmaul respirations
d. The presence of large amounts of ketones in the urine

Answer: a. Profound neurological symptoms due to severe dehydration and hyperosmolarity. Explanation: HHS is often distinguished from DKA by profound neurological symptoms, including altered mental status or coma, primarily due to severe dehydration and hyperosmolarity.

837. What is the typical acid-base status in a patient with HHS?
a. Metabolic acidosis
b. Respiratory alkalosis
c. Metabolic alkalosis
d. Normal acid-base balance or mildly altered due to dehydration

Answer: d. Normal acid-base balance or mildly altered due to dehydration. Explanation: Patients with HHS typically have a normal acid-base balance or only mildly altered status, unlike the metabolic acidosis seen in DKA, as the ketone production is not as pronounced in HHS.

838. How does the treatment approach for fluid replacement in HHS compare to that in DKA?
a. More aggressive fluid replacement is needed in HHS due to more severe dehydration.
b. Less fluid is required in HHS as dehydration is not as significant.
c. Fluid replacement protocols are identical for both HHS and DKA.
d. Fluids are contraindicated in HHS.

Answer: a. More aggressive fluid replacement is needed in HHS due to more severe dehydration. Explanation: HHS typically involves more severe dehydration than DKA, necessitating more aggressive fluid replacement to correct the hyperosmolarity and improve renal perfusion.

839. What role do ketones play in the diagnosis of HHS versus DKA?
a. Ketones are elevated in both conditions, making them non-discriminatory.
b. The absence or minimal presence of ketones is a distinguishing feature of HHS.
c. Ketones are only present in HHS.

d. The presence of ketones indicates HHS rather than DKA.

Answer: b. The absence or minimal presence of ketones is a distinguishing feature of HHS. Explanation: HHS is characterized by the absence or minimal presence of ketones in the blood and urine, differentiating it from DKA, where ketone production is a hallmark feature.

840. What is a common precipitating factor for HHS?
a. Recent insulin overdose
b. Acute infectious process, such as pneumonia or urinary tract infection
c. Sudden discontinuation of antidiabetic medications
d. Intense physical exercise

Answer: b. Acute infectious process, such as pneumonia or urinary tract infection. Explanation: HHS is often precipitated by an acute illness such as pneumonia or urinary tract infection, especially in elderly patients with type 2 diabetes, leading to severe dehydration and hyperglycemia.

841. In managing HHS, what is the significance of monitoring serum osmolality?
a. It helps in diagnosing HHS as serum osmolality is typically normal.
b. Elevated serum osmolality is a diagnostic criterion for HHS and guides hydration therapy.
c. Serum osmolality is typically decreased in HHS and needs correction.
d. Monitoring serum osmolality is irrelevant in the management of HHS.

Answer: b. Elevated serum osmolality is a diagnostic criterion for HHS and guides hydration therapy. Explanation: Serum osmolality is a critical parameter in diagnosing and managing HHS, with elevated levels indicating hyperosmolarity, which guides the extent and rate of fluid replacement therapy.

842. How does the insulin requirement in the initial treatment of HHS compare to DKA?
a. Higher doses of insulin are required in HHS due to severe insulin resistance.
b. Lower doses of insulin are typically needed in HHS than in DKA.
c. Insulin is not used in the treatment of HHS.
d. Insulin requirements are the same for both HHS and DKA.

Answer: b. Lower doses of insulin are typically needed in HHS than in DKA. Explanation: Lower doses of insulin are generally required in the initial treatment of HHS compared to DKA, as the primary issue in HHS is profound dehydration and hyperosmolarity rather than severe insulin deficiency.

843. What is a potential complication of overly rapid correction of hyperglycemia in HHS?
a. Cerebral edema
b. Diabetic foot ulcers
c. Thyroid storm

d. Adrenal insufficiency

Answer: a. Cerebral edema. Explanation: Overly rapid correction of hyperglycemia in HHS, similar to DKA, can lead to cerebral edema, a serious complication due to osmotic shifts affecting the brain.

844. Why is it important to assess for underlying causes in a patient presenting with HHS?
a. Underlying causes are rare in HHS and identifying them can prevent future episodes.
b. Most cases of HHS are idiopathic, making treatment straightforward.
c. Identifying and treating underlying causes, such as infections, can significantly impact the patient's recovery and prognosis.
d. HHS is always secondary to dietary indiscretion, and assessing for underlying causes can help with nutritional counseling.

Answer: c. Identifying and treating underlying causes, such as infections, can significantly impact the patient's recovery and prognosis. Explanation: HHS is often precipitated by other acute illnesses or conditions, such as infections or medications. Identifying and treating these underlying causes are crucial for effective management and recovery.

845. What is a key component of the "Sepsis Six" bundle to be administered within the first hour of recognizing sepsis?
a. Immediate initiation of antifungal therapy
b. Administration of broad-spectrum antibiotics
c. High-dose corticosteroid therapy
d. Insertion of an intra-aortic balloon pump

Answer: b. Administration of broad-spectrum antibiotics. Explanation: The "Sepsis Six" bundle includes the administration of broad-spectrum antibiotics within the first hour of recognizing sepsis. This early intervention is crucial for combating the underlying infection and preventing further progression of sepsis.

846. Which physiological parameter is crucial for the early identification of septic shock?
a. Core body temperature above 39°C (102.2°F)
b. Mean arterial pressure (MAP) less than 65 mmHg
c. Heart rate below 50 bpm
d. Respiratory rate of 12 breaths per minute

Answer: b. Mean arterial pressure (MAP) less than 65 mmHg. Explanation: A mean arterial pressure (MAP) less than 65 mmHg is a critical parameter for identifying septic shock, indicating compromised systemic perfusion that requires immediate management to restore adequate blood flow and prevent organ dysfunction.

847. In the context of sepsis, what is the significance of lactate monitoring?

a. It helps to assess nutritional status.
b. It indicates the level of physical activity.
c. It is a marker of tissue hypoperfusion and oxygenation.
d. It determines the patient's hydration status.

Answer: c. It is a marker of tissue hypoperfusion and oxygenation. Explanation: Lactate monitoring in sepsis is significant as elevated lactate levels can indicate tissue hypoperfusion and inadequate oxygenation, which are critical concerns in septic patients that require urgent correction to prevent organ failure.

848. What is the goal of fluid resuscitation in the early management of sepsis?
a. To increase diuresis and reduce fluid overload
b. To restore intravascular volume and maintain organ perfusion
c. To reduce heart rate and improve myocardial efficiency
d. To decrease blood viscosity and improve microcirculation

Answer: b. To restore intravascular volume and maintain organ perfusion. Explanation: The goal of fluid resuscitation in the early management of sepsis is to restore intravascular volume, ensuring adequate blood flow to organs and tissues, thus maintaining organ perfusion and preventing sepsis-induced tissue damage.

849. Which diagnostic test is essential in the early treatment bundle for sepsis to identify the causative pathogen?
a. Electrocardiogram (ECG)
b. Blood cultures before antibiotic administration
c. Complete blood count (CBC) with differential
d. Urinalysis

Answer: b. Blood cultures before antibiotic administration. Explanation: Obtaining blood cultures before antibiotic administration is essential in the early treatment bundle for sepsis. It helps identify the causative pathogen, allowing for targeted antimicrobial therapy, which is crucial for effective sepsis management.

850. How does the implementation of the "hour-1 bundle" improve sepsis outcomes?
a. By delaying interventions until the causative agent is identified
b. Through rapid initiation of specific, evidence-based interventions
c. By focusing exclusively on ventilatory support
d. Through the use of invasive monitoring to guide therapy

Answer: b. Through rapid initiation of specific, evidence-based interventions. Explanation: The "hour-1 bundle" improves sepsis outcomes through the rapid initiation of specific, evidence-based interventions within the first hour of sepsis recognition, including antimicrobials, fluid resuscitation, and lactate measurement, aiming to quickly address the underlying infection and support vital organ functions.

851. In sepsis management, what is the primary reason for administering vasopressors after fluid resuscitation?
a. To induce diuresis and prevent fluid overload
b. To decrease heart rate and reduce myocardial oxygen demand
c. To maintain adequate blood pressure and organ perfusion
d. To promote vasodilation and increase blood flow to extremities

Answer: c. To maintain adequate blood pressure and organ perfusion. Explanation: Vasopressors are administered after fluid resuscitation in sepsis management primarily to maintain adequate blood pressure and ensure organ perfusion, especially when fluids alone are insufficient to stabilize hemodynamics.

852. What role does source control play in the management of sepsis?
a. It involves controlling the patient's body temperature through external cooling.
b. It includes identification and management of the infectious source, such as drainage of abscesses.
c. It is focused on controlling the patient's heart rate through beta-blockers.
d. It pertains to the regulation of serum potassium levels.

Answer: b. It includes identification and management of the infectious source, such as drainage of abscesses. Explanation: Source control is a critical component in the management of sepsis, involving the identification and management of the infectious source, such as drainage of abscesses, debridement of infected tissue, or removal of infected devices, to eliminate the focus of infection and facilitate recovery.

853. Why is glucose control important in sepsis management?
a. Hyperglycemia is a preferred metabolic state in sepsis.
b. Glucose serves as the primary nutrient for infectious agents.
c. Tight glucose control has been shown to reduce mortality in septic patients.
d. Glucose control is unrelated to sepsis outcomes and is not a management priority.

Answer: c. Tight glucose control has been shown to reduce mortality in septic patients. Explanation: Tight glucose control is important in sepsis management as hyperglycemia can exacerbate inflammatory responses and is associated with worse outcomes. Maintaining glucose levels within a target range has been shown to reduce mortality and improve outcomes in septic patients.

854. What is the primary difference between Systemic Inflammatory Response Syndrome (SIRS) and sepsis?
a. SIRS is always triggered by an infectious process, whereas sepsis can be caused by non-infectious agents.
b. SIRS and sepsis are essentially the same condition, with no significant differences.
c. SIRS can be triggered by infectious and non-infectious processes, whereas sepsis is specifically associated with infection.
d. Sepsis requires the presence of organ dysfunction, which is not a criterion for SIRS.

Answer: c. SIRS can be triggered by infectious and non-infectious processes, whereas sepsis is specifically associated with infection. Explanation: SIRS is a clinical response that can be triggered by a wide range of infectious and non-infectious processes, characterized by systemic inflammation. Sepsis, on the other hand, is a dysregulated response to an infection that leads to life-threatening organ dysfunction.

855. Which of the following is a criterion for the diagnosis of SIRS?
a. Core body temperature > 38°C or < 36°C
b. Blood glucose level > 140 mg/dL in the absence of diabetes
c. Platelet count > 400,000/mm³
d. Isolated leukocytosis > 15,000/mm³

Answer: a. Core body temperature > 38°C or < 36°C. Explanation: SIRS criteria include two or more of the following: core body temperature > 38°C or < 36°C, heart rate > 90 beats per minute, respiratory rate > 20 breaths per minute or PaCO2 < 32 mm Hg, and white blood cell count > 12,000/mm³, < 4,000/mm³, or > 10% immature (band) forms.

856. What defines septic shock?
a. Hypotension responsive to fluid resuscitation
b. Sepsis-induced hypotension requiring vasopressors to maintain MAP ≥65 mm Hg and serum lactate >2 mmol/L despite adequate fluid resuscitation
c. Sepsis with a serum lactate level >4 mmol/L without hypotension
d. Sepsis with multiorgan dysfunction syndrome (MODS)

Answer: b. Sepsis-induced hypotension requiring vasopressors to maintain MAP ≥65 mm Hg and serum lactate >2 mmol/L despite adequate fluid resuscitation. Explanation: Septic shock is a subset of sepsis in which underlying circulatory and cellular/metabolic abnormalities are profound enough to substantially increase mortality. It is specifically defined by sepsis-induced hypotension that persists despite adequate fluid resuscitation, requiring vasopressors to maintain a mean arterial pressure (MAP) ≥65 mm Hg and a serum lactate level >2 mmol/L, indicating tissue hypoperfusion.

857. What is the role of lactate measurement in the context of sepsis?
a. To confirm the presence of an infection
b. As a direct marker of bacterial load in the bloodstream
c. To assess the severity of sepsis and guide resuscitation efforts
d. To identify the source of infection

Answer: c. To assess the severity of sepsis and guide resuscitation efforts. Explanation: Serum lactate levels are used to assess the severity of sepsis and the adequacy of tissue perfusion. Elevated lactate levels indicate tissue hypoxia and can guide resuscitation efforts, with serial measurements used to monitor the response to treatment.

858. In the management of septic shock, why is early goal-directed therapy (EGDT) important?
a. It focuses solely on antibiotic administration within the first hour.
b. It provides a structured approach for optimizing tissue oxygenation and perfusion in the early stages of septic shock.
c. It prioritizes invasive monitoring techniques over clinical assessment.

d. It delays fluid resuscitation until the source of infection is identified.

Answer: b. It provides a structured approach for optimizing tissue oxygenation and perfusion in the early stages of septic shock. Explanation: Early goal-directed therapy (EGDT) is important in the management of septic shock because it provides a structured protocol for early intervention, focusing on optimizing intravascular volume, tissue oxygenation, and perfusion within the first 6 hours of recognizing septic shock, thereby improving outcomes.

859. How does the "sepsis bundle" improve outcomes in patients with sepsis and septic shock?
a. By delaying interventions until a definitive diagnosis is made to avoid unnecessary treatments
b. By providing a set of specific, time-sensitive interventions to be performed within the first hour of recognizing sepsis and septic shock
c. By focusing on long-term rehabilitation post-sepsis
d. By emphasizing the use of corticosteroids in all septic patients

Answer: b. By providing a set of specific, time-sensitive interventions to be performed within the first hour of recognizing sepsis and septic shock. Explanation: The "sepsis bundle" consists of evidence-based practices

860. What triggers the systemic inflammatory response seen in sepsis?
a. Uncontrolled hyperglycemia
b. The presence of pathogens in the bloodstream
c. Autoimmune reactions targeting healthy tissue
d. Genetic predisposition to inflammatory conditions

Answer: b. The presence of pathogens in the bloodstream. Explanation: Sepsis is triggered by the presence of pathogens in the bloodstream, leading to a systemic inflammatory response. This response is the body's effort to fight off these pathogens, but it can become excessive and cause widespread tissue damage, leading to organ dysfunction.

861. How does sepsis lead to hypotension and shock?
a. By causing dehydration and reduced oral intake
b. Through vasodilation and increased vascular permeability
c. By inducing chronic hypertension and vascular damage
d. Through direct toxic effects of bacteria on cardiac myocytes

Answer: b. Through vasodilation and increased vascular permeability. Explanation: Sepsis leads to hypotension and shock primarily through vasodilation and increased vascular permeability. These effects are mediated by inflammatory cytokines, causing blood vessels to dilate and become leaky, resulting in fluid loss from the circulatory system and decreased vascular resistance, ultimately leading to reduced tissue perfusion and shock.

862. What is the role of cytokines in the pathophysiology of sepsis?
a. They enhance insulin sensitivity and glucose uptake.

b. They promote vasoconstriction and increase blood pressure.
c. They mediate immune responses and can cause systemic inflammation.
d. They stimulate diuresis and help in fluid resuscitation.

Answer: c. They mediate immune responses and can cause systemic inflammation. Explanation: Cytokines are key mediators in the immune response and play a significant role in the pathophysiology of sepsis. While they are essential for fighting off infections, their overproduction in sepsis can lead to systemic inflammation, tissue damage, and organ dysfunction.

863. In sepsis, what causes disseminated intravascular coagulation (DIC)?
a. Direct inhibition of coagulation factors by bacterial toxins
b. Excessive anticoagulant production by the liver
c. The immune response leading to widespread activation of the coagulation cascade
d. Depletion of coagulation inhibitors due to renal failure

Answer: c. The immune response leading to widespread activation of the coagulation cascade. Explanation: In sepsis, the immune response can lead to the widespread activation of the coagulation cascade, contributing to the development of disseminated intravascular coagulation (DIC). This results in the formation of microthrombi throughout the vasculature, which can impede blood flow to organs and contribute to multi-organ dysfunction, while simultaneously consuming clotting factors and platelets, leading to an increased risk of bleeding.

864. How does endothelial dysfunction contribute to organ failure in sepsis?
a. By restricting blood flow to vital organs
b. Through the uncontrolled release of growth hormones
c. By enhancing nutrient and oxygen exchange at the cellular level
d. Through the promotion of vasodilation and maintenance of vascular tone

Answer: a. By restricting blood flow to vital organs. Explanation: Endothelial dysfunction in sepsis contributes to organ failure by disrupting the normal regulatory functions of the endothelium, including vasodilation, anticoagulation, and barrier function. This can lead to increased vascular permeability, edema, and impaired distribution of blood flow to vital organs, exacerbating organ dysfunction.

865. What mechanism is primarily responsible for the sepsis-induced impairment in oxygen utilization at the cellular level?
a. Hyperoxia leading to oxidative stress
b. Mitochondrial dysfunction and impaired aerobic metabolism
c. Overproduction of erythropoietin leading to polycythemia
d. Increased affinity of hemoglobin for oxygen, reducing its availability to tissues

Answer: b. Mitochondrial dysfunction and impaired aerobic metabolism. Explanation: Sepsis-induced impairment in oxygen utilization at the cellular level is primarily due to mitochondrial dysfunction and impaired aerobic metabolism.

Despite adequate oxygen delivery, septic cells may be unable to effectively utilize oxygen due to mitochondrial damage, contributing to cellular and organ dysfunction.

866. In sepsis, what leads to the phenomenon known as "capillary leak syndrome"?
a. Hypertrophy of smooth muscle cells in the capillary walls
b. Increased production of antidiuretic hormone (ADH)
c. Inflammatory mediators causing increased capillary permeability
d. Compression of capillaries by external edema

Answer: c. Inflammatory mediators causing increased capillary permeability. Explanation: "Capillary leak syndrome" in sepsis is caused by inflammatory mediators that increase the permeability of capillary walls. This allows fluid and proteins to leak from the vascular space into the interstitial tissue, leading to edema, hypotension, and further complicating organ dysfunction.

867. How does the activation of the complement system affect the progression of sepsis?
a. It provides immediate, direct clearance of pathogens without inflammation.
b. It amplifies the inflammatory response and can lead to tissue damage.
c. It suppresses the immune response to prevent excessive inflammation.
d. It directly stimulates the production of red blood cells to improve oxygen delivery.

Answer: b. It amplifies the inflammatory response and can lead to tissue damage. Explanation: The activation of the complement system in sepsis amplifies the inflammatory response, enhancing the ability of the immune system to fight infection. However, this can also lead to collateral tissue damage, exacerbating the severity of sepsis and contributing to organ dysfunction.

868. What initial pharmacological treatment is indicated for a patient presenting with symptoms of ACS without contraindications?
a. Intravenous beta-blockers
b. Sublingual nitroglycerin
c. Oral antidiabetic medications
d. Intramuscular anticoagulants

Answer: b. Sublingual nitroglycerin. Explanation: Sublingual nitroglycerin is often used as an initial treatment in ACS to relieve chest pain by dilating the coronary arteries and improving blood flow to the ischemic myocardium, provided there are no contraindications like hypotension or use of phosphodiesterase inhibitors.

869. In the management of ACS, what role does aspirin play when administered upon presentation?
a. It acts as a vasodilator to increase coronary blood flow.
b. It serves as an antipyretic to manage fever associated with inflammation.
c. It functions as an antiplatelet agent to prevent thrombus extension.
d. It is used as an anticoagulant to dissolve existing clots.

Answer: c. It functions as an antiplatelet agent to prevent thrombus extension. Explanation: Aspirin is a cornerstone in the management of ACS due to its antiplatelet properties, which inhibit platelet aggregation and prevent the extension of the thrombus that is compromising coronary blood flow.

870. Which medication is essential for stabilizing plaque in ACS and reducing the risk of recurrent myocardial infarction?
a. Statins
b. Calcium channel blockers
c. Diuretics
d. ACE inhibitors

Answer: a. Statins. Explanation: Statins are essential in the management of ACS for their role in stabilizing atherosclerotic plaques, reducing cholesterol levels, and decreasing the risk of recurrent myocardial infarction by improving endothelial function and reducing inflammation.

871. For a patient with ACS and persistent chest pain after nitroglycerin, which medication class is indicated for additional anti-ischemic effects?
a. Thiazolidinediones
b. Beta-blockers
c. Selective serotonin reuptake inhibitors
d. Oral hypoglycemic agents

Answer: b. Beta-blockers. Explanation: Beta-blockers are indicated for patients with ACS and persistent chest pain after nitroglycerin administration, as they reduce myocardial oxygen demand by decreasing heart rate, blood pressure, and myocardial contractility, providing additional anti-ischemic effects.

872. In ACS management, what is the primary indication for using anticoagulants like heparin?
a. To control blood pressure
b. To reduce cholesterol levels
c. To prevent further thrombosis in the coronary arteries
d. To alleviate chest pain

Answer: c. To prevent further thrombosis in the coronary arteries. Explanation: Anticoagulants like heparin are used in ACS management to prevent further thrombosis within the coronary arteries, thus reducing the risk of myocardial infarction by inhibiting the coagulation cascade.

873. When is the use of Glycoprotein IIb/IIIa inhibitors considered in the management of ACS?
a. As first-line treatment for all ACS patients
b. In patients undergoing percutaneous coronary intervention (PCI)
c. In patients with a contraindication to aspirin

d. As a replacement for beta-blockers in patients with asthma

Answer: b. In patients undergoing percutaneous coronary intervention (PCI). Explanation: Glycoprotein IIb/IIIa inhibitors are considered in the management of ACS for patients undergoing PCI, as they inhibit the final common pathway of platelet aggregation, reducing the risk of thrombotic complications during and after the procedure.

874. What is the role of dual antiplatelet therapy (DAPT) in the management of ACS?
a. It is used to manage hypertension associated with ACS.
b. It provides synergistic antiplatelet effects to reduce the risk of stent thrombosis.
c. It replaces the need for statin therapy in lipid management.
d. It is the primary treatment for heart failure symptoms in ACS patients.

Answer: b. It provides synergistic antiplatelet effects to reduce the risk of stent thrombosis. Explanation: Dual antiplatelet therapy, typically aspirin and a P2Y12 inhibitor, is crucial in ACS management, especially post-PCI, providing synergistic antiplatelet effects that significantly reduce the risk of stent thrombosis and recurrent ischemic events.

875. In ACS, what is the indication for the use of ACE inhibitors within the first 24 hours?
a. To increase heart rate and improve myocardial contractility
b. To manage hyperlipidemia and stabilize atherosclerotic plaques
c. To reduce mortality, particularly in patients with LV systolic dysfunction
d. To relieve chest pain by dilating the peripheral vasculature

Answer: c. To reduce mortality, particularly in patients with LV systolic dysfunction. Explanation: ACE inhibitors are indicated within the first 24 hours of ACS, especially in patients with evidence of left ventricular systolic dysfunction, heart failure, or hypertension, to reduce mortality by preventing adverse remodeling, reducing preload and afterload, and improving survival.

876. How do P2Y12 inhibitors contribute to the management of ACS when added to aspirin therapy?
a. They act as direct thrombin inhibitors to dissolve clots.
b. They provide additional antiplatelet action by inhibiting the ADP receptor on platelets.
c. They are used as antihypertensive agents to control blood pressure.
d. They enhance the cholesterol-lowering effect of statins.

Answer: b. They provide additional antiplatelet action by inhibiting the ADP receptor on platelets. Explanation: P2Y12 inhibitors, when added to aspirin therapy in ACS management, contribute by providing additional antiplatelet action. They inhibit the ADP receptor on platelet surfaces, preventing ADP-mediated activation and aggregation of platelets, thus reducing the risk of recurrent thrombotic events.

877. A patient with chest pain and shortness of breath has the following ECG rhythm: . Which intervention takes top priority?
a. Synchronized cardioversion
b. Adenosine administration
c. Heparin bolus
d. Assessing for a pulse

Answer: d. Assessing for a pulse. Explanation: This rhythm is atrial fibrillation. The priority is determining hemodynamic stability. If pulseless, immediate defibrillation is needed (not synchronized cardioversion). Other interventions depend on the patient's clinical status.

878. You're monitoring a patient post-cardiac surgery who develops a new, wide-complex tachycardia at a rate of 180 bpm. They become hypotensive. Which is the most appropriate immediate action?
a. Administer amiodarone IV
b. Synchronized cardioversion
c. Initiate overdrive pacing
d. Obtain a 12-lead ECG

Answer: b. Synchronized cardioversion. Explanation: Wide-complex tachycardia with hypotension indicates ventricular tachycardia (VT). Synchronized cardioversion is the treatment of choice for unstable VT. Antiarrhythmics take time, overdrive pacing is for some supraventricular arrhythmias, and while a 12-lead is helpful, it delays lifesaving treatment.

879. A patient in the ICU has frequent runs of non-sustained ventricular tachycardia on their telemetry monitor. Which electrolyte abnormality would be the most important to correct?
a. Hypomagnesemia
b. Hyperkalemia
c. Hyponatremia
d. Hypercalcemia

Answer: a. Hypomagnesemia. Explanation: Low magnesium levels predispose patients to ventricular arrhythmias, including torsades de pointes, a form of polymorphic VT. Correcting this electrolyte imbalance is crucial before other antiarrhythmic interventions.

880. A patient's ECG shows regular wide QRS complexes with a rate of 110 bpm. Atrial activity isn't clearly discernible. Which additional finding would help differentiate between VT and SVT with aberrancy?
a. Presence of a carotid pulse
b. Blood pressure 150/85 mmHg
c. Left bundle branch block morphology
d. Fusion beats

Answer: d. Fusion beats. Explanation: Fusion beats occur when a supraventricular impulse partially conducts down the ventricles, blending with a ventricular beat. This is highly suggestive of VT. The presence of a pulse or BP doesn't reliably differentiate, and LBBB morphology can occur in both arrhythmias.

881. A patient with new-onset atrial fibrillation is being considered for rate control medication. Which medication class would be contraindicated in a patient with a history of COPD?
a. Calcium channel blockers (diltiazem, verapamil)
b. Beta-blockers (metoprolol, atenolol)
c. Potassium channel blockers (amiodarone)
d. Digoxin

Answer: b. Beta-blockers (metoprolol, atenolol). Explanation: Beta-blockers can worsen bronchospasm and should be used cautiously, if at all, in patients with COPD. The other options may be considered for rate control.

882. A patient on a continuous amiodarone infusion develops hypotension and bradycardia. Which is the most appropriate first-line intervention?
a. Discontinue the amiodarone infusion.
b. Administer atropine.
c. Initiate dopamine infusion.
d. Consider temporary pacing.

Answer: a. Discontinue the amiodarone infusion. Explanation: Hypotension and bradycardia are common amiodarone side effects. Stopping the infusion is the first step to allow its effects to wear off. Other interventions may be needed subsequently depending on the patient's response.

883. A patient with chronic atrial fibrillation on warfarin (Coumadin) is admitted for elective cardioversion. Which lab result is essential to review before proceeding?
a. International Normalized Ratio (INR)
b. Partial thromboplastin time (PTT)
c. Hemoglobin and hematocrit
d. Serum potassium level

Answer: a. International Normalized Ratio (INR). Explanation: Warfarin increases the risk of bleeding. The INR assesses its anticoagulant effect and determines if it's safe to proceed with cardioversion. PTT monitors heparin, and while bleeding risk and electrolyte balance are important, they are less directly tied to warfarin therapy.

884. You're analyzing a 12-lead ECG of a patient with an irregular rhythm. The P waves vary in shape and are followed by narrow QRS complexes. Which type of arrhythmia is most likely?
a. Multifocal atrial tachycardia (MAT)
b. Atrial flutter
c. Sinus arrhythmia
d. First-degree AV block

Answer: a. Multifocal atrial tachycardia (MAT). Explanation: MAT is characterized by varying P wave morphology (at least 3 different shapes) due to multiple atrial foci firing irregularly. Atrial flutter has typical "sawtooth" waves, sinus arrhythmia has a regular variation, and first-degree block shows prolonged PR interval, not P wave changes.

885. A patient is started on procainamide for recurrent ventricular arrhythmias. Which potential side effect requires close monitoring?
a. Hypotension
b. QT interval prolongation
c. Hyperkalemia
d. Thrombocytopenia

Answer: b. QT interval prolongation. Explanation: Procainamide is a Class Ia antiarrhythmic and can prolong the QT interval, increasing the risk of torsades de pointes. Monitoring the QT interval on ECG is essential.

886. A patient with paroxysmal supraventricular tachycardia (PSVT) is hemodynamically stable. You've attempted vagal maneuvers without success. Which medication is the next appropriate step?
a. Diltiazem IV
b. Adenosine IV
c. Lidocaine IV
d. Procainamide IV

Answer: b. Adenosine IV. Explanation: Adenosine is the first-line medication for PSVT due to its ability to transiently block AV nodal conduction, often terminating the re-entry circuit. The other medications may be used in certain situations, but not as the initial treatment in a stable patient.

887. A patient presents to the ED with a blood pressure of 240/130 mmHg and a severe headache. They have no history of hypertension. Which finding would suggest a hypertensive emergency rather than urgency?
a. Normal creatinine and BUN
b. Chest tightness
c. Blurred vision
d. Urine dipstick positive for protein

Answer: c. Blurred vision. Explanation: Blurry vision can indicate papilledema or retinal changes suggestive of hypertensive encephalopathy, a life-threatening complication needing rapid BP reduction. The other findings may be present in either urgency or emergency.

888. You're caring for a patient with a suspected aortic dissection. Their blood pressure is 195/110 mmHg. Which initial blood pressure management goal is most appropriate?
a. Reduce systolic BP to <120 mmHg within 1 hour

b. Decrease mean arterial pressure (MAP) by 20% within 30 minutes
c. Lower diastolic BP to <90 mmHg over 24 hours
d. Gradually reduce systolic BP to <140 mmHg over 12 hours

Answer: a. Reduce systolic BP to <120 mmHg within 1 hour. Explanation: Aortic dissection necessitates fast BP control to prevent further propagation of the tear. Rapidly lowering the systolic BP to <120 mmHg is the guideline-driven goal.

889. A patient admitted with hypertensive encephalopathy is prescribed intravenous labetalol. Which potential adverse effect warrants close monitoring?
a. Hyperkalemia
b. Tachycardia
c. Bronchospasm
d. Acute renal failure

Answer: c. Bronchospasm. Explanation: Labetalol is a mixed alpha and beta-blocker. The beta-blocking effect can worsen bronchospasm, especially in patients with underlying lung disease.

890. A patient with malignant hypertension has a blood pressure of 230/140 mmHg, despite receiving an IV vasodilator. Which additional medication class might be indicated?
a. Beta-blocker
b. Loop diuretic
c. Calcium channel blocker
d. ACE inhibitor

Answer: b. Loop diuretic. Explanation: Malignant hypertension often involves volume overload. Adding a potent diuretic aids in blood pressure control by reducing volume. The other options may be used in specific situations, but diuresis often plays a key role.

891. A patient with a known pheochromocytoma develops a hypertensive crisis with a blood pressure of 260/150 mmHg. Which medication should be avoided?
a. Nicardipine IV infusion
b. Phentolamine IV
c. Labetalol IV
d. Sodium nitroprusside IV

Answer: c. Labetalol IV. Explanation: Unopposed beta-blockade in pheochromocytoma can cause paradoxical worsening of hypertension due to excess circulating alpha stimulation. Alpha-blockers (phentolamine) and vasodilators are preferred.

892. A patient receiving intravenous nitroprusside for hypertensive emergency develops altered mental status and weakness. Which intervention is the priority?
a. Increase the nitroprusside infusion rate
b. Obtain a 12-lead EKG
c. Discontinue the nitroprusside infusion
d. Administer intravenous sodium bicarbonate

Answer: c. Discontinue the nitroprusside infusion. Explanation: These symptoms suggest cyanide toxicity, a potential complication of nitroprusside. Stopping the infusion is crucial. The other interventions may be needed, but not as the immediate priority.

893. A patient has been treated for a hypertensive emergency, and their blood pressure is now 160/95 mmHg. They report mild nausea. Which oral medication would be a good transition agent?
a. Metoprolol
b. Hydralazine
c. Clonidine
d. Lisinopril

Answer: d. Lisinopril. Explanation: ACE inhibitors offer gradual, controlled blood pressure reduction. Beta-blockers can cause rebound hypertension, hydralazine often requires multiple doses, and clonidine might cause excessive sedation after recent IV antihypertensive therapy.

894. A patient with chronic hypertension is admitted with a blood pressure of 200/120 mmHg but has no acute symptoms. Which medication class would be most appropriate for initial management?
a. Parenteral vasodilators
b. Oral beta-blockers
c. Intravenous calcium channel blockers
d. Long-acting oral antihypertensives

Answer: d. Long-acting oral antihypertensives. Explanation: This is a hypertensive urgency. Gradual reduction with oral medications is appropriate. Parenteral medications are typically reserved for more severe or symptomatic presentations.

895. A patient's blood pressure is adequately controlled after a hypertensive emergency. Before discharge, which diagnostic test is essential for further workup?
a. CT scan of the head
b. Renal ultrasound
c. Echocardiogram
d. Serum cortisol level

Answer: b. Renal ultrasound. Explanation: Secondary causes of hypertension should be investigated, and renal artery stenosis is a common culprit in severe cases. CT of the head might be indicated if there were neurological findings, echo for longstanding hypertension, and cortisol levels to screen for endocrine causes.

896. A patient with hypertensive urgency reports flushing and palpitations after taking their newly prescribed antihypertensive medication. Which medication class is most likely responsible?
a. Calcium channel blockers
b. ACE inhibitors
c. Diuretics
d. Beta-blockers

Answer: a. Calcium channel blockers. Explanation: Flushing and palpitations are common side effects of dihydropyridine calcium channel blockers (like amlodipine, nifedipine). The other classes are less likely to cause these specific symptoms.

897. What hemodynamic change is most indicative of cardiac tamponade?
a. Decreased systemic vascular resistance
b. Elevated left ventricular ejection fraction
c. Pulsus paradoxus greater than 10 mmHg
d. Increased pulmonary capillary wedge pressure

Answer: c. Pulsus paradoxus greater than 10 mmHg. Explanation: Pulsus paradoxus, an exaggerated decrease in systolic blood pressure during inspiration by more than 10 mmHg, is a classic hemodynamic change indicative of cardiac tamponade, reflecting the impaired filling of the right ventricle due to increased intrapericardial pressure.

898. In the context of cardiac tamponade, which echocardiographic finding is commonly observed?
a. Left ventricular hypertrophy
b. Right ventricular dilation
c. Pericardial effusion with diastolic collapse of the right ventricle
d. Aortic dissection

Answer: c. Pericardial effusion with diastolic collapse of the right ventricle. Explanation: Echocardiography in cardiac tamponade often reveals pericardial effusion with diastolic collapse of the right ventricle, indicating increased pericardial pressure impairing the cardiac chambers' ability to expand and fill during diastole.

899. Which clinical manifestation is typically associated with cardiac tamponade?
a. Widened pulse pressure
b. Jugular venous distension
c. Hyperactive precordium
d. Wheezing on auscultation

Answer: b. Jugular venous distension. Explanation: Jugular venous distension is a typical clinical manifestation of cardiac tamponade, resulting from increased central venous pressure due to the heart's inability to expand fully during diastole, leading to venous back-up.

900. What is the immediate treatment of choice for hemodynamically significant cardiac tamponade?
a. Intravenous beta-blockers
b. Pericardiocentesis
c. High-dose diuretics
d. Oral anticoagulation

Answer: b. Pericardiocentesis. Explanation: Pericardiocentesis, the aspiration of fluid from the pericardial space, is the immediate treatment of choice for hemodynamically significant cardiac tamponade to relieve pressure on the heart and improve cardiac function.

901. How does cardiac tamponade affect systolic blood pressure during the respiratory cycle?
a. Systolic blood pressure increases significantly during inspiration.
b. Systolic blood pressure remains unchanged during the respiratory cycle.
c. Systolic blood pressure decreases significantly during inspiration.
d. Systolic blood pressure increases during expiration.

Answer: c. Systolic blood pressure decreases significantly during inspiration. Explanation: In cardiac tamponade, systolic blood pressure decreases significantly during inspiration due to reduced left ventricular filling and output, a phenomenon contributing to pulsus paradoxus.

902. Which of the following best describes the pathophysiology of cardiac tamponade?
a. Decreased pericardial fluid leading to enhanced ventricular filling
b. Accumulation of fluid in the pericardial space, leading to decreased ventricular filling
c. Thickening of the ventricular walls, reducing myocardial contractility
d. Inflammation of the myocardium, leading to reduced ejection fraction

Answer: b. Accumulation of fluid in the pericardial space, leading to decreased ventricular filling. Explanation: The pathophysiology of cardiac tamponade involves the accumulation of fluid in the pericardial space, which increases intrapericardial pressure and restricts cardiac filling during diastole, leading to decreased ventricular filling and cardiac output.

903. What is the effect of cardiac tamponade on heart sounds?
a. Loud S1 and S2 sounds
b. Split S2 sound
c. Muffled or distant heart sounds
d. High-pitched systolic murmur

Answer: c. Muffled or distant heart sounds. Explanation: Cardiac tamponade typically leads to muffled or distant heart sounds due to the insulating effect of the fluid in the pericardial space, which dampens the transmission of sound.

904. In cardiac tamponade, what does the term "Beck's triad" refer to?
a. Hypertension, bradycardia, and bounding pulses
b. Jugular venous distension, muffled heart sounds, and hypotension
c. Tachycardia, wheezing, and pulsus paradoxus
d. Cyanosis, pulmonary edema, and tachypnea

Answer: b. Jugular venous distension, muffled heart sounds, and hypotension. Explanation: Beck's triad for cardiac tamponade consists of jugular venous distension, muffled heart sounds, and hypotension, reflecting the effects of increased intrapericardial pressure on venous return, sound transmission, and arterial pressure.

905. How does the "water bottle" sign on a chest X-ray relate to cardiac tamponade?
a. It indicates lung congestion secondary to heart failure.
b. It describes the enlarged cardiac silhouette resembling a water bottle, suggestive of pericardial effusion.
c. It is a sign of pneumothorax adjacent to the cardiac border.
d. It signifies calcification of the pericardium.

Answer: b. It describes the enlarged cardiac silhouette resembling a water bottle, suggestive of pericardial effusion. Explanation: The "water bottle" sign on a chest X-ray in the context of cardiac tamponade describes the enlarged, globular-shaped cardiac silhouette, which resembles a water bottle, indicative of significant pericardial effusion.

906. Which hemodynamic monitoring finding is characteristic of cardiac tamponade?
a. Decreased central venous pressure (CVP)
b. Equalization of diastolic pressures in all four chambers
c. Lowered pulmonary artery wedge pressure
d. Elevated left ventricular preload

Answer: b. Equalization of diastolic pressures in all four chambers. Explanation: In cardiac tamponade, hemodynamic monitoring often reveals equalization of diastolic pressures in all four chambers of the heart due to the external pressure exerted by the pericardial effusion, limiting the heart's ability to expand fully during diastole.

907. What is the primary pathophysiological feature of cardiogenic shock?
a. Decreased systemic vascular resistance leading to hypotension
b. Inadequate cardiac output despite sufficient preload
c. Excessive preload leading to acute heart failure
d. Hyperdynamic left ventricular function with tachycardia

Answer: b. Inadequate cardiac output despite sufficient preload. Explanation: Cardiogenic shock is primarily characterized by the heart's inability to pump blood effectively, leading to inadequate cardiac output despite sufficient preload. This results from severe impairment of the heart's pumping function due to myocardial infarction, cardiomyopathy, or arrhythmias.

908. Which hemodynamic parameter is typically elevated in cardiogenic shock?
a. Central venous pressure (CVP)
b. Pulmonary capillary wedge pressure (PCWP)
c. Cardiac index (CI)
d. Systemic vascular resistance (SVR)

Answer: b. Pulmonary capillary wedge pressure (PCWP). Explanation: In cardiogenic shock, the pulmonary capillary wedge pressure (PCWP) is typically elevated due to backward failure of the left ventricle, leading to pulmonary congestion and increased left atrial pressures, which is reflected in the PCWP measurement.

909. What is the goal of using inotropic agents in the management of cardiogenic shock?
a. To reduce heart rate and myocardial oxygen demand
b. To increase systemic vascular resistance
c. To improve myocardial contractility and increase cardiac output
d. To promote diuresis and reduce preload

Answer: c. To improve myocardial contractility and increase cardiac output. Explanation: The use of inotropic agents in cardiogenic shock aims to enhance myocardial contractility, thereby increasing cardiac output. This helps to improve perfusion to vital organs in the setting of impaired cardiac function.

910. How does invasive hemodynamic monitoring assist in the management of cardiogenic shock?
a. By directly measuring intra-arterial blood pressure and heart rate
b. By providing real-time data on cardiac filling pressures, cardiac output, and systemic vascular resistance
c. By visualizing coronary artery patency and assessing for blockages
d. By monitoring electrolyte levels and acid-base balance

Answer: b. By providing real-time data on cardiac filling pressures, cardiac output, and systemic vascular resistance. Explanation: Invasive hemodynamic monitoring, such as with a pulmonary artery catheter, offers crucial real-time data on cardiac filling pressures (CVP, PCWP), cardiac output/index, and systemic vascular resistance, guiding the optimization of fluid status, inotropic support, and afterload reduction in cardiogenic shock.

911. In cardiogenic shock, why is mechanical circulatory support, such as intra-aortic balloon pump (IABP), considered?
a. To mechanically reduce preload and fluid volume
b. To provide rhythm regularization similar to a pacemaker

c. To decrease afterload and myocardial oxygen demand while improving coronary perfusion
d. To increase systemic vascular resistance and blood pressure

Answer: c. To decrease afterload and myocardial oxygen demand while improving coronary perfusion. Explanation: Mechanical circulatory support devices like the intra-aortic balloon pump (IABP) are used in cardiogenic shock to decrease afterload (thus reducing myocardial oxygen demand) and augment diastolic coronary perfusion, helping to stabilize the patient and support the failing heart.

912. What is the significance of measuring lactate levels in a patient with cardiogenic shock?
a. High lactate levels indicate increased aerobic metabolism.
b. Low lactate levels confirm the absence of shock.
c. Elevated lactate levels suggest tissue hypoperfusion and anaerobic metabolism.
d. Lactate levels are used to assess renal function in shock patients.

Answer: c. Elevated lactate levels suggest tissue hypoperfusion and anaerobic metabolism. Explanation: In cardiogenic shock, elevated lactate levels are a marker of tissue hypoperfusion and the shift to anaerobic metabolism, indicating the severity of shock and the urgency for intervention to restore adequate perfusion.

913. What role does early revascularization play in cardiogenic shock secondary to acute myocardial infarction?
a. It is primarily used to reduce preload and fluid accumulation.
b. It aims to restore coronary blood flow and myocardial perfusion, improving cardiac function.
c. Its main purpose is to increase heart rate and improve cardiac output.
d. It is used to decrease systemic vascular resistance and afterload.

Answer: b. It aims to restore coronary blood flow and myocardial perfusion, improving cardiac function. Explanation: In cardiogenic shock caused by acute myocardial infarction, early revascularization (through percutaneous coronary intervention or bypass surgery) is critical to restore blood flow to the ischemic myocardium, thereby improving cardiac function and patient outcomes.

914. When considering fluid management in cardiogenic shock, what is the primary concern?
a. Rapid fluid infusion to increase preload and improve cardiac output
b. Avoiding fluid overload to prevent worsening pulmonary congestion and edema
c. Using hypotonic solutions to reduce afterload
d. Prioritizing colloid over crystalloid solutions to enhance oncotic pressure

Answer: b. Avoiding fluid overload to prevent worsening pulmonary congestion and edema. Explanation: In cardiogenic shock, careful fluid management is crucial to avoid fluid overload, which can exacerbate pulmonary congestion and edema due to the heart's impaired pumping ability. Fluid therapy must be judiciously managed, often guided by invasive hemodynamic monitoring.

915. Which parameter is most directly improved by vasodilator therapy in cardiogenic shock?
a. Heart rate
b. Myocardial contractility
c. Systemic vascular resistance
d. Central venous pressure

Answer: c. Systemic vascular resistance. Explanation: Vasodilator therapy in cardiogenic shock is primarily aimed at reducing systemic vascular resistance (afterload), which can improve cardiac output by decreasing the workload on the heart and facilitating easier ejection of blood into the aorta.

916. You're assessing a patient with shortness of breath and chest tightness. During inspiration, you notice their systolic blood pressure drops by more than 15 mmHg. Which condition is most likely responsible?
a. Acute aortic regurgitation
b. Left ventricular failure
c. Hypovolemia
d. Cardiac tamponade

Answer: d. Cardiac tamponade. Explanation: Pulsus paradoxus is an exaggeration of the normal inspiratory decrease in systolic BP. It's most pronounced in cardiac tamponade, as the constricted pericardial space limits cardiac filling during inspiration.

917. A patient with COPD exacerbation is on non-invasive positive pressure ventilation (NIPPV). Which method is the most reliable for assessing pulsus paradoxus in this patient?
a. Palpating the radial pulse while observing chest rise
b. Auscultating blood pressure during inspiration and expiration
c. Observing the waveform on an arterial line monitor
d. Using a standard blood pressure cuff while the patient breathes normally

Answer: c. Observing the waveform on an arterial line monitor. Explanation: NIPPV creates positive intrathoracic pressure changes, interfering with traditional pulsus paradoxus assessment. An arterial line allows direct visualization of pressure variations throughout the respiratory cycle.

918. You are unable to palpate a patient's radial pulse during inspiration but can easily palpate it during expiration. Their blood pressure is 110/80 mmHg at expiration and 85/70 mmHg during inspiration. How would you quantify this pulsus paradoxus?
a. 15 mmHg
b. 20 mmHg
c. 25 mmHg
d. Unable to determine with the information given

Answer: b. 20 mmHg. Explanation: Pulsus paradoxus is defined as the difference between the inspiratory and expiratory systolic blood pressure. In this case, it's 110 - 90 = 20 mmHg.

919. A patient with pericarditis is being evaluated for possible cardiac tamponade. Which additional assessment finding would support this diagnosis?
a. Elevated jugular venous pressure (JVP)
b. Loud S3 gallop
c. Hepatomegaly
d. New-onset atrial fibrillation

Answer: a. Elevated jugular venous pressure (JVP). Explanation: Cardiac tamponade impairs venous return to the heart, leading to elevated JVP. An S3 gallop and hepatomegaly suggest heart failure, while atrial fibrillation can have various causes.

920. A patient in the ICU develops pulsus paradoxus without other new clinical findings. Which diagnostic test would be the most helpful for initial evaluation?
a. Chest x-ray
b. Echocardiogram
c. 12-lead electrocardiogram (ECG)
d. Arterial blood gas (ABG)

Answer: b. Echocardiogram. Explanation: Pulsus paradoxus can suggest several conditions, including tamponade, asthma, and COPD. An echocardiogram provides the most direct assessment of cardiac chamber size, pericardial effusion, and diastolic function.

921. A patient with septic shock and respiratory distress has a pulsus paradoxus of 18 mmHg. Their blood pressure remains low despite fluid resuscitation. Which intervention might improve their hemodynamics?
a. Albumin infusion
b. Initiation of NIPPV
c. Intubation and mechanical ventilation
d. Pericardiocentesis

Answer: c. Intubation and mechanical ventilation. Explanation: Positive pressure from NIPPV can worsen pulsus paradoxus and hemodynamics in tamponade. Intubation allows for control of intrathoracic pressures while addressing respiratory distress. If tamponade is confirmed, pericardiocentesis may be needed.

922. A patient presents with hypotension, muffled heart sounds, and jugular venous distention. You suspect cardiac tamponade but cannot reliably assess for pulsus paradoxus due to their clinical condition. Which is the most appropriate next step?
a. Administer a fluid bolus
b. Proceed with emergent pericardiocentesis
c. Initiate a dopamine infusion

d. Obtain a STAT chest x-ray

Answer: b. Proceed with emergent pericardiocentesis. Explanation: This classic presentation of Beck's Triad (hypotension, muffled heart sounds, JVD) is highly suggestive of tamponade. In an unstable patient, immediate pericardiocentesis is both diagnostic and lifesaving.

923. A patient post-cardiac surgery has a blood pressure of 100/70 mmHg with a 10 mmHg pulsus paradoxus. They are asymptomatic. Which is the most appropriate action?
a. Close observation with frequent vital sign checks
b. Administer an IV fluid bolus
c. Notify the surgeon for possible re-exploration
d. Obtain an emergent echocardiogram

Answer: a. Close observation with frequent vital sign checks. Explanation: A mild pulsus paradoxus after cardiac surgery is common and may not indicate tamponade. Close monitoring is initially appropriate, especially if the patient is stable.

924. A patient with asthma has a significant pulsus paradoxus during an acute exacerbation. Which finding on physical exam would help differentiate this from cardiac tamponade?
a. Wheezing on lung auscultation
b. Distant heart sounds
c. Peripheral edema
d. Inspiratory crackles

Answer: a. Wheezing on lung auscultation. Explanation: Wheezing is a hallmark of asthma and wouldn't be expected in cardiac tamponade. The other findings could be present in either condition.

925. A patient has a newly noted pulsus paradoxus. Which historical detail would raise the greatest concern for a serious underlying cause?
a. Recent viral respiratory infection
b. Long-standing history of hypertension
c. Prior radiation therapy to the chest
d. Family history of coronary artery disease

Answer: c. Prior radiation therapy to the chest. Explanation: Radiation can cause constrictive pericarditis, which can present with pulsus paradoxus. The other factors are less directly linked to conditions typically causing significant pulsus paradoxus.

926. A patient presents with severe shortness of breath and fatigue. Arterial blood gas (ABG) shows: pH 7.20, PaCO2 80 mmHg, PaO2 55 mmHg, HCO3 25 mEq/L. Which type of acute respiratory failure is present?

a. Type I hypoxemic respiratory failure
b. Type II hypercapnic respiratory failure
c. Combined hypoxemic and hypercapnic respiratory failure
d. Ventilatory failure with metabolic compensation

Answer: b. Type II hypercapnic respiratory failure. Explanation: The elevated PaCO2 is the hallmark of Type II failure, indicating ventilatory impairment. The low PaO2 is hypoxemia, and the normal HCO3 indicates no primary metabolic disturbance.

927. A patient with COPD is admitted for worsening dyspnea. Their ABG reveals a pH of 7.30, PaCO2 65 mmHg, PaO2 60 mmHg, and HCO3 32 mEq/L. Which acid-base disturbance is primarily responsible for their presentation?
a. Acute respiratory acidosis
b. Chronic respiratory acidosis
c. Acute respiratory acidosis superimposed on chronic respiratory acidosis
d. Metabolic alkalosis

Answer: c. Acute respiratory acidosis superimposed on chronic respiratory acidosis. Explanation: The elevated PaCO2 and low pH are typical of acute respiratory acidosis. However, the elevated HCO3 indicates renal compensation, which occurs in chronic respiratory acidosis.

928. You're caring for a patient with ARF on high-flow nasal cannula. Despite receiving 60% FiO2, their oxygen saturation remains 88%. Which intervention is the most appropriate next step?
a. Initiate non-invasive positive pressure ventilation (NIPPV)
b. Increase FiO2 to 100%
c. Intubate and initiate mechanical ventilation
d. Obtain a chest x-ray

Answer: a. Initiate non-invasive positive pressure ventilation (NIPPV). Explanation: This patient is showing signs of refractory hypoxemia. NIPPV provides positive airway pressure which helps recruit alveoli and improves oxygenation. While intubation might be necessary, NIPPV is a less invasive option to try first.

929. A patient with acute respiratory failure has been intubated and placed on mechanical ventilation. Their initial PaO2 is 70 mmHg with FiO2 0.8 (80%). To improve oxygenation, which ventilator adjustment would be most appropriate?
a. Increase tidal volume
b. Increase respiratory rate
c. Increase positive end-expiratory pressure (PEEP)
d. Initiate pressure support ventilation

Answer: c. Increase positive end-expiratory pressure (PEEP). Explanation: PEEP helps prevent alveolar collapse and improves oxygenation in ARF. Increasing tidal volume or rate primarily affects ventilation (CO2 removal) more than oxygenation. Pressure support assists patient-initiated breaths but doesn't directly impact oxygenation.

930. A patient with ARF is on mechanical ventilation with PEEP of 10 cmH2O and FiO2 of 0.6 (60%). Their ABG shows persistent hypoxemia. Which additional strategy might be beneficial?
a. Administer intravenous bicarbonate
b. Switch to pressure-control ventilation mode
c. Prone positioning
d. Administer inhaled nitric oxide

Answer: c. Prone positioning. Explanation: Prone positioning can improve oxygenation in severe ARF by redistributing ventilation and perfusion. Bicarbonate is for metabolic acidosis, switching modes won't directly improve oxygenation, and nitric oxide is for specific cases like pulmonary hypertension.

931. You're titrating down the FiO2 on a patient recovering from ARF. They become tachypneic and their oxygen saturation drops below 90%. Which is the most likely explanation?
a. Development of a pneumothorax
b. Increasing work of breathing
c. Pulmonary embolism
d. Exacerbation of the underlying condition

Answer: b. Increasing work of breathing. Explanation: The tachypnea and oxygen desaturation suggest the patient is struggling to breathe with the lower oxygen support. The other options might cause these findings but are less likely in this specific scenario of weaning oxygen.

932. A patient with pneumonia and ARF is on mechanical ventilation in the assist-control mode. You notice they are taking very rapid, shallow breaths. Which adjustment should you consider first?
a. Switch to the SIMV mode of ventilation
b. Administer a sedative medication
c. Increase the set tidal volume
d. Paralyze the patient

Answer: b. Administer a sedative medication. Explanation: Rapid, shallow breathing suggests the patient is anxious or uncomfortable. Sedation reduces their respiratory drive, allowing better synchronization with the ventilator. The other options may be necessary but aren't the first priority.

933. A mechanically ventilated patient with ARDS has a PaO2/FiO2 ratio of 120. How would you classify the severity of their ARDS according to the Berlin Definition?
a. Mild ARDS
b. Moderate ARDS
c. Severe ARDS

d. No ARDS present

Answer: a. Mild ARDS. Explanation: The Berlin Definition classifies ARDS as: Mild (PaO2/FiO2 200-300), Moderate (PaO2/FiO2 100-200), Severe (PaO2/FiO2 <100).

934. A patient in respiratory failure has increasing peak inspiratory pressures (PIP) on the ventilator. Which factor is the most likely cause?
a. Decreasing pulmonary compliance
b. Development of bronchospasm
c. Patient agitation and dyssynchrony
d. Inadequate PEEP settings

Answer: a. Decreasing pulmonary compliance. Explanation: Increasing PIPs suggest decreased lung compliance or increased airway resistance. Diseases like ARDS and pneumonia decrease compliance. The other options could raise PIPs, but the primary change here is likely stiffening lungs.

935. A patient with ARF on mechanical ventilation has a sudden drop in oxygen saturation and hypotension. Their breath sounds are absent on the left side. Which intervention takes the highest priority?
a. Increase PEEP on the ventilator
b. Perform needle decompression of the left chest
c. Order a STAT chest x-ray
d. Initiate a dopamine infusion

Answer: b. Perform needle decompression of the left chest. Explanation: This presents as a tension pneumothorax, a life-threatening emergency. Immediate decompression relieves pressure. The other options are important, but secondary to relieving the immediate threat.

936. What is the primary mechanism by which the Intra-aortic Balloon Pump (IABP) provides hemodynamic support?
a. Increasing myocardial oxygen supply by inflating during systole
b. Decreasing afterload by deflating just before systole
c. Enhancing left ventricular ejection by inflating during diastole
d. Reducing preload by deflating during diastole

Answer: b. Decreasing afterload by deflating just before systole. Explanation: The IABP enhances cardiac function primarily by decreasing afterload. It deflates just before systole, reducing aortic pressure and the heart's workload, and inflates during diastole, increasing coronary blood flow.

937. In which situation is the use of a Ventricular Assist Device (VAD) most appropriate?
a. As a permanent solution for patients with acute reversible myocardial injury
b. For temporary support in patients with chronic end-stage heart failure not eligible for transplantation

c. As a bridge to decision-making in patients with acute decompensated heart failure
d. For long-term support in patients with refractory heart failure awaiting heart transplantation

Answer: d. For long-term support in patients with refractory heart failure awaiting heart transplantation. Explanation: VADs are most appropriately used as a bridge to transplantation, providing long-term support for patients with refractory heart failure who are awaiting heart transplantation, or as destination therapy for those not eligible for transplantation.

938. What is the key hemodynamic effect of IABP therapy in patients with cardiogenic shock?
a. Increased pulmonary artery pressure
b. Increased right ventricular preload
c. Improved coronary artery perfusion
d. Decreased venous return to the heart

Answer: c. Improved coronary artery perfusion. Explanation: IABP therapy improves coronary artery perfusion by increasing diastolic pressure during balloon inflation, which enhances blood flow to the coronary arteries, crucial for patients with cardiogenic shock.

939. Which of the following is a potential complication of IABP insertion?
a. Hyperkalemia
b. Aortic dissection
c. Pulmonary embolism
d. Hepatic failure

Answer: b. Aortic dissection. Explanation: Aortic dissection is a recognized, though infrequent, complication of IABP therapy, resulting from mechanical stress on the aortic wall by the balloon, especially in patients with atherosclerotic disease.

940. For a patient with left ventricular failure, which type of VAD would be most suitable?
a. Right Ventricular Assist Device (RVAD)
b. Left Ventricular Assist Device (LVAD)
c. Biventricular Assist Device (BiVAD)
d. Total Artificial Heart (TAH)

Answer: b. Left Ventricular Assist Device (LVAD). Explanation: An LVAD is most suitable for patients with left ventricular failure, as it directly assists the left ventricle in pumping blood to the systemic circulation, alleviating symptoms and improving organ perfusion.

941. How does IABP therapy affect systolic blood pressure?
a. Increases by augmenting left ventricular systolic pressure

b. Decreases due to reduced aortic impedance
c. Remains unchanged as IABP only affects diastolic pressure
d. Fluctuates significantly with each balloon inflation and deflation

Answer: b. Decreases due to reduced aortic impedance. Explanation: IABP therapy can lead to a slight decrease in systolic blood pressure due to reduced afterload from balloon deflation just before systole, which decreases aortic impedance and the heart's workload.

942. In the context of VAD therapy, what is the significance of "pulsatility index"?
a. It measures the level of cytokines in the blood due to device-induced hemolysis.
b. It indicates the degree of blood flow pulsatility, which can help assess VAD function and patient hemodynamics.
c. It determines the risk of thrombus formation within the device.
d. It assesses the adequacy of anticoagulation therapy in VAD patients.

Answer: b. It indicates the degree of blood flow pulsatility, which can help assess VAD function and patient hemodynamics. Explanation: The pulsatility index in VAD therapy helps monitor the device's performance and the patient's hemodynamic status by indicating the degree of pulsatile blood flow, which can vary with changes in the patient's condition or device function.

943. What role does IABP play in the management of acute mitral regurgitation due to papillary muscle rupture?
a. It directly repairs the mitral valve lesion.
b. It reduces mitral valve regurgitation by decreasing left ventricular systolic pressure.
c. It increases regurgitant flow across the mitral valve by increasing left atrial pressure.
d. It has no role in the management of mitral regurgitation.

Answer: b. It reduces mitral valve regurgitation by decreasing left ventricular systolic pressure. Explanation: IABP can help manage acute mitral regurgitation due to papillary muscle rupture by decreasing left ventricular systolic pressure (afterload), thereby reducing the volume of regurgitant flow across the mitral valve.

944. Which statement best describes the impact of VAD support on cardiac output?
a. It decreases cardiac output by increasing afterload.
b. It has no significant impact on cardiac output but stabilizes blood pressure.
c. It significantly increases cardiac output by mechanically assisting ventricular ejection.
d. It transiently increases cardiac output but leads to long-term myocardial atrophy.

Answer: c. It significantly increases cardiac output by mechanically assisting ventricular ejection. Explanation: VAD support significantly increases cardiac output by mechanically assisting or taking over the ejection function of the failing ventricle(s), thereby improving systemic perfusion and end-organ function.

945. In patients with VADs, what is a critical consideration to prevent device-related complications?

a. Regular monitoring for signs of gastrointestinal bleeding
b. Frequent adjustments of the device's pulsatility index
c. Vigilant infection control practices and anticoagulation management
d. Daily calibration of the device's electrical components

Answer: c. Vigilant infection control practices and anticoagulation management. Explanation: Infection control and anticoagulation management are critical in patients with VADs to prevent device-related complications such as infections (including driveline and systemic infections) and thromboembolic events, ensuring the device's optimal function and patient safety.

946. A patient develops respiratory distress 24 hours after a traumatic injury. Chest x-ray shows bilateral infiltrates. PaO2 is 65 mmHg on FiO2 of 0.8 (80%). No signs of cardiac dysfunction are present. Does this meet criteria for ARDS?
a. Yes, all Berlin criteria are met.
b. Yes, but a pulmonary artery wedge pressure (PAWP) is needed to confirm.
c. No, the timing suggests a different etiology.
d. No, the PaO2/FiO2 ratio is not low enough.

Answer: a. Yes, all Berlin criteria are met. Explanation: ARDS diagnosis includes: acute onset, bilateral opacities, PaO2/FiO2 ratio ≤ 300, and no evidence of cardiogenic edema. This case fits, even without a PAWP measurement.

947. A patient with ARDS is on mechanical ventilation. Their plateau pressure is 35 cmH2O. Which intervention is crucial to reduce the risk of further lung injury?
a. Administer a neuromuscular blocking agent.
b. Decrease the tidal volume.
c. Increase the respiratory rate.
d. Switch to high-frequency oscillatory ventilation (HFOV).

Answer: b. Decrease the tidal volume. Explanation: Protective lung ventilation in ARDS prioritizes low tidal volumes (4-6 mL/kg ideal body weight) to minimize overdistention of alveoli. This reduces plateau pressures, a key marker of lung stress.

948. You're setting up mechanical ventilation for a patient with severe ARDS. Which initial tidal volume target would be in line with lung-protective strategies?
a. 4-6 mL/kg ideal body weight
b. 6-8 mL/kg ideal body weight
c. 8-10 mL/kg ideal body weight
d. 10-12 mL/kg ideal body weight

Answer: a. 4-6 mL/kg ideal body weight. Explanation: ARDS necessitates smaller tidal volumes to reduce the risk of ventilator-induced lung injury (VILI). 6-8 mL/kg may be used in non-ARDS patients, but here the priority is lung protection.

949. A mechanically ventilated patient with ARDS has worsening hypoxemia despite high PEEP and FiO2. Which recruitment maneuver would be the most reasonable next step?
a. Increasing the inspiratory flow rate
b. Administering inhaled albuterol
c. Performing a bronchoscopy
d. Prone positioning

Answer: d. Prone positioning. Explanation: Prone positioning redistributes ventilation and perfusion, improving oxygenation in severe ARDS. Increasing flow rate won't help collapsed alveoli, albuterol is for bronchospasm, and bronchoscopy is primarily diagnostic, unless there's a mucus plug.

950. A patient with ARDS on mechanical ventilation has an oxygen saturation of 89%, PEEP of 15 cmH2O, and FiO2 of 1.0 (100%). Which adjunct therapy might be considered?
a. Nitroglycerin infusion
b. Inhaled nitric oxide
c. Intravenous furosemide (Lasix)
d. Extracorporeal membrane oxygenation (ECMO)

Answer: d. Extracorporeal membrane oxygenation (ECMO). Explanation: ECMO is considered in refractory ARDS when conventional therapies fail. Nitroglycerin is for cardiac issues, nitric oxide helps in specific cases (pulmonary hypertension), and Lasix is for volume overload, not primarily for oxygenation.

951. A patient with ARDS has a rising PaCO2 despite increased minute ventilation. Which is the most likely explanation?
a. Development of respiratory alkalosis
b. Increasing dead space ventilation
c. Oversedation suppressing respiratory drive
d. Worsening pulmonary edema

Answer: b. Increasing dead space ventilation. Explanation: ARDS causes ventilation-perfusion (V/Q) mismatch, with areas of lung receiving ventilation but not blood flow (dead space). This makes it hard to eliminate CO2. The other options are possible but less likely the primary cause in this scenario.

952. You're concerned about fluid overload in a patient with ARDS. Which assessment tool would be most helpful to guide fluid management?
a. Chest x-ray
b. Central venous pressure (CVP) monitoring
c. Pulmonary artery wedge pressure (PAWP)

d. Daily weights

Answer: c. Pulmonary artery wedge pressure (PAWP). Explanation: PAWP is the most accurate assessment of left-sided filling pressures in ARDS. It helps differentiate hydrostatic vs. permeability edema, aiding fluid decisions. CVP is less reliable in ventilated patients, X-rays are not specific enough, and daily weights are a lagging indicator.

953. A patient with ARDS is developing signs of systemic inflammatory response syndrome (SIRS). Which management principle is essential?
a. Empiric broad-spectrum antibiotics
b. Aggressive volume resuscitation
c. Liberal use of corticosteroids
d. Source control and supportive care

Answer: d. Source control and supportive care. Explanation: The focus in ARDS is treating the underlying cause (infection, trauma, etc.) and providing support (lung-protective ventilation, preventing complications). Antibiotics are used if infection is confirmed, fluid management is conservative, and steroids are controversial.

954. A patient with ARDS on mechanical ventilation has a heart rate of 130 bpm and low blood pressure. Which intervention should you prioritize?
a. Administer IV fluids
b. Increase PEEP
c. Initiate a vasopressor
d. Assess for bleeding or occult blood loss

Answer: d. Assess for bleeding or occult blood loss. Explanation: New-onset tachycardia and hypotension in ARDS raise suspicion for a complication like hemorrhage, sepsis, or tension pneumothorax. Immediate assessment is crucial before blindly giving fluids or vasopressors, which may be harmful depending on the cause.

955. A patient with ARDS has been on mechanical ventilation for several days. Which complication should you be especially vigilant for?
a. Deep vein thrombosis (DVT)
b. Ventilator-associated pneumonia (VAP)
c. Acute kidney injury (AKI)
d. Stress ulcers

Answer: b. Ventilator-associated pneumonia (VAP). Explanation: Patients with ARDS on mechanical ventilation are at very high risk for VAP. Prevention bundles (oral care, head of bed elevation, etc.) and early recognition are crucial. The other complications are important risks but VAP is a major concern in this population.

956. What is a primary risk factor for the development of a pulmonary embolism (PE)?

a. Hypertension
b. Prolonged immobilization
c. Hyperthyroidism
d. Hypoglycemia

Answer: b. Prolonged immobilization. Explanation: Prolonged immobilization, such as during long flights or in patients with prolonged bed rest, significantly increases the risk of deep vein thrombosis, which can lead to PE by a thrombus dislodging and traveling to the pulmonary arteries.

957. Which diagnostic test is considered the gold standard for confirming the presence of a pulmonary embolism?
a. Chest X-ray
b. Pulmonary function test
c. CT pulmonary angiography (CTPA)
d. Electrocardiogram (ECG)

Answer: c. CT pulmonary angiography (CTPA). Explanation: CTPA is considered the gold standard for diagnosing PE as it provides detailed images of the pulmonary arteries, allowing for the direct visualization of any thrombi.

958. In the initial management of PE, what is the purpose of administering anticoagulant therapy?
a. To dissolve the existing clot
b. To prevent the extension of the existing clot and the formation of new clots
c. To relieve symptoms of dyspnea and chest pain
d. To reduce pulmonary artery pressure

Answer: b. To prevent the extension of the existing clot and the formation of new clots. Explanation: The primary goal of anticoagulant therapy in PE is to prevent the enlargement of the existing clot and the formation of new thrombi, thus reducing the risk of further embolic events.

959. Which clinical sign is often associated with a large or massive PE?
a. Wheezing
b. Unilateral leg swelling
c. Hemoptysis
d. Right ventricular strain on ECG

Answer: d. Right ventricular strain on ECG. Explanation: Right ventricular strain on ECG, indicated by signs such as a new right bundle branch block, is often associated with a significant PE, reflecting the increased load on the right heart due to obstructed pulmonary circulation.

960. For a patient with a confirmed PE and a high risk of bleeding, which of the following might be considered over standard anticoagulation therapy?

a. Systemic thrombolysis
b. Inferior vena cava (IVC) filter placement
c. Increased fluid administration
d. Beta-blocker therapy

Answer: b. Inferior vena cava (IVC) filter placement. Explanation: In patients with PE who have a high risk of bleeding, an IVC filter may be considered to prevent further emboli from reaching the pulmonary circulation when anticoagulation is contraindicated or poses significant risks.

961. What is the role of D-dimer testing in the workup of suspected PE?
a. To confirm the diagnosis of PE
b. To rule out PE in patients with a low pre-test probability
c. To determine the size of the pulmonary embolus
d. To assess the effectiveness of anticoagulation therapy

Answer: b. To rule out PE in patients with a low pre-test probability. Explanation: D-dimer testing is useful in excluding PE in patients with a low pre-test probability, as a negative result makes the diagnosis of PE unlikely in this group.

962. In the context of PE, what does a "saddle" embolus refer to?
a. A small clot located in a distal pulmonary artery
b. A clot that straddles the bifurcation of the pulmonary trunk into the left and right pulmonary arteries
c. Multiple small emboli distributed throughout the pulmonary vasculature
d. An embolus causing isolated right ventricular failure

Answer: b. A clot that straddles the bifurcation of the pulmonary trunk into the left and right pulmonary arteries. Explanation: A "saddle" embolus refers to a large thrombus located at the bifurcation of the main pulmonary artery, often causing severe hemodynamic compromise due to obstruction of blood flow to both lungs.

963. Following the initiation of anticoagulation therapy for PE, what is an important consideration for long-term management?
a. Transitioning to aspirin therapy after 6 months
b. Assessing for the need for lifelong anticoagulation based on risk factors for recurrence
c. Discontinuing anticoagulation after resolution of symptoms
d. Switching to thrombolytic therapy for maintenance

Answer: b. Assessing for the need for lifelong anticoagulation based on risk factors for recurrence. Explanation: Long-term management after PE involves assessing the risk of recurrence to determine the duration of anticoagulation therapy, with some patients requiring lifelong anticoagulation due to high risk of recurrent PE.

964. What imaging finding is classically associated with PE on a CT pulmonary angiogram?

a. Pleural effusion
b. Enlarged aortic root
c. Filling defect in the pulmonary artery
d. Consolidation in the lung parenchyma

Answer: c. Filling defect in the pulmonary artery. Explanation: A filling defect in the pulmonary artery on a CT pulmonary angiogram is a classic sign of PE, indicating the presence of a thrombus within the vessel.

965. A patient involved in a motor vehicle accident arrives in the ED short of breath, tachycardic, and with decreased breath sounds on the right side. Which intervention takes immediate priority?
a. Obtain a STAT chest x-ray
b. Administer 100% oxygen
c. Prepare for needle decompression
d. Assess for subcutaneous emphysema

Answer: c. Prepare for needle decompression. Explanation: This presents as a potential tension pneumothorax, a life-threatening emergency. Needle decompression to release pressure is done before confirmation with imaging. Oxygen is important but secondary.

966. Following needle decompression, a patient with a suspected tension pneumothorax has improved breath sounds. What's the definitive next step?
a. Observe for signs of recurrent tension
b. Initiate non-invasive positive pressure ventilation (NIPPV)
c. Chest tube insertion
d. High-resolution CT scan of the chest

Answer: c. Chest tube insertion. Explanation: Needle decompression is a temporizing measure. All patients with a tension pneumothorax need a chest tube for definitive treatment. Careful observation is needed, but chest tube placement shouldn't be delayed.

967. A trauma patient has just undergone chest tube insertion for a left-sided pneumothorax. What finding on the chest tube drainage system would be most concerning?
a. Bubbling in the suction control chamber
b. Absence of tidaling in the water seal chamber
c. 500mL of sanguineous output in the first hour
d. Continuous bubbling in the water seal chamber

Answer: d. Continuous bubbling in the water seal chamber. Explanation: Continuous bubbling indicates a persistent air leak. Some bubbling in the suction chamber is expected, no tidaling may mean a blocked tube, and initial drainage after trauma is common.

968. You are assisting with chest tube placement. Where is the anatomically correct location for insertion in the case of a simple pneumothorax?
a. 2nd intercostal space, mid-clavicular line
b. 4th to 5th intercostal space, mid-axillary line
c. 8th to 9th intercostal space, mid-axillary line
d. 5th intercostal space, anterior axillary line

Answer: b. 4th to 5th intercostal space, mid-axillary line. Explanation: This is the standard location, aiming for the apex of the lung where air accumulates. The 2nd intercostal space is too high, and more posterior or anterior lines are used for fluid drainage, not primarily for air.

969. A patient with a chest tube for a pneumothorax complains of sudden chest pain and shortness of breath. The chest tube is dislodged. Which action is the immediate priority?
a. Reinsert the chest tube at the bedside
b. Cover the insertion site with an occlusive dressing
c. Obtain a portable chest x-ray
d. Connect a new chest tube drainage system

Answer: b. Cover the insertion site with an occlusive dressing. Explanation: This prevents air from entering the pleural space, which could worsen a pneumothorax. Addressing this is more urgent than replacing the chest tube system or obtaining imaging.

970. A mechanically ventilated patient with a pneumothorax has a persistent air leak despite chest tube placement. Which troubleshooting step should be considered first?
a. Increase suction pressure on the chest tube system
b. Clamp the chest tube briefly to assess for changes
c. Obtain a bronchoscopy to evaluate the airways
d. Reposition the patient to facilitate drainage

Answer: b. Clamp the chest tube briefly to assess for changes. Explanation: Clamping helps differentiate between an ongoing leak from the lung and a leak within the system itself. Increasing suction without addressing the source is unlikely to help, and bronchoscopy is invasive if a simpler solution exists.

971. A patient with a chest tube has no fluctuations (tidaling) in the water seal chamber. Which is the most likely cause?
a. The lung has fully re-expanded
b. There is a kink in the chest tube tubing
c. The suction control chamber is not filled to the correct level
d. The patient has developed a bronchopleural fistula

Answer: b. There is a kink in the chest tube tubing. Explanation: Absence of tidaling usually indicates an obstruction. Full re-expansion is a positive sign, suction level wouldn't affect tidaling, and a fistula would cause continuous bubbling.

972. A patient with a pneumothorax and chest tube has an oxygen saturation of 85% despite a high-flow oxygen mask. Which additional intervention may be indicated?
a. Increasing the chest tube suction pressure
b. Initiating positive pressure ventilation (PPV)
c. Aggressive pulmonary hygiene (coughing, deep breathing)
d. Administering a diuretic

Answer: b. Initiating positive pressure ventilation (PPV). Explanation: PPV can help stent open the collapsed lung and improve oxygenation in severe cases. Increasing suction won't help if the lung is collapsed, and pulmonary hygiene or diuretics won't acutely address the pneumothorax.

973. A patient's chest tube is accidentally disconnected from the drainage system. What is the most appropriate immediate action?
a. Reconnect the chest tube to the drainage system.
b. Place the end of the chest tube in a bottle of sterile water.
c. Clamp the chest tube close to the patient's chest.
d. Irrigate the chest tube with normal saline.

Answer: b. Place the end of the chest tube in a bottle of sterile water. Explanation: This creates a temporary water seal, preventing air from re-entering the pleural space. Reconnecting without a water seal is risky, clamping close to the chest could lead to tension pneumothorax, and irrigation isn't the priority.

974. A patient one week post-lung transplant has a small air leak noted on their chest tube. The lung remains well-expanded on x-ray. Which management approach is most appropriate?
a. Water seal the chest tube
b. Emergency surgical repair
c. Observation and continued chest tube suction
d. Pleurodesis

Answer: c. Observation and continued chest tube suction. Explanation: Small, stable air leaks after lung surgery are common and often resolve on their own with continued suction. Water seal is premature, surgery is too invasive at this point, and pleurodesis is for persistent leaks.

975. What is the first-line pharmacological treatment for acute asthma exacerbation?
a. Oral corticosteroids
b. Short-acting beta-agonists (SABAs) via nebulizer or metered-dose inhaler
c. Long-acting beta-agonists (LABAs)
d. Anticholinergic inhalers

Answer: b. Short-acting beta-agonists (SABAs) via nebulizer or metered-dose inhaler. Explanation: SABAs, such as albuterol, are the first-line treatment for acute asthma exacerbations due to their rapid onset of action in relieving bronchoconstriction.

976. During an acute COPD exacerbation, what is the role of systemic corticosteroids?
a. To immediately relieve airway obstruction
b. To reduce inflammation and improve airflow
c. To prevent future exacerbations
d. To act as a rescue medication for sudden symptoms

Answer: b. To reduce inflammation and improve airflow. Explanation: Systemic corticosteroids are used during acute COPD exacerbations to reduce airway inflammation, thereby improving airflow and reducing the severity of the exacerbation.

977. In the management of asthma exacerbations, what is the purpose of administering ipratropium bromide?
a. To provide long-term control of asthma symptoms
b. To act as an anti-inflammatory agent
c. To provide additive bronchodilation when combined with SABAs
d. To increase mucociliary clearance

Answer: c. To provide additive bronchodilation when combined with SABAs. Explanation: Ipratropium bromide, an anticholinergic, is often added to SABA treatment in acute asthma exacerbations for additional bronchodilation, particularly in severe cases.

978. What is the significance of measuring peak expiratory flow (PEF) in the acute management of asthma?
a. To determine the need for hospitalization
b. To assess the severity of the exacerbation and monitor response to treatment
c. To identify the presence of a respiratory infection
d. To calculate the dose of inhaled corticosteroids

Answer: b. To assess the severity of the exacerbation and monitor response to treatment. Explanation: PEF measurement is a crucial component of assessing the severity of an asthma exacerbation and the patient's response to treatment, guiding further management decisions.

979. Why are long-acting beta-agonists (LABAs) contraindicated as monotherapy in asthma?
a. Due to the risk of increasing asthma-related mortality
b. Because they can cause rebound bronchoconstriction
c. Due to their potential to induce tolerance
d. Because they are less effective than SABAs

Answer: a. Due to the risk of increasing asthma-related mortality. Explanation: LABAs are contraindicated as monotherapy in asthma due to evidence suggesting an increased risk of asthma-related death when used without inhaled corticosteroids.

980. For a patient with COPD exacerbation, what is the role of supplemental oxygen therapy?
a. To treat underlying hypoxemia
b. To prevent respiratory infection
c. To reduce carbon dioxide retention
d. To stimulate hypoxic respiratory drive

Answer: a. To treat underlying hypoxemia. Explanation: In COPD exacerbations, supplemental oxygen is provided to correct hypoxemia, with careful monitoring to avoid excessive oxygenation, which can lead to CO2 retention in susceptible individuals.

981. What is the rationale behind using combination inhalers containing both a corticosteroid and a LABA in the management of COPD?
a. To provide immediate relief of symptoms
b. To reduce the frequency and severity of exacerbations
c. To decrease the use of oral corticosteroids
d. To promote mucociliary clearance

Answer: b. To reduce the frequency and severity of exacerbations. Explanation: Combination inhalers with corticosteroids and LABAs are used in COPD to reduce the frequency and severity of exacerbations by providing anti-inflammatory effects and sustained bronchodilation.

982. How does noninvasive ventilation (NIV) benefit patients with acute COPD exacerbation?
a. By curing the underlying lung disease
b. By improving survival and reducing the need for intubation
c. By permanently improving lung function
d. By reducing the risk of future exacerbations

Answer: b. By improving survival and reducing the need for intubation. Explanation: NIV, such as CPAP or BiPAP, is used in acute COPD exacerbations to improve ventilation, reduce the work of breathing, improve gas exchange, and ultimately reduce the need for endotracheal intubation and improve survival.

983. In acute asthma management, what is the role of magnesium sulfate?
a. To act as a primary bronchodilator
b. To serve as a substitute for inhaled corticosteroids
c. To reduce airway inflammation

d. As an adjunct therapy in severe exacerbations refractory to standard treatments

Answer: d. As an adjunct therapy in severe exacerbations refractory to standard treatments. Explanation: Intravenous magnesium sulfate may be used as an adjunct treatment in severe asthma exacerbations that are not responding adequately to initial treatments like SABAs and corticosteroids, due to its bronchodilating properties.

984. What monitoring is essential after initiating bronchodilator therapy in an acute exacerbation of asthma or COPD?
a. Continuous electroencephalographic (EEG) monitoring
b. Frequent assessment of respiratory rate and pattern, oxygen saturation, and level of distress
c. Daily chest X-rays
d. Hourly measurement of serum electrolytes

Answer: b. Frequent assessment of respiratory rate and pattern, oxygen saturation, and level of distress. Explanation: After initiating bronchodilator therapy in acute exacerbations, it's crucial to frequently monitor the patient's respiratory rate, breathing pattern, oxygen saturation, and subjective feeling of distress to evaluate response to treatment and adjust therapy as needed.

985. A patient with a history of chronic heart failure presents with acute shortness of breath, an S3 heart sound, and jugular venous distension. Which of the following interventions is MOST appropriate initially?
A) Administer high-flow oxygen.
B) Begin continuous nitroglycerin infusion.
C) Initiate high-dose loop diuretics intravenously.
D) Start non-invasive positive pressure ventilation (NIPPV).

Answer: C) Initiate high-dose loop diuretics intravenously.
Rationale: The patient's symptoms suggest acute decompensated heart failure with volume overload. High-dose loop diuretics are effective in rapidly reducing preload, improving symptoms of congestion like shortness of breath and jugular venous distension.

986. In a patient with septic shock, which hemodynamic parameter is MOST likely to be observed?
A) Increased systemic vascular resistance (SVR)
B) Decreased cardiac output
C) Increased central venous pressure (CVP)
D) Decreased pulmonary artery occlusion pressure (PAOP)

Answer: B) Decreased cardiac output
Rationale: Septic shock is characterized by distributive shock physiology, where there is profound vasodilation leading to decreased SVR. Despite an initial increase in cardiac output due to compensatory mechanisms, it eventually decreases due to myocardial depression associated with sepsis.

987. Which of the following EKG changes is MOST indicative of hyperkalemia?
A) ST-segment depression
B) Peaked T waves
C) Prolonged PR interval
D) Presence of a U wave

Answer: B) Peaked T waves
Rationale: Peaked T waves are an early electrocardiographic sign of hyperkalemia, reflecting the effects of increased extracellular potassium levels on cardiac myocyte repolarization.

988. A patient with acute pulmonary edema is receiving furosemide. Which of the following outcomes indicates effective treatment?
A) Decreased respiratory rate
B) Increased urine output
C) Increased blood pressure
D) Decreased heart rate

Answer: B) Increased urine output
Rationale: Furosemide, a loop diuretic, effectively reduces preload by increasing renal excretion of sodium and water, leading to increased urine output. This decrease in intravascular volume helps alleviate symptoms of pulmonary edema.

989. In assessing a patient for fluid responsiveness, which of the following is the MOST reliable indicator?
A) Heart rate
B) Blood pressure
C) Central venous pressure (CVP)
D) Passive leg raise test

Answer: D) Passive leg raise test. Rationale: The passive leg raise test temporarily increases venous return, mimicking a fluid bolus. An increase in cardiac output or blood pressure in response to this maneuver indicates fluid responsiveness, making it a reliable bedside assessment.

990. A patient with a right ventricular myocardial infarction would likely exhibit which of the following hemodynamic patterns?
A) High CVP with low PAOP
B) Low CVP with high PAOP
C) High CVP with high PAOP
D) Low CVP with low PAOP

Answer: A) High CVP with low PAOP
Rationale: Right ventricular infarction impairs right ventricular function, leading to increased CVP due to venous congestion. However, left ventricular filling (and thus PAOP) may be reduced due to decreased right ventricular output, leading to a low PAOP.

991. Which medication is MOST appropriate for treating a patient with cardiogenic shock who has a low cardiac output and high systemic vascular resistance?
A) Dobutamine
B) Norepinephrine
C) Dopamine at high doses
D) Hydrochlorothiazide

Answer: A) Dobutamine
Rationale: Dobutamine, a beta-1 agonist, increases myocardial contractility and cardiac output without significantly increasing SVR, making it suitable for patients with cardiogenic shock who already have elevated SVR.

992. A patient's arterial blood gas reveals a pH of 7.32, PaCO2 of 50 mmHg, and HCO3- of 26 mEq/L. This is indicative of:
A) Metabolic acidosis
B) Metabolic alkalosis
C) Respiratory acidosis
D) Respiratory alkalosis

Answer: C) Respiratory acidosis
Rationale: The elevated PaCO2 with a slightly increased HCO3- and decreased pH indicates respiratory acidosis, likely due to hypoventilation. The body attempts to compensate by retaining bicarbonate.

993. For a patient with acute decompensated heart failure and renal insufficiency, which of the following medications should be used cautiously?
A) ACE inhibitors
B) Beta-blockers
C) Loop diuretics
D) NSAIDs

Answer: D) NSAIDs. Rationale: NSAIDs can exacerbate heart failure by causing sodium and water retention and can further impair renal function, making them a poor choice in patients with heart failure and renal insufficiency.
A patient with septic shock is being treated with fluid resuscitation and norepinephrine. Which of the following best indicates an improvement in their condition?
A) Increase in heart rate
B) Increase in urine output
C) Decrease in body temperature
D) Decrease in white blood cell count

Answer: B) Increase in urine output
Rationale: An increase in urine output indicates improved renal perfusion, suggesting that the patient's hemodynamic status is improving with treatment. It reflects better tissue perfusion, a key goal in the management of septic shock.

994. A patient with an acute anterior ST-elevation myocardial infarction (STEMI) develops hypotension and bradycardia. EKG reveals new right ventricular infarct pattern. Which intervention has the highest priority?
a. Aggressive fluid resuscitation
b. Atropine administration
c. Emergent cardiac catheterization
d. Temporary transvenous pacing

Answer: a. Aggressive fluid resuscitation
Explanation: Right ventricular infarcts often lead to preload-dependent cardiac output. Fluids help maintain right heart filling and are crucial. Atropine and pacing may be needed, but fluids are often the first-line intervention.

995. You are caring for a patient with decompensated heart failure and a blood pressure of 80/50 mmHg. PAWP is 28 mmHg, and cardiac index is 1.8 L/min/m2. Which pharmacological intervention would be most appropriate?
a. Dobutamine infusion
b. Furosemide IV
c. Nitroglycerin infusion
d. Norepinephrine infusion

Answer: a. Dobutamine infusion Explanation: This patient has cardiogenic shock. The low cardiac index and elevated PAWP suggest poor contractility. Dobutamine increases contractility; the others are less likely to be the primary solution.

996. A patient with severe COPD exacerbation is on non-invasive positive pressure ventilation (NIPPV). Despite optimal settings, the patient remains tachypneic and increasingly fatigued. ABG shows pH 7.25, PaCO2 70 mmHg, PaO2 58 mmHg. What is the next best step?
a. Increase inspiratory pressure support (IPAP)
b. Administer intravenous bicarbonate
c. Initiate heliox therapy
d. Intubate and initiate mechanical ventilation

Answer: d. Intubate and initiate mechanical ventilation
Explanation: The worsening ABG and fatigue indicate impending respiratory failure. NIPPV is insufficient – they need mechanical ventilation for full support. Increasing IPAP risks overdistention, bicarbonate is not for primary ventilation issues, and heliox is adjunctive.

997. A mechanically ventilated patient with ARDS has worsening hypoxemia despite FiO2 of 1.0 and PEEP of 16 cmH2O. Which adjunctive therapy is most likely to improve oxygenation?
a. Prone positioning
b. Inhaled nitric oxide
c. High-frequency oscillatory ventilation (HFOV)
d. Neuromuscular blockade with cisatracurium

Answer: a. Prone positioning
Explanation: Prone positioning redistributes ventilation and perfusion in ARDS, often dramatically improving oxygenation. Nitric oxide is for specific scenarios, HFOV is complex, and paralysis is for vent synchrony, not primary oxygenation.

998. A patient with a traumatic head injury develops a fixed and dilated pupil on the right side. Which of the following is the most urgent priority?
a. Administer hypertonic saline
b. Obtain an emergent CT scan of the head
c. Increase the PEEP setting on the ventilator
d. Initiate hyperventilation to lower PaCO2

Answer: b. Obtain an emergent CT scan of the head
Explanation: This suggests uncal herniation, a neurosurgical emergency. CT confirms the diagnosis and guides intervention. Hypertonic saline helps intracranial pressure but needs a diagnosis first.

999. A patient in the ICU develops new-onset seizures. After initial stabilization, which diagnostic test would be the most helpful in determining the underlying etiology?
a. Lumbar puncture
b. Head CT without contrast
c. Continuous EEG monitoring
d. Serum electrolyte panel

Answer: c. Continuous EEG monitoring
Explanation: Seizures can have numerous causes including metabolic and structural problems. EEG monitoring helps detect ongoing seizure activity, even subclinical seizures which are common in ICU patients.

1,000. A patient with septic shock develops oliguria and rising creatinine. Urine studies show a fractional excretion of sodium (FeNa) <1%. Which is the most likely pathophysiological mechanism?
a. Acute tubular necrosis (ATN)
b. Prerenal azotemia
c. Intrinsic renal disease
d. Post-renal obstruction

Answer: b. Prerenal azotemia
Explanation: Low FeNa suggests the kidney is avidly retaining sodium, implying decreased perfusion (prerenal). ATN usually has FeNa >1%, and obstruction shouldn't cause a low FeNa.

1,001. A patient is admitted with diabetic ketoacidosis (DKA). Initial labs show: potassium 5.8 mEq/L, glucose 450 mg/dL, anion gap 24. Which intervention is contraindicated in the initial management?
a. Intravenous insulin infusion
b. Aggressive fluid resuscitation
c. Potassium replacement
d. Sodium bicarbonate infusion

Answer: d. Sodium bicarbonate infusion
Explanation: Bicarbonate is rarely needed in DKA; it can worsen acidosis and cause other complications. Insulin, fluids, and potassium are cornerstones of DKA management.

Copyright © 2024 Kylie Smithfeild

All rights reserved. No part of this publication may be reproduced, distributed, or transmitted in any form or by any means, including photocopying, recording, or other electronic or mechanical methods, without the prior written permission of the publisher, except in the case of brief quotations embodied in critical reviews and certain other noncommercial uses permitted by copyright law.

ISBN
ISBN: 978-1-964079-02-8

Made in the USA
Coppell, TX
21 April 2024

31531125R00206